GW01607443

PATHS TO THE ABSOLUTE

JOHN GOLDING

PATHS TO THE ABSOLUTE

Mondrian, Malevich, Kandinsky, Pollock, Newman, Rothko and Still

With 172 illustrations, 64 in colour

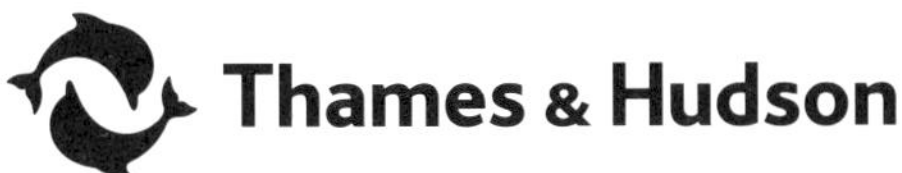

For Helen and Phil

This is the forty-eighth volume of the A.W. Mellon Lectures in the Fine Arts, which are delivered annually at the National Gallery of Art, Washington, D.C.
The volumes of lectures constitute Number XXXV in the Bollingen Series, sponsored by the Bollingen Foundation.

First published in Great Britain in 2000 by Thames & Hudson Ltd, London
Published in the United States of America in the Bollingen Series
by Princeton University Press, Princeton, N.J.

ISBN 0-500-23775-1

Printed in Italy by Artegrafica

Contents

Preface

There is in existence no standard work on the origins, birth and dissemination of abstract art in the twentieth century, let alone a definitive study of the subject: its manifestations are too diverse, its ramifications too complex. Michel Seuphor's pioneering *L'Art abstrait, ses origines, ses premières maîtres*, published in Paris in 1950, remains a useful work of reference, but it is dictionary-like in structure. In this respect it anticipates most subsequent works on the subject, although these are in fact surprisingly few.

Two historically important exhibitions underline divergent approaches towards abstraction and changing critical attitudes. Alfred Barr's epoch-making 'Cubism and Abstract Art' was mounted in New York at The Museum of Modern Art in 1936. As its title implied, the exhibition stressed the formalistic implications of abstraction and its antecedents. Looking back over the twentieth century, it is clear that Cubism remains its pivotal visual movement. Cubism was concerned with questioning the nature of perceived reality. In doing so, it reinvented the language, the very syntax of painting and sculpture. Cubism was also the threshold over which many artists passed in arriving at abstraction; and Cubism's concerns were largely formalistic. Of the great pioneering abstractionists only Kandinsky chose to ignore Cubism in his own work, although he was of course fully aware of its development and its significance. Barr's catalogue is broken down into sections, preceded by short but important essays, and it is notable that the passages on Kandinsky, the first under the heading 'Abstract Expressionism in Germany', are the most awkward.

The Spiritual in Art: Abstract Painting 1890–1985, co-ordinated by Maurice Tuchman, and staged at the Los Angeles County Museum of Art in 1986, has been the largest and most comprehensive exhibition of abstraction to date. It subsequently travelled to The Museum of Contemporary Art in Chicago and to the Gemeentemuseum in The Hague. The exhibition was accompanied by a weighty catalogue containing a wealth of essays by distinguished art historians. These texts reflected a tendency to concentrate on the philosophical and Symbolist background to abstraction and on its connections with Theosophy, the occult, and various other esoteric systems of thought which informed many of its early manifestations. This allowed for the inclusion in the exhibition of many minor and virtually forgotten figures, some of whom produced works of questionable aesthetic value or appeal.

When I was invited to deliver the forty-sixth series of A.W. Mellon Lectures in the Fine Arts, I sought for a subject that might reflect something of a lifetime spent as a teacher of twentieth-century art at both an academic and a studio level, and also something of my own interests as a practising painter. The idea came to me that it might be fruitful to examine aspects of the work of the three greatest European pioneering abstract painters – Mondrian, Malevich and Kandinsky – and to compare and contrast these with some of the concerns of their great American successors – Pollock, Newman, Rothko and Still – who in the 1940s and 1950s succeeded in endowing abstraction with a renewed sense of purpose. It was they who reaffirmed the fact that, at its best and most profound, abstract painting is heavily imbued with meaning, with content, and that, in order to make this content palpable, new formal pictorial innovations must be found to express it.

The lectures (which in my slightly revised texts I refer to as essays) are basically monographic in their organization. But they also attempt to examine the ambitions shared by all seven artists and simultaneously to indicate the different visual means by which each reached his goal. It is of deep significance that of these artists five reached artistic maturity notably late in life. Even the two most temperamental and impetuous, Malevich and Pollock, were well into their thirties before they stormed the citadel of abstraction. It remains a source of some wonder, given the fact that abstraction has been with us as a fact of life for over eighty years, that it was only in the second half of the 1950s and in the 1960s that there came into existence a generation of artists who felt that they could turn directly and immediately to abstraction as a viable idiom. Countless younger artists, originally exhilarated by the prospects opened up by the pioneering European abstractionists, and subsequently an even greater number who sought to emulate the new American abstraction, came to recognize to their grief, often to their very artistic extinction, that they were not after all certain of what it was they were trying to say or express through the various abstract idioms they had adopted. Each of the artists here examined, on the other hand, had been inspired by the fact that he was on the path to some new, ultimate pictorial truth or certainty, to a visual absolute.

August 1999 J.G.

I

Mondrian and the architecture of the future

Piet Mondrian was the purest and most single-minded of the great pioneering abstractionists. He felt simplicity to be the ideal state of humankind; and there is a sense in which he himself was a simple man. However, the apparent simplicity of his own art is also dangerously deceptive. Similarly, he came to reject totally the use of symbols; and yet although his abstraction is informed by the idealistic philosophy with which he became imbued, he reached his initial conclusions through hermetic systems of thought saturated with symbolic content.

Mondrian was born in 1872. That is to say, he was ten years older than Picasso and Braque, the inventors of Cubism, the style which was to be the catalyst for his own equally radical visual revolution. More than half of Mondrian's total output belongs to the years between 1890 and 1907; but it was only after this that Mondrian began to hit his stride. His natural gifts as an artist were not outstanding; and he was a slow starter. Mondrian was the son of the principal of a Protestant elementary school and he grew up in an atmosphere of Calvinism that was liberal but
1 still imbued with a strong Puritan heritage. The view of the Jacobskerk in the village of Winterswijk seen from the garden of his family home, painted early in 1898, tells a tale. The picture is stylistically unremarkable within the context of contemporary Dutch landscape painting; but it has about it a moody intensity, and in the light of Mondrian's subsequent development it is interesting to note the way in which the sullen, grey sky is caught up between the skeletal black branches of the trees in the foreground and pressed forward onto the surface of the picture. If this early picture tells us something about the role of religion in provincial Dutch
2 life at the turn of the century, *Composition II with Blue*, for example, painted some forty years later, says something about art as icon, about art as substitute for religious belief.

Through his Uncle Frits, who had taken over the family barber's shop in The Hague and was himself a painter, Mondrian came into contact with the school of art which bore the city's name. The Hague School combined traditional Dutch principles with the influence of the Barbizon School and other pre-Impressionist French art; and by the time that Mondrian encountered it, it was becoming increasingly conservative in outlook. Amsterdam, where Mondrian registered at the Rijksakademie in 1892, was livelier and more receptive to contemporary trends

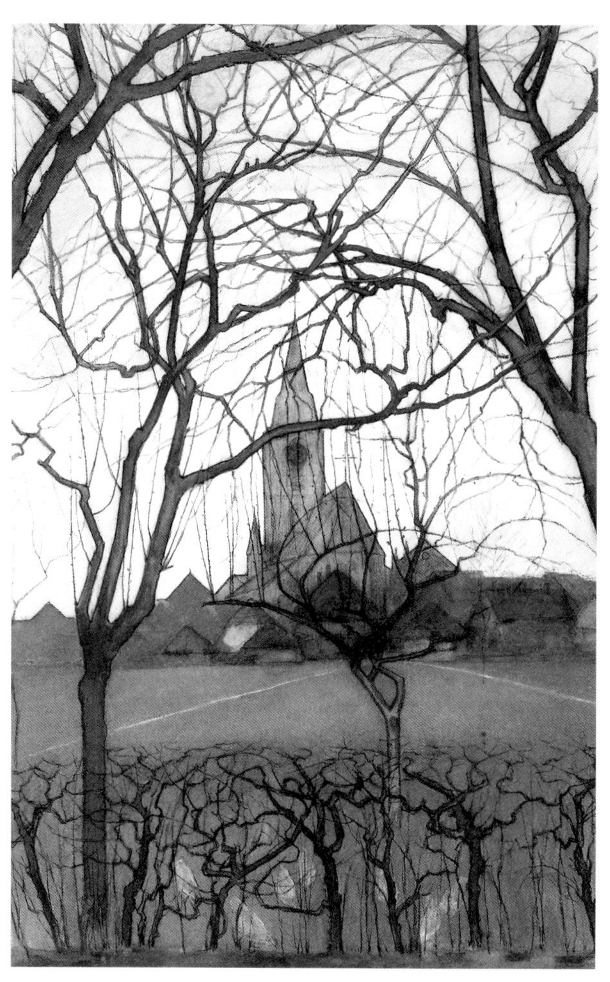

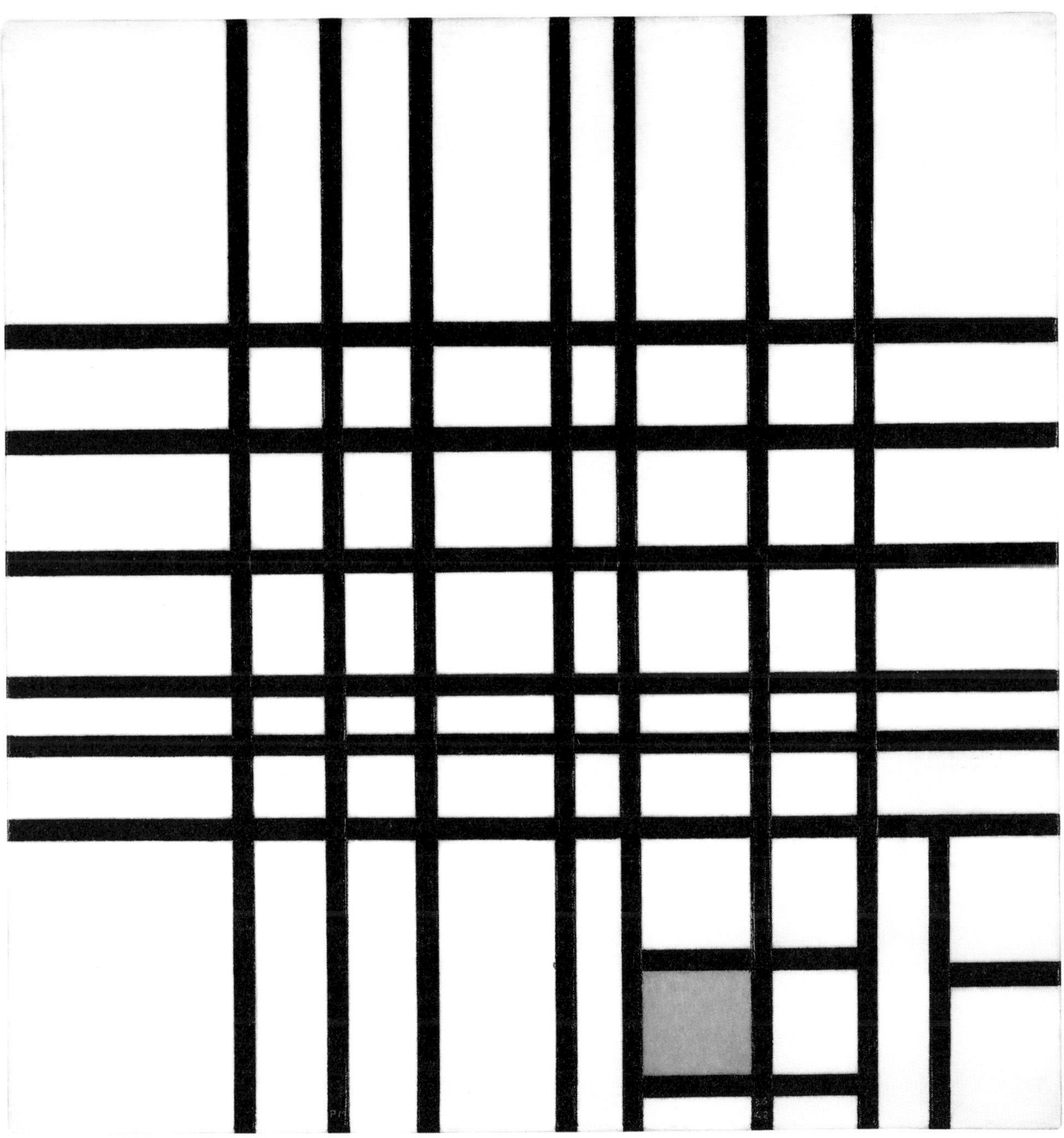

1 Mondrian, *The Jacobskerk, Winterswijk,* pencil, charcoal, pastel, watercolour and gouache on paper, 1898.

2 Mondrian, *Composition II with Blue,* oil on canvas, *c.* 1936–42.

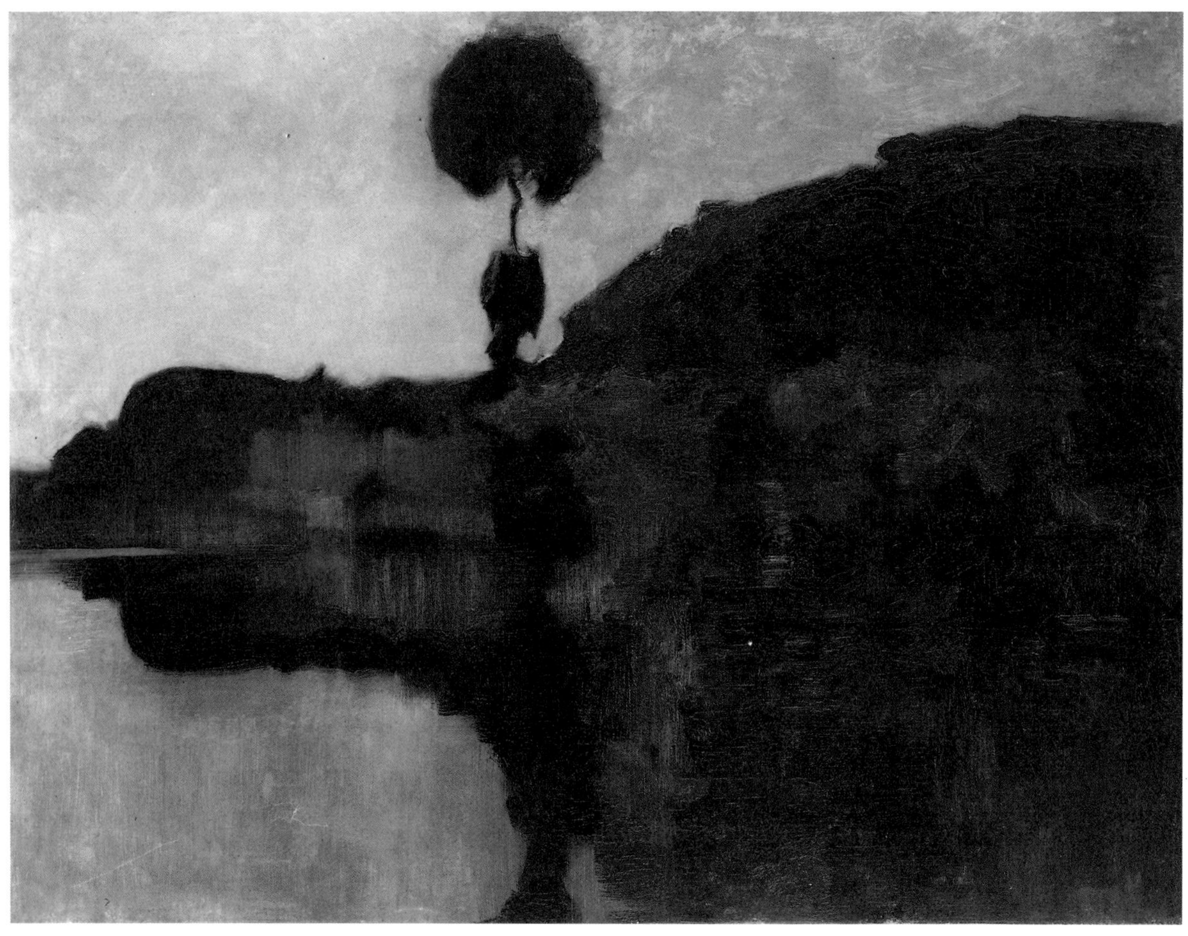

3 Mondrian, *Evening on the Gein with Isolated Tree*, oil on canvas, *c.* 1907–8.

from abroad; but although Mondrian absorbed some of the current interest in Symbolism, he was still standing apart from progressive trends, just as he belonged to and yet stood apart from the city's bohemian community. And the truth is that as a painter Mondrian was ultimately an autodidact, struggling against his own technical limitations.

But between 1906 and 1907 Mondrian's art begins to take on a new dimension. While remaining within the context of a conservative Dutch landscape tradition, his paintings now start to catch and to hold the eye, partly because they begin to acquire a bolder, more reductive look, but above all because they now begin to generate what can only be described as a feeling of expectancy; this is experienced particularly strongly in a work such as *Evening on the Gein with Isolated Tree* 3
(*c.* 1907–8). These paintings are totally still and devoid of movement, yet they have about them a feeling of suppressed drama; the light comes almost invariably from behind, and is most often slowly sinking. Looking at them, we sense that something is about to happen. Twilight, for Mondrian at this stage in his career, was the hour of revelation and heightened sensibility, just as it was for Kandinsky. Mondrian had also by now begun to work in series, unlike his Dutch contemporaries

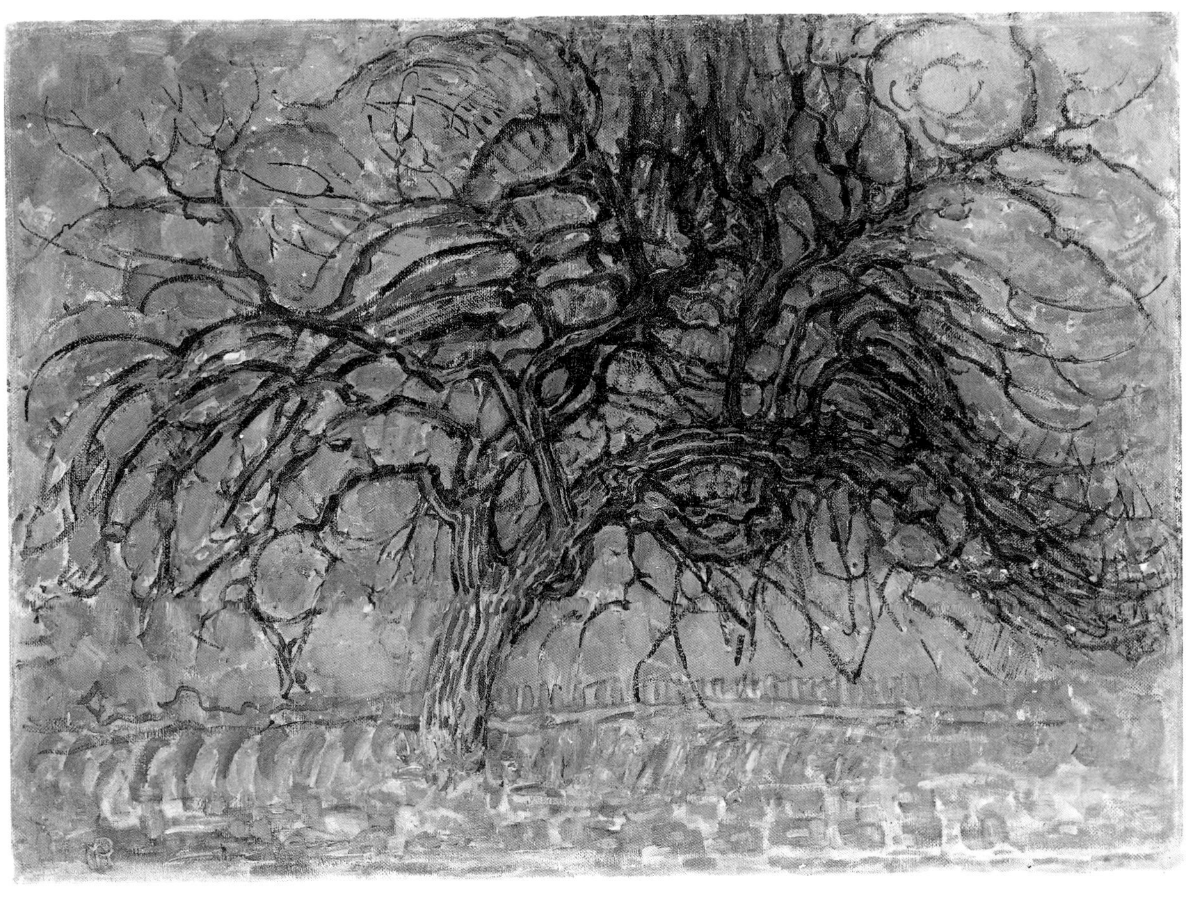

4 Mondrian, *Evening; Red Tree*, oil on canvas, 1908.

and peers; in other words, he was thinking in terms of themes and not in terms of individual motifs.

Mondrian wrote extensively about art, as also – at even greater length – did Malevich and Kandinsky. At the same time each painter insisted that in practice he proceeded purely intuitively and was not primarily a theoretician. Rather, all three were overwhelmed by the wealth of possibilities opening up to art as they sensed before them a network of shining paths into a new abstract hinter-world. And they felt the need to talk about it. In their writings they were not so much justifying their own art, and not one of the three men discusses his own art in any depth; rather they were in their different ways proclaiming the arrival of new sensibilities which could speak of new pictorial truths. In this respect their art had a moral cast in a way that the art of the Impressionists, to take a single example, did not. Mondrian's writings are often turgid and repetitive. They are further flawed by contradictions; and in this respect they are in marked contrast to his paintings, which so uniquely reconcile visual oppositions.

The most revealing of Mondrian's texts from the point of view of his own development as a painter is also the most accessible, and it came to be his own particular favourite. *Natural Reality and Abstract Reality*, written 1919–20, takes the form of a 'Trialogue' – a three-way conversation between a Naturalistic Painter ('X'), a Layman ('Y') and what Mondrian calls an Abstract-Real Painter ('Z'), i.e. himself. It has as a subtitle *While Strolling from the Country to the City.*[1] The first scene is set in a river landscape (like that of *Evening on the Gein*) and the moon has risen. All three men agree on the beauty and inspiration to be found in nature. However, Z, the Abstract-Real Painter, says, 'We need not look past the natural, but we should in a sense see through it.'[2] In a high proportion of Mondrian's work of this period the landscape is reflected in water, echoing and reversing the imagery above it and thus not only negating recession but also challenging the hierarchies of perceived reality. Z also remarks on the way twilight flattens things out, and there is already a tendency in Mondrian's mind to equate flatter effects with enhanced spirituality or with the generalized essence of things brought forward to confront the viewer directly.

In the autumn of 1908 Mondrian paid a short visit to the village of Domburg in Zeeland; he was to return there often. The circle of artists working there under the unofficial leadership of Jan Toorop, who had produced his own very radical branch of Dutch Symbolism, was the most avant-garde to be found in Holland at the time. It introduced Mondrian to Neo-Impressionism. It is also highly likely that Mondrian had visited the Van Gogh retrospective, recently mounted in Amsterdam, which highlighted his French work; *Evening; Red Tree* of 1908 speaks 4
eloquently of Van Gogh's influence. The first Domburg visit transformed Mondrian into a modernist. He heightened his palette and yet altered and restricted it from painting to painting in such a way that harmonies glow and generate an intense, at times unnaturalistic, sense of light, a mystic light with symbolic implications; this can be experienced in *Mill in Sunlight*, also of 1908. But Mondrian's first 5
contacts with French Post-Impressionism were largely at second hand; and even when he became conversant with developments in the Parisian art world at first hand – and this was true even of his encounters with Cubism – they never came to him as the revelation that they did to Malevich and Kandinsky; rather he sought from them aspects that confirmed his own already determined artistic convictions. Of all great twentieth-century painters he is the most internalized and his development the most purely linear.

Scene Four in *Natural Reality and Abstract Reality* shows 'A mill from close up, dark and sharply silhouetted against a bright night sky – its arms arrested in the form of a cross'. A pivotal image of Mondrian's, *Red Mill at Domburg* of 1911, 6
comes instantly to mind. Z stresses the fact that the closeness of the mill makes the use of normal perspective impossible (one cannot situate it against a horizon line). And here Z is already suggesting to us that one of the many ways into abstraction can involve a move up into the very breast of perceived reality and into the heart of what an individual canvas or series of canvases may be depicting. As with Mondrian's visual sources, so with his intellectual sources. Out of his personal background he formulated his own attitude to life, and he turned to outside intellectual stimulus for confirmation about what he already knew and felt: this separates him sharply from both Malevich who allowed himself to be bombarded by, and Kandinsky who sought out a vast range of both mainline and esoteric cross-currents of thought. In 1909 Mondrian wrote: '. . . my work remains entirely outside the occult realm, although I try to attain occult knowledge for myself in order to gain a better understanding of things.'[3] Theosophy, which flour-

ished as a cult during the 1890s and the first two decades of the twentieth century, might perhaps be described as a sort of Western Buddhism. Its goal was transcendental knowledge. It sought to destroy the boundaries between all religions and to transform observation of the natural world into 'the inner eye'. Helena Petrovna Blavatsky had founded the Theosophical Society in 1875. Mondrian claimed to have encountered Blavatsky's writings only in 1908; but he was aware of Theosophy earlier. At the time when Mondrian encountered Jan Toorop and his Domburg circle they were becoming increasingly interested in Theosophy and it was then that Mondrian recognized that its cosmology was what he himself had been looking for. Blavatsky's *The Secret Doctrine* came out in 1888; and it was to his friend Theo van Doesburg that Mondrian would confide that he got 'everything' from it.[4]

Today the lack of intellectual rigour which is one of the chief characteristics of Blavatsky's writings makes them hard to take. She was, however, astonishingly widely read and her books offer a short cut to a vast panorama of occult thought and religion. Indeed, to artists who saw themselves as being in a period of acute transition the tenets of Theosophy must have seemed marvellously suggestive and adaptable. Blavatsky was receptive to art and she sought common meanings and hidden, occult truths in the symbols and signs of art in all its manifestations. One of Mondrian's greatest debts to Theosophy was his subsequent and abiding belief that all life is directed towards evolution, and that the goal of art is to give expression to this principle. From Theosophy he also derived the idea that progress towards ultimate revelation comes through the balance and reconciliation of opposing forces and that this reconciliation may have to be achieved through the destruction of any principle or belief that is becoming too dominant. Rudolf Steiner, who was to found the dissenting Anthroposophical movement in 1913, also played a part in Mondrian's intellectual orientation. Mondrian subscribed to his proposition that the exalted knowledge sought by the Theosophist could be drawn from the observation of ordinary day-to-day visual phenomena, through 'conscious observation'. Steiner lectured in Holland not only on Theosophy but also on Goethe and Hegel. Mondrian's subsequent adherence to the three primary colours – red, yellow and blue – owes much to Goethe's colour theories, and it was his own very personal blend of the spiritual tinged initially by the occult (as encouraged by Theosophy), together with the Platonic idealism of Hegel, that was ultimately to confirm the premises of his art.

Mondrian's fealty to Blavatsky can perhaps be explained by the fact that she saw religion and art as being on parallel paths and acknowledged that the aim of both was to transcend matter. An added attraction lay in the fact that, as far as art was concerned, she laid down no rules. Yet there is a sense in which Mondrian was to go beyond Theosophy when he entered his fully evolved abstract style. By 1919 he was beginning to reject certain aspects of Theosophical doctrine and soon he was complaining that the Theosophists 'could never achieve the experience of equivalent relationship' and hence never experience 'real, fully human harmony'.[5] In short, for Mondrian art was beginning to become a substitute for religious experience. And with his rejection of Theosophy Mondrian left behind a world of vast, intangible and amorphous ideas to re-enter one of the most constricted of all worlds: that of the self-contained, small-scale easel painting. But there is no doubt that it was his contacts with Theosophy that turned Mondrian into the painter-philosopher he was to become.

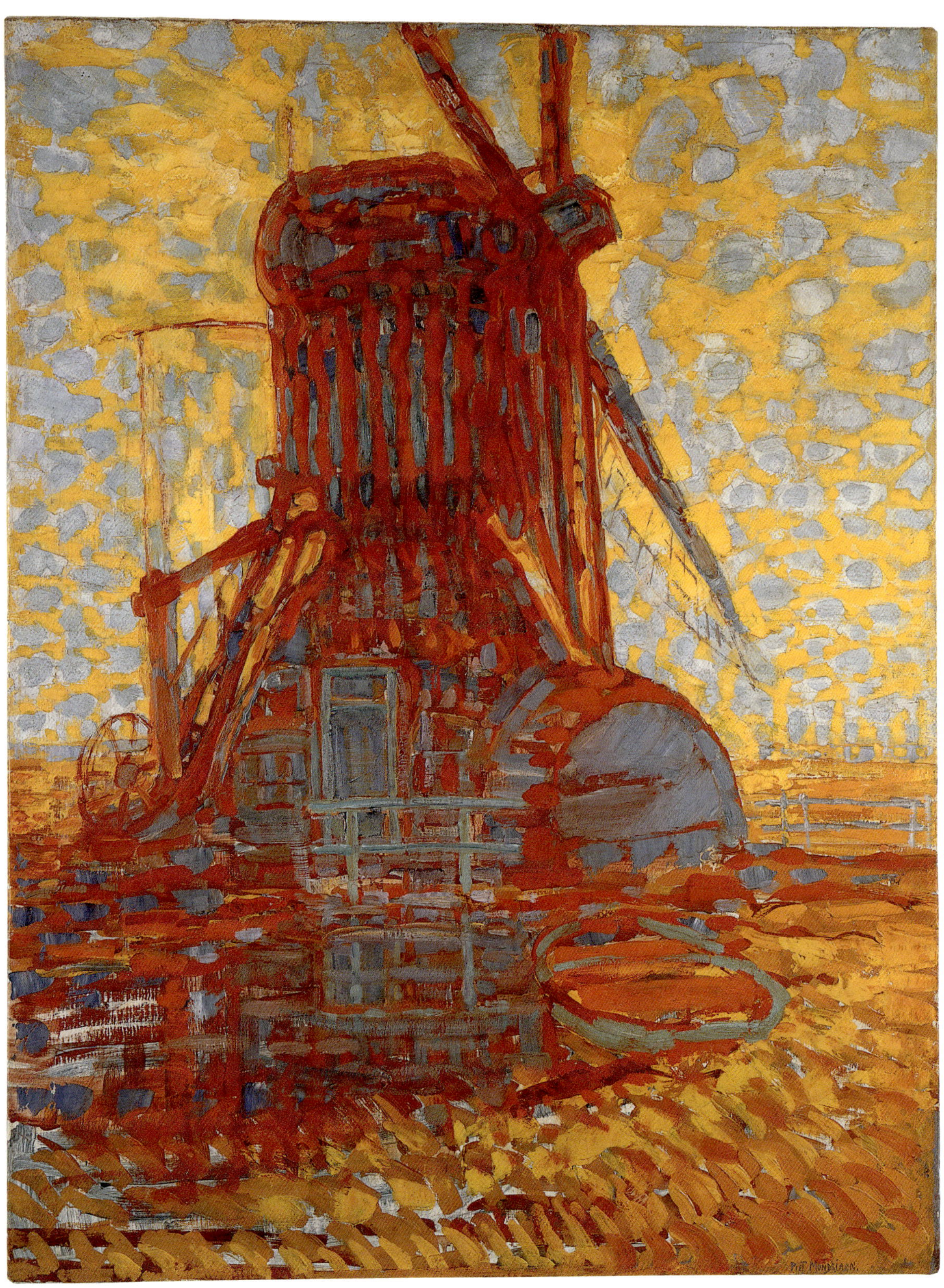
PIET MONDRIAAN.

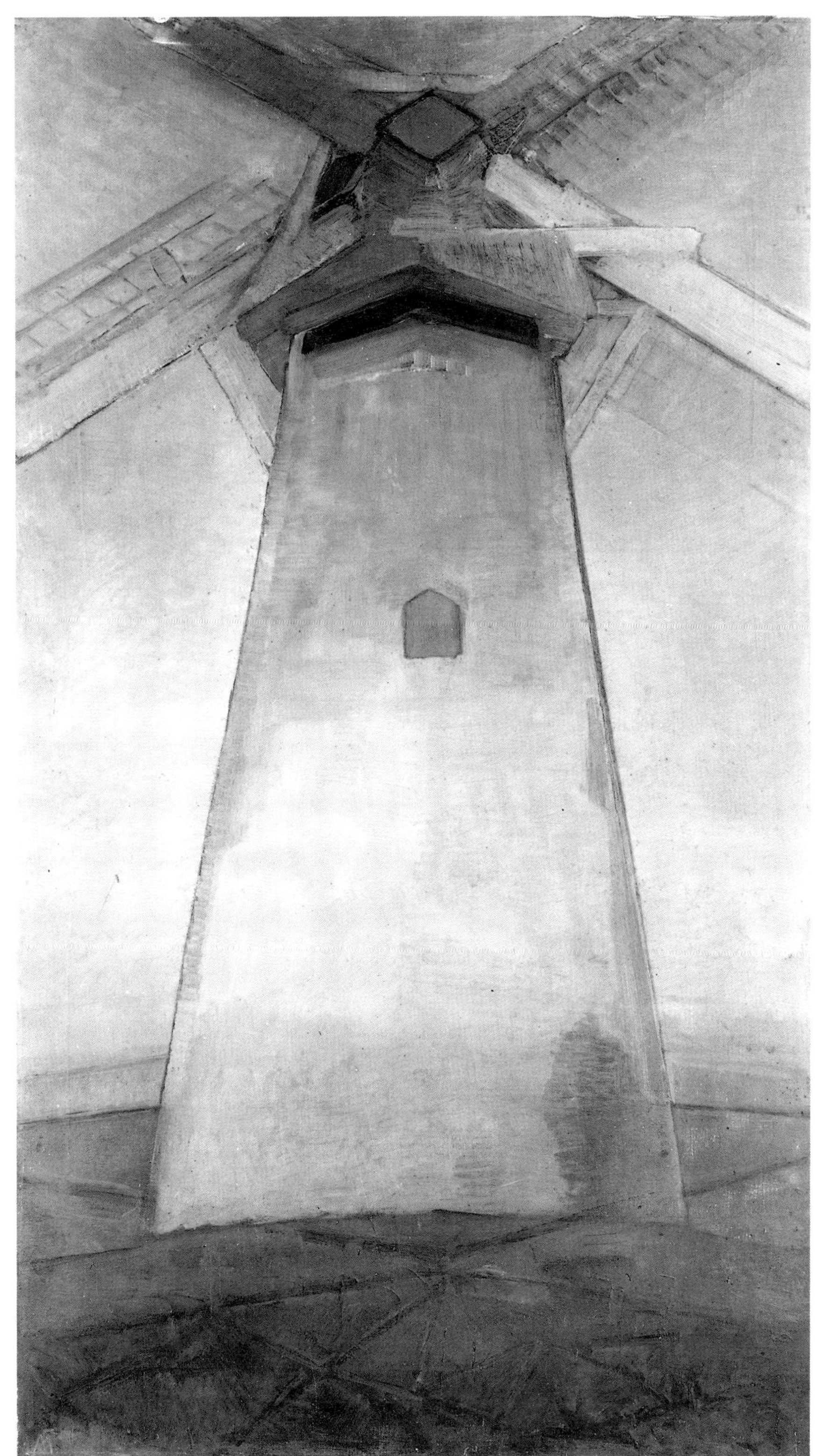

5 Mondrian,
Mill in Sunlight,
oil on canvas, 1908.

6 Mondrian,
Red Mill at Domburg,
oil on canvas, 1911.

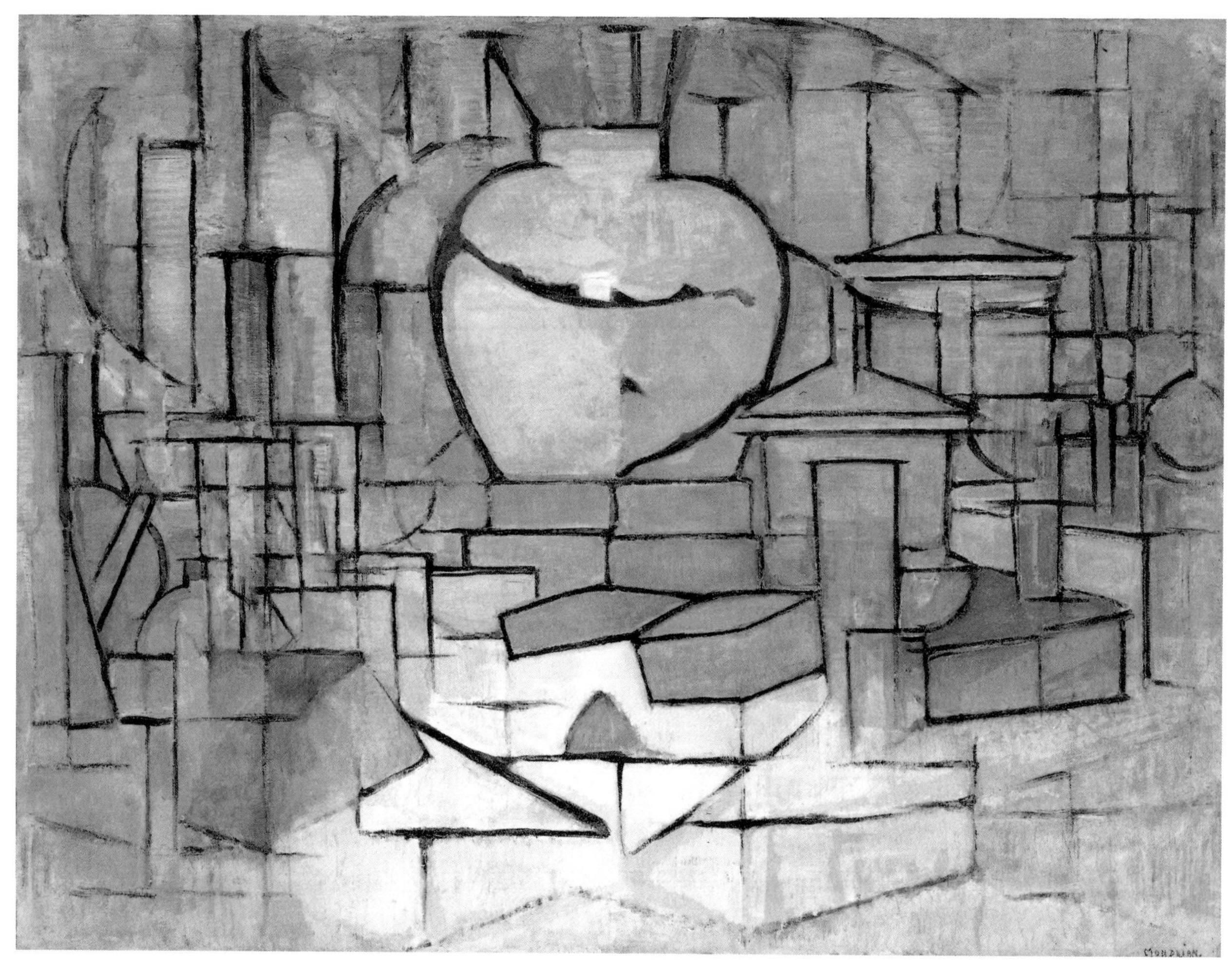

7 Mondrian, *Still Life with Ginger Pot II*, oil on canvas, 1911–12.

The works that illustrate most directly Mondrian's involvement with Theosophical ideas are a handful of figure pieces executed between 1908 and 1911, and they are the least satisfactory of his entire career. On the other hand, the principles of Theosophy inform the landscapes which also show his awakened interest in Post- and Neo-Impressionism, and they helped to endow these pictures with the haunting, numinous air that characterizes them. Mondrian came to see them as transitional in his development. However, it was the contacts with Cubism that marked the true turning-point in his career. As a prelude to his immersion in Cubism he turned to Cézanne, and through Cézanne he learned how to give equal pictorial weight to every single area of the picture surface. This can already be seen

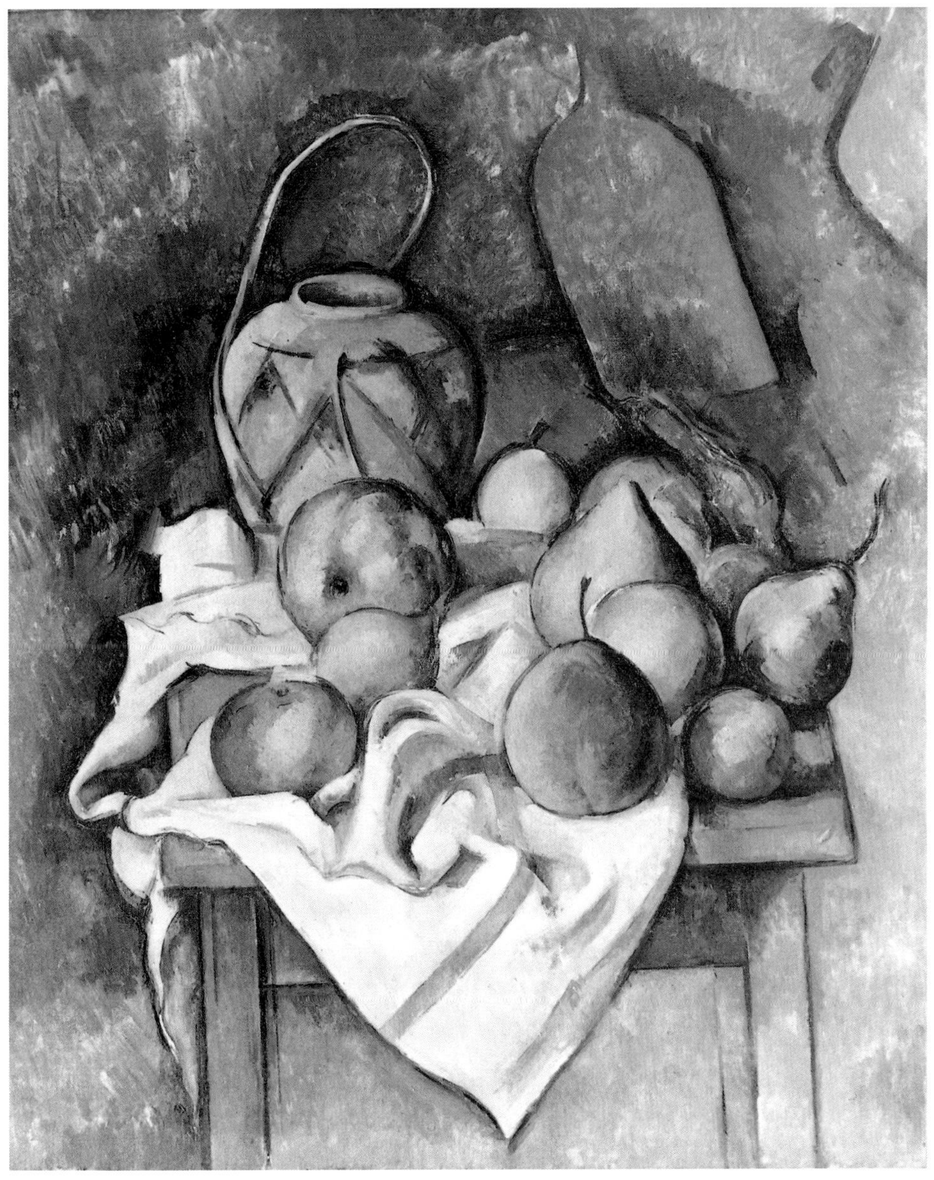

8 Cézanne, *Still Life with Ginger Jar*, oil on canvas, *c.* 1895.

7 in *Still Life with Ginger Pot II* of 1912, begun in Amsterdam and finished in Paris.
And here we come to one of the greatest and most revealing enigmas of twentieth-
8 century art. It was through Cézanne's example that in the first decade of this
century still life became the supreme vehicle for formalistic experiment. In the final analysis Cézanne's still lifes were more directly responsible for helping to shape the Cubist revolution than were his figure pieces or his landscapes. Yet it says something about the nature of abstract art that not one of the great twentieth-century abstractionists moved into non-figuration through still life. Each artist saw his work as being charged with esoteric or hidden meaning; and even the symbolic implications of a large proportion of still lifes executed throughout the ages simply

did not seem to be sufficiently charged with the spiritual and emotive content that could be found in depictions of the human form and of nature and its forces.

Although Mondrian was to turn his back so completely on nature, he had matured as a landscape painter; and it was through the obliteration of what had meant most to him visually that he achieved his triumph and his goal. In the early summer of 1911 Mondrian visited Paris for ten days and must have seen Cubist works on display at the Salon des Indépendants. That autumn, as a committee member, he helped to judge submissions to the first international exhibition of the Moderne Kunstkring (Modern Art Circle, founded in 1910) at the Stedelijk Museum, Amsterdam; the exhibition included twenty-eight works by Cézanne and examples of the early Cubism of Picasso and Braque, hitherto unknown in Holland. A few months later, Mondrian moved to Paris. He had come to realize that his art must meet the challenge of what was going on there. Basically, Mondrian was not interested in travel, but he always knew instinctively where his art required him to be.

Mondrian never became a Cubist. He particularly admired the work of Picasso, but he was never interested in the use of a multiple viewpoint, a method which was central to Picasso's Cubism and which enabled him to render his painted subjects in what might be described as sculptural plenitude. Mondrian may well have read into Cubism a search for formal certainties, whereas in fact Cubism was totally open-ended in its attempt to get to grips with the creation of a revolutionary formal vocabulary by which to render perceived visual reality in a new, completely unnaturalistic manner. The subsequent careers of both its initial creators, Picasso and Braque, demonstrate that this was their prime concern. But Mondrian also saw Cubism in clear-headed fashion, and he recognized that the abandonment of traditional, single-viewpoint perspective destroyed the window through which, for centuries past, Western artists had been looking out upon the external world. Through the Abstract-Real Painter Z he expressed his thoughts thus: 'Cubism understood that perspective representation confuses and weakens the appearance of things . . . Precisely because it sought to represent them as completely as possible Cubism came to represent them in several projections simultaneously.'[6] The phrasing is clumsy but the meaning is precise.

Mondrian made full use of the grids or scaffoldings of high Analytic Cubism, but put them to new ends, right from the start. He was not concerned with opening his subjects into the space around them and then in exploring the tactility, the palpability of this space; this had been Braque's prime concern, although Picasso also saw the grid as a more flexible way of feeling his way around the contours of things, coaxing more of the image up onto the picture plane. Mondrian wanted, on the contrary, to destroy the distinction between figure and ground, between matter and non-matter. The planes into which he dissolves the image and the space that surrounds it are invariably strictly frontal, and they reaffirm the flatness of the pictorial support. Although these planes hover and hang in front of and behind each other, they do not slide in and out of space as happens in contemporary canvases by Picasso and Braque. Similarly, lights and darks are not angled against each other to produce a sensation of volume and depth; and the blacks of Mondrian's scaffoldings already begin to read as dark elements in their own right.

The greatest of Mondrian's Cubist-inspired canvases was undoubtedly *Tableau* 9
No. 2, Composition No. VII, derived from studies of paired, as opposed to single, trees; and because of this it is instructive to compare this work with the only two-

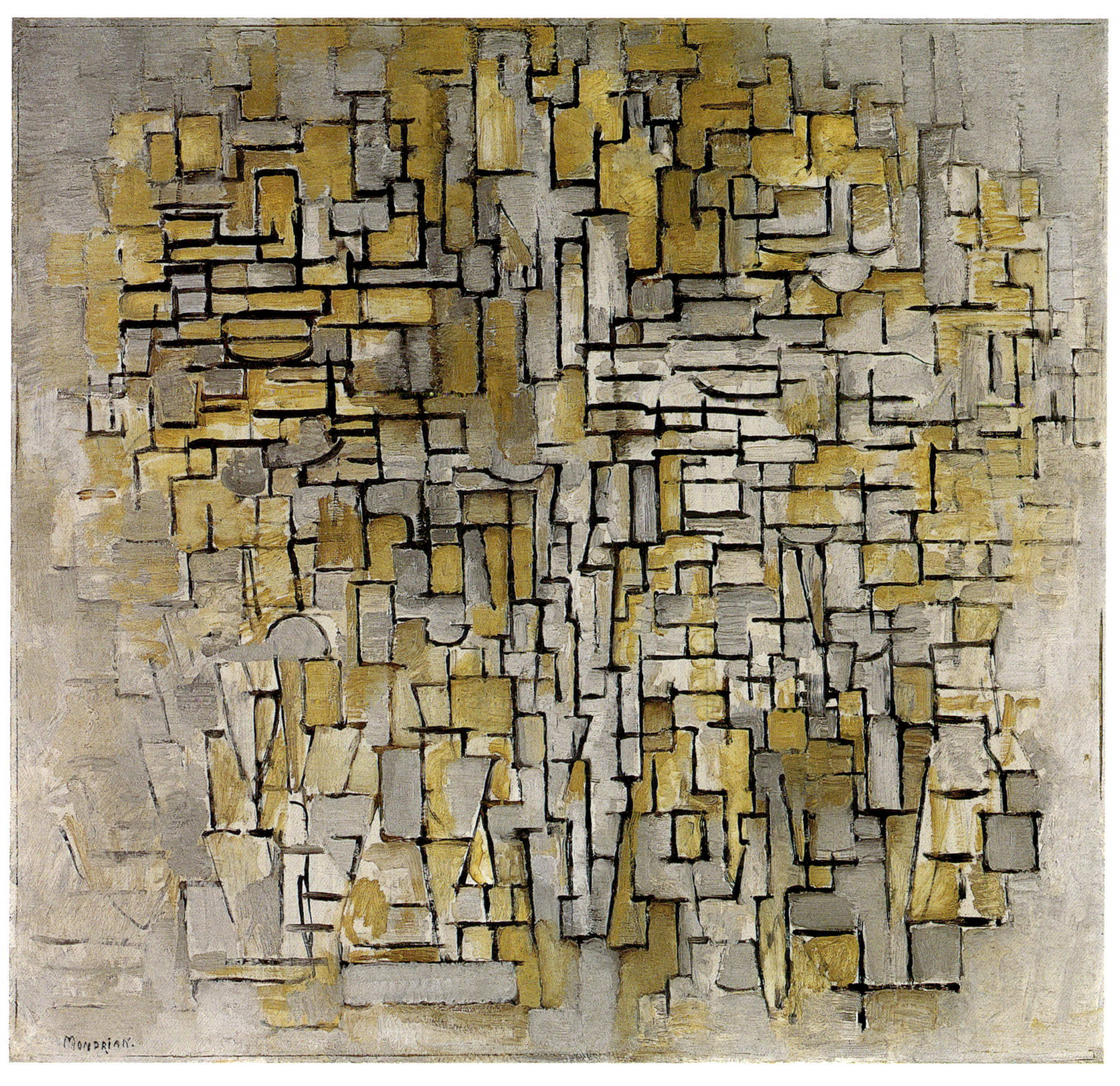

9 Mondrian,
Tableau No. 2,
Composition No. VII,
oil on canvas, 1913.

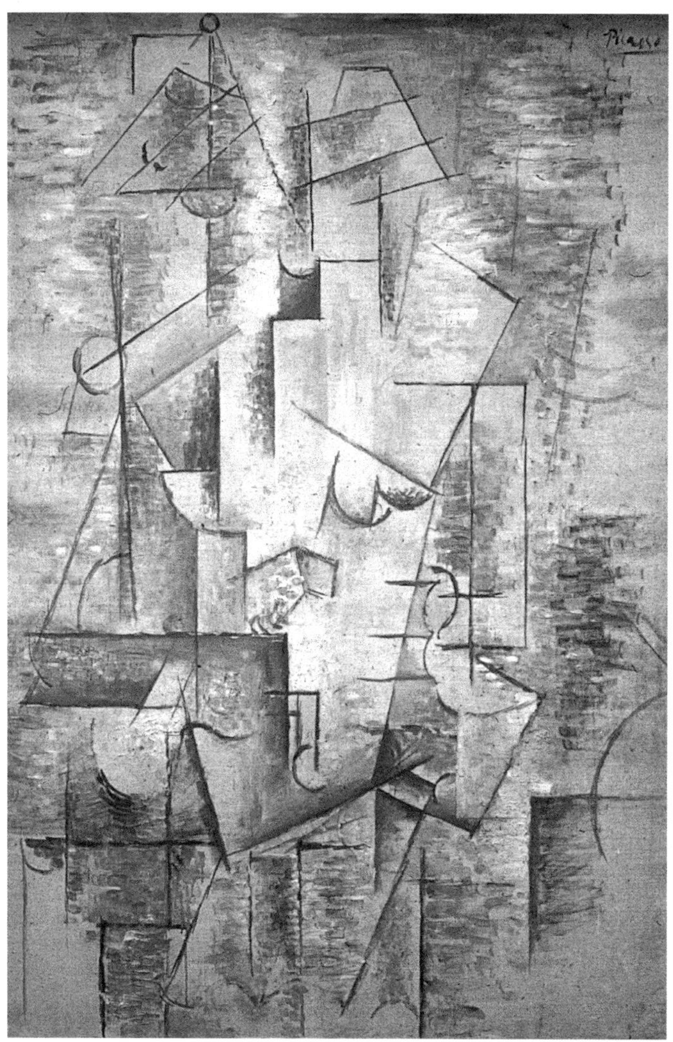

10 Picasso, *Soldier and Girl*, oil on canvas, 1911.

figure composition of Picasso's Analytic Cubist phase, *Soldier and Girl* of 1911. 10
Although he was fast putting natural appearances behind him, Mondrian still
loved the subject-matter that he was disguising and coming to renounce: hence the
painting's potency and beauty. Yet Mondrian was aware of the fact that the iconog- 11
raphy of Cubism was urban and that the Cubists had turned their backs on landscape because the volumetric and spatial sensations they were seeking to convey became too diffuse when related to distant views. From the depiction of trees he turned to compositions based on architectural motifs. Although these have about them a pellucid beauty, they do not move and excite us in the way that the tree-inspired paintings do, quite simply because the underlying subject did not really touch Mondrian's heart. In other words, for Mondrian these motifs are in a sense artificial.

Mondrian eased himself into a monochrome Cubist palette gently, by the use of tints of grey. Subsequently, during the latter of part of 1913 and 1914, when colour begins to creep back into his paintings, he makes use of tinted primaries: pale

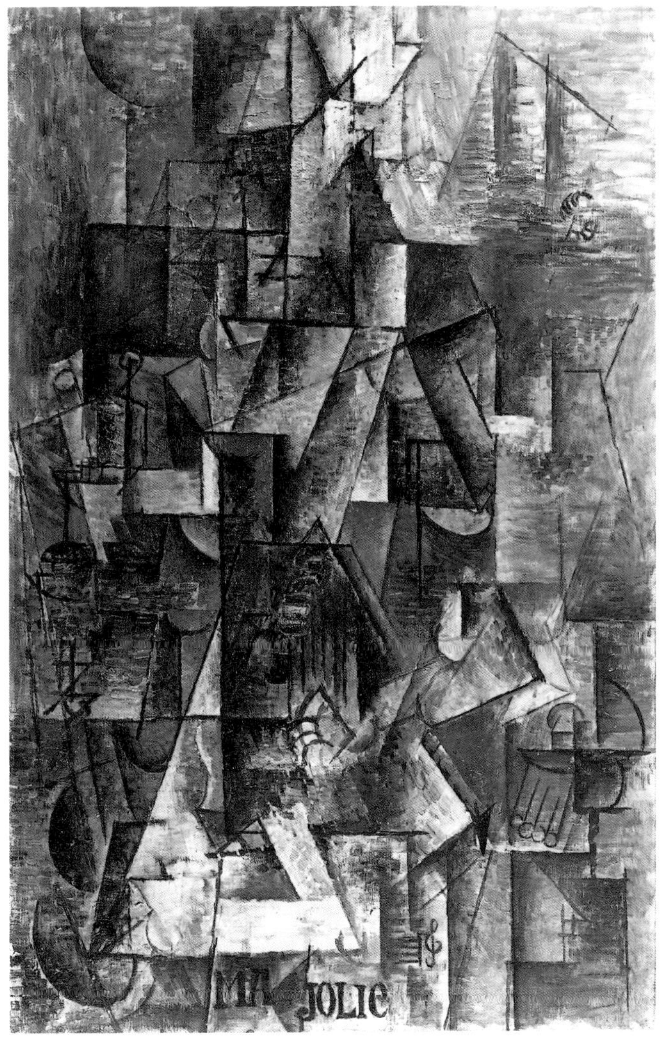

11 Picasso, *Ma Jolie* (*Woman with a Zither or Guitar*), oil on canvas, 1911–12.

radiant yellows (often derived from earth pigments), silvery blues, and pinks (reds reduced by the admixture of a lot of white). The pinks almost invariably weaken the impact of these canvases. From architectural façades Mondrian next turned to images which incorporate the internal geometry of gutted buildings. These are in a sense internalized cityscapes in that they include the inner, abandoned hearts of houses, and it is perhaps because of this that they possess once again a haunting quality that the slightly earlier façade paintings lack. Like the Cubists, Mondrian
12 was fascinated by oval formats.[7] By keeping the edges of his canvases blurred or indistinct he was able to explore the internal relations between lines and planes more independently and also to explore more freely the varying relationships between the vertical and the horizontal that were becoming increasingly important to him.

In 1914 Mondrian returned to Holland to see his father, who was ill; and there he was caught by the outbreak of war. Times were hard for him, but in retrospect one can see that it was fundamental and indeed even necessary for him to reassess

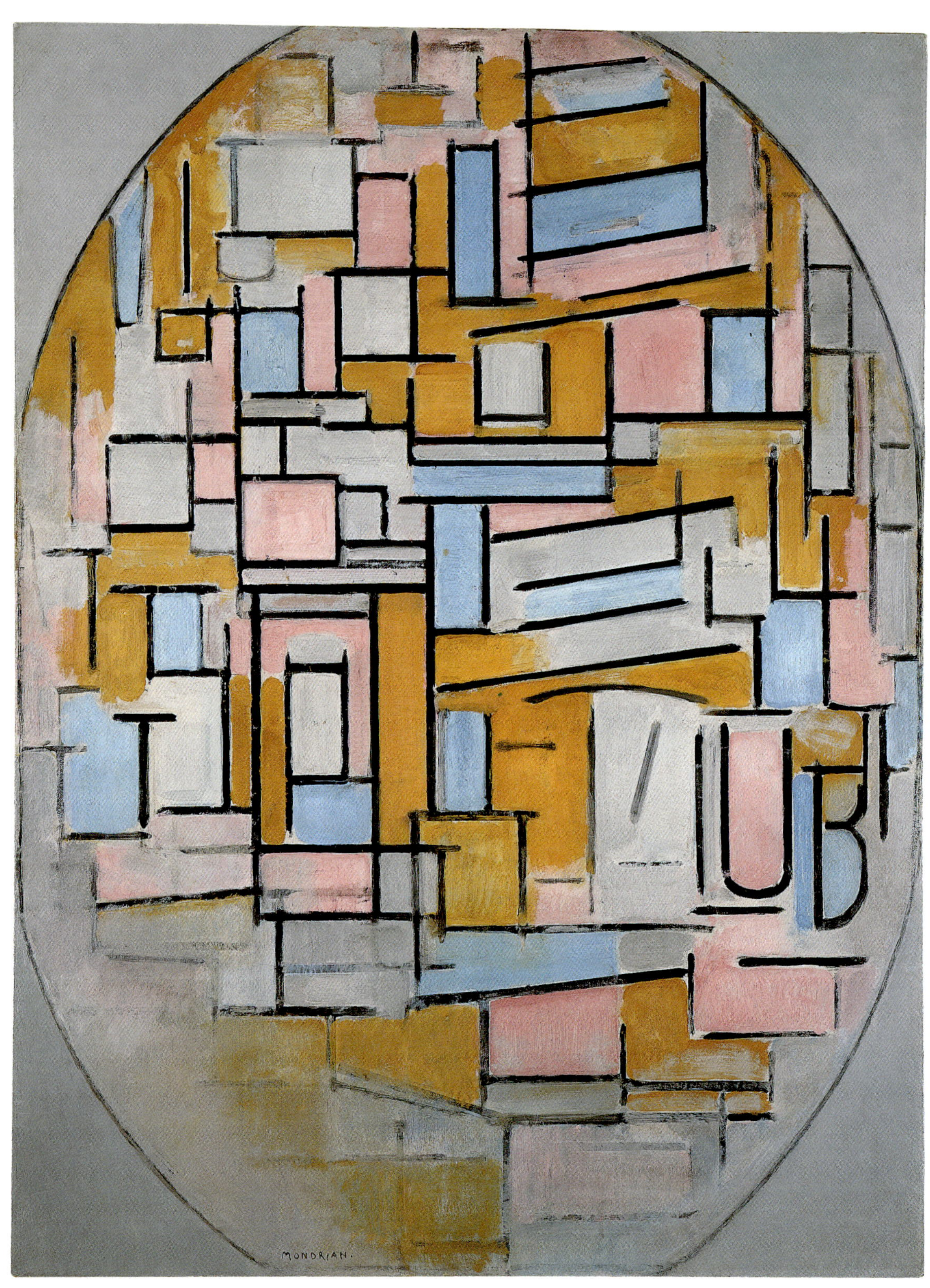
MONDRIAN.

12 Mondrian, *Composition in Oval with Colour Planes 2*, oil on canvas, 1914.

13 Mondrian, *Composition 1916*, oil on canvas (with wooden strip at bottom edge).

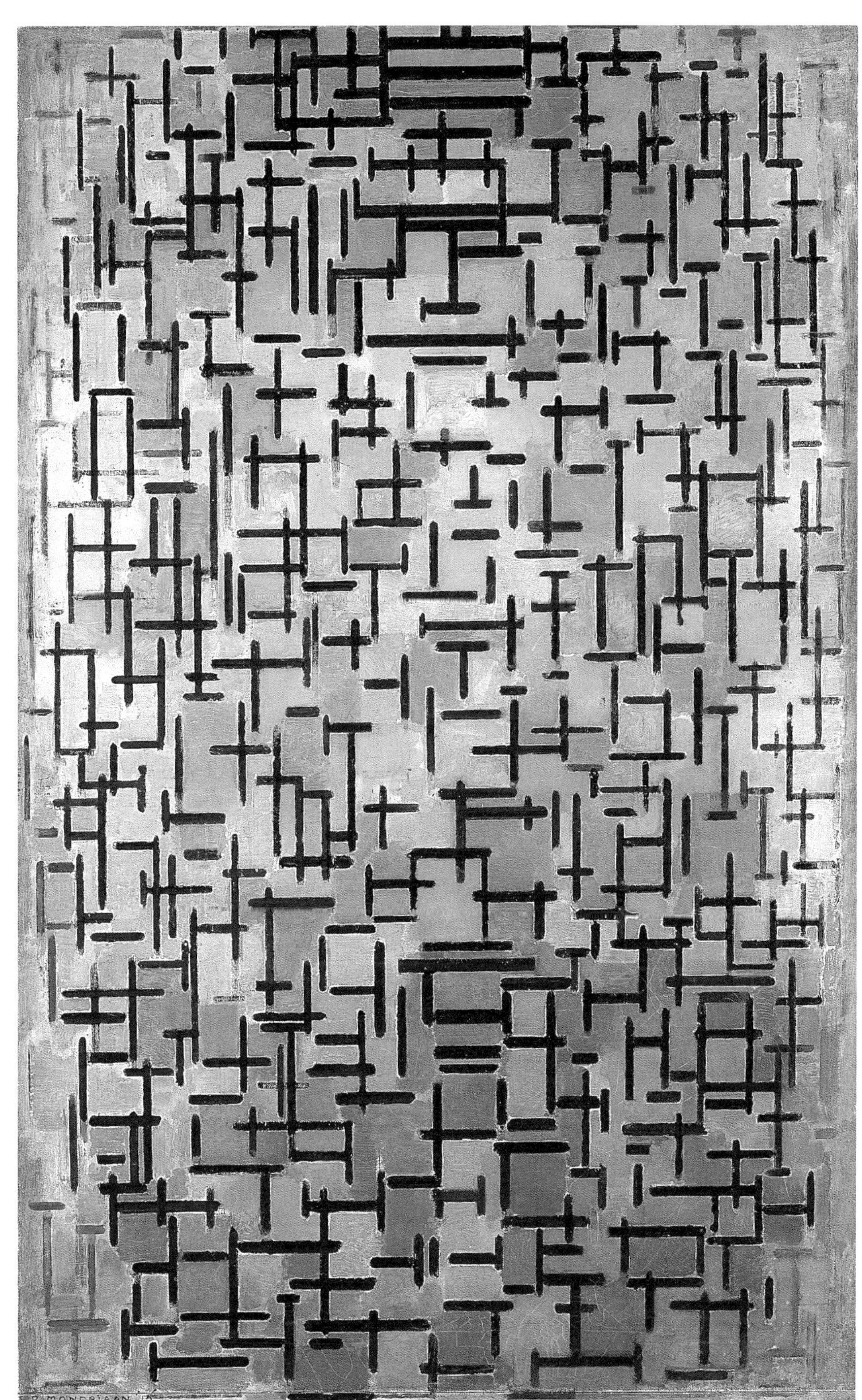

the discoveries he had made in Paris in the light of his earlier sources of inspiration. In the autumn of 1914 he revisited Domburg where, in addition to discovering modern art, he had originally fallen under the spell of the dunes and the sea. Scene 3 of the 'Trialogue' is set at night with stars shining in a bright sky above a wide expanse of water. The Abstract-Real Painter exalts the scene's beauty over that of tree- and riverscapes which he has come to find too particularized, too arbitrary in their configurations and, because of this, too reflective of what he calls 'the tragic' – the individually or subjectively emotive which he is now seeking to obviate. While at Domburg, Mondrian was drawing a lot, thinking out loud in black and white, and there he produced his so-called 'plus and minus' series in which he rendered church façades, dunes, the sea and the sky by short calligraphic, linear markings and notations that relate at a distance to his earlier experiments in divisionist and pointillist techniques.

The monochrome works on paper are precursors of one of the most profound and magical oil paintings ever produced by Mondrian, *Composition No. 10 in* 14
Black and White; Pier and Ocean of 1915. Here, a rough oval is described within the horizontal format of the canvas and this is filled with a network of vertical and horizontal lines, subtly and infinitely varied in length, which touch, cross, or hover independently to create a feeling of perfect equilibrium. However, they also pulse and shimmer, as does the sea itself when at rest. Perceived reality – the pier, the sea, the sky – may stand behind the configurations conveyed by the lines, but it is the lines themselves and their relationship to the white ground on which they are imposed and into which they are embedded that have become the subject of the painting: their pulse, their rhythm have become the pictorial image. Theosophy was still on Mondrian's mind, but now he knew what reductive conclusions he wanted to extract from it (and here the diagrams that Blavatsky made use of in *The Secret Doctrine*, the glyphs and symbols lifted from ancient and occult wisdom, may not be irrelevant). Blavatsky also writes, 'In all Cosmogonies "Water" plays the same important part. It is the base and source of material existence.'[8] Mondrian's ambitions to reproduce in his works the ebb and flow of water, of the sea, were pivotal to his move into a purely abstract idiom.

When 'Composition 10' was shown at an exhibition at the Stedelijk Museum in October 1915, the artist and critic Theo van Doesburg wrote: 'Spiritually this work is more important than all the others. It conveys the impression of Peace; the stillness of the soul.'[9] The review provoked a correspondence between the two men and after some hesitation Mondrian agreed to collaborate on a new periodical, *De Stijl*, which soon acquired a subtitle, *Monthly Review for New Art, Science and Culture*. De Stijl became an exciting new art movement and, largely through the periodical, an international force. Mondrian's first article for *De Stijl*, which was to become the first chapter of a book, *The New Plastic in Painting*, came out on 1 November 1917. One of the most remarkable and telling features about *New Plastic* is that it contains only one, indirect, mention of Theosophy, and this in connection with a reference to Kandinsky's *On the Spiritual in Art*. Here Mondrian suggests that Theosophy is simply another expression of the same spiritual movement that is being seen in painting. Mondrian now says of style what he had previously said of religion: that there is a single universal content which is embedded in a series of different forms that are the product of their particular age. 'Art – although an end in itself, like religion – is the means through which we can know the universal . . .'.[10] The parallels between art and religion are restated and made

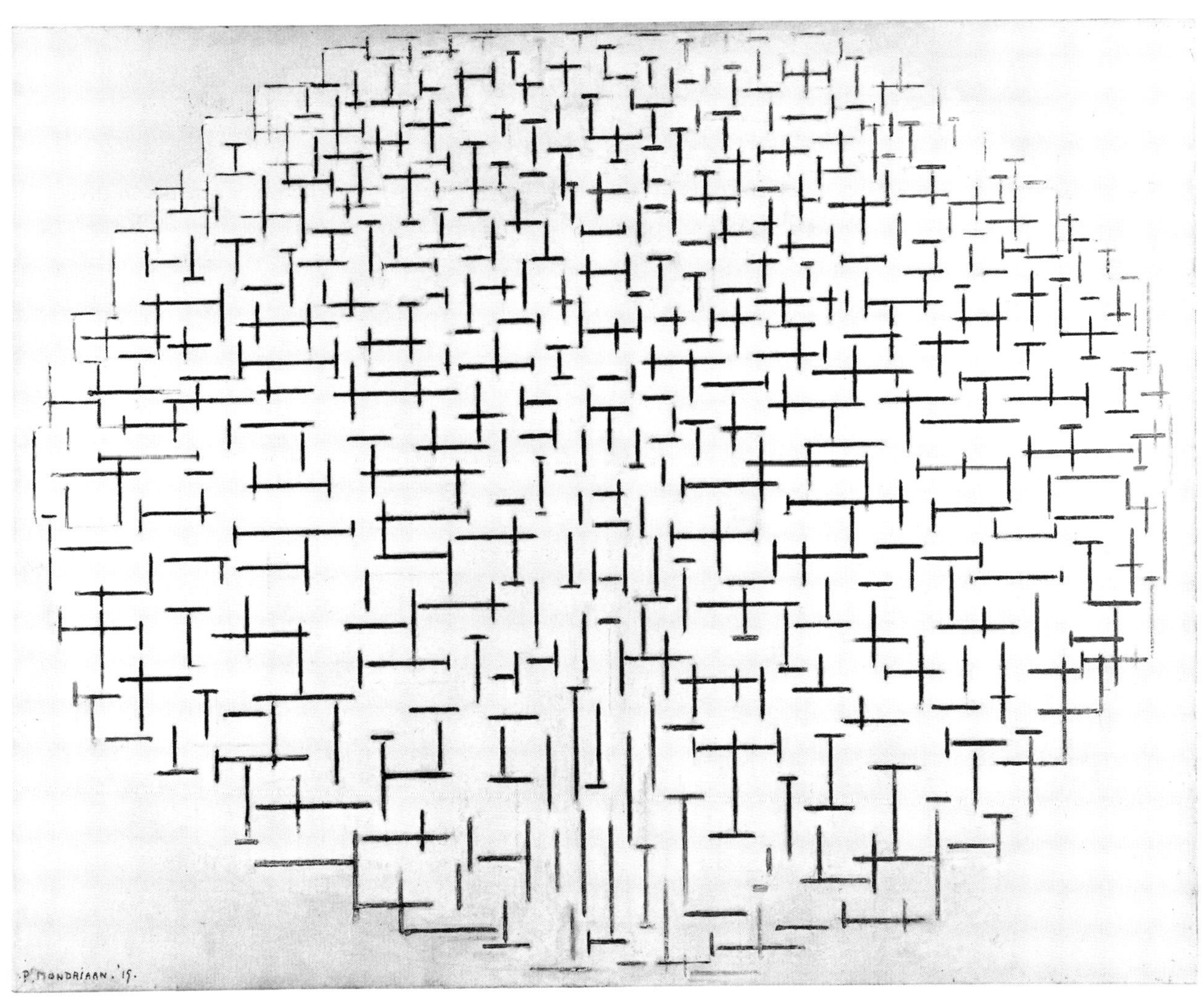

14 Mondrian,
Composition No. 10
in Black and White;
Pier and Ocean,
oil on canvas, 1915.

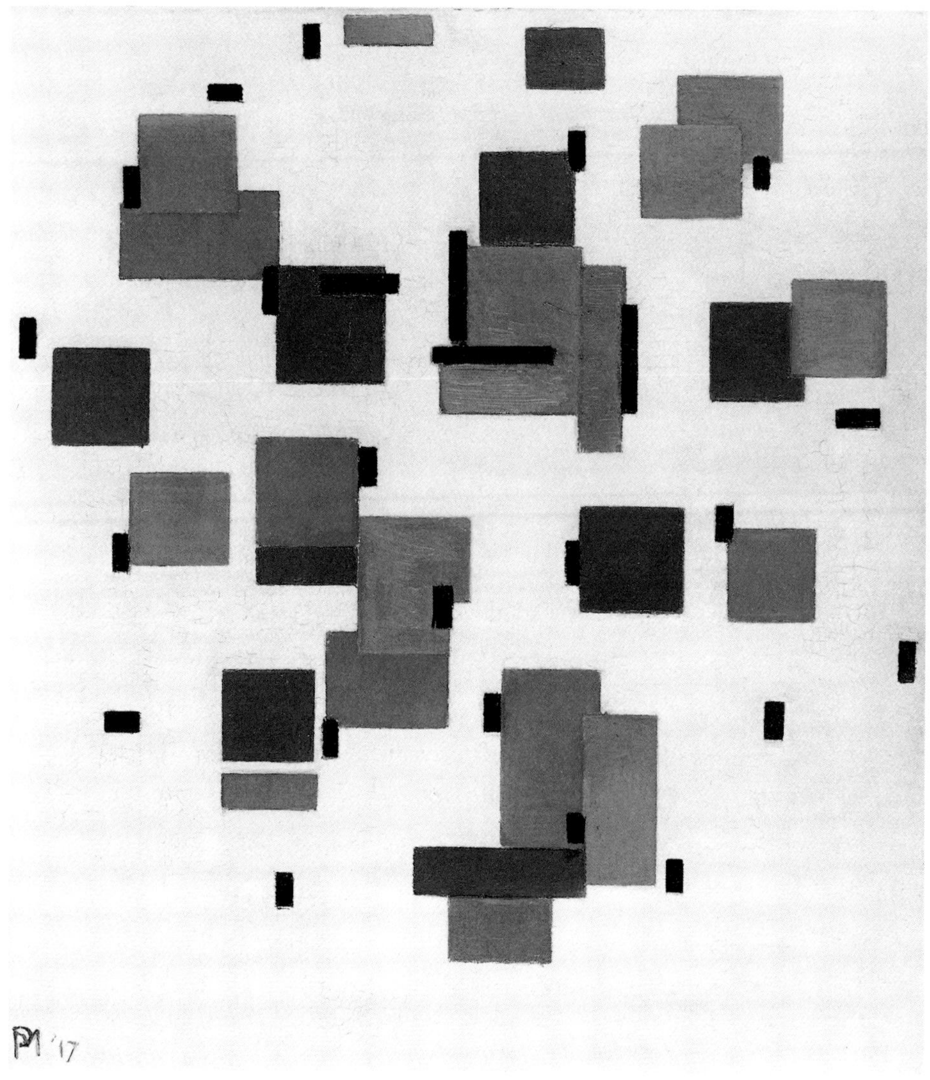

15 Mondrian, *Composition in Colour B*, oil on canvas, 1917.

even more explicit in other later writings.'The new art is the old art *free of all oppression* . . . , in this way art becomes religion.'[11] Already in *The New Plastic* Mondrian had written: 'As pure creation of the human *spirit*, art is expressed as pure aesthetic creation manifested in abstract form.'[12] It was the reductiveness and purity of the new art that was particular to his time: 'The growing profundity of the whole of modern life can be purely reflected in *painting*.'[13]

With *Composition* of early 1916, another pivotal work for Mondrian, the artist 13
moved back into colour, using it more boldly and richly than at any point since his virtual abandonment of it following his encounter with monochromatic Analytic Cubism. Here the black lines help to define the colour planes, although they do not always correspond to them, and they assume an equal importance. Mondrian was now moving fast towards abstraction, but this work owes much of its extraordi-

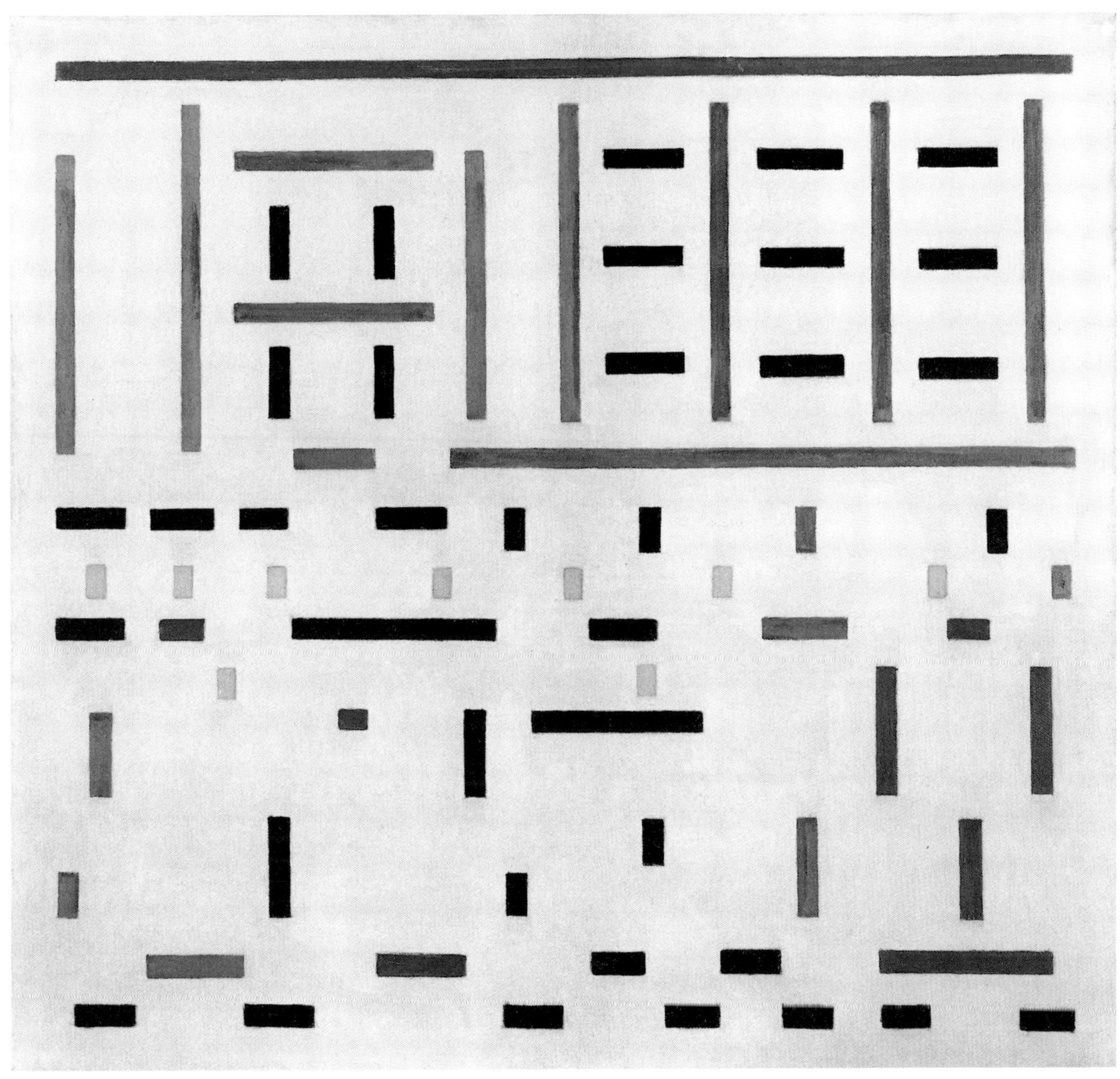

16 Bart van der Leck, *Geometrical Composition I*, oil on canvas, 1917.

nary presence to the fact that it has as its starting-point studies of the Domburg church façade. Mondrian had long since put aside the traditional religious beliefs of his family background, but the motif that formed his starting-point here was still charged for him with symbolic and emotive connotations. Architecture may still be
15 standing somewhere behind *Composition in Colour B* of 1917, but Mondrian was now on the cusp of pure abstraction.

Discussions between Mondrian, van Doesburg and the painter Bart van der Leck (the two figures associated with *De Stijl* who during the years 1917–18 meant most to Mondrian) concentrated on how far it was possible to go in restricting and purifying the means of painting, and on whether it was desirable or indeed permissible for the new art to have a starting-point in the natural world. For a while Mondrian kept an open mind on the latter issue. Earlier, in a letter of 1914, he had written:

'Nature (or the visible) inspires me, arouses in me the emotion that stimulates creation.'[14] Inevitably, however, as his art came to feed increasingly on its own processes, he distanced himself from perceived reality: 'When one does not describe or depict anything human – then, through complete negation of the self, a work of art emerges that is a monument of Beauty, far above anything human, yet most human in its depth and universality!'[15]

Mondrian was influenced by van der Leck – an example of an artist of genius 16
being prepared to learn from an infinitely lesser talent. When the two men became friendly in 1916, van der Leck was attempting to revive an interest in monumental, muralistic art, and had evolved a schematized, almost cartoon-like style which reduced figures and their surroundings to flat, bold coloured cutouts. After his contact with Mondrian, he sometimes further reduced and concealed his imagery in a diagrammatic manner, with the result that his art appeared at times to be totally abstract. Mondrian must have found van der Leck's work coarse, and while he disagreed with van der Leck's assertion that colour should always be used at full strength or hue, as if direct from the tube, he was impressed by the boldness of his younger colleague, and van der Leck's example helped Mondrian to eliminate the last vestiges of Cubist syntax from his work.

It was probably as a result of his theoretical discussions with members of the De Stijl circle that in some of his works of 1918 and 1919 Mondrian experimented with a modular grid structure based on a division of the canvas into eight sections.
One of these works, *Composition with Grid 1* (1918), was the first of Mondrian's 17
'lozenge' paintings. As is true of all Mondrian's work, this example loses its scintillation and presence in reproduction; and it might be fair to say that paintings by Mondrian suffer more in reproduction than do those of the other great painters of his age. I myself believe that originally the first four 'lozenge' or 'diamond' compositions were probably conceived and worked on as square paintings and only subsequently rotated through 45° or placed on one of their corners. Even in the early lozenge pictures total symmetry is avoided or destroyed by the way in which the interacting black or dark-grey lines are of different thicknesses, widened to left or right, above or below.

The lozenge pictures punctuate Mondrian's career. Although Mondrian insisted that there was no radical distinction between the diamond shapes and other more conventional formats, he seems to have used them to verify or to question successive visual conclusions, by, so to speak, standing things on their heads. It was with the early lozenge paintings that Mondrian made his total breakthrough into abstraction. Initially they almost certainly took as their starting-point the very firmament itself. In the 'Trialogue' Mondrian writes, '. . . because of the multitude of stars [the universal] now reveals itself as multiplicity. We no longer have to merely think of it as multiplicity. It is now visible as such.'[16] Owing to their unconventional positioning these paintings cannot be viewed as windows onto nature; horizontals inscribed on them cannot be read as implied horizons; and, as on oval canvases, the juxtaposition of vertical to horizontal becomes starker because their relationships cannot be related to the paintings' edges. Conceptually, because they are based on flexible geometric structures, these works are by implication infinitely extensible, but the unusual diamond formats forbid our eyes to acknowledge this. We are forced to accept these canvases as finite objects made up of discrete parts which are nevertheless inseparable from the matrix in which they are embedded. For the first time in the history of art the totality of the pictorial surface has become the pictures' very image: we are not looking at imagery within a picture, but rather viewing the entire picture surface itself *as* imagery.

18 Of *Composition with Grid 8; Checkerboard with Dark Colours* (1919) Mondrian wrote: 'at this moment I am working on something which is a reconstruction of a starry sky, and yet it is without a given in nature. So he who says one should start from a given in nature can be just as right as he who says one should not.'[17] But Mondrian also emphasizes that even if he was inspired by the infinity of the night sky, the work was conceived of as an abstract painting right from the start. The work also demonstrates why Mondrian soon abandoned the modular grid. His interest in the occult had undoubtedly made him aware of the secret power of geometry, but he wished it to remain secret and he was not in any case interested in geometry as such. More important still, when a modular structure is imposed on a conventional picture format with top, bottom and sides, the module is by implication more insistently extensible and can in the imagination be continued beyond its support; and Mondrian was seeking to discover how to render the universal and the infinite in paintings that were themselves palpably finite. This aim had been achieved in the first lozenge pictures. He now had to find ways of conveying the same conclusions within the traditional picture format.

Despite the fact that Mondrian derived obvious stimulus from his association with De Stijl, there are indications that he no longer felt completely at home in Holland. Then perhaps the Dutch landscape continued to haunt him and he was by now anxious to turn his back on nature as completely as possible. Relations with van der Leck had cooled. Mondrian endorsed wholeheartedly van Doesburg's attempts to broaden the perspectives of *De Stijl* to allow the journal to embrace as wide a variety of art forms as possible, though secretly he must have resented the fact that in it painting was not being given the supremacy that he felt it deserved. When he eventually broke with van Doesburg, it was not simply because of personal disputes, but because he resented the increasing importance that was being accorded to architecture by van Doesburg's ally van der Leck. Mondrian agreed that painting and architecture should advance hand in hand, always provided that it was acknowledged that painting must point the way forward. On the other hand, Mondrian used to describe his own paintings as architecture. And although his own influence was to be incalculable, he was aware of the fact that it was architects and environmentalists who had best understood what he stood for. It was at this moment that he declared, '. . . there must be a destruction of the natural and the reconstruction of it in accordance with the spirit.'[18]

On 22 June 1919, Mondrian returned to Paris, taking with him the unfinished manuscript of his 'Trialogue'. Its closing scene is set in the studio of the Abstract-Real Painter and it describes Mondrian's own studio in the rue des Coulmiers. He had always been conscious of the appearance of his working spaces and now he created the first of his interiors which mirrored very directly his pictorial concerns by attaching rectangular pieces of cardboard, painted in primary colours and grey and white, to the off-white walls of the studio. His two easels and the few pieces of furniture, mostly made by himself out of abandoned crates and boxes, were similarly painted. He moved to a new studio in the rue du Départ in 1921,[19] and this was to become the most famous of his working and living places. Strangers, often foreigners, would knock on the door and ask to have a look. The interior was small, with virtually no facilities, and here Mondrian lived and worked. One can imagine him in the evening, sitting in the only comfortable chair, studying the walls

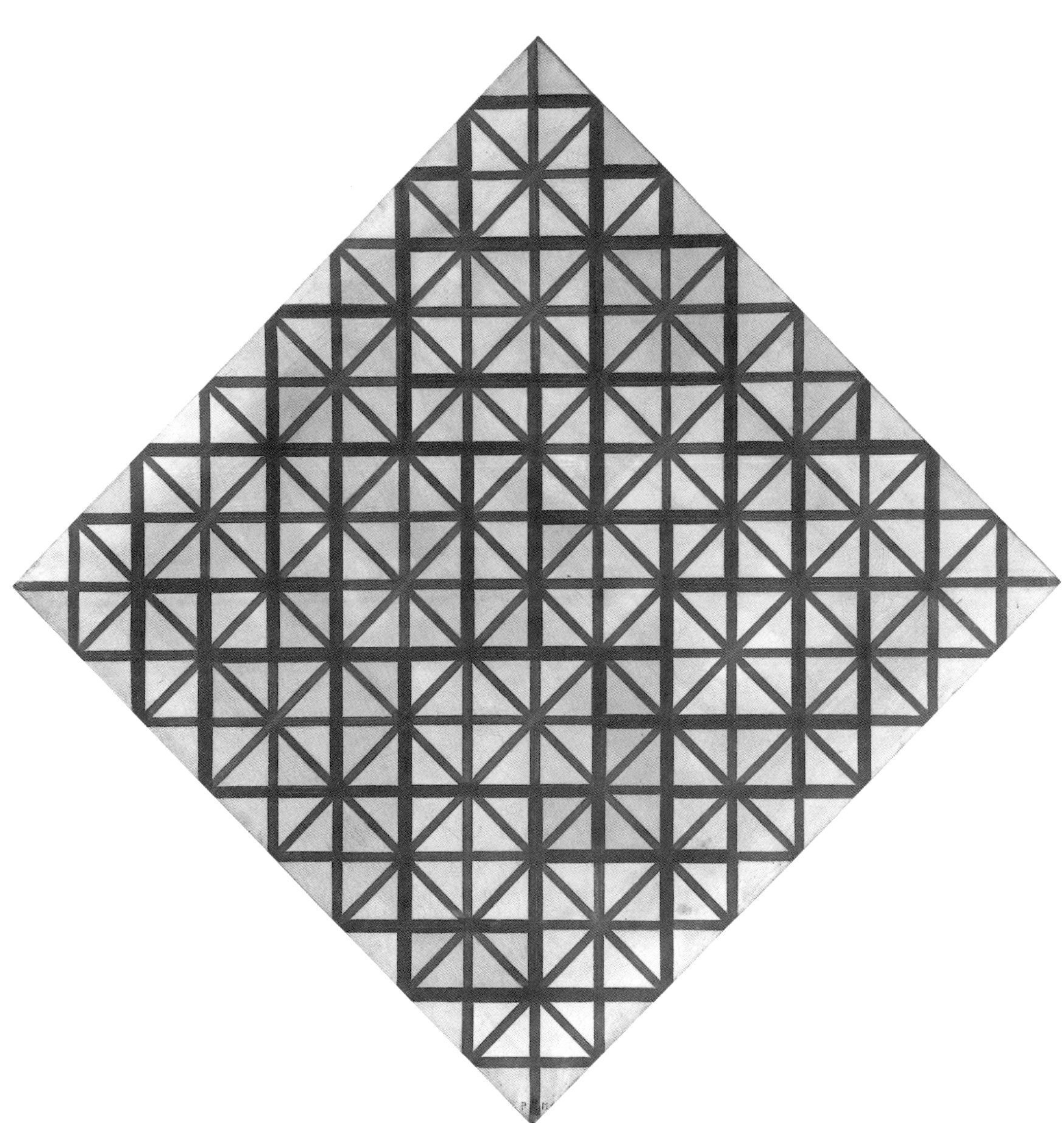

17 Mondrian, *Composition with Grid 1 (Lozenge)*, oil on canvas, 1918.

and the coloured shapes imposed on them, getting up from time to adjust one of them. In the 'Trialogue' the layman Y says, 'I am no by no means surprised that this studio is yours. It breathes your ideas; it is altogether different from most.'[20] We all live in our minds to a greater or lesser extent, and the surroundings of many of us reflect our personal concerns and natures. In the case of Mondrian, however, the environments he created for himself were diagrams of his mind, and he lived in them in spiritual, if not physical, comfort.

Already before his return to Paris, Mondrian had evolved his characteristic method of composition, although he was to alter it subtly from painting to painting, so that by the end of his life he had produced an astonishing number of variations on a basically simple formula. *Composition with Colour Planes and Grey Lines 1* of 1918 is a pivotal work. An irregular grid of relatively thick lines 19

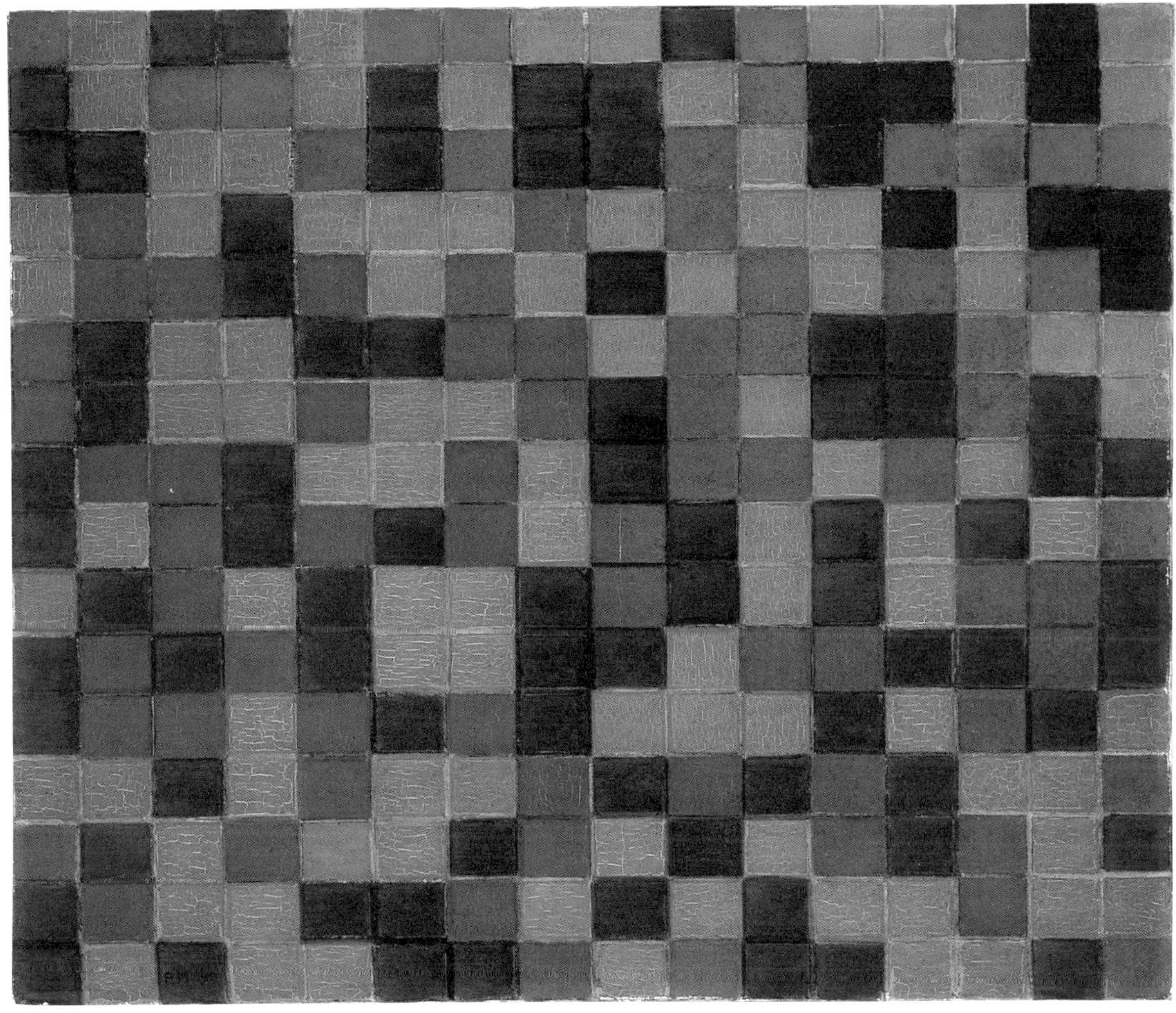

organizes the picture surface; all of them are either vertical or horizontal – some extend to the outer edges of the canvas, some do not, thus ensuring that the picture does not look like a fragment of a larger whole. The rectilinear shapes or planes created by the grid are of an ochre-like yellow, a tinted cobalt-blue, and faded roses or pinks, offset by others of white or of the palest grey; some of these are cut off by the picture's outer edges, in turn affirming that the coloured planes could be continued outwards and have an existence independent of their linear corset. Only in one instance are two areas of the same colour placed adjacent to each other; and the individual colours call to their counterparts across the picture surface. Here the yellows appear to stand forward from the picture surface, but some do so more than others because the size of the planes that they describe are unequal and thus condition the optical effects of colouristic saturation. The blues are distributed in

18 Mondrian, *Composition with Grid 8; Checkerboard with Dark Colours*, oil on canvas, 1919.

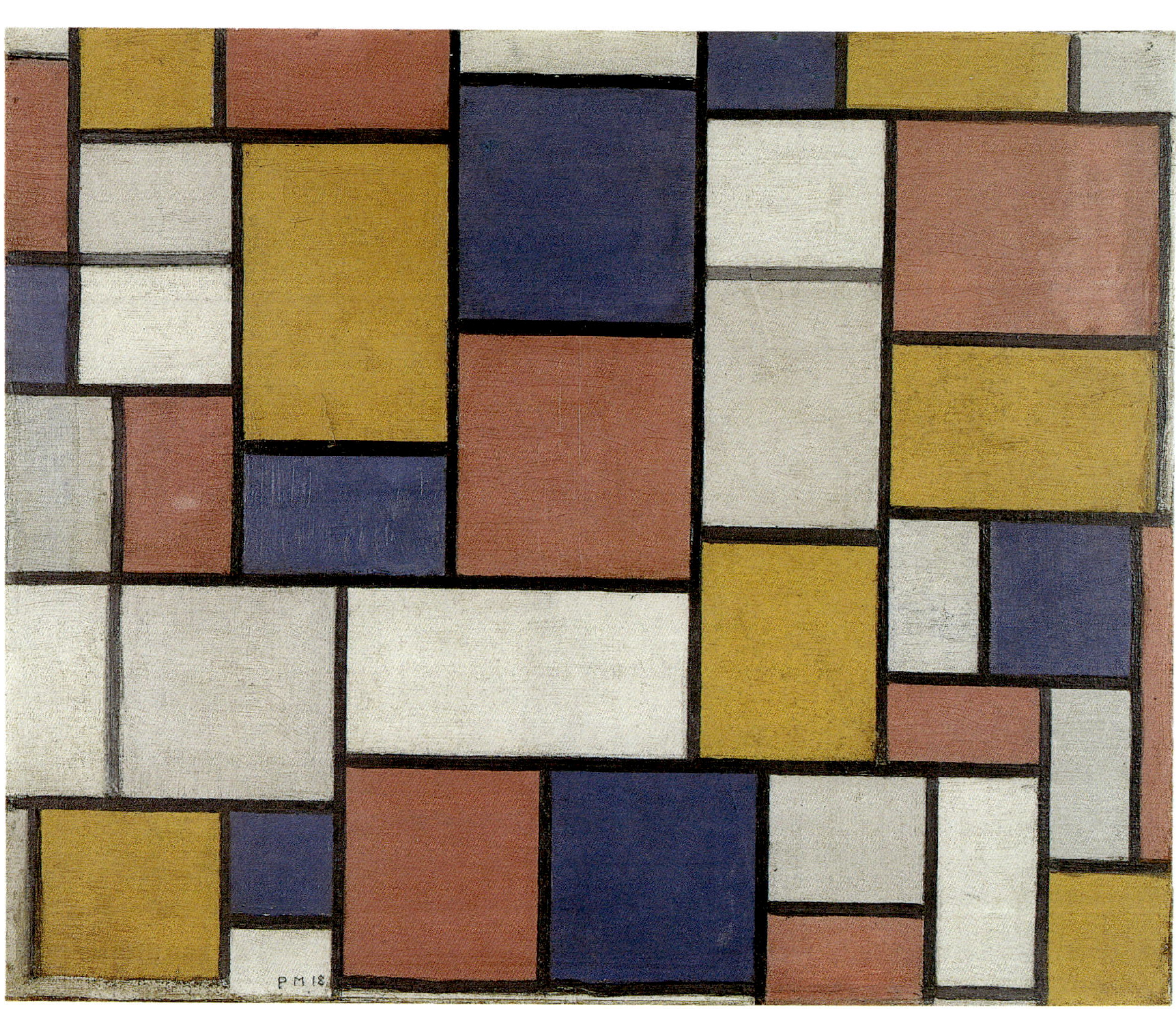
PM 18

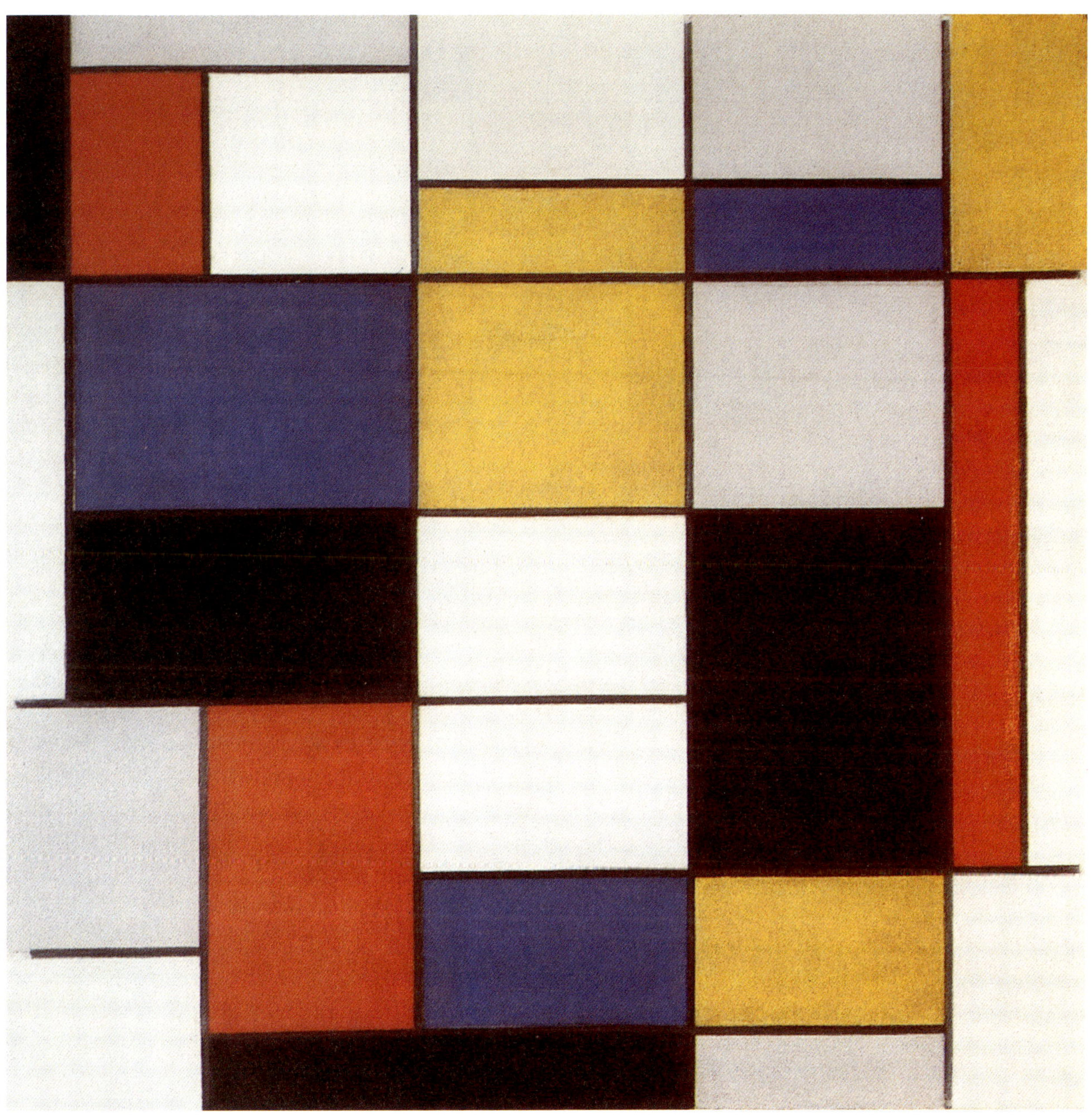

19 Mondrian, *Composition with Colour Planes and Grey Lines 1*, oil on canvas, 1918.

20 Mondrian, *Composition A; Composition with Black, Red, Grey, Yellow and Blue*, oil on canvas, 1920.

such a way that some appear to hang behind the linear grid while others advance. The rose-coloured planes are the most passive and static.

It is true that the artists associated with the periodical *De Stijl* were obsessed with the concept of flatness.True, too, that the scaffoldings Mondrian was evolving – somehow reminiscent of the leaded armatures of stained-glass windows – stress the two-dimensionality of the picture plane more insistently than had been done by any other artist hitherto. This two-dimensionality is reinforced by the fact that the individual rectangles or planes defined or imprisoned by the linear framework invariably exist parallel to the picture plane. When confronted by objects that are rigorously flat, we are always aware of this quality. In 1920 Mondrian began exhibiting his pictures without frames, but soon realized that this practice exposed them to the risk of damage; he then attached white strips of wood to the edges. Subsequently, in the late 1920s, he began suspending or affixing the canvases and the attached wooden strips to rectangular wooden bases. These devices again reinforce the flatness of the pictures themselves and their status as objects. Yet, contrary to received opinion, Mondrian's art invariably involves simultaneous spatial sensations, and indeed spatial activity of a totally new pictorial kind. This is something which he himself came to acknowledge and to accept with satisfaction.[21] Because each individual element in a painting by Mondrian is different from every other one, and because each is so uncannily and strongly characterized by its own particular identity, the viewer becomes absorbed into the spatial interplay between their pictorial parts. The spatial tensions are what gives Mondrian's art that sense of dynamic tautness that he was now coming to seek. Having achieved it, he can hold the spectator's eye in thrall almost indefinitely. He was coming increasingly to believe that equilibrium could exist within dissonance. It is these dissonances that henceforth endow Mondrian's pictures with what he would have called their 'rhythm', their visual throb. Through spatial tensions he is able to achieve dynamism within stability. 20

The first work finished by Mondrian in Paris in 1920, *Composition A; Composition with Black, Red, Grey, Yellow and Blue*, pleased him, and he felt that it surpassed anything he had yet produced. It is now that red emerges in his work as a colour in its own right. In Theosophy red was seen as earthbound and sensual. Mondrian was not, or was no longer, concerned with colour symbolism, but in his letters he makes it clear that he always regarded red as the most physical and least spiritual of the three primary colours.[22] This belief cost him a great effort in reaffirming red's identity. Henceforth his blues are invariably tied to the blacks, while the yellows are married to the whites and pale greys, while the reds assert only their own presence.

Now, because Mondrian's colours have become true primaries and are brighter and purer, the whites and greys (and even the blacks) are made to look more luminous. Colours and non-colours (blacks, whites and greys) find an exact equivalence. Most of the linear gridding is rendered in black, but some lines are grey. Scientific analysis has revealed that although the linear compositional frameworks of this period undergo alteration, they remained the most constant element in the paintings, whereas the colours of the shapes defined by them were being constantly altered. There remained one further step to be taken in the realization of Mondrian's fully developed Neo-Plasticism: the reaffirmation of the importance of the grid or the reassertion of equivalence or balance between line and colour. It was, after all, through linear notation that Mondrian had brought himself to the

21 threshold over which he stepped into abstraction. He achieved this in a slightly later painting of 1920, *Composition with Yellow, Red, Black, Blue and Grey,* in which all the linear elements are rendered in black and have been thickened so that they become more insistent and achieve a pictorial importance equal to that of the coloured shapes they define. Though relatively small, this painting instantly arrests and holds the eye.

It has been suggested that it was through Mondrian's increasing immersion in the philosophy of Hegel that he re-examined his earlier intellectual influences and rid himself of a lot of the woolliness of Theosophical thought,[23] and there may be a certain amount of truth in this. But if he rejected his early sources of visual inspiration, Mondrian never totally turned his back on what had nourished the formation of his own mind. He had been aware of Hegel's ideas certainly since his involvement with those of Rudolf Steiner, and possibly earlier. Then his interest in Hegel was undoubtedly quickened by his contacts with van Doesburg and De Stijl, which was deeply Hegelian in its orientation. A fundamental paradox in Hegel's view of art lay, it could be argued, in the fact that on the one hand he saw it as one of humanity's greatest achievements and even at times as a self-revelation of God or of the absolute. On the other hand, he felt that art had been in decline since classical antiquity, or at least since the Renaissance. This was coupled with the fact that he was disturbed by the lack of religious content or feeling in the art of his own day. Because of this he now placed art below religion, and both of them below philosophy, as a means of attaining the absolute. His famous predictions about the death of art are in fact veiled in ambiguity, and he also acknowledged that the art of the future could not be predicted and that art might be subject to a new rebirth. To this extent he was unwittingly presenting future artists, who read him as offering a 'tabula rasa', with the sense that art's promised land lay in the search for a new absolute, even if that goal were to prove unattainable. For Mondrian art had replaced religion, and hence Hegel's dissatisfaction with or reservations about its present state would have been to a large extent obviated. Theosophy had in any case taught Mondrian to see things in terms of opposing forces and of the flux of both mind and matter that could absorb or eradicate the dichotomies which Hegel faced so fearlessly in his philosophy and his aesthetics. But there can be no doubt that the unconscious attempt to fuse a Hegelian dialectic onto the principles of flow and evolution underlying Theosophy sharpened and quickened Mondrian's art. Through a Hegelian dialectic Mondrian pushed further his view of opposing forces or elements as complementing or reinforcing each other to arrive at more dynamic conclusions.

In this respect another – albeit at first glance unlikely – source of inspiration was Mondrian's belated interest in Italian Futurism. He had certainly been aware of it in his pre-war Paris years, though visually it had absolutely nothing to offer him. However, on his return to Paris he had come to feel that French art was lagging behind the aesthetic developments that he himself had helped to promote in Holland, and that it was now from the urban environment of Paris rather than from any new visual manifestation in French painting that he was drawing sustenance. From the start the Futurists had exalted the modern city, the shock of the new and the rejection of traditional values in art and indeed in life generally. Futurist aesthetic values stood at the opposite end of the spectrum from Mondrian's insofar as the spiritual in art interested them not at all. However, in his writings between 1920 and 1924 Mondrian mentions Futurism just as frequently as he does Cubism, although subsequently his enthusiasm for the Italians lapses while he

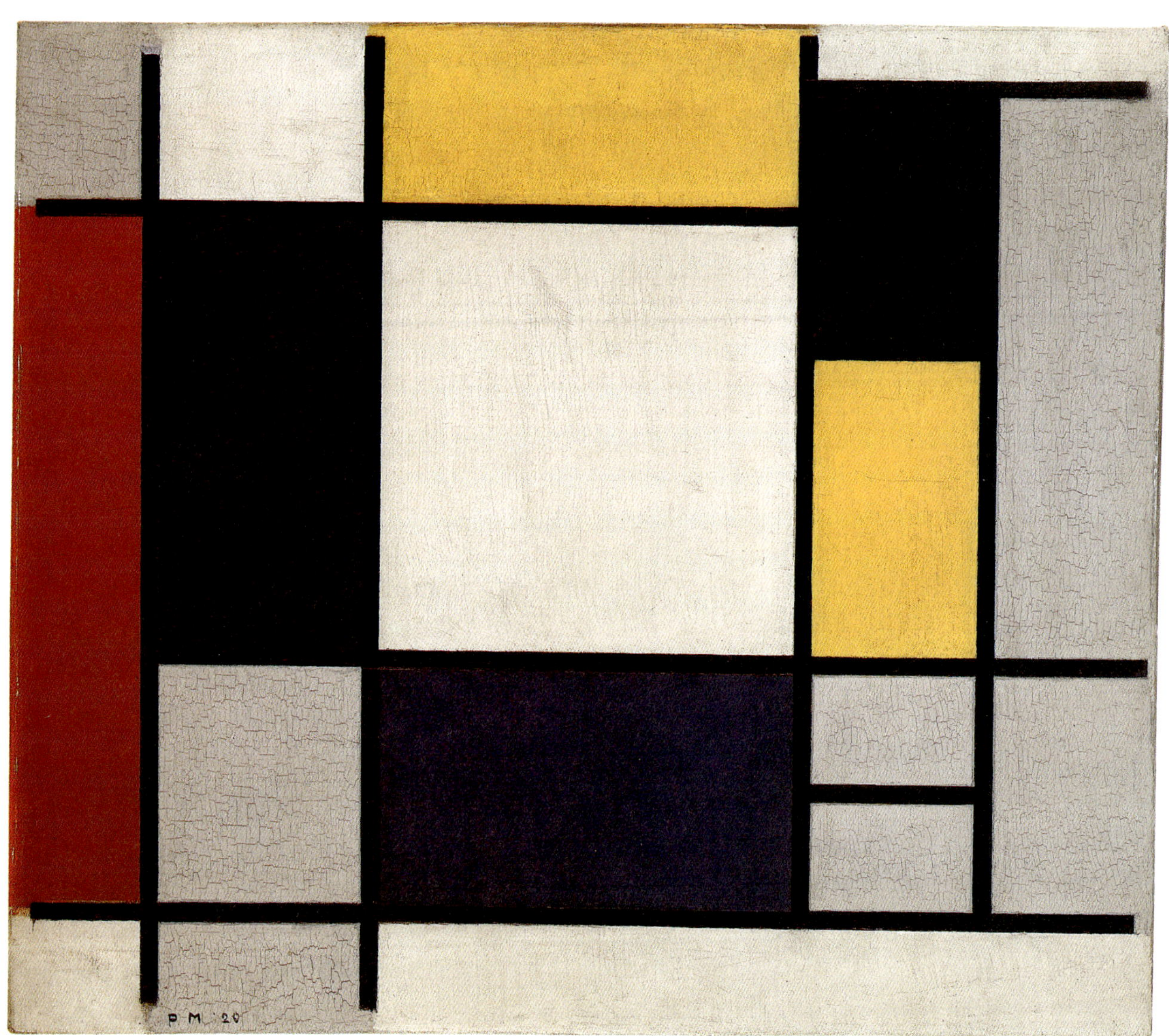

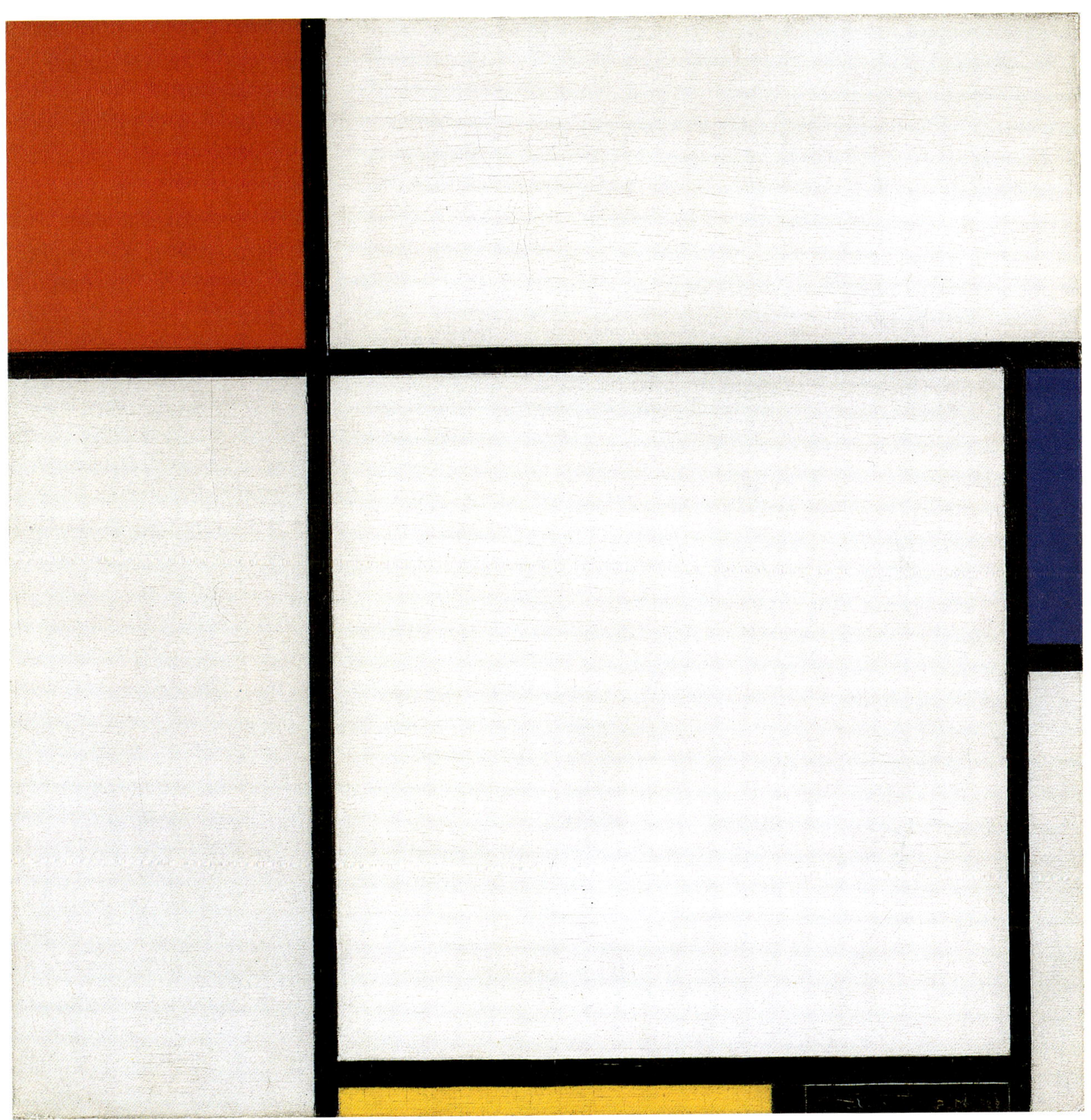

21 Mondrian,
Composition with Yellow, Red, Black, Blue and Grey,
oil on canvas, 1920.

22 Mondrian,
Composition with Red, Blue, Yellow and Black,
oil on canvas, 1929.

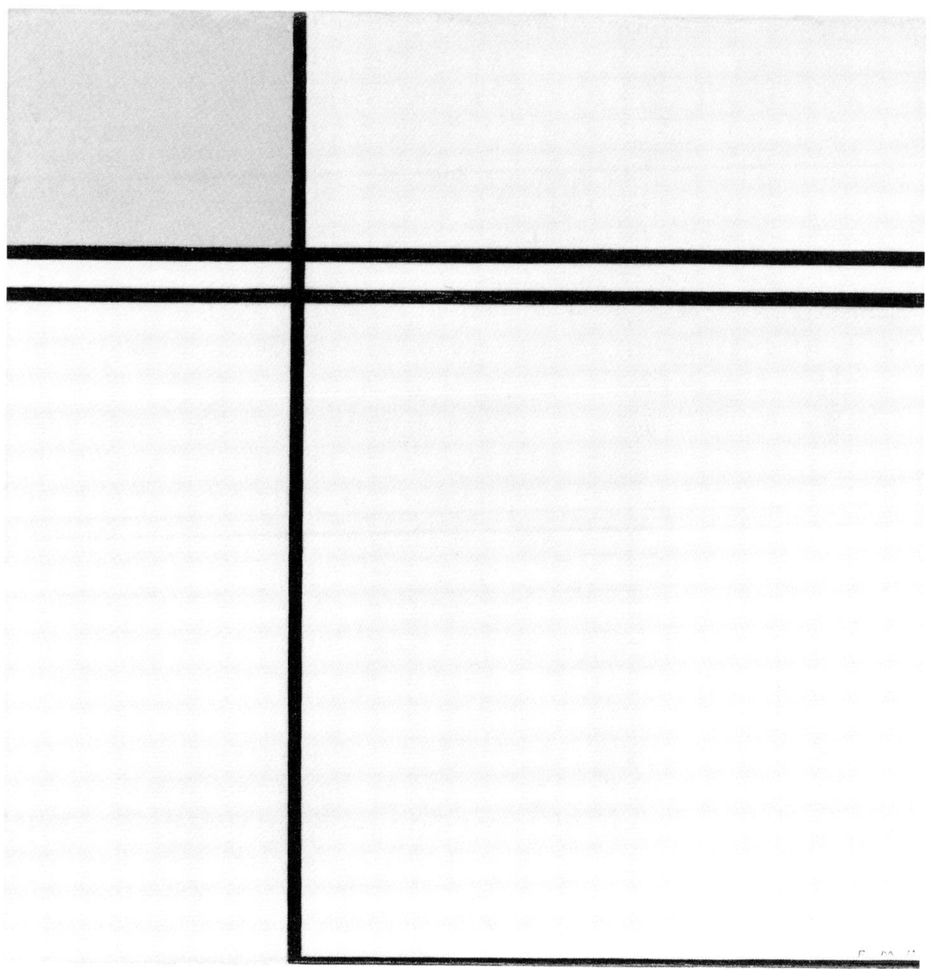

23 Mondrian, *Composition with Yellow and Double Line*, oil on canvas, 1932.

24 Mondrian, *Trafalgar Square*, oil on canvas, 1939–43.

continues to reaffirm his debt to Cubism, thus underlying the formalist orientation of his own art, which he saw as illustrating or at least going hand in hand with his spiritual preoccupations.

Throughout the 1920s Mondrian slowly purified his vision, and the years 1929–30 represent a highpoint in his achievement. By now he had evolved a formal 22
vocabulary of total clarity. Each of the compositional types that had been created within the rigours of his Neo-Plastic principles had been honed down and refined to its simplest expression and then altered or put onto a slightly different track in order to open up new lines of enquiry. Hitherto Mondrian's art had continued to generate that sense of expectancy, that breathlessness, which had characterized his art ever since his realization that nature was not something to be contemplated but rather to be looked into, and beyond, as a key to a higher reality. The feeling of expectancy now vanishes, and this can perhaps be associated with Mondrian's gradual elimination of greys and their replacement with the whites to which they

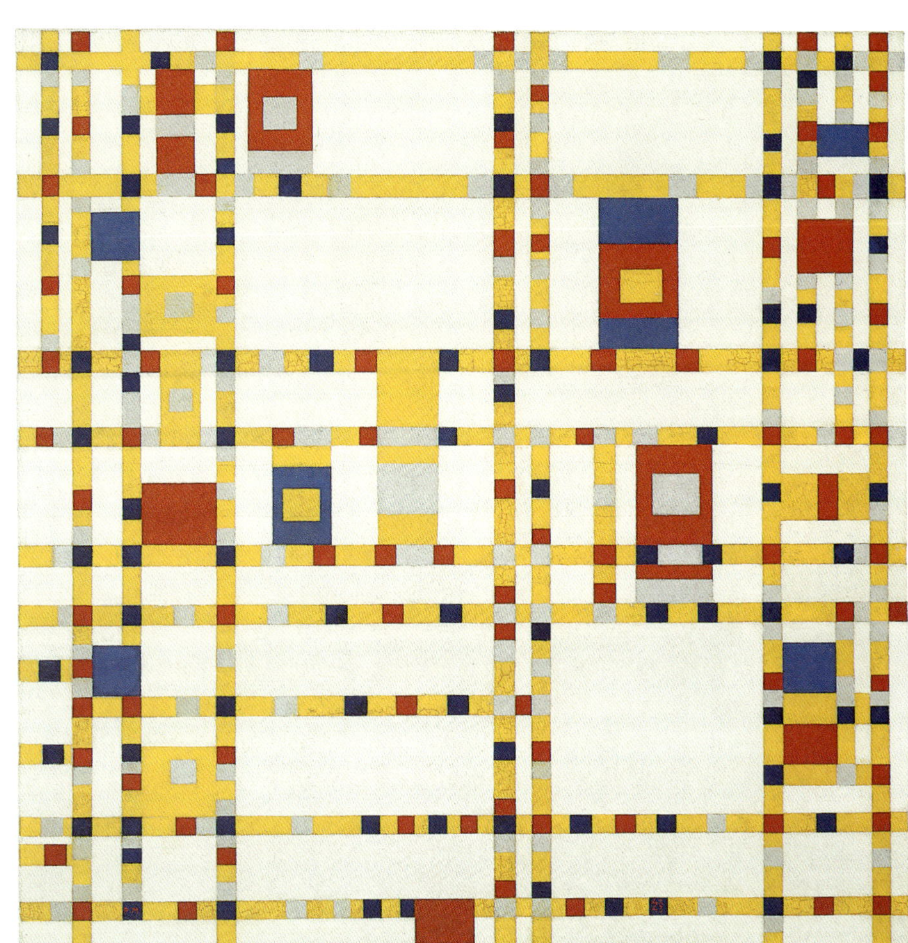

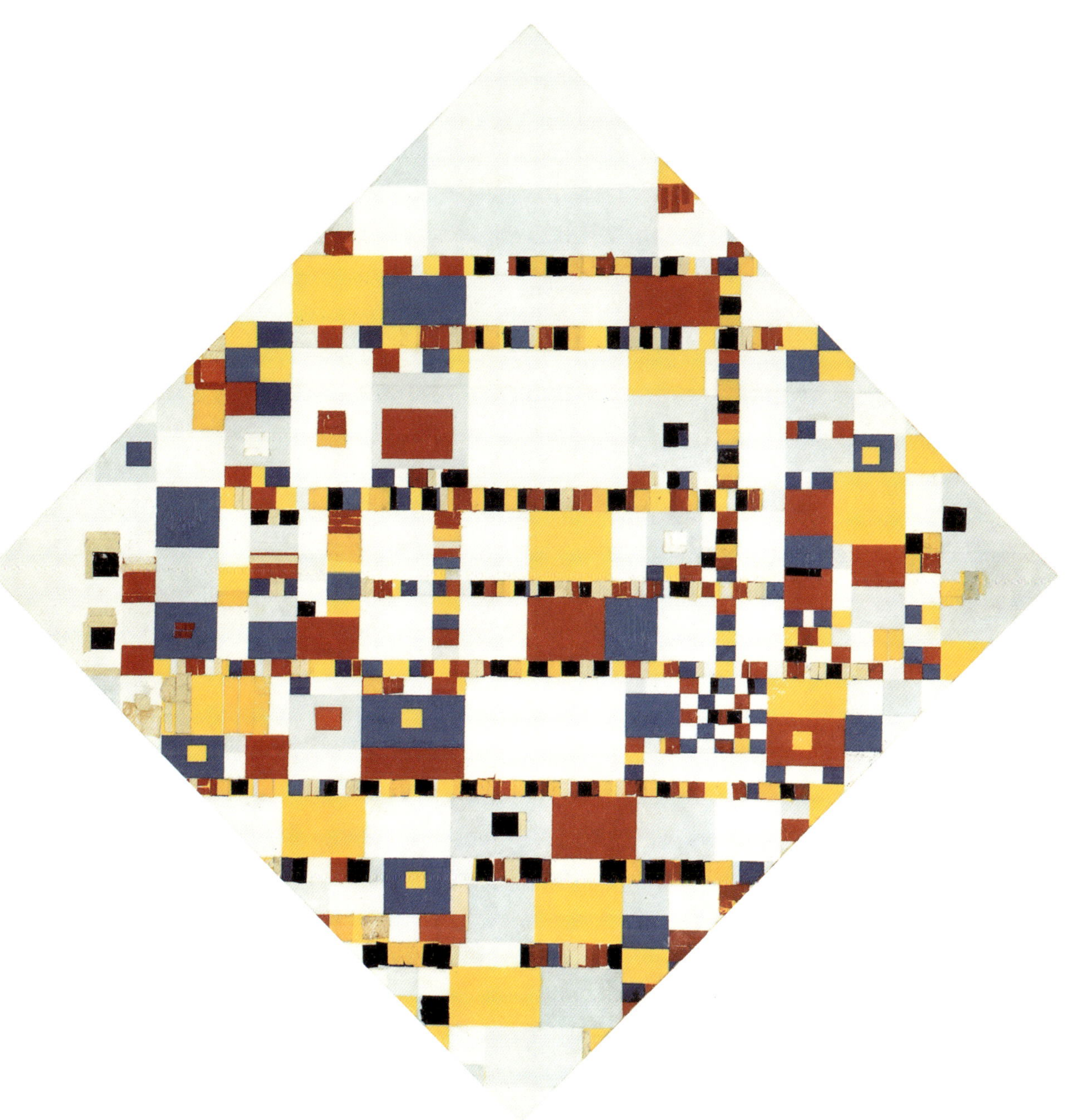

25 Mondrian, *Broadway Boogie Woogie*, oil on canvas, 1942–3.

26 Mondrian, *Victory Boogie Woogie* (unfinished), oil on canvas, 1942–4.

had always been allied; from the start his greys had tended to be in lighter tints rather than tonally muted towards the dark and the shadowy.

One of Mondrian's first teachers in Holland had commented on his ability to handle greys emotively in his landscapes, and it is with his virtual rejection of them (though they continue to put in the occasional appearance) that he finally puts behind him any nostalgia for the natural world which had originally nurtured his vision. There is a sense in which, while he had achieved total abstraction a decade earlier, abstraction now in turn reaches back towards him and embraces and enfolds him. Up till 1930 Mondrian's whites had been subliminally tinted by his primaries. Now they are purified; but Mondrian's control of optical effects had also become so sure and skilful that he could make each white shape appear to be personalized, just as each of his canvases seems to possess a personality all of its own. Because of their variety, and because they read differently according to the size and placing of the planes they define, the whites also recede or advance in spatial interplay. With the virtual suppression of grey, Mondrian's art becomes harder, sharper, more abrasive in feel. Henceforth his art is characterized by a more immediate scintillation, a new syncopation. These sensations are reinforced by the 23
introduction in 1932 of the double line. Mondrian was becoming dissatisfied with his blacks; as usual when he became unhappy with the use of any one of his component pictorial elements, it was because he felt he was employing it too easily and too well. The use of double black lines, thin at first, introduced a new complexity into his pared-down means: the whites which appear between the black lines now read like lines themselves and by implication they bisect a larger black plane behind them.

The increased syncopation in Mondrian's work forces upon us the recognition of a new and in some ways surprising element in the ongoing formation of his art. On returning to Paris, Mondrian had discovered jazz, which he referred to as 'this music bombshell'.[24] It became, after painting, his great passion in life, even though he saw jazz as a somewhat imperfect realization of the 'Universal' which he felt his 'free rhythm' could accomplish in painting. His essay 'Jazz and Neo-Plastic', published in 1927,[25] is a paean to jazz; and there is little doubt that jazz helped him to elaborate this concept of a 'free' and 'open' rhythm. After 1932 the black lines take on a more aggressive, independent quality – at times they appear to constrict or even to threaten the very existence of the coloured squares and rectangles between them. Mondrian's paintings now challenge the eye in a new way. Because of their boldness they attract our attention instantly. They purify and sharpen our visual responses. The earlier works of the classical phase constitute small, individual universes in which we can lose ourselves indefinitely; the syncopation of the new paintings of the 1930s forces us to look at them and then to look over and over again. They induce in effect a new way of seeing. Through Mondrian's incalculable influence on twentieth-century architecture and industrial design these works have, directly or indirectly, affected the visual sensibilities of a vast proportion of people alive today.

During the 1930s Mondrian's writings reveal an increasing social consciousness. Through his apprehension of Hegel he too came to feel that art might one day die. However, he saw this as happening at a safe and comfortable distance from himself and even then only when art, and painting in particular, had established what the utopian future would look like. He had dedicated the French edition of *Neo-Plasticism* (1920) to the 'men of the future'[26] and was now convinced that art could

transform not only the quality of life but the whole future of humankind. He continued to paint what one might call 'head-sized' pictures, landscapes of the mind; but in other works the scale is increased and we sense that his concerns are becoming more environmental. From the inception of his move into abstraction he had been acutely concerned as to how his paintings should be placed, lit and viewed. The titles that he attached to works begun in the late 1930s, many of which were subsequently reworked when he was living in New York, sometimes bear place
24 names such as *Place de la Concorde* or *Trafalgar Square*, and these confirm the environmental bias.

Mondrian never attained the goal of the absolute, nor would he have wished to do so. Despite the fact that its evolution seems so beautifully self-contained, his art was basically about processes, and his credo is encapsulated in two words he often used: 'always further'.[27] Through his art he had come to realize that the only way forward was to reject every visual certainty he had reached in order to look ahead to a new and hopefully higher one. But if he had not arrived at the absolute, he also sensed that it was out there and beyond him, a goal that made the ongoing processes of art worthwhile, and indeed morally essential. And we must hope that Mondrian recognized that time and again in his canvases he had reached out towards the absolute and had touched it.

Towards the end of his life, in 1943, he declared, 'I think that the destructive element is too much neglected in art.'[28] By now Mondrian had come to see his entire life's work as a series of destructive acts. The last and in a sense the boldest of his acts of destruction would take place in his studios on East 56th and East 59th Streets in New York. In 1938, with the threat of war looming in Europe, Mondrian wrote from Paris to the painter Ben Nicholson, asking him for an invitation to visit England; he had no desire to return to Holland and maybe subconsciously he was wary of the spell that its trees and waterways and skies might once again cast upon him. After spending two years in London, Mondrian was forced by German bombing raids to vacate his Hampstead studio. He set sail for the United States and arrived in New York in October 1940. He fell in love with the city at once, and the close bond between Neo-Plasticism and the metropolitan existence was reinforced as never before.

In another statement of 1943 Mondrian declared that, 'Only now . . . I become conscious that my work in black, white and little color planes has been merely "drawing" in oil color.'[29] At the age of seventy-one he was quite prepared to begin his artistic life anew. In a letter to a friend he talks of the need he feels to destroy the powerful network of black line that it had taken him half a lifetime to evolve.[30] In 1933, in his *Lozenge Composition with Four Yellow Lines*, Mondrian had for the first time used colour as line, but this had remained an isolated experiment. In New York he looked afresh at earlier Paris and London canvases that he had had shipped over to him, and began introducing into them coloured bands that read both as lines and as small shapes or planes. In New York Mondrian also devised a new method of working, attaching strips of coloured adhesive paper to the surfaces of his canvas (in order to avoid monotony some of them were trimmed). After moving the strips about experimentally, and when he had achieved the effects he was seeking, the strips of paper were removed and the same areas painted in with thick impasto. Now he began to experiment with the use of coloured linear ele-
25 ments. In his last two canvases, *Broadway Boogie Woogie* (1942–3) and the
26 unfinished *Victory Boogie Woogie* (1942–4), the coloured lines have in turn been

broken down into an infinity of tiny shapes – red, blue, yellow, black, white and grey. He had opened up a a whole new world of possibilities in painting, destroying the concept of line as being independent of colour. Of *Broadway Boogie Woogie* he said, '. . . even about this picture I am not quite satisfied. There is still too much of the old in it.'[31] It is deeply significant that *Victory Boogie Woogie* employs the experimental lozenge format. In New York, when asked why he was reworking earlier canvases rather than simply painting new ones, he replied, 'I don't want pictures. I just want to find things out.'[32]

2

Malevich and the ascent into ether

Although Mondrian turned his back so conclusively on nature, he nevertheless found his way into abstraction through the sensations initially inspired in him by the landscape of Holland (admittedly largely man-made), harnessed to a relatively limited range of ideological beliefs. Kasimir Malevich, on the other hand, achieved abstraction through his apprehension of the human body; allied to this was his belief in ideal proportion and what was to become an obsession with the mystic properties of geometry.[1] He developed in particular a startlingly original attitude
28 to the human head and physiognomy. A fine self-portrait of 1908–9 conveys something of the vividness and intensity of his own personality. It is of great significance that this work is painted in a square format. The portrait has about it a strongly fin-de-siècle feeling and there are symbolic, almost Munch-like overtones in the juxtaposition of warm and cool halves of the artist's face, and in the red and green oppositions that dominate the colouristic harmonies of the painting. A later por-
29 trait, the *Finished Portrait of Ivan Kliun* executed in 1913 in Malevich's Cubo-Futurist manner, shows the head of his friend and disciple sawn apart; Kliun's right eye looks both outwards and inwards while its counterpart has been removed to reveal an imaginary world containing cubistic depictions of a wooden house, a chimney stack and billowing smoke: the viewer is thus led into Kliun's
42 mind. Malevich was to refer to his *Black Square* of 1915, his most famous canvas, in terms of facial imagery.

Kasimir Severinovich Malevich was born in the Ukraine, of Polish descent, in 1878. Although younger than Mondrian, he was still marginally older than the Cubists who were – as in the case of Mondrian – to transform the development of his art. Despite the fact that the fragments of an autobiography that survived him are more revelatory than the crumbs of personal comment left by Mondrian, Malevich remains an enigmatic figure. He came from fairly simple stock, attended agricultural college for a couple of years but appears to have had no very rigorous academic education. He wrote prolifically, and from his writings it becomes clear that he became much more widely read than Mondrian, though in a wild, disorganized fashion. His highly personal literary style can strike beautiful and memorable chords, but his writings are also extremely difficult to follow, even by native speakers of Russian.

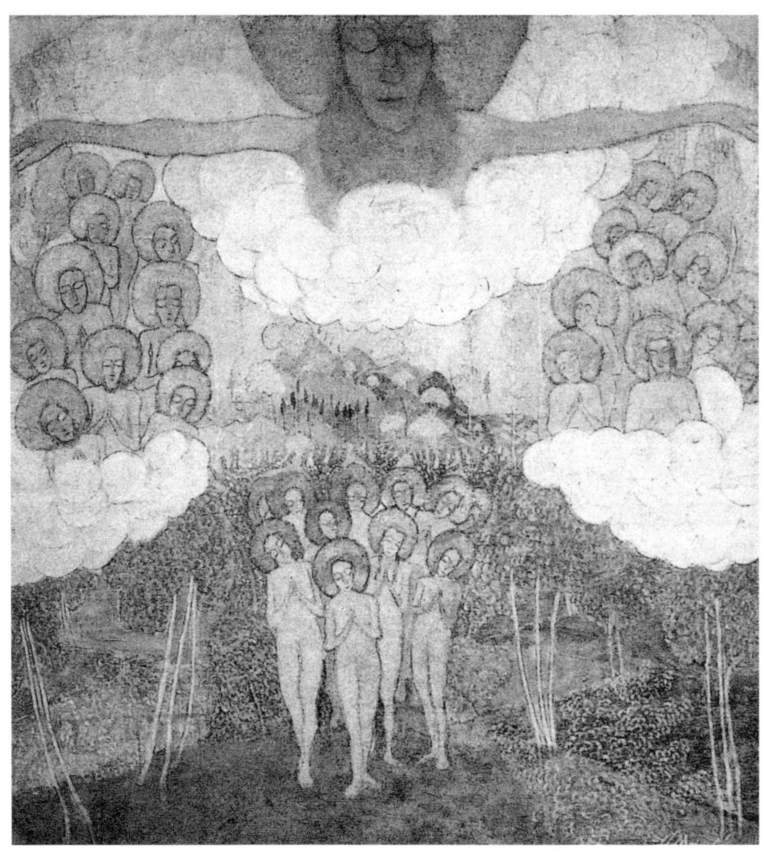

27 Malevich, *The Triumph of Heaven* (study for a fresco), tempera on cardboard, 1907.

As a painter Malevich began by believing that it was his mission to capture and transcribe nature faithfully. Next he turned to a somewhat timid form of Impressionism.The first major turning-point in Malevich's career came in 1907, when he moved permanently to Moscow. His arrival there coincided with the first independent exhibition by a new group of Symbolist artists who adopted the name Blue Rose. The influence of the group's founder, Pavel Kuznetsov, can be felt in Malevich's 'Yellow Series' – studies for frescoes first shown in 1908. Russian Symbolism was in some respects a disorganized affair, capable of accommodating almost every aesthetic tendency and certainly more flexible than the Symbolism that Mondrian had encountered in Amsterdam and, at the same time, less factionalized than the Symbolism that Kandinsky had by now already come to know in Munich. In the 'Yellow Series' the pantheism that characterized so much Blue Rose work takes on a genuinely mystical dimension, and the naked figures which appear throughout the series do not so much commune with their landscape surroundings as become literally absorbed into nature. While these are archetypally Symbolist works, they are totally devoid of the submerged eroticism that pervades so much other contemporary Russian Symbolist art; and they radiate some of the innocent spirituality that characterizes so many anonymous provincial Russian icons. In the panel entitled *The Triumph of Heaven* the transcendental being above is all head and arms, 27 but mostly head. In another panel, embedded once again in a square format, the artist's own head replaces that of the deity.

In the spring of 1908 Malevich must have visited the first 'Golden Fleece' exhibition in Moscow. This included a large section of recent French art. As a survey of French avant-garde painting it was in many ways both more comprehensive and more succinct than any comparable exhibition mounted in France; and the work of French artists was juxtaposed to that of emergent Russian painters. Malevich met two of them, Mikhail Larionov and Natalia Goncharova, in 1910, and they invited him to take part in the first 'Jack of Diamonds' group exhibition, an attempt to unite the Paris-oriented Russian avant-garde with their counterparts who had settled in Munich; a smattering of recent French art was included. The 'Golden Fleece' and the 'Jack of Diamonds' catapulted Malevich into the twentieth century. He was particularly drawn to the art of Goncharova, but over the next two to three years it was her partner, Larionov, who was to be the driving force behind the group of artists that revolved around them. The attempt by Larionov and Goncharova to give certain aspects of French Post-Impressionism a specifically Russian flavour, by injecting into it aspects of icon painting and local folk and peasant art, struck a natural chord in Malevich's make-up.

During the course of 1911–12 Malevich executed a set of large gouaches depicting different aspects of Russian labour and society. These are bursting with vitality, raw and deliberately clumsy, and totally unselfconscious. They represent the side of his nature complementary to that embodied in the mystical, somewhat etiolated images of the 'Yellow Series'. Malevich was now acutely aware of the most recent developments in French art, from Cézanne through to Cézanne's greatest and most
30 direct heirs: Matisse, Picasso and Braque. He was by now also frequenting the collections of the rich merchant Sergei Shchukin, in his day the greatest collector of
31 French Post-Impressionist painting. Indeed, Malevich's *Bather* of 1911 shows how immediately, and also how recklessly he was now reacting to every aspect of French modernism, and in this particular work to Matisse's *La Danse* of 1910, which was received into Shchukin's collection in the year that *Bather* was painted. Through the Shchukin collection, and through contemporary exhibitions which also followed developments in Germany and subsequently in Italy, young Russians were able to gain a more concentrated view of what was going on elsewhere in Europe than would have been possible if they had been living in Paris, Munich or Milan. In just the same way, thirty years later, emergent American abstractionists were given, through the displays and programme of the Museum of Modern Art in New York, a more historical introduction into modernist art than was available to their progenitors and contemporaries in Europe.

But Malevich's creations in the gouaches remain supremely individual and also supremely Russian, like characters out of Russian literature. Although Malevich's work is never literary in a narrative or descriptive way, of all the painters under consideration here he was, with the possible exception of Kandinsky, the one who learned and profited most from his literary contemporaries and friends. From time to time he even tried to recreate in visual terms the way in which his writer friends were experimenting with words.

In 1912 Larionov and Goncharova ceded, as it were, from themselves. They were feeling their native Russian oats and felt that the 'Jack of Diamonds' association was giving too much prominence to developments in foreign and, in particular, French art. They now organized a new exhibiting society, the 'Donkey's Tail',

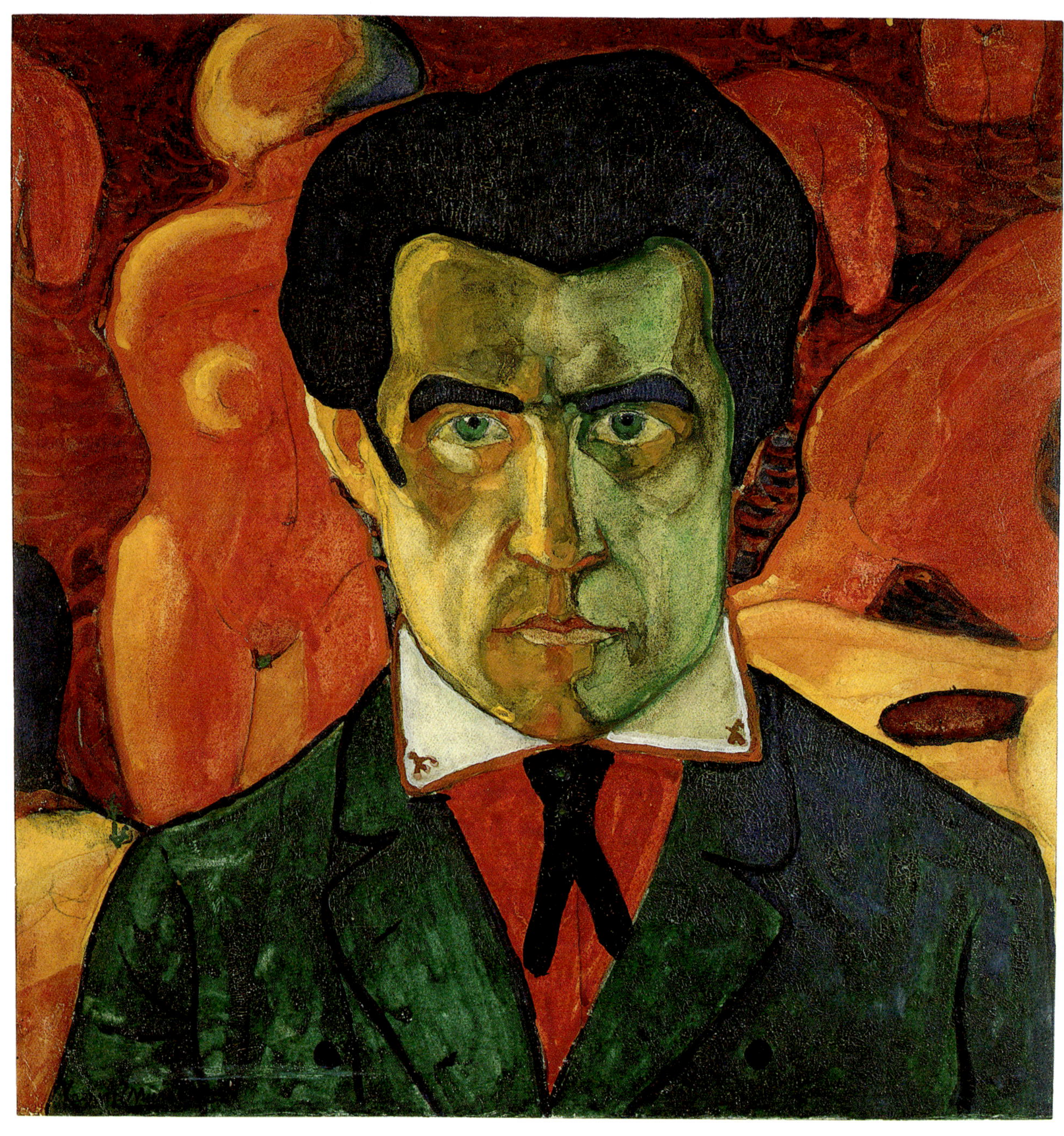

28 Malevich,
Self-Portrait, gouache on paper, *c.* 1908–9.

29 Malevich,
Finished Portrait of Ivan Kliun, oil on canvas, 1913.

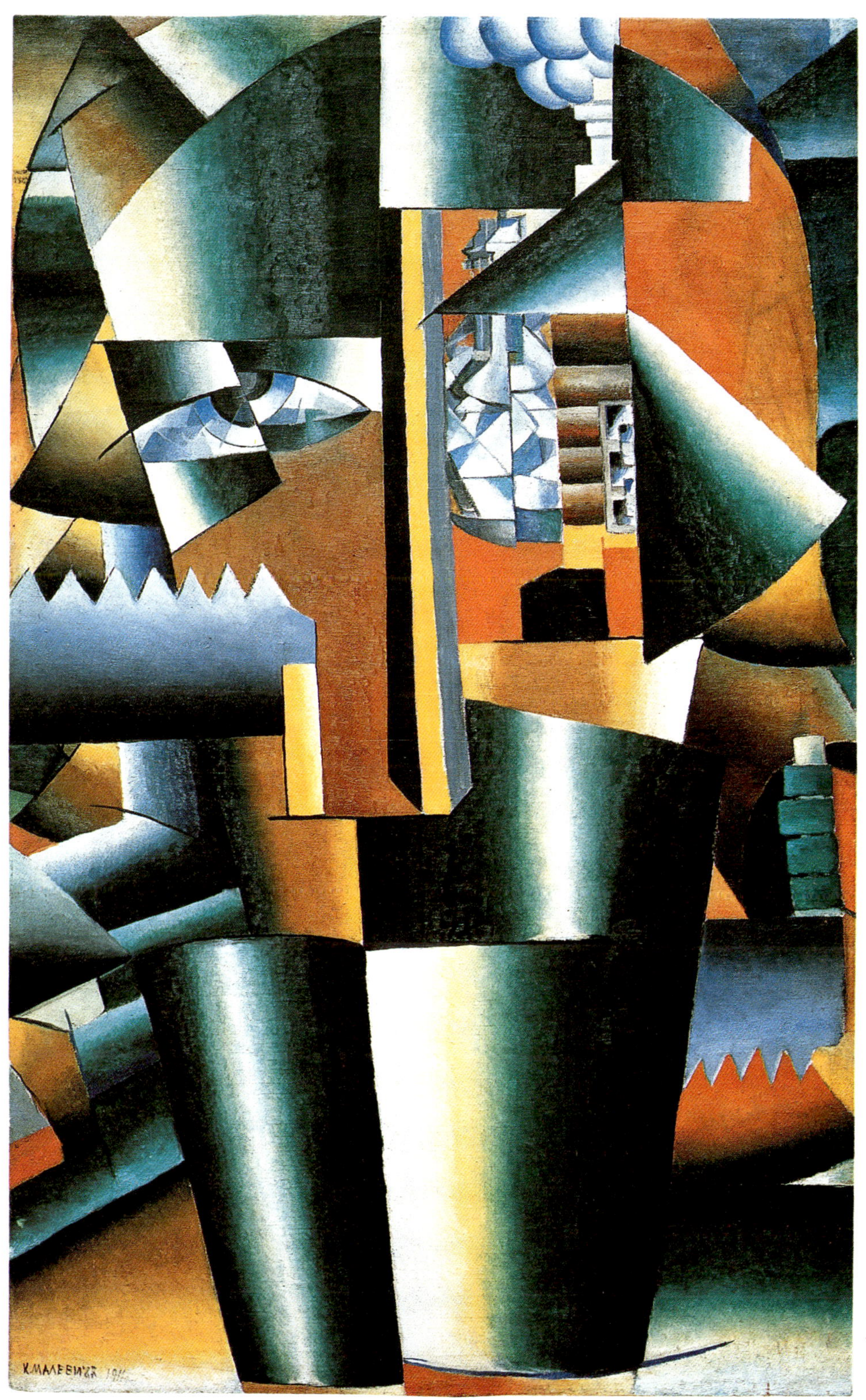
К.МАЛЕВИЧЪ

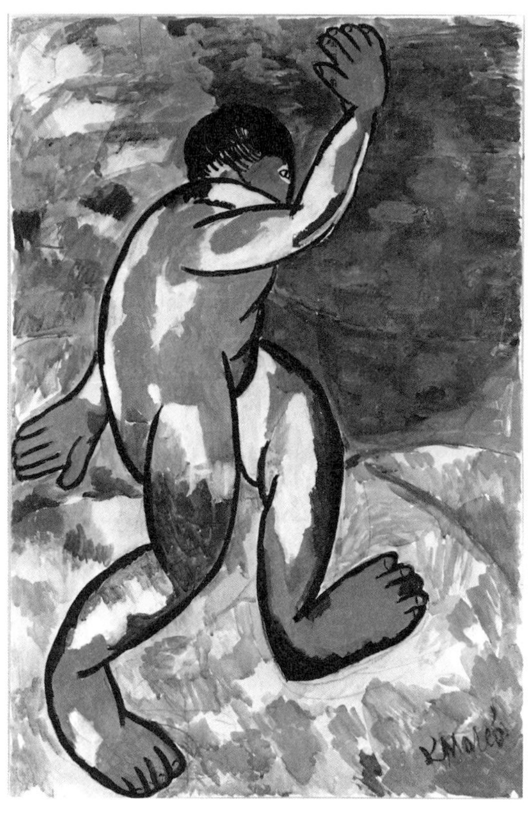

30 Malevich, *Bather*, gouache on paper, 1911.

31 Matisse, *La Danse*, oil on canvas, 1910.

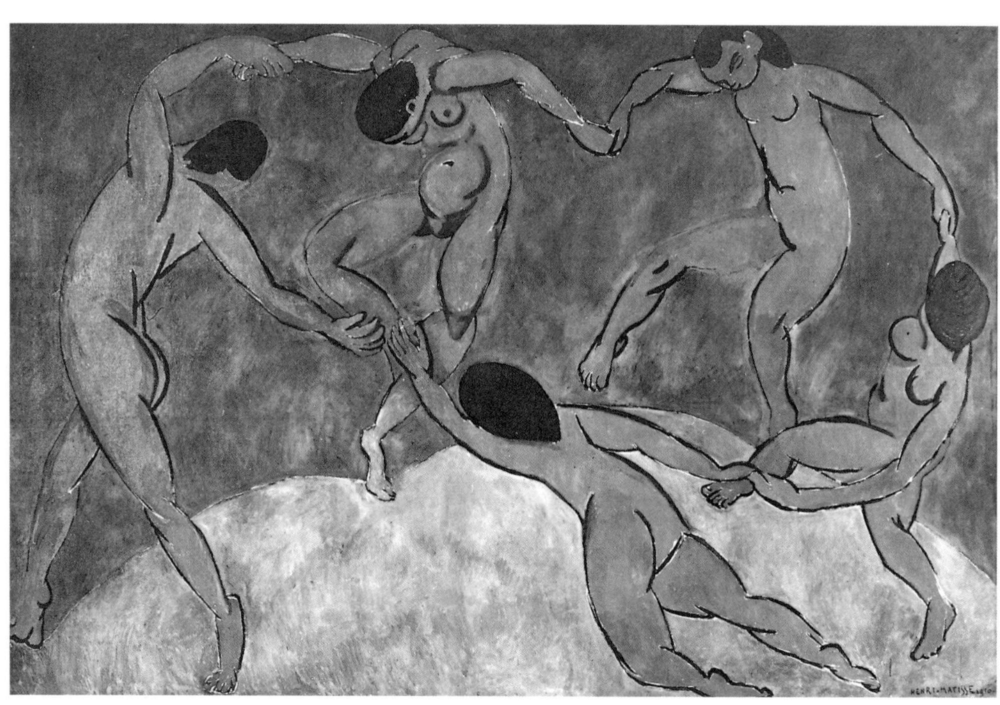

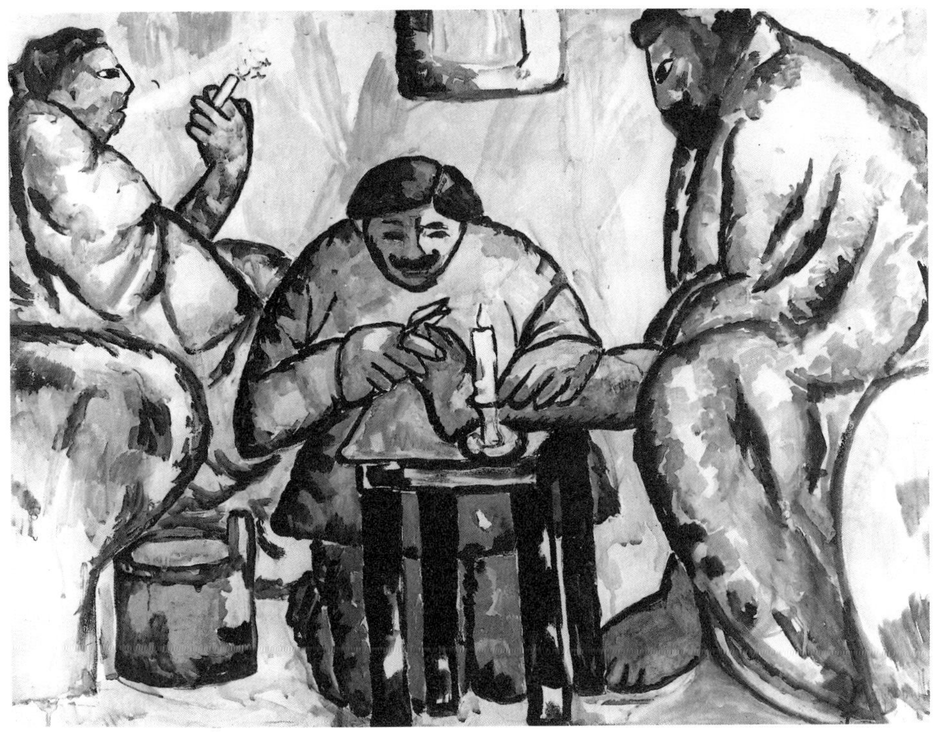

32 Malevich, *The Chiropodist at the Bath House*, gouache on paper, *c.* 1911–12.

taking with them Malevich and Vladimir Tatlin, the man who was to become Malevich's only true peer in the formation of a new and totally revolutionary Russian art. At the first 'Donkey's Tail' exhibition held in March 1912 Malevich
32 showed a group of his 'occupational' gouaches, including *The Chiropodist at the Bath House* with its echoes of Cézanne – a premonition of the fact that when he came to subscribe to the principles of a Hegelian dialectic he also came to see Cézanne as having initiated a phase in art which was to terminate in himself.

The founders of the 'Donkey's Tail' now expressed a certain contempt for Cubism; this was because they were exhilarated by their contacts with Italian Futurism which, at a visual level, was using French Cubism to 'modernize' its own external façade; simultaneously the Italians began denigrating Cubism's achievements. The Russians first learned of Futurism through its pamphlets or manifestos. These were almost invariably blueprints for art that was about to be produced, rather than justifications or explanations of literature, painting and sculpture already in existence, and this explains why the influence of Italian Futurism was to be incalculable and yet entirely disproportionate to that of its artistic and intellectual achievements: it provided artists all over the world with instant aesthetic do-it-yourself kits. The products of Russian Futurism were be more truly original and certainly more daring and lethally iconoclastic than anything that the Italians achieved. One of the reasons why Futurism fell on such particularly fertile soil in Russia was that, although the Russian artists were becoming increasingly aware of their own artistic heritage, they were not frightened or intimidated by it as the Italians were by theirs. This fear was one of the factors that ultimately short-circuited the parent movement.

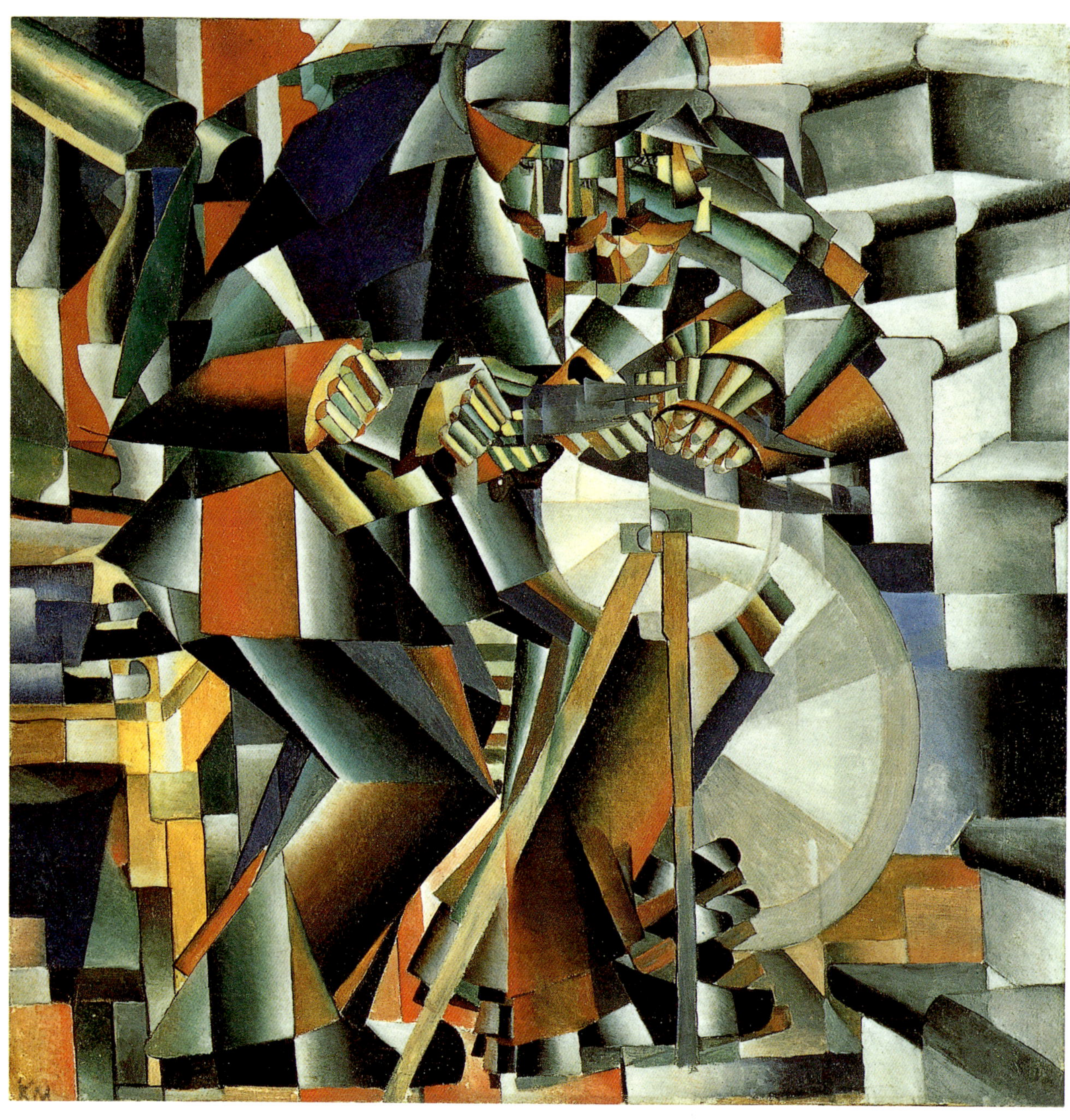

33 Malevich,
The Knife Grinder:
Principle of Flickering,
oil on canvas, 1913.

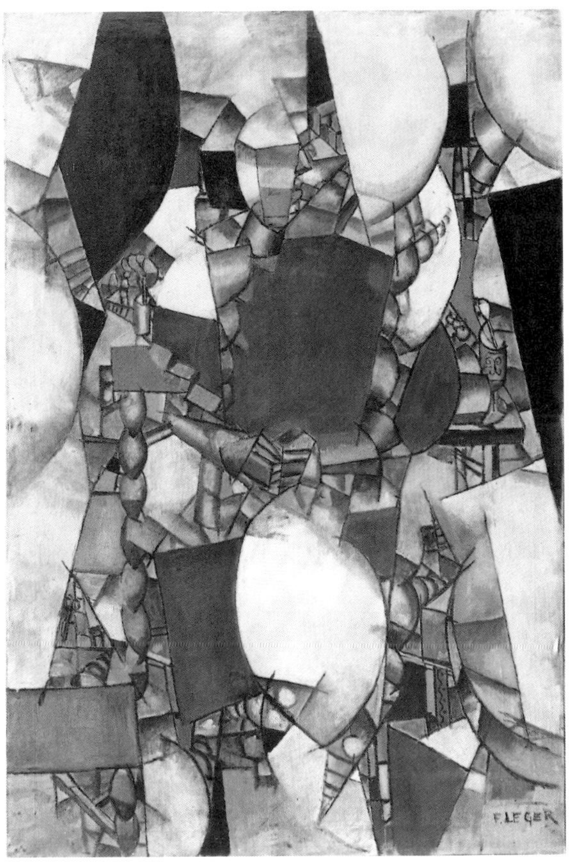

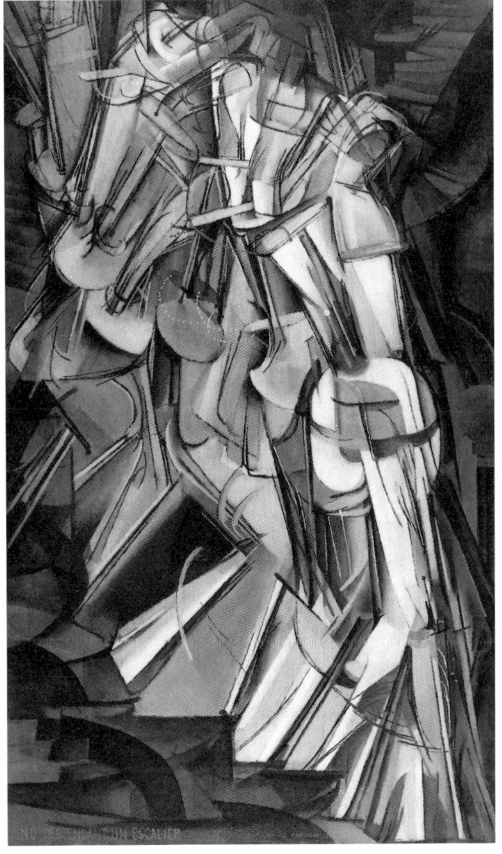

34 Fernand Léger, *Woman in Blue*, oil on canvas, 1912.

35 Marcel Duchamp, *Nude Descending a Staircase, No. 2*, oil on canvas, 1912.

The impact of Futurism on Malevich was to be decisive, but most immediately it
encouraged him to look at Cubism in a new way and to formulate his own independent variant of it. Malevich's researches at this point parallel very closely those
of Fernand Léger, who was at this time acquiring a following in Russia which was
particularly receptive to his own, very independent brand of Cubism; photographs
of Léger's work as well as that of other artists associated with Cubism were avidly
studied and passed from hand to hand in Russian studios. Léger's *Essai pour Trois
Portraits* (1910–11), shown in Moscow in February 1912, was to inspire a poem
by Benedikt Livshits that appeared in *A Slap in the Face of Public Taste*, a document launched late in that year and one that, more than any other, ushered in the
first phase of Russian Futurism. Malevich's intellect, though untutored, was vora-
cious and quick, and he recognized instinctively that, of all artists working in
Western Europe, Léger more than any other was able to retain a French predisposi-
tion for purely formal values and yet subscribe to the Futurists' vision of a modern,
mechanized urban scene and society and to their insistence on the dynamic frag-
33 mentation of matter. *The Knife Grinder: Principle of Flickering* of 1912–13,
Malevich's most sophisticated work to date, reads in effect like a marriage between
34, 35 Léger's *Woman in Blue* and Duchamp's *Nude Descending a Staircase, No. 2* which,
because of its cinematic depiction of motion, has affinities with contemporary

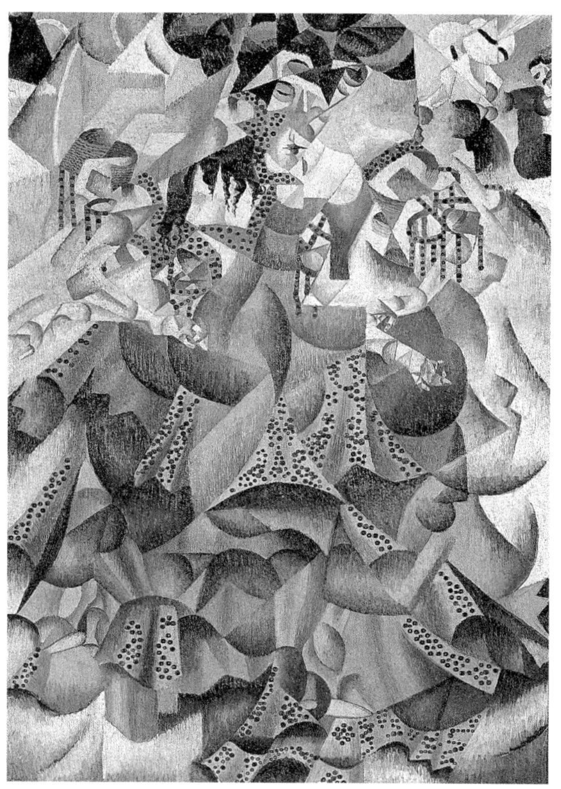

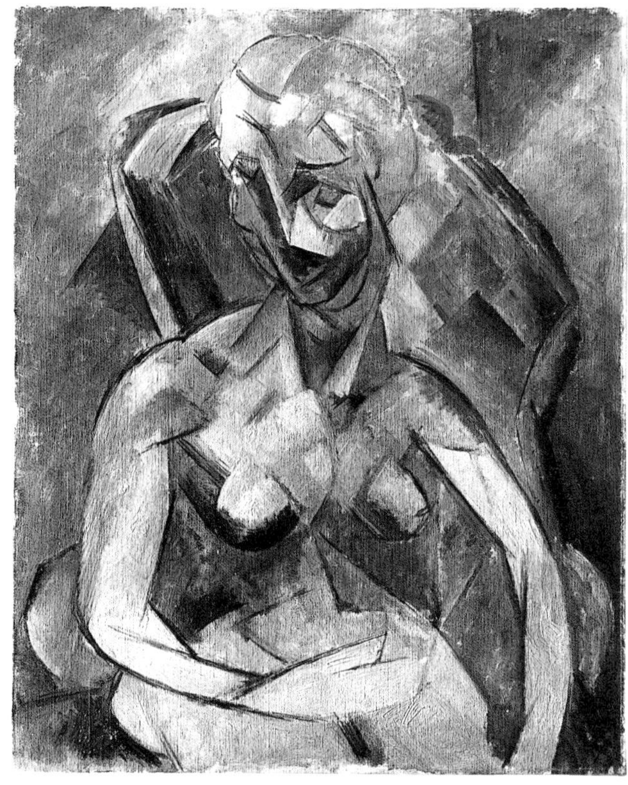

36 Gino Severini, *Blue Dancer,* oil on canvas, 1912.

37 Picasso, *Female Nude in an Armchair,* oil on canvas, 1909–10.

Italian Futurism. Both works hung in the 'Section d'Or' exhibition mounted in Paris in the autumn of 1912.[2] A comparison of Malevich's canvas with Severini's *Blue Dancer* executed in Paris, also in 1912, reinforces the sensation of flickering 36
movement that Malevich used as his subtitle.

Simultaneously Malevich was getting to grips with Cubism proper – as it had been invented by Picasso and Braque. His *Head of a Peasant Girl* of 1913, for 38
example, shows his reaction to Picasso's *Female Nude in an Armchair* of winter 37
1909–10 in the Shchukin collection, although it demonstrates that, like Mondrian, Malevich was not fundamentally interested in Picasso's use of multiple viewpoints. On the other hand, while Mondrian responded to the transparency and crystalline quality of Picasso's Analytic Cubism, Malevich responded to its physical, sculptural properties; Malevich's image appears to have been fashioned out of sheet metal, bent and twisted by a powerful fist.

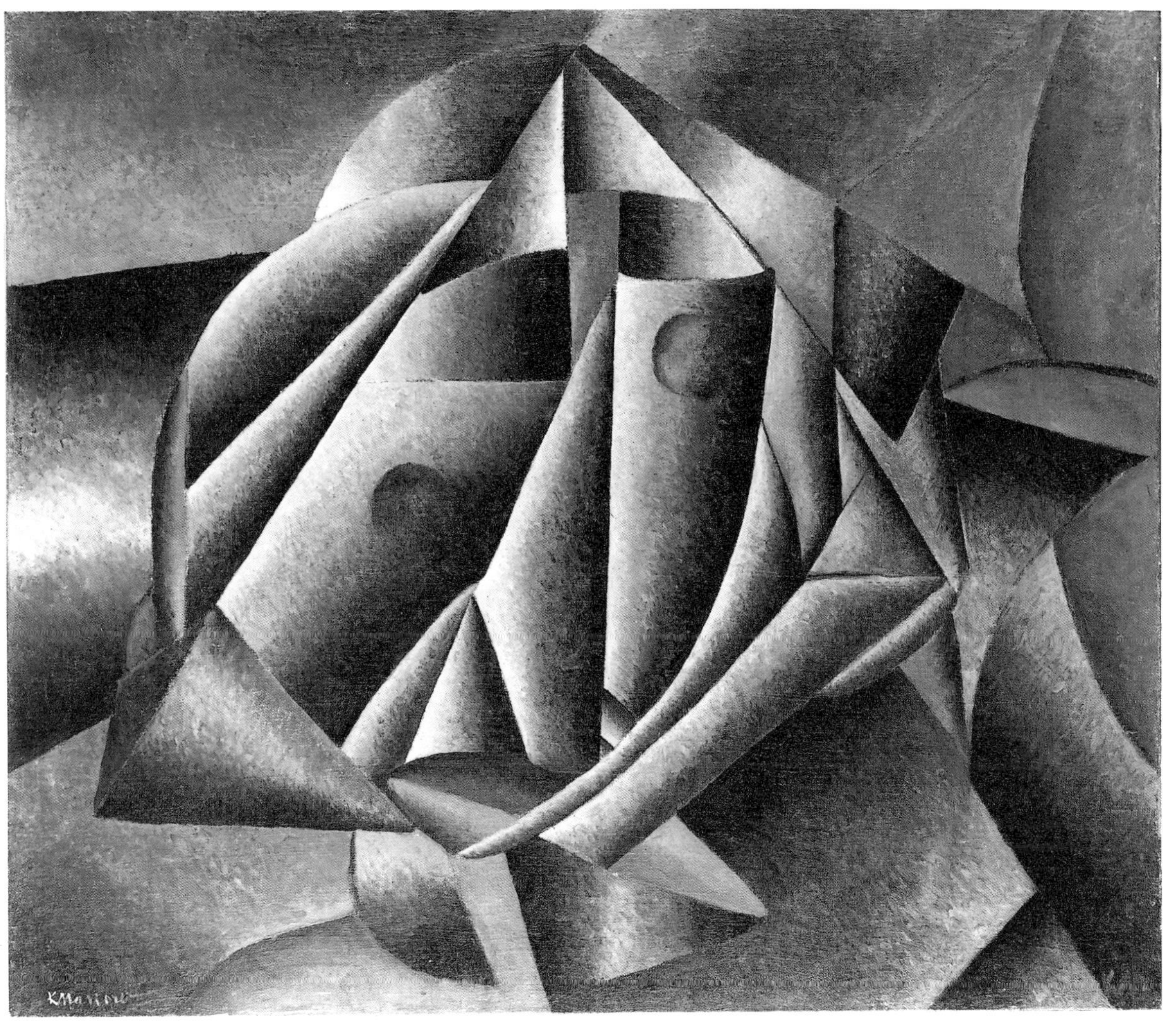

38 Malevich, *Head of a Peasant Girl*, oil on canvas, 1913.

But it is in the next phase of Malevich's work, initiated towards the end of 1913 under the very direct stimulus of Picassos's new, Synthetic Cubist manner, that more mysterious, complex developments began to take place – developments that were to lead Malevich into pure abstraction. And it is in a sense ironic that Cubism, which was concerned with depicting perceived reality in a totally new, fuller way, should have been the threshold over which both Mondrian and Malevich stepped into abstraction. Again, it is significant that neither of them was interested in Cubism's attempt to look at objects in greater plenitude. Mondrian may have overestimated the Cubists' concern with pure form, but he understood perfectly the basic tenets of the early, analytic phase of Cubism and that what he was taking from it was basically inimical to the movement itself; and he was never really interested in the second phase, Synthetic Cubism, that was ushered in by the invention of *papier collé* in 1912 (although it may have indirectly influenced the slab-like appearance of some of his works of 1917). Apart from anything else, the anti-aestheticism that characterized so much of Picasso's Synthetic Cubism would have been totally foreign to Mondrian. Malevich's understanding of the earlier phases of Cubism was as personal as Mondrian's but earthier and certainly more idiosyncratic. On the other hand, he totally misunderstood the intentions and grammar of Synthetic Cubism, and it was this misunderstanding that enabled him to produce such startlingly original results.

Synthetic Cubism largely reversed the premises of Analytic Cubism. Forms became simpler and bolder and now, instead of beginning with a clearly legible subject which would subsequently be dissected and analyzed in the light of the new Cubist use of a variable viewpoint, the Cubists were instead building up their canvases in a more abstract fashion, using flat interlocking planes which were subsequently qualified in such a way that they took on representational significance, or onto which the artists laid their subjects.

In Picasso's Synthetic Cubist canvases the subject is always immediately identifiable, and Picasso himself would undoubtedly have seen the abstract pictorial substructure of his work as reinforcing the materiality of his subjects, as helping to lend them weight and substance. Malevich, on the other hand, viewed the areas of *papier collé* in Cubist works, and the flat slab-like forms derived from them, as new configurations working in some way *against* the subject, as undermining and challenging its importance and supremacy. Malevich's own output of 1914 is at first glance strongly Cubist in appearance. But although many of his canvases do seem to have a starting-point in concrete reality, in much of his work the subject defies a logical visual and intellectual reconstruction – the kind of reconstruction which is essential to the mechanics of Cubism – and many of his paintings are in fact medleys of disconnected fragments buried in an abstract pictorial architecture.
In *Woman at the Advertising Column* of 1914, for example, the subject can to a 39
certain extent be reconstructed with the help of the title. But the figure's pictorial identity is now menaced rather than reinforced by the large oblongs and quadrilaterals – more dominant and aggressive as independent pictorial shapes than those found in Cubist paintings – that are so daringly balanced in a space which now often seems to be suspended in front of the figure and at times in front of the picture plane.

Woman at the Advertising Column was shown at the 'Tramway V' exhibition mounted in Petrograd in February 1915, together with other Cubo-Futurist canvases and his own complementary 'Alogic' works which were even more fanciful in their use of imagery and often employ both visual and verbal puns. But by the end of the year Malevich had, in his own words, transformed himself 'into the zero of form'.[3] In December 1915, at '0.10 – The Last Exhibition of Futurist Painting', he asserted his primacy as the most innovative painter working in Russia when he launched the Suprematist movement by showing forty-six totally abstract works,
dominated in the catalogue by the *Black Square*, which was hung, icon-like, across 40
the corner of his space. Following Futurist practice, the paintings were accompanied by a manifesto.

The *Suprematist Manifesto* (originally entitled *From Cubism to Suprematism in Art, to the New Realism of Painting, to Absolute Creation*) is, in a sense, Malevich's literary masterpiece. It has about it an apocalyptic, almost biblical grandeur that its Italian prototypes never achieved. In it Malevich has much to say in praise of Futurism, although he does not specifically distinguish between its Italian and

39 Malevich, *Woman at the Advertising Column*, oil and collage on canvas, 1914.

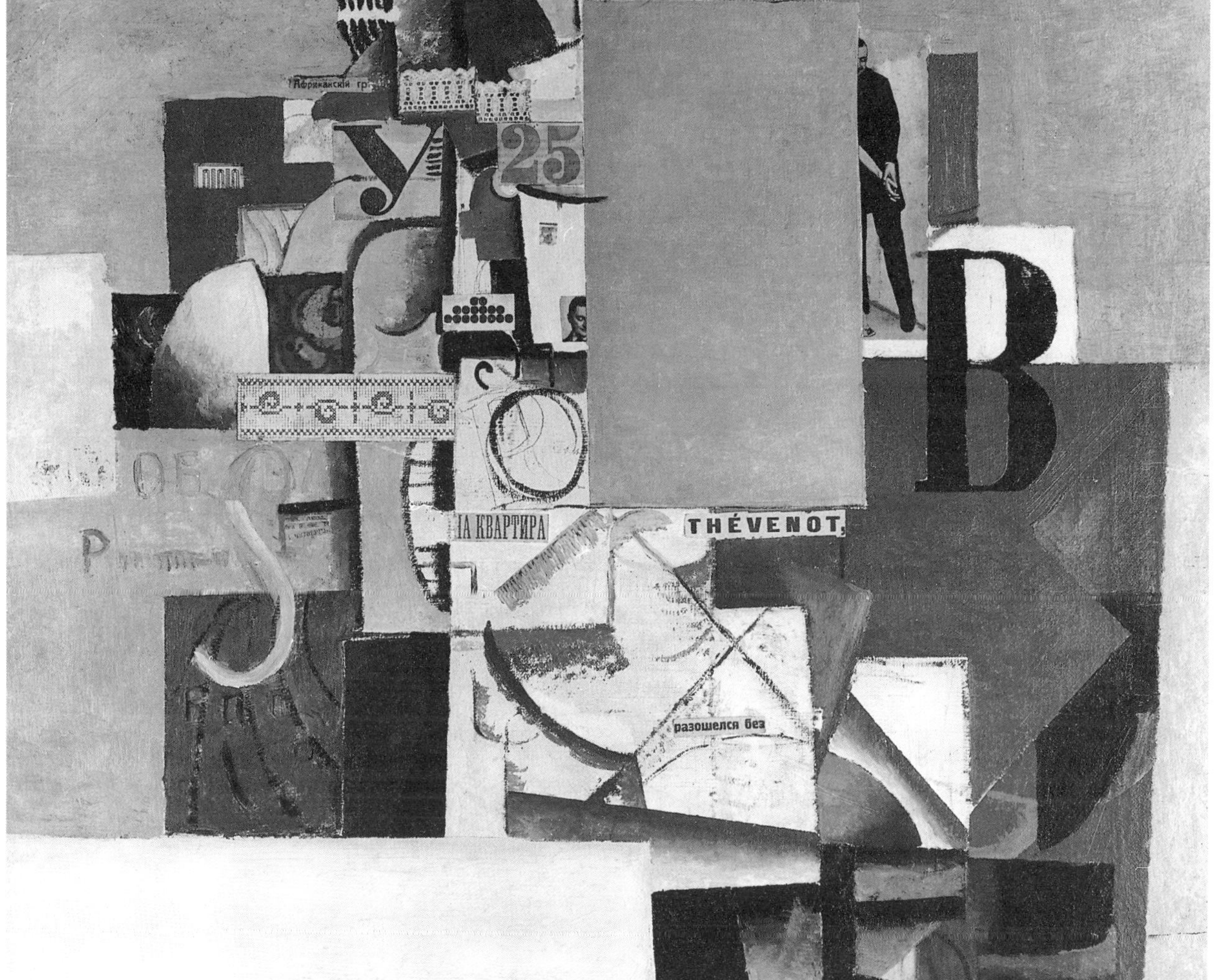
Африканский гр
У
25
В
IA КВАРТИРА
THÉVENOT,
разошелся без

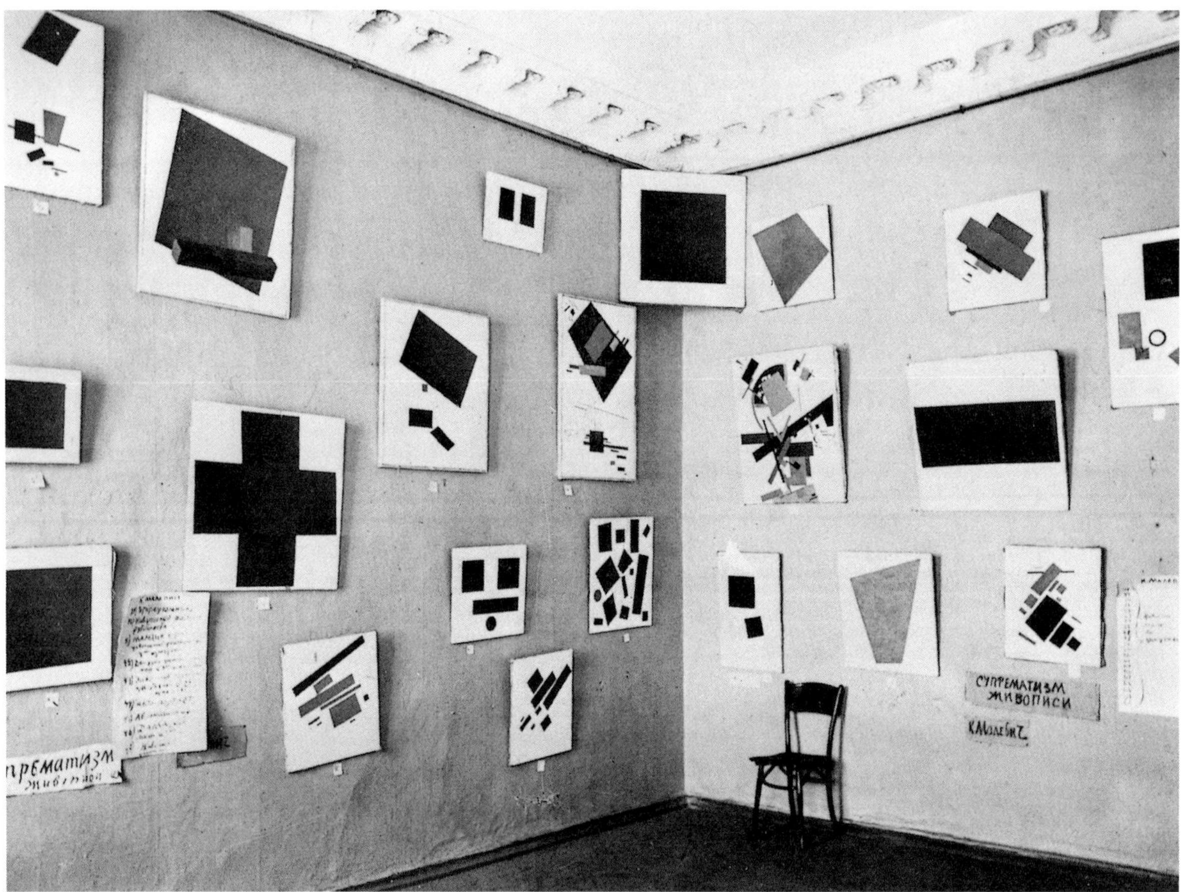

40 Abstract paintings by Malevich at the exhibition 0.10, which opened in Petrograd on 30 December 1915, with *Black Square* (see ill. 42) dominating the display.

Russian manifestations. He does, however, condemn the Futurists for being too interested in the outward appearance of things. On the other hand, he approves of the way in which, through their depiction of motion and speed, the Futurists have succeeded in destroying the 'wholeness of things'. He then makes it clear, however, that 'we [the Suprematists] have abandoned Futurism, and we, the most daring, have spat upon the altar of its art' – in itself, of course a very Futurist thing to say. In the manifesto Malevich devotes more space to Futurism than he does to Cubism, yet the verbal emphasis on Futurism, in the face of the much greater visual impact of Cubism on his work, brings us perhaps to to an understanding of the way in which he achieved his pictorial vision. He was dazzled and excited by the appearance of Cubist art, but was apprehending it through a Futurist aesthetic – an aesthetic that was in many ways antithetical to its aims. And Malevich's writings confirm what our eyes tell us when we compare his paintings of 1912–14 to those of his French mentors.

The Cubists had begun by fragmenting and analyzing their subjects, in Braque's case in order to get closer to them and to touch them visually – and by opening objects up into the space around he sought also to touch optically the space

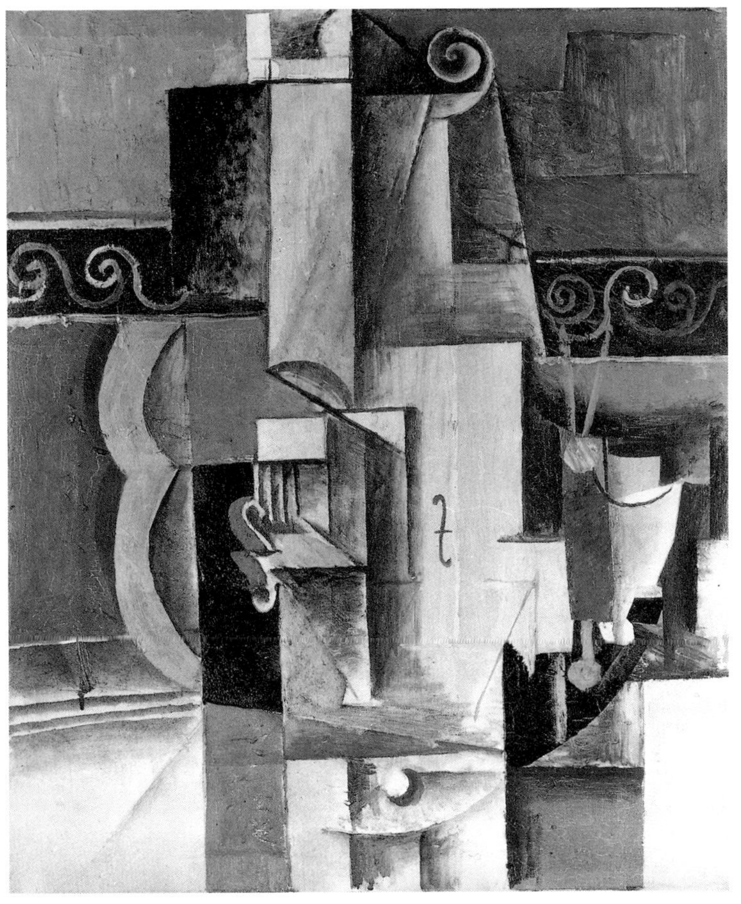

41 Picasso, *Table with Violin and Glasses*, oil on canvas, 1913.

between them. Picasso exploited the use of a variable viewpoint to possess his subjects more completely. Malevich saw Picasso and Braque, on the contrary, as destroying the identity of things. 'The Cubists, thanks to their pulverisation of the object, left the field of objectivity . . .', he declared in 1919.[4] In Synthetic Cubism abstract pictorial elements are assembled or transformed into identifiable presences or subjects that confront their counterparts in the tangible world around us; they are assemblages, aggregates. Malevich, by contrast, saw Synthetic Cubist pictures as cracking apart dynamically. He talked of Cubism as being 'stuffed with
41 explosiveness' and was convinced that 'all matter disintegrates into a large number of component parts which are fully independent'. Malevich had encountered only a few Synthetic Cubist works in the original, and one of them was richly if soberly coloured.[5] He was almost certainly acquainted with Cubist *papiers collés* only in the form of black-and-white reproductions and hence could have imagined them as being highly coloured, and he saw their component parts as dissociating themselves one from another and spinning off into their white paper or canvas supports, rather than as overlapping in shallow depth to recreate or suggest traditional subject-matter in a new fashion. In the same way, the letters stencilled or painted

onto Cubist paintings are always used associatively as clues or keys to help the spectator identify and reconstruct the subject. Malevich speaks of them as dissociative or dislocating elements, denying the importance or significance of subject-matter.

The *Black Square*, emblem of Suprematism, is a static form; it hovers motionless against its white support. But in the manifesto there is a constant emphasis on movement and dynamic tensions. 'Art', Malevich insists, 'is the ability to construct . . . on the basis of weight, speed and movement.' In the same way the *Black* 42
Square was the most reduced, the most minimal canvas yet to have been produced, but we find its author declaring that 'art should not proceed towards reduction, or simplification, but towards complexity'. Relatively recent X-ray examination has revealed that the black square in fact obliterates a composition of coloured shapes underneath it. And to understand its meaning for Malevich we need to appreciate the fact that for him that it represented a dynamically charged synthesis of all his own previous pictorial achievements and was capable of being split apart once more to produce hitherto unimagined pictorial configurations. Malevich also talks of the 'face' of the *Black Square*. In the manifesto he writes: 'Any painting surface is more alive than any face . . . a surface lives, it has been born. It is the face of the new art. The *Square* is a living, royal infant.' By contrast with Mondrian, Malevich remained a figure/ground artist, a painter of abstract images distinguishable from their surrounds.

By the time that Malevich had produced the *Black Square*, and its accompanying verbal pyrotechnics, he had been influenced also, often at second hand, by a vast, amorphous body of philosophical and speculative literature, ranging from Russian Symbolist reinterpretations of eighteenth- and early nineteenth-century German ideology, through to Nietzsche and Walt Whitman and on to the contemporary philosophy of Bergson. M.V. Lodyzhenski's *The Super Consciousness and Ways to Achieve it*, published in 1911, was particularly influential in Russian Cubo-Futurist circles and Malevich himself had fallen under the spell of other occultists and pseudo-scientists fascinated with ideas about the fourth dimension, which had already been disseminated by the turn of the century.

The concept of the fourth dimension had been brought to public attention in particular by the American architect Claude Bragdon. Bragdon's book *Man the Square*, strongly influenced by Theosophy, was published in 1912. Malevich's close friend, the composer-painter Mikhail Matiushin, had introduced him to Howard Hinton's popularizing treatise *The Fourth Dimension*, originally issued in 1904. Most important of all, for Malevich personally, was P.D. Uspensky, a devotee of Helena Petrovna Blavatsky (founder of the Theosophical Society), who in his writings invokes amongst many other sources, Plato, Plotinus and the Upanishads. Malevich had always been interested in geometry, but it is now, between 1913 and 1915, that it becomes for him an obsessive concern; he was interested both by its scientific and its mystical interpretations as propounded by mathematicians from the distant past through to those of the immediate present. Concepts of the fourth dimension differed, but all its advocates agreed that it represented a space outside sensory perception and that it reversed the dialogue as to what was real and unreal, or logical and illogical, in our perception of the three-dimensional universe around us, which is in fact illusory. Many of the writers on the fourth dimension and virtually every painter interested in the concept agreed that it involved or implied a recognition of infinity, although paradoxically this infinite space is also often equated with flatness;

42 Malevich, *Black Square*, oil on canvas, 1915.

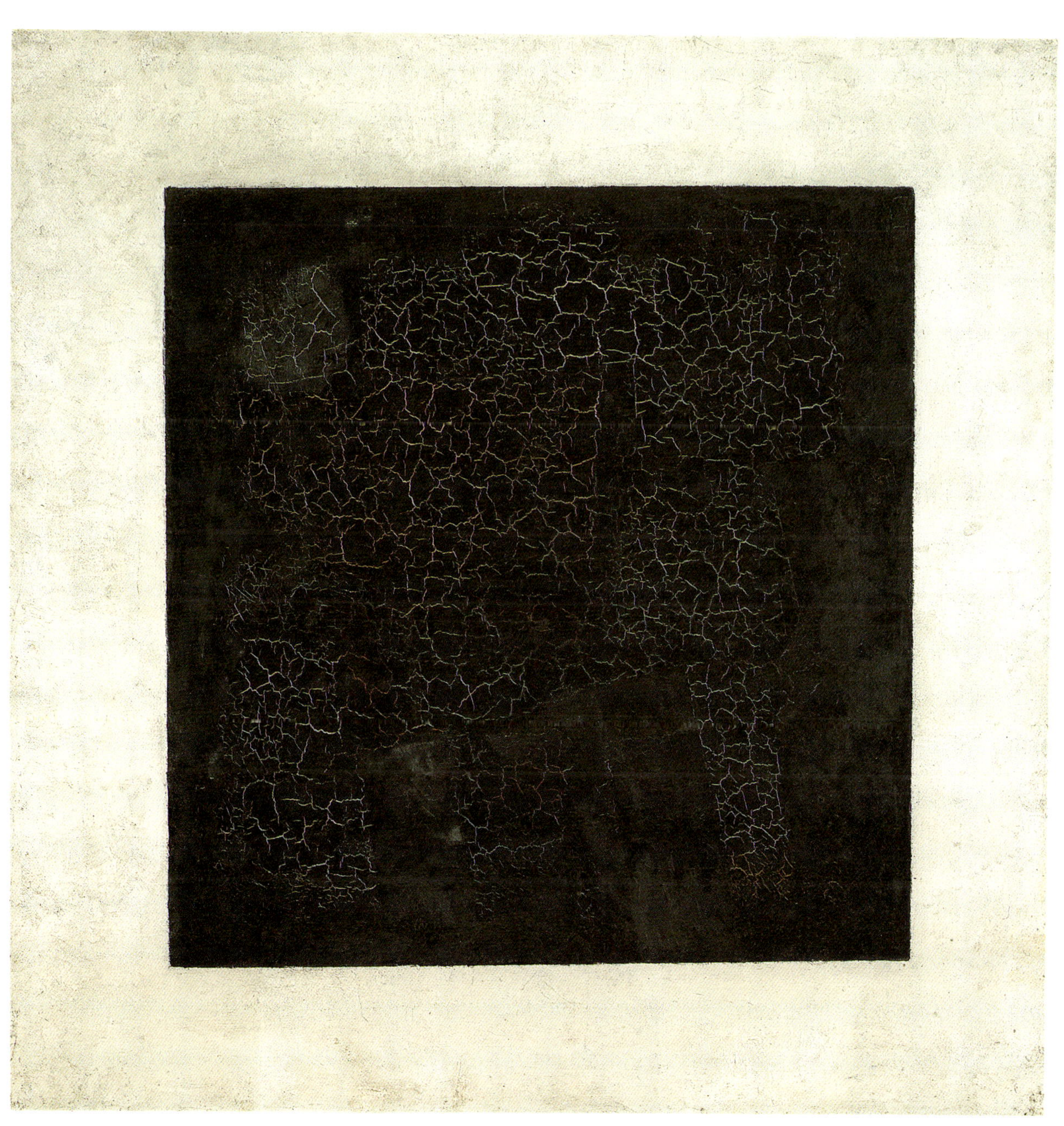

what has to be distrusted is the three-dimensional space in which we believe ourselves to live and which is captured through traditional, illusionistic pictorial means.

It is this welter of intellectual speculation that makes the *Suprematist Manifesto* such an exhilarating, but also difficult and baffling, document. On the other hand, it becomes more accessible to us if we view it not as a consistent aesthetic or philosophical credo, but simply as an apocalyptic speculation on the nature of painting and how it might develop in the hands of Malevich and his potential followers (and these were soon to close ranks behind him). The manifesto is most forcefully experienced if we let its rhetoric wash over us in successive waves rather than if we try to distil or analyze its content.

There are other, purely visual, factors that must be taken into consideration in discussing the genesis of Malevich's abstraction; and because Malevich, like most painters, lived primarily through his eyes and worked with his hands, these factors are as important – possibly even more important – than the intellectual speculation with which they went hand in hand. In 1913 Vladimir Tatlin visited Picasso's studio in Paris, where the reliefs in wood and metal and cardboard he saw hanging on the walls came to him as a revelation. Picasso's relief constructions had in turn been inspired by a simple tribal mask that he owned; it is one of the wonders of our age that such a simple tribal artifact, which could justifiably be called primitive, should have given birth indirectly to Russian Constructivism, one of the most technologically visionary of all twentieth-century art movements. Tatlin had in fact misinterpreted Picasso's intentions, which were to reinvent the language of representational art; he saw them, rather, as speculative abstractions. Tatlin had shown a series of 'painterly reliefs' at 'Tramway V', early in 1915, opposite works by Malevich such as *Woman at the Advertising Column*, and they may have helped to encourage Malevich to make his own leap into the unknown. At '0.10' works by these two artists once again confronted each other across the exhibition hall and
the configurations seen in Tatlin's very recent 'corner reliefs' prefigure, or at least 43
parallel, those found in Malevich's work of late 1915 or early 1916.

In 1913 Malevich had executed the sets and costumes for *Victory over the Sun*, a Futurist opera, which had a prelude by Khlebnikov, like Malevich a visionary but unlike him a dreamer, whose dreams at the time, oddly enough, were of a mathematical nature. The prelude refers to time travel, reincarnation and magic. The 'non-sense' libretto was by Aleksei Kruchenykh and the music by Mikhail Matiushin. The libretto does not mention a black square but Malevich talks of it in contemporary letters to Matiushin and emphasizes its supreme importance to him, and it is surely because of this that he dated the origins of Suprematism to 1913. Scene Two of the opera depicts the hiding of the sun and culminates in a definitive eclipse – in other words with the destruction of cycles of days and seasons, or the elimination of traditional ways of measuring time; the scene ends with the arrival
of the aviator's 'iron bird'. The design for Act I, Scene Three depicts the funeral of 44
the sun; its coffin is perhaps the black square shown in the backdrop – the costume designs for the pallbearers show them displaying black squares on their chests and hats. By the end of the opera the 'aviator' or Futurist strongman replaces the sun as
the focus. The rectangular format of *The Aviator*, a cardinal painting of 1914, is in 45
fact a double square. The lighting of the opera was one of its most innovative features and at times only parts of the performers in their jagged, bright costumes were visible, so that they must have looked like mobile abstractions and premonitions of things to come. It remains a mystery whether any of the back-cloths

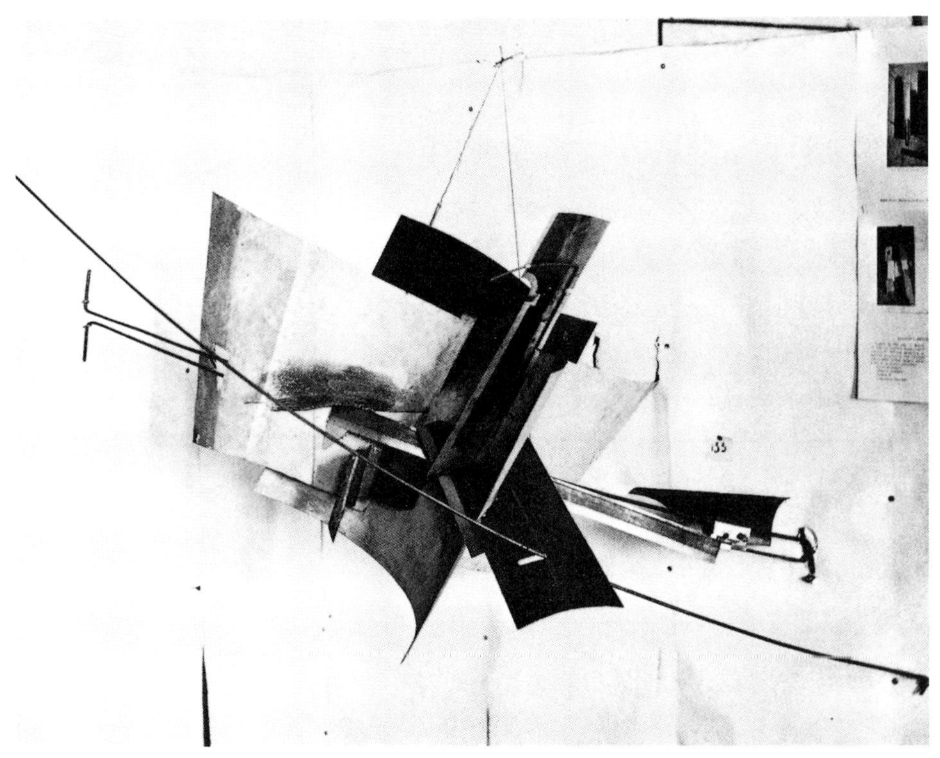

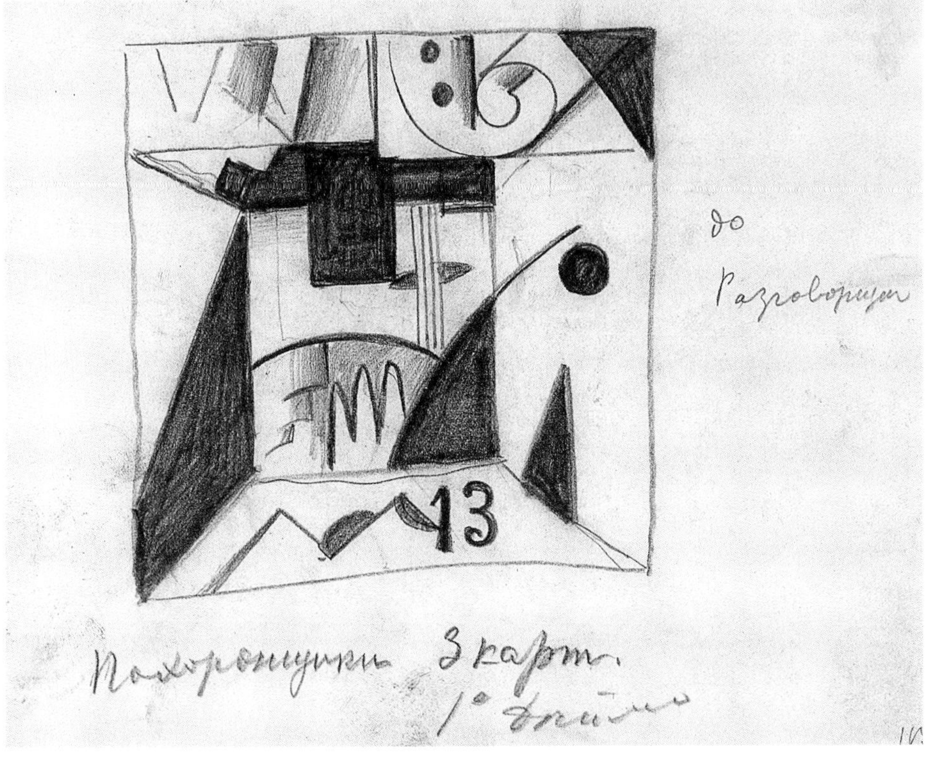

43 Vladimir Tatlin, *Corner Counter-Relief*, iron, aluminium and primer, displayed at the exhibition 0.10, Petrograd, 1915.

44 Malevich, set design for Act I, Scene Three of *Victory over the Sun*, pencil on paper, 1913.

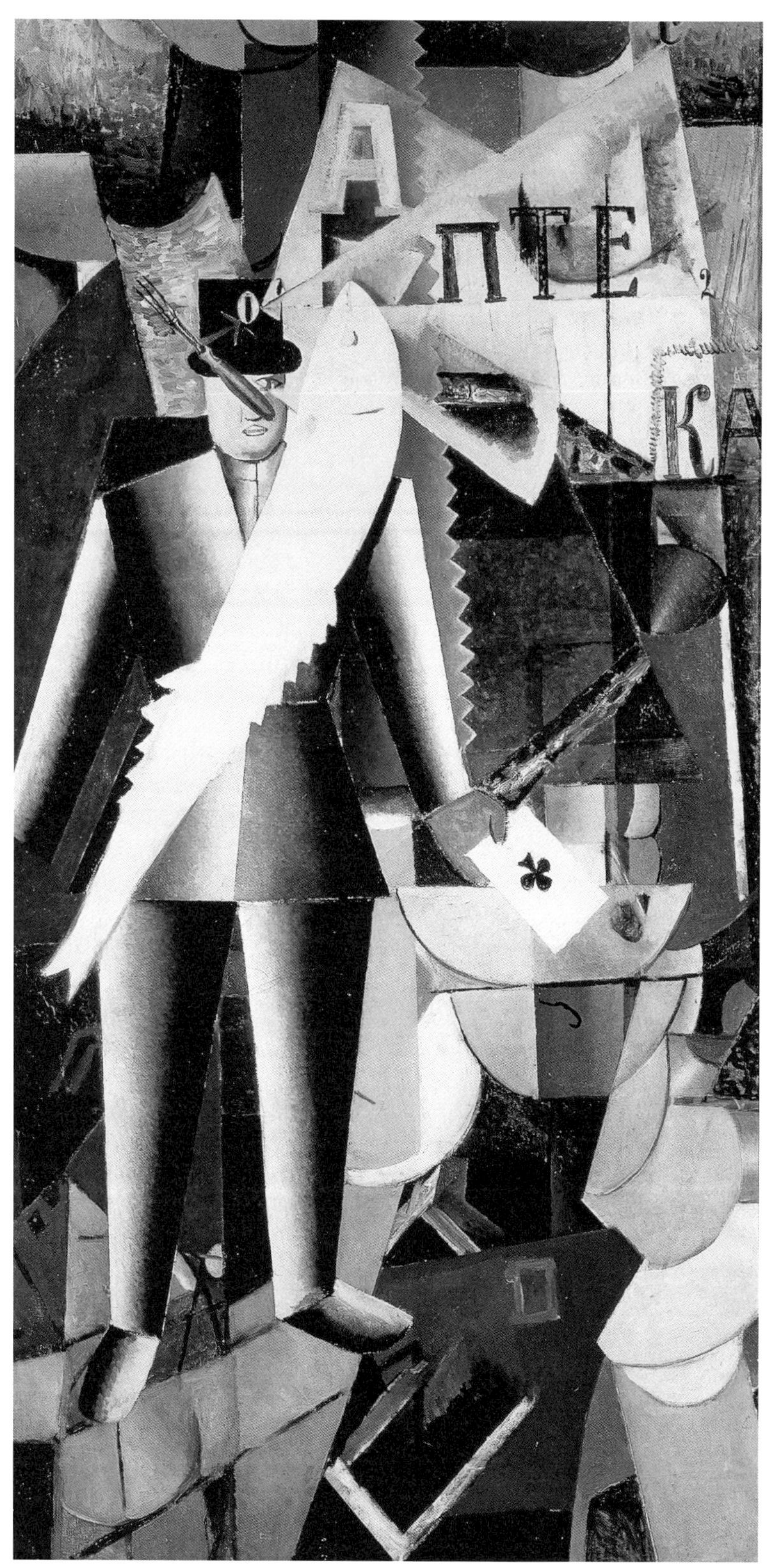
А
ПТЕ
КА

actually represented a simple black square; a surviving design shows a square bisected diagonally into black and white areas. It is possible that when Malevich saw what he had conceived as a simple symbolic emblem hanging motionless under the searing theatrical arc lights, it appeared to him, all of a sudden, to be wonderfully numinous, filled with some breathless, expectant, hidden truth.

It might be fair to say that Malevich's abstraction sprang, Athena-like, ready formed from the brow of its creator; this distinguishes Malevich's approach very sharply from that of both Mondrian and Kandinsky, who had sensed and inched their way into abstraction over a period of many years. It is this that makes Malevich's art so exhilarating. When we see a group of his abstractions, we feel that we are indeed travellers in new galaxies where traditional views of space and time have ceased to exist. But whereas Mondrian, when he had achieved abstraction, turned his back on the natural world, Malevich's attitude towards the study of nature remained more passive, more sympathetic. Although in 1913 he had already sensed that it was possible to convey a sense of profundity through simple, non-referential pictorial forms, and had found confirmation of this in his first Suprematist works of 1915, he was on occasion still accepting more earthbound starting-points to provoke their configurations. Some of the Suprematist canvases
46 at '0.10', for example, bore descriptive titles like *Painterly Realism of a Football Player: Colour Masses in the Fourth Dimension.* Many contemporary Suprematist drawings can be read in terms of body imagery and are concerned with the age-old search for ideal proportion. There are even in his writings from time to time undercurrents of nostalgia for the green pastures and meadows of his youth.

But already, in his first Suprematist paintings, Malevich had found what was to be the true subject of his art. It was to be an art about flight, about man's ascent into the ether, into that mysterious light-carrying medium believed by occultists and many early scientists to fill all empty space. His text *The Non-Objective World* was published by the Bauhaus in 1927; here, under the heading 'The Environment which Stimulates the Suprematist', he used as illustrations photographs of aeroplanes flying in formation and aerial views of towns – one of the fruits of new technologies developed during the First World War.[6] These clearly formed the basis for many of the compositions of tipping, tilted planes and shapes that began to appear almost immediately in his Suprematist canvases.The concept of powered flight was one about which Russia was obsessive in the period before 1917 – Kandinsky was to talk of 'the current craze for aeronautics'[7] – and it became one of the leitmotifs of the great revolution itself. In his writings Malevich pays tribute to modern technology and appears to subscribe, here and there, to the Futurist cult of the machine.

Ultimately, however, Malevich was not interested in machines in themselves, or even in what they could be made to symbolize; one sometimes even senses that he disliked and distrusted them. His visions of flight were of a more cosmological nature. They had to do with extraterrestrial, interplanetary travel in a future world where accepted concepts of space and time no longer had a place. His coloured shapes against white grounds suggest totally new perspectives. Shapes of different weights and proportions overlap and intercept, but it is impossible to gauge the distances that separate them. In his paintings there is no near, no far, no up, no down.[8] Tilted shapes suggest recession into depth, flat frontal ones hover in an indeterminate space. Similarly, the painted white backgrounds reaffirm the flatness of the pictorial support and yet suggest infinity, an unbounded space beyond

45 Malevich, *The Aviator,* oil on canvas, 1914.

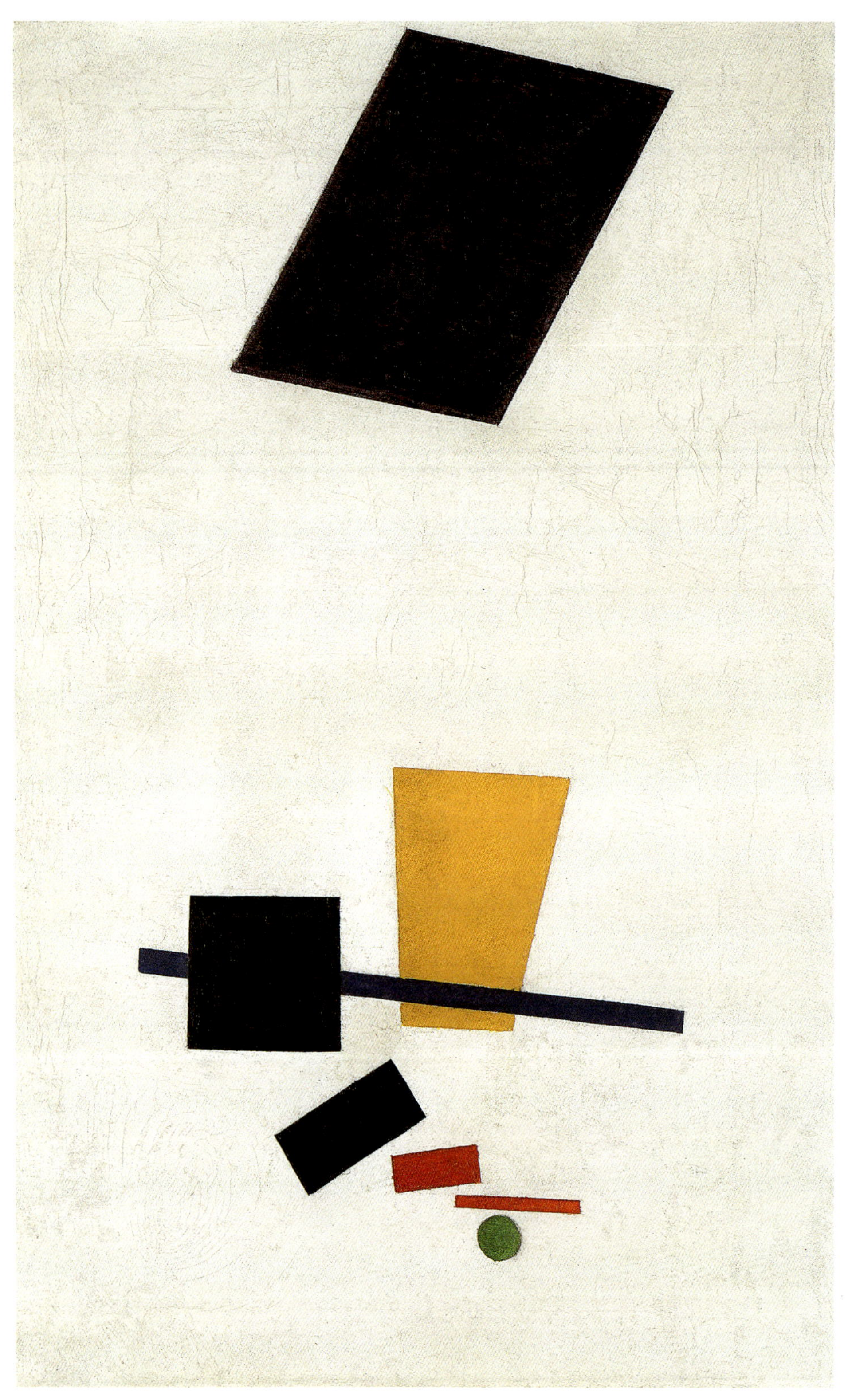

46 Malevich, *Painterly Realism of a Football Player: Colour Masses in the Fourth Dimension*, oil on canvas, 1915.

47 Malevich, *Suprematist Painting: Aeroplane in Flight*, oil on canvas, 1915.

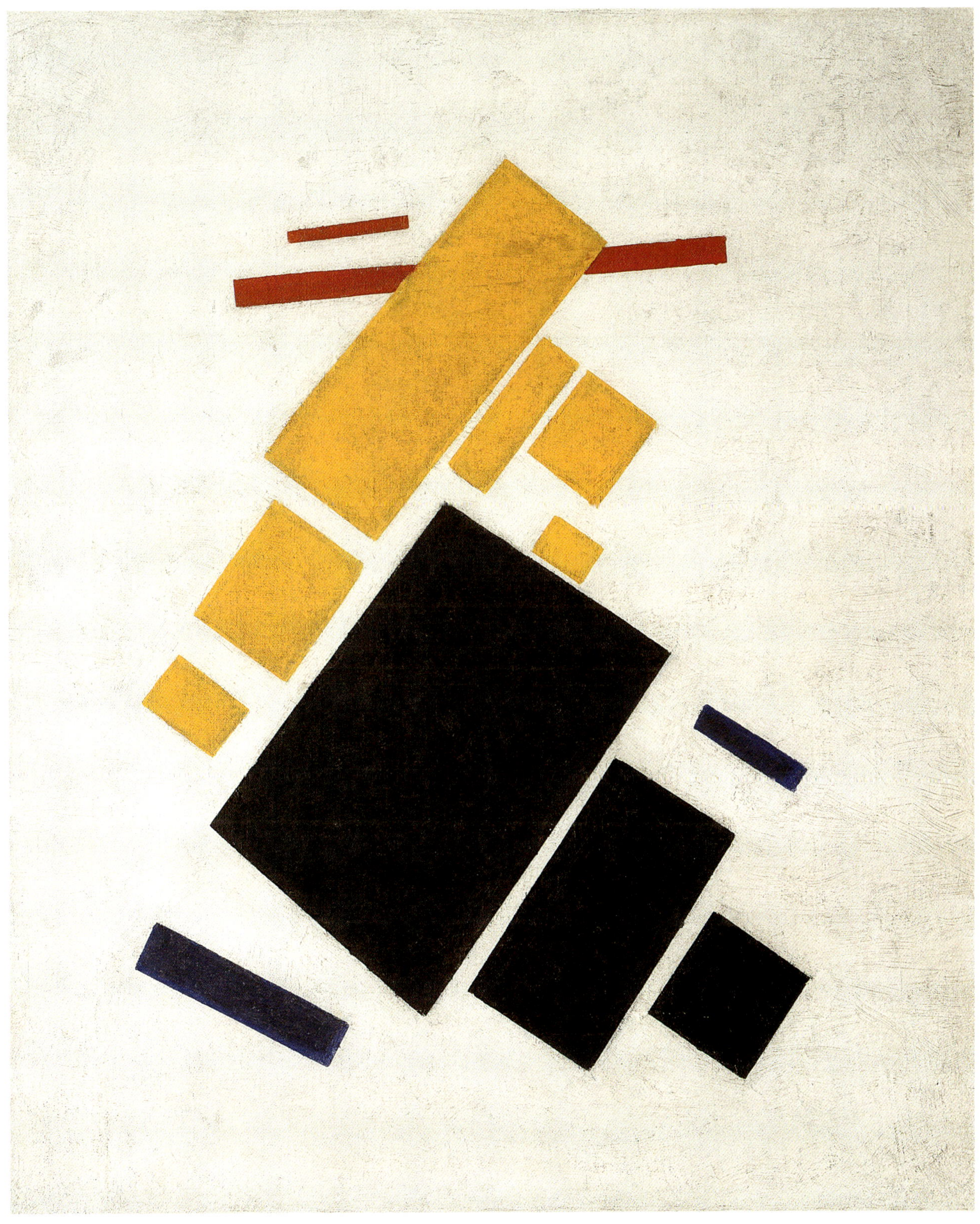

human ken. If the Cubists had turned their backs on traditional, single-viewpoint perspective and Mondrian had created a new kind of pictorial space, it might perhaps be fair to say that Malevich was imagining a new, 'perspective-less' perspective. And if the concept of flight took on new dimensions during the First World War, as an instrument of both power and destruction, it is surely also of the deepest significance that Russian artists, who in the years between 1907 and 1914 had been exposed to developments in Western Europe in such a compressed way, were now, during the war years, finding themselves cut off from outside inspiration and having to work in almost complete isolation. It is this isolation that further fostered and nourished the total originality of Malevich's vision.

Malevich subsequently came to distinguish three main phases in the evolution of Suprematism;[9] although it is difficult to fit the stylistic development of Suprematism quite so neatly into a Hegelian system of evolution, the distinctions remain useful in charting the development of Malevich's thought. The first phase was black and corresponds, Malevich tells us, to economy. His use of the word is baffling until one realizes that it is derived from the German nineteenth-century philosopher Richard Avenarius, whose *Philosophy as a Reflection on the World, according to the Minimal Waste of Energies*, published in 1876, appeared in Russian translation in 1913. Avenarius rejected all processes of deductive reasoning and claimed that truth could be apprehended through immediate perception. He suggested that, if these truths seemed contradictory, 'economy' of thought could be produced by formulating a compromise that synthesizes the two. Thus, '. . . different groups of ideas have been reduced to one'.[10] Malevich was not one for compromises, but he probably saw Avenarius's proposals as endorsing his view of the *Black Square*, as digesting and compressing a lot of previous art; and the concept of shapes representing ideas which come together to form new ones was central to Malevich's art. But it is also revealing that Malevich's attention should have been caught by an engaging, but minor and eccentric, thinker at the same time as he was attempting to come to terms with the over-arching splendours of Hegel's world-view.

The second stage of Suprematism is the red phase, which corresponds to revolution. In fact as the installation of '0.10' suggests – and this is confirmed by the fact that the original *Black Square* of 1915 (and there are several later ones) is painted over an earlier composition of coloured shapes – the black, and the first coloured, Suprematist paintings were being executed at the same time. But when Malevich made his categories, in 1920, he was looking for ways to harness his art to the ideologies of the great revolution of 1917, ideologies which were subsequently to work towards his own artistic and physical destruction. And again this forces on us the recognition that, just as Suprematism was born during the period of isolation imposed on Russia by external events during the First World War, so its basic premises were established before the advent of Russia's internal cataclysm. Most deeply revealing of all, perhaps, is the fact that Malevich himself seems to have realized, if only unconsciously, that the final – white – phase of Suprematism, which he equates with 'pure action', was even less adaptable to the here and now than Suprematism's earlier manifestation had been. Rather, it is a blueprint for a purer and better world.

48 Malevich, *Suprematist Painting*, oil on canvas, 1916–17.

It is hard to establish an exact sequence or chronology for Suprematism, but the move seems to have been from relatively simple compositions, in both black and colour, to works of greater complexity. The most elaborate works exhibited in

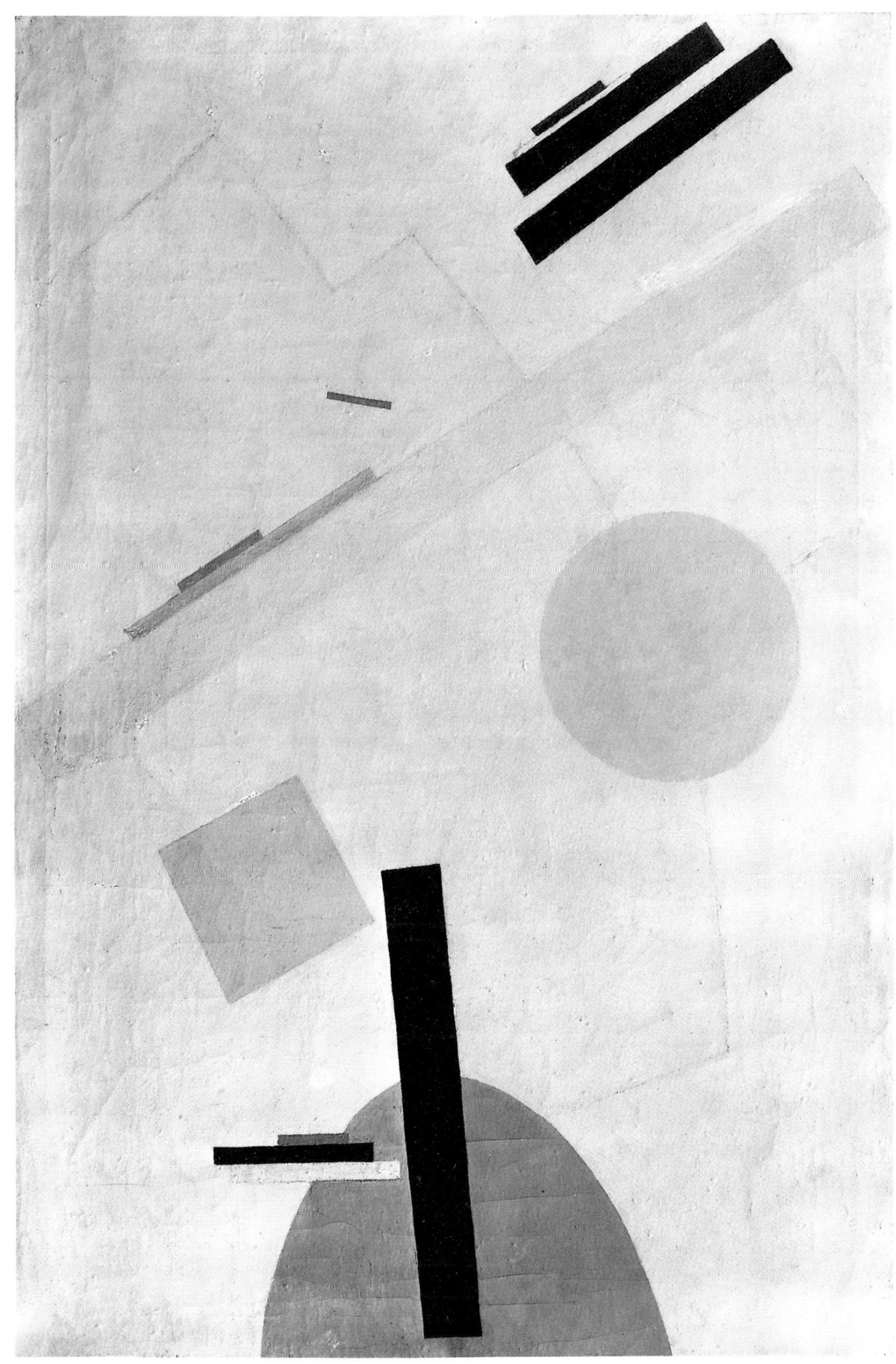

49 Malevich,
Suprematist Painting,
oil on canvas, 1917–18.

50 Malevich,
Suprematist Painting,
oil on canvas, 1917–18.

'0.10' were probably the latest. The subtitles sometimes attached to works which
Malevich himself would later have placed in his second, or red, phase are still relatively straightforward and descriptive in nature, for example *Suprematism: Eight* 47
Red Rectangles, or *Suprematist Painting: Aeroplane in Flight*. Next, perhaps, are
works where smaller shapes tend to drift off towards the edges of the canvas as if in 48
an attempt to wing their way out into the space beyond the pictorial arena. These
were succeeded by a number of paler paintings in which the centre of the canvas 49
tends to empty out and the larger forms now also brush the edges of the canvas or
are cut off on reaching them. The titles of these paintings become more symbolic:
Composition of Suprematist Elements Expressing the Sensation of Metallic Sounds 50
(Pale Metallic Colours) is one example. The white backgrounds are now sometimes subliminally divided into two by curving or jagged lines, as if infinity itself
were being torn apart.

There then comes a break, manifested by the 'fading away' pictures – works
which appear to be an attempt to release form from the two-dimensional picture
plane. At least one canvas showing a tilted form was exhibited at '0.10', although
it did not yet constitute 'fading away'. And it has been suggested that the tilted
forms which first make their appearance in Malevich's work in 1913–14 may
reflect diagrams of Bragdon's and ideas of Uspensky's describing cubes of the
fourth dimension passing through the screen of our familiar space.[11] The subtitles
of the 'Suprematist Whites' become frankly mystical: *Mystic Waves from Outer*
Space is one. The series reaches a climax in the *White Square on White*. And it 51
would be nice to think that the *Black Square* had split apart, forming new configurations that had taken on bright colour, and that as they wheeled and drifted to the
edges of the canvas they had become pale and faded, and as these new configurations revolved through an infinite space they had regrouped or reassembled to
form the purified white square. Unfortunately, however, as the genesis of the *Black*
Square, itself suggests, things were not that simple.

In 1919, however, Malevich was able to claim: 'The blue colour of the sky has been defeated by the Suprematist system, has been broken through and entered white as the real concept of infinity.'[12] And a year later, 'What is the canvas? What do we see represented on it? . . . a window through which we discover life . . . blue does not give a true impression of the infinite. The rays of vision are caught in a cupola and cannot penetrate the infinite. The Suprematist infinite white allows the beam to pass on without encountering any limit.'[13] During the years following the launch of the *Suprematist Manifesto* Malevich's thought was evolving at the same dizzying and heady rate as the evolution of his painting itself. His intellectual sources, as has been suggested, are astonishingly and bafflingly disparate, and again they can best be apprehended if we consider them as sheltering under Malevich's own characteristically eccentric Hegelian umbrella.

The third and final stage of Hegel's view of evolution, as propounded in the 1820s, is that in which spirit detaches itself from nature and achieves total freedom, thus becoming 'pure universal form . . . in which the spiritual essence attains the consciousness and feeling of itself'.[14] It was this state of advanced spirituality that Malevich felt had at last been brought to a conclusion by himself. Of all the visual arts, Hegel had been prepared to admit only painting as one of the achievements of the third phase of the evolution of the world spirit, precisely because painting is in a sense the most abstract of the visual arts, conveying as it does a sensation of illusion on a flat surface. In his initial *Suprematist Manifesto*

51 Malevich,
White Square on White,
oil on canvas, 1918.

Malevich had in turn placed an almost moral emphasis on the need to respect the two-dimensionality of the canvas support and, although his art of previous and succeeding years had been richly layered in overlapping pictorial planes, he also felt that it was the flatness of much recent painting, and of his own Suprematism in particular, that marked an advance on what had gone before. He personally had no difficulty in reconciling this flatness with infinite space because so many of his intellectual mentors, and particularly those with an interest in the speculative and mystic properties of geometry, had suggested that with the elimination of three-dimensional or illusionistic pictorial depiction, a fourth dimension – and indeed even a fifth – could be given expression or explained diagrammatically on a two-dimensional plane.

Even within the compressed development of his own Suprematism, however, Malevich's thought and his attitude towards painting had changed. The most significant document for an understanding of his new position is perhaps 'God is not Cast Down' written in 1920 and published in 1922. He was now reconsidering the very nature and future of art. It soon becomes obvious that God, as viewed by Malevich, is an embodiment of the super-artist; and he suggests that man himself in the guise of artist – a being possibly even more exalted than Nietzsche's own *Übermensch* or superman – can reach perfection 'through all he produces, so that he can achieve a state of rest' and that man himself can then 'act no longer as man but as God'.

In 1920 Malevich announced the death of easel painting. 'There can be no question of painting in Suprematism,' he declared, 'painting was done was done for long ago.'[15] In his essay on poetry of 1919 he had condemned craftsmanship out of hand: 'The poet is not a craftsman, craftsmanship is nonsense.' And this view helps to suggest why, despite his belief in the perfectibilty of geometry, his own work is so often almost aggressively rough-hewn. At the same time in *On the New Systems in Art* he had given a hint of how he had come to see his Suprematism when he wrote: '. . . The important thing in art is signs flowing from the creative brain.'

One of the peculiarities of Malevich's writing is the use, in his discussions of creativity, of the image of the human skull. He writes, 'Is not the whole universe a strange skull in which meteors, suns, comets and planets rush [throb] endlessly?'[16] And Malevich's latter-day Suprematist paintings are no longer paintings in the traditional sense at all. Rather, they are signs, messages, pictorial planets, emanating from the artist's skull – in itself, white, spherical, translucent – and directed out through infinite space toward some ultimate, unknowable Godhead, seat of perfection, purity and, despite Malevich's earlier insistence on speed, yes, now one of infinite repose.

Lissitzky, the most gifted of Malevich's disciples of the next generation, and a more educated and hence more accessible writer, was to clarify his master's position in a lecture entitled 'New Russian Art', delivered in 1922. In it he draws a distinction between two kinds of signs. One type, he posits, is derived from our knowledge of the outside world and natural phenomena and can be easily read and identified, since the idea exists before the pictorial sign for it is identified. He goes on: 'Now the second possibility: A sign is designed, much later it is given its name, and later still its meaning becomes clear. So we do not understand the signs, the shapes, which the artist created, because man's brain has not yet reached the corresponding state of development.'[17] If Mondrian was a prophet, Malevich was a true mystic – as both his images and his words confirm. He came to see his art as

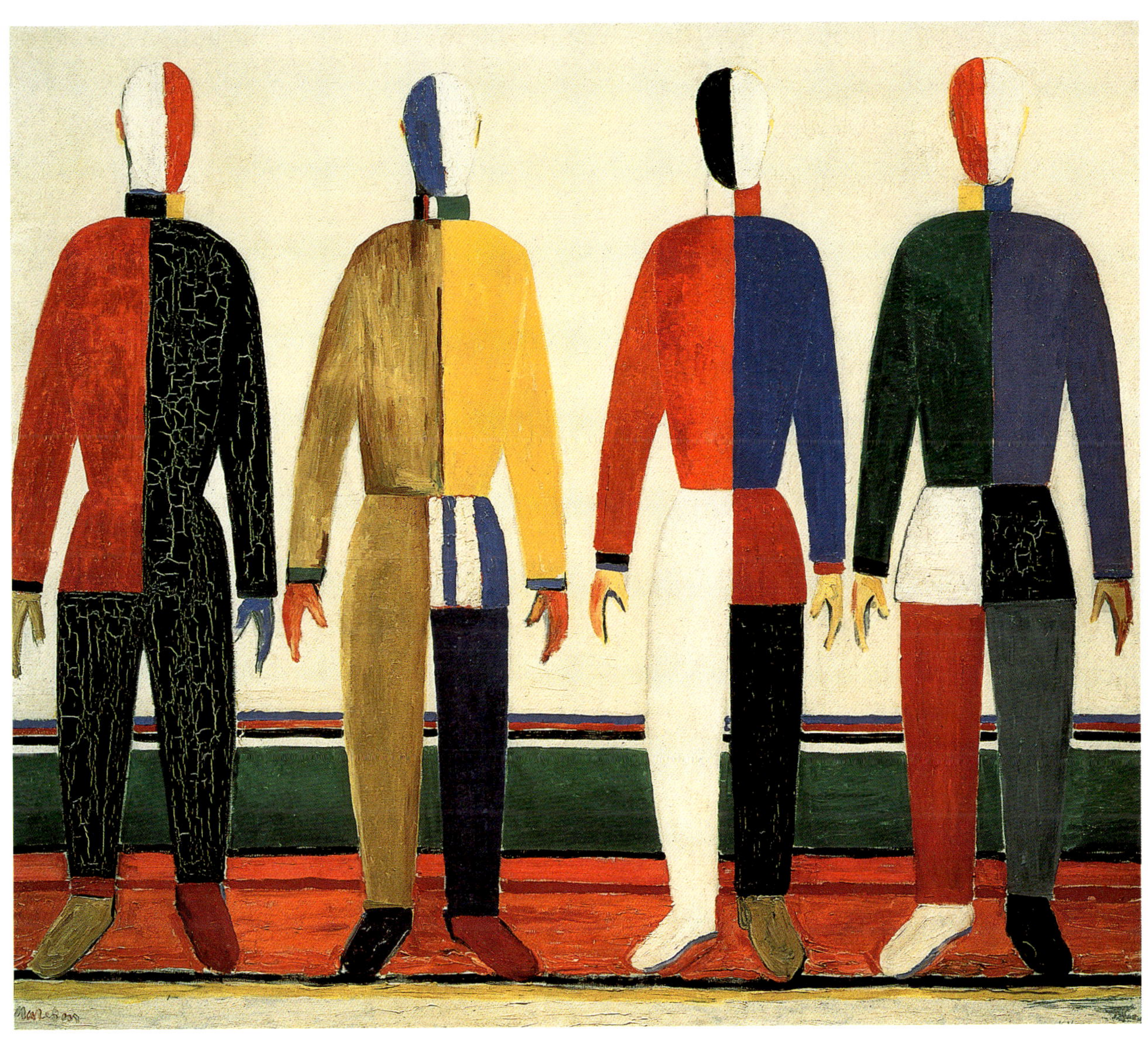

52 Malevich,
The Sportsmen, oil on canvas, *c.* 1928–32.

opening up a vast panorama of possibilities; and certainly his followers, such as Lissitzky, viewed his art in this light.

But with his white 'beam' paintings, and above all with *White Square on White*, Malevich must have realized that he had brought to a close a whole chapter in the history of art. And to this extent he had reached an absolute: he said, 'If someone knows the absolute he has known zero.'[18] There is even a sense in which, by throwing open a window onto what he sensed might be the art of the future, he had slammed shut the door on immediate developments in his own art.

Malevich is the true father of what we have come to call 'minimal' and 'conceptual' art. But he is also the prototype for countless subsequent abstract artists who having reached their goal – or at least a distillation of the ideas and sensations they were seeking to evoke – only find themselves in the tragic position of wondering how to go further, how to avoid the endless repetition of the climax of their achievement, a repetition that might ultimately only drain their art of much of its original impact or meaning. Mondrian knew how to renew himself by constantly kicking the visual ladder from under himself. Kandinsky's endlessly inquiring mind produced for him, throughout his career, a succession of alternative possibilities. But it could be argued that, within the cycle of his own art, Malevich had succumbed to the principle of destruction inherent in a Hegelian system of dialectics. Mondrian had equated art with religion and his faith sustained him. Kandinsky, despite his orthodox religious beliefs and his quest for spirituality, eventually turned himself into an artistic scientist. Malevich's religious beliefs appear to have been passionate but unorthodox and his propensity for extremes, coupled with the pace of the Russian Revolution which caught him up while he was in the latter stages of Suprematism, meant that he placed an absolutely unrealizable burden on art by coming to view it as a panacea for philosophy, education, politics and ultimately for society itself.

As he imposed ever greater burdens on Suprematism, Malevich was transforming it from being a new view of art into a new concept of the cosmos. German transcendentalism, as seen through Russian eyes, had been part of his heritage since his Symbolist days. By now, like Mondrian, he was rejecting any symbolic content to his art, despite the fact that his followers saw his images as signs, or reductive symbols. A figurative painter making use of symbols might assert that they endow his work with added layers of meaning. Yet if the signs appearing in non-figural art seem to be 'standing in' for something else, they might also appear to be challenging the conclusions, the veracity of purely abstract art. It was the recognition of this situation that prompted Malevich's renunciation of symbolic content in his work while continuing to insist that the important thing in art is 'signs flowing from the creative brain.'[19]

After producing his Suprematist 'Whites', Malevich virtually ceased painting for some five years. He threw himself into a frenzy of revolutionary activity, serving on committees, designing decorations for rallies and parades, seeking to serve a cause in which at first he believed entirely. He was writing furiously and, as early as 1917, was advertising his teaching programmes for workers. In 1919 he began his intensive period as a teacher. A moving photograph, taken probably late in 1919, shows his new team departing from Moscow for their new headquarters, the art school in Vitebsk, an industrial town some 300 miles to the west. His students, many of them little more than children, wore black squares stitched to their sleeves and they adopted as their slogan 'Art into Life'. In 1920, on the anniversary of the

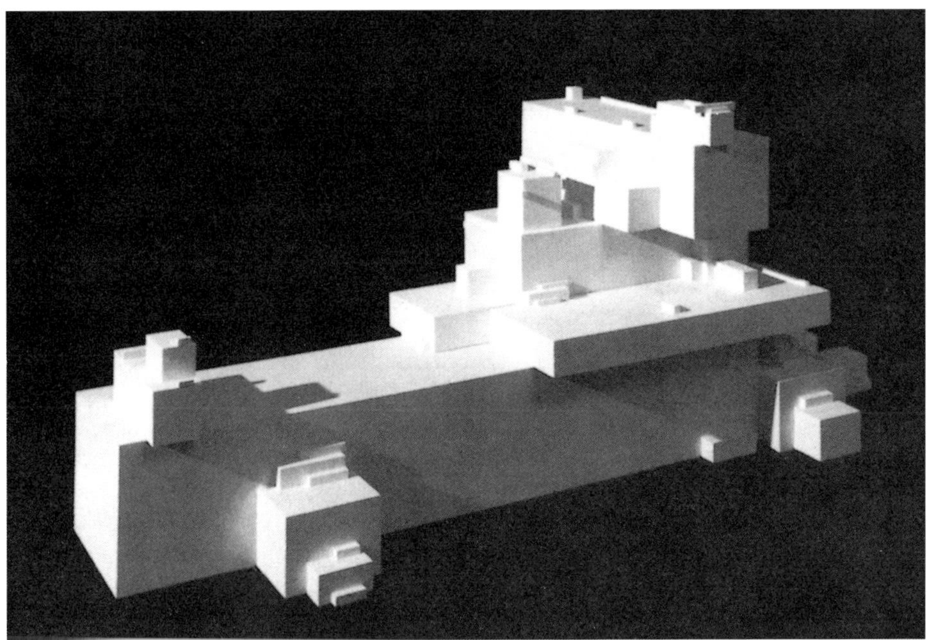

53 Malevich, *Alpha*, model in plaster of Paris, 1920.

Revolution and under Malevich's direction, they set about transforming the grimy town into a pageant of colour signs. The great film director Sergei Eisenstein was to write: 'All the main streets are covered with white paint on the red-brick walls, and against this white background are green circles, reddish-orange squares, blue rectangles. This is Vitebsk 1920. Kasimir Malevich's brush has passed over its walls. "The squares of the town are our palette" is the message that these walls convey.'[20]

When Malevich resumed painting, around 1923, he would often work in the company of his students and sometimes they would be delegated to complete his canvases. Many of these works take on a heraldic air and lack the quality of mystery and cosmic vision that had characterized Malevich's own, more personal, Suprematist messages – although from time to time his own uncanny sense of touch, the very feeling of his hand, continues to make itself felt. In keeping with his social concerns and his conviction that traditional easel painting was dead, he turned his attention to architecture and, together with his students in Vitebsk, and subsequently Petrograd, he executed many architectural designs and a group of
53 models in plaster of Paris. And yet he continued to cling to the conviction that art was neither utilitarian nor at the service of any one rigid, political credo – a position that was bringing him increasingly into conflict with colleagues on both the left and the right. He maintained, moreover, that the aims and pursuits of art and science were very different. The architectural models may once again best be seen as messages and designs, or blueprints for builders of the future. He called his constructions 'blind architecture' and referred to them as 'planits'. And even in these solid three-dimensional structures there persists the obsession with the white purity of flight. A note attached to one of the drawings reads: 'Thanks to its construction the *planit* is easy to clean. It can be washed daily. The material is matte

white glass . . . the *planit* will be accessible from all sides to the earth dweller, who will be able to be in it and on top of it.'[21]

And yet throughout the 1920s, and increasingly so as the decade progressed, things became difficult for Malevich. In a retrospective held in 1929 at the Tretyakov Gallery in Moscow the most recent work exhibited by him recapitulated the peasant themes that he had first tackled in 1912–13 and, placed next to their earlier counterparts, these canvases look somewhat cold and emasculated. He was now being openly attacked as a 'bourgeois' artist, and the director of the Tretyakov, Fedor Kumpan, was given a long prison sentence for having mounted the exhibition.

Harder still to assess is a totally new phase in Malevich's art. *The Sportsmen*, of 52
around 1928–32, one of the largest and most important of this new group of paintings, was shown in an exhibition called 'Art from the Imperialist Epoch' as an example of pre-revolutionary bourgeois art, even though the paint upon it was barely dry. What was in Malevich's mind? Was he trying to adapt to the edict of 1929 that proclaimed that all artists must henceforth depict in their work the establishment of a socialist society? Contemporary drawings confirm that he was still trying to understand the human figure in terms of ideal or divine proportion. And some of these late paintings have about them an air of innocent optimism that is strangely heartbreaking. Are these faceless peasants and sportsmen the men and women of the future who may yet participate in a renewed Suprematist world and environment? One or two of the late single-figure pieces emanate some of the same mystical fervour that had characterized the Suprematist 'Whites'.

Malevich was gradually being broken by the system. With his death in 1935 in Leningrad, Suprematism enjoyed a strange revival. His body was placed in a Suprematist coffin of his own design, executed by a disciple, but without the cross on the lid that Malevich had indicated. A *Black Square* was placed above his body for the wake. A second square was attached to the lorry that transported the coffin to Moscow for cremation. His ashes were buried, as he had requested, in the countryside near his dacha at Nemchinovka, where he had formulated many of the tenets of Suprematism. Over them was placed a monument on which was inscribed a final square.

3
Kandinsky and the sound of colour

Vasily Kandinsky is the most complex of the pioneering abstractionists, and both his character and his art embody the contradictions which he himself saw as one of the governing characteristics of the spirit of his times. The literature on him is wider and more controversial than that devoted to any other abstract painter. He himself wrote extensively, and his *On the Spiritual in Art* remains possibly the most influential single statement to have been produced by any twentieth-century artist. It first arrived at the very end of 1911 and there were two further editions in 1912. It brought him instant and greater fame than he had achieved hitherto as a painter. Kandinsky followed a more tortuous path into abstraction than did either Mondrian or Malevich, investigating the relationship of figures to landscape and subsequently of figures to a cosmos dissolved into compositions of a colouristic richness hitherto unenvisaged.

Kandinsky came from a cultivated and privileged background, and was more truly cultured, more widely travelled and infinitely better read, than either of his two peers. At Moscow University he studied economics, law and ethnography. Mondrian and Malevich had found their artistic vocations early on, but although Kandinsky was more naturally gifted than either of them, it was only in 1896, when he was thirty, that he decided to become a painter. When he did so, it was out of a sense of moral conviction, out of a belief that it was through art that the world might be altered and reformed. Like all the early abstractionists, he was in revolt – and most vociferously – against the materialism of much nineteenth-century society and thought and against positivistic philosophy. The nineteenth-century, he declared, 'distinguished itself as a time far remote from inner creation'.[1] And yet he owed, and continued to owe, more to the nineteenth century than did Mondrian or Malevich. Kandinsky distrusted developments in contemporary science, and claimed that knowledge of splitting the atom had destroyed his own universe;[2] none the less he was of a scientific disposition. Although he was not a mystic, he did believe in mysticism and steeped himself in a vast body of mystic lore. The work of his most historically significant period, the years between 1910 and 1914, is fundamentally tragic, and yet he willed himself into optimism. About his own work he was simultaneously candid and secretive. He was at once the most programmatic and the most romantic of the early abstractionists.

What divided Kandinsky most sharply from Mondrian and Malevich, apart from his background, was his attitude to Symbolism. Mondrian had explored it briefly and then, as the formalistic concerns of his work had come to carry within themselves the truths he sought to express, he would have considered it demeaning to them to acknowledge that they were standing in for something else – meaning for him was embedded in form. Malevich's headlong rush into early twentieth-century modernism turned him into an iconoclast. As he came to see himself as looking only forwards, he, too, rejected symbolic content in his art, although it could be argued that it was the ethos of Symbolism that had in fact prepared him for the advent of his epiphanies. Kandinsky, on the other hand, was formed by the Symbolism of three countries: Russia, Germany and France. He remained deeply steeped in it, and there is a sense in which he became the Symbolist *par excellence*, even when he felt he had gone beyond the three figures who more than any others had been his Symbolist heroes: the painter Arnold Böcklin, the writer Maurice Maeterlinck and the composer Richard Wagner. In what is perhaps the most frequently quoted of his aphorisms, Kandinsky asked himself, 'Speaking of the hidden by means of the hidden. Is this not content?'[3] It would be hard to think of two short sentences that so encapsulate the whole mystique of Symbolism. When we look at a painting by Kandinsky, we are simultaneously looking at what it is concealing, veiling.

In his *Reminiscences* of 1912–13,[4] the most accessible of all his writings, Kandinsky talks of three early and formative revelations he experienced. In the summer of 1896 he saw one of the *Haystacks* paintings by Monet at the French Industrial and Art Exhibition in Moscow and was deeply moved by it without at first being aware of what it represented; Monet himself, looking at his own paintings in the gloaming, doubtless felt similar sensations. Subsequently Kandinsky had a comparable experience when he saw one of his own paintings standing on its side – its literal subject-matter all of a sudden seemed to him totally irrelevant. Then he attended a performance of Wagner's *Lohengrin* at the Court Theatre in Moscow. To him the music caught the spirit of Moscow at his, Kandinsky's, twilight hour; he saw the music in terms of colour, and sensed that painting could possess the same emotive and spiritual qualities as music. Thousands of sensitive young artists the world over have succumbed to Wagner in analogous ways. However, the third of Kandinsky's revelations was unique to him, and it prepared the way for the other two. In 1889, before he turned to art as a vocation, he was commissioned by the Russian Imperial Society of Friends of Natural History, Anthropology and Ethnogrophy to go alone to the province of Vologda, some 300 miles north of Moscow, to study its folk art.

The paper that he subsequently published on the pagan religion of its people, the Zyrians, an East Finnish tribe, also recognized the effects of the Christianity that had been imposed on their beliefs and of the 'duoverie' – that is to say the dual faith, pagan and Christian – that resulted. Kandinsky himself clung to the Russian Orthodox Church throughout his life, but came also to see life and art in terms of clashes, contrasts, fusions. In his *Reminiscences* he describes the importance to him of folk art and of the way it proliferates in the lives of the people whose habits he was studying in the Vologda region: 'I shall never forget the great wooden houses covered with carving: They taught me to move within the picture, to live in the picture. I still remember how I entered the living room for the first time and stood rooted to the spot before the unexpected scene. Every object was covered with brightly coloured, elaborate ornaments . . . The 'red' [or icon] corner, thickly, completely covered with painted and printed pictures of the saints . . . I felt surrounded on all sides by the painting, into which I had thus penetrated.'[5] It was to be one of Kandinsky's greatest achievements that in his first full maturity he created individual works of art, single canvases, that function as environmental entities.

Whereas the abstractions of both Mondrian and Malevich involved not simply reductiveness but that quality of distillation which is one of the characteristics of so much great abstract art, Kandinsky, an equally great artist, achieved abstraction through the proliferation of imagery, through endowing his pictures with such a multiplicity of images that eventually one image cancels out another and the
54 canvas surface becomes a single, throbbing whole. *Motley Life*, painted in Paris in 1907, represents the climax of Kandinsky's early 'Russian' phase. He was unhappy in France and although Paris was to be of crucial importance to his development, this was also a period of intense nostalgia for the homeland of which he could be critical but where his heart still lay. The picture represents a pageant of Russian life from medieval times onwards: the costumes, for example, are of different periods. It is a work conceived of in terms of opposites. Youth meets old age, birth encounters death, battle finds its counterpart in play, and so on. It has also been suggested, convincingly, that *Motley Life* sums up the experience of Kandinsky's trip to the Vologda region, in that characters of pagan mythology are juxtaposed with
55 symbols of Orthodox Christianity.[6] *Composition X* is the last of Kandinsky's great series of canvases which he categorized as 'Compositions' and which he considered to be his most important achievements, his definitive statements. It was painted in 1939, once again in Paris, and although the two pictures are at first glance worlds apart, the affinities between them are startling. Both works provide the viewer's eye with more visual data than it can easily digest.

In 1896 Kandinsky moved to Munich to study painting. He felt the artistic climate in Russia was '*retardataire*', although subsequently in 1909 he was also to say that Munich understood little of painting.[7] He brought with him to Munich an awareness of the early manifestations of Russian Symbolism which stressed the apocalyptic and moral aspects of art and also a belief in its healing, redemptive properties. These beliefs were to remain central to his aesthetic. And the strain of mysticism in Russian Orthodox religion married more naturally to a Symbolist aesthetic than did more artificial attempts to graft esoteric and occult beliefs onto traditional religious beliefs and practice in Western Europe. In Germany, Kandinsky kept up with developments in the work of the second generation of literary Symbolists back in Russia – men like Bely, Blik and Ivanov – just as he later kept abreast of the pictorial Neo-Primitivism of Larionov and Goncharova and then subsequently of Russian Cubo-Futurism. He never really engaged with Cubism, however, and it was this that helped to keep his ties with the nineteenth century so alive. He also disliked iconoclasm and came to feel that the argumentativeness of later Russian Symbolists and the aggressive factionalism of the new modernists were inimical to his own great crusades and concern for the spiritual.

The Symbolist climate in Germany had affinities with that of Russia, but was more rigorously theoretical; this was not surprising in view of the fact that Russia was borrowing simultaneously from an amalgam of German Idealist and Romantic thought that the Germans took for granted as strands of their natural heritage. Like Symbolists elsewhere, the Germans were passionately interested in 'Synthetisme' – the interrelationships between the arts – and this was to be a prime

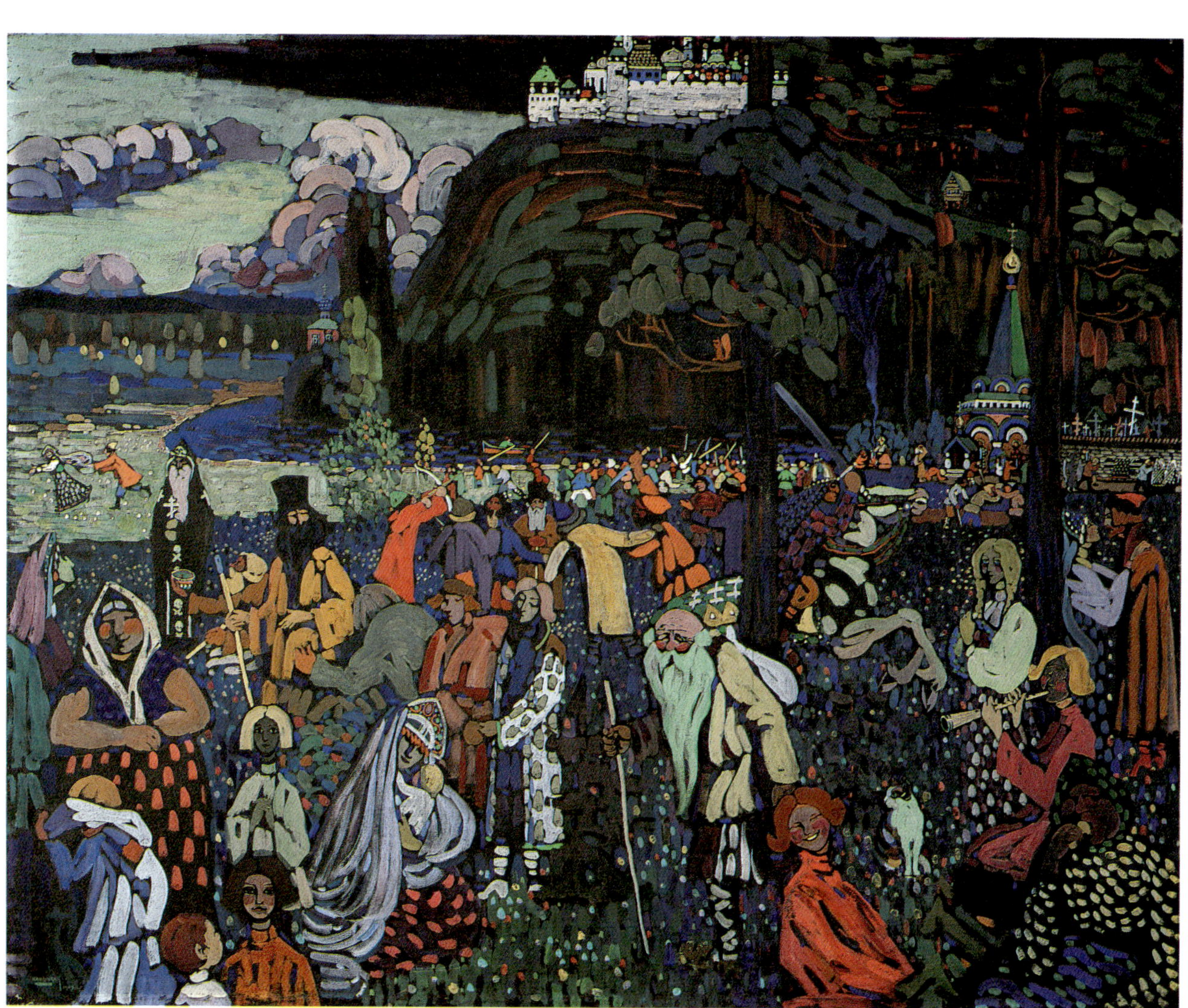

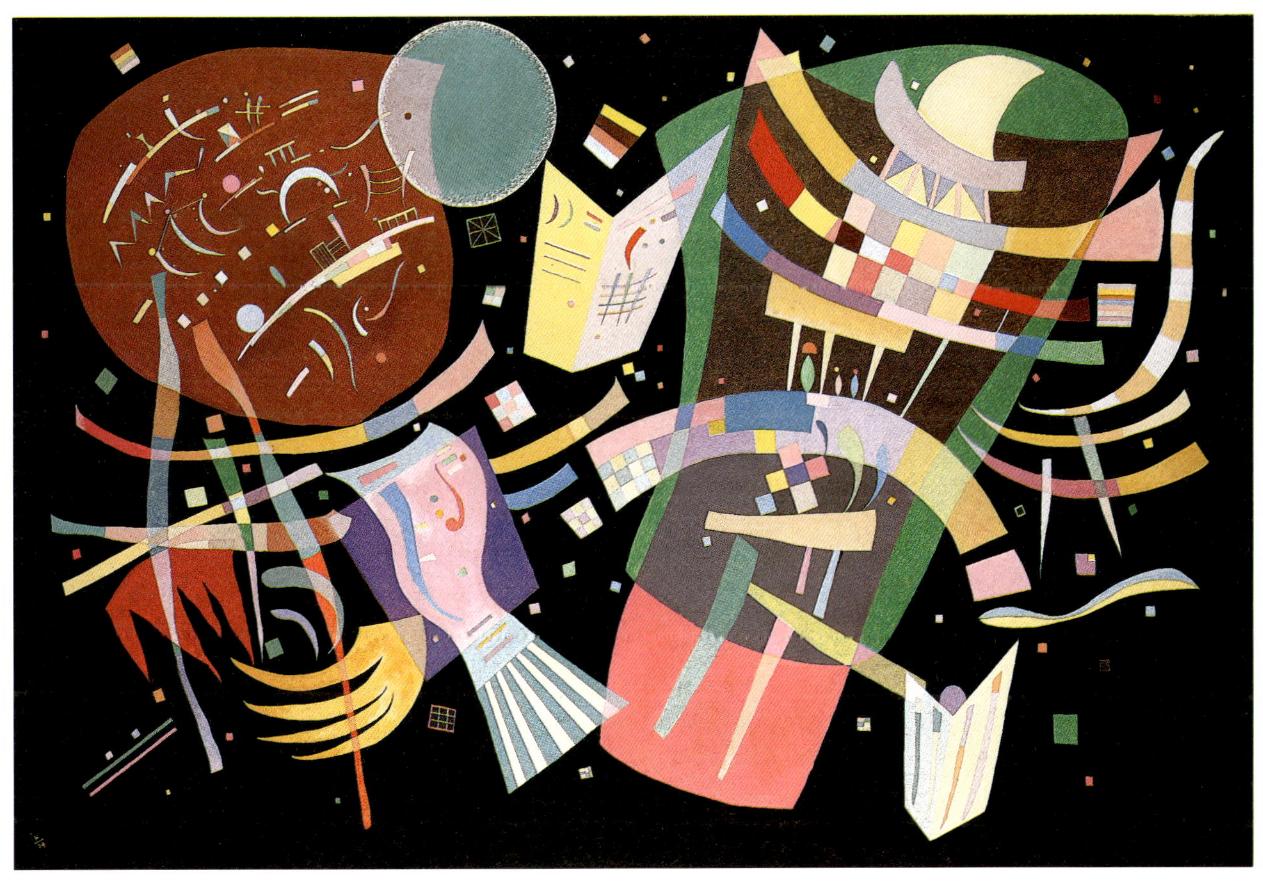

54 Kandinsky, *Motley Life*, tempera on canvas, 1907.

55 Kandinsky, *Composition X*, oil on canvas, 1939.

concern of Kandinsky's. However, the German Symbolists were simultaneously concerned with the other side of the coin, with what separated the arts from each other; and possibly it was in part at least because of this dichotomy that they failed to give truly great visual expression to their aesthetic ambitions. It was left to Kandinsky to do so. In the closing years of the nineteenth century Munich was also experiencing an extraordinary flowering in the applied or decorative arts, and men like Hermann Obrist and August Endell were advocating the use of abstract motifs long before Kandinsky entered the realm of abstraction. While stimulated by this climate, Kandinsky was also made deeply aware of the fact that the drift towards the decorative could damage his own profounder aspirations. When, after *Motley Life*, he abandoned his coloured drawings on black grounds, works which he rated more highly than his more naturalistic notations in oils, it was because they were being praised for their decorative properties. During 1906 and 1907 Kandinsky was also spending a considerable amount of time in France, at Sèvres outside Paris. There he was involved with the Symbolist journal *Les Tendances Nouvelles*, and this association further helped to widen his already broad Symbolist horizons.[8] But Symbolism in France was on the wane, and Kandinsky must have recognized that many of its most recent visual products were becoming etiolated. This he must have found disturbing.

Kandinsky had come to Paris to learn as a painter. He realized that French painting was in advance of developments elsewhere and he was stunned by the works of the Fauve painters, who had burst upon the Paris public at the Salon d'Automne in 1905, and above all by those of Matisse. He described Gauguin as 'more profound, more concentrated'[9] than Manet, whose works he in truth preferred. Cézanne came increasingly to be a father figure to him. But it was Matisse, he felt, who kept Cézanne's artistic legacy most alive. His unhappiness in France and the subsequent temporary mental breakdown he experienced were surely the result of the fact that Fauve painting opened up to him a new world of pictorial possibilities, while at the same time the aspect of Fauvism which most attracted him – its colouristic and formalistic 56 hedonism – was a reaction against and, to a large extent, a rejection of what had formed and what was continuing to form his own intellectual and spiritual landscape. He clung to Neo-Impressionism, one of Fauvism's sources, because he found its theoretical bias graspable and its concern with colour symbolism (rejected by the Fauves) sympathetic.

Soon after his return to Germany and during the convalescence from his breakdown Kandinsky said, 'Only music can save me now.'[10] There is a very real sense in which it did, but his time in Paris had transformed his visual sensibilities. The colouristic abstraction of Fauvism had alerted him to the fact that the apocalyptic vision he was coming to seek must be visionary not only in terms of its spiritual charge but also in its visual impact. It was in the Fauve-influenced landscapes produced between 1908 and 1910, and above all those executed at Murnau in Upper 57 Bavaria, that he became a true modernist. During this period his landscapes become notably larger in scale. Some of them contain figures, but in others one senses that the stage is being set, cleared and prepared for major dramas yet to come; it is valid to talk of Kandinsky's art in terms of theatre for he also wrote plays in which colours as well as actors were among the protagonists. He was a natural colourist but, like many great colourists, he matured as such only relatively late in his career.

In 1911 Kandinsky proclaimed that 'a general interest in abstraction is being reborn both in the superficial form of the movement towards the spiritual and in the forms of occultism, spiritualism, monism, the "new" Christianity, Theosophy and religion in its broadest sense.'[11] The term 'abstraction' is evidently being applied very broadly and not in a specifically painterly context; but the use of the word 'reborn' pulls one up short. Clearly Kandinsky was re-examining his sources. In 1909 he had attended a lecture given in Berlin by Rudolf Steiner, founder of the Anthroposophical movement and of the German Theosophical Society. Steiner's influence on German artistic and intellectual life, though short-lived, was to be incredibly potent. He was a genuine visionary and seer, and although his belief in spirit forms and astral auras awoke scepticism in some, he was, or could be, a more rigorous thinker than Madame Blavatsky, his original mentor. Steiner did at times write pedantically, but he was at the same time an apocalyptic thinker in a way that Blavatsky was not. His expositions of the Gospels, and in particular of *The Revelation of Saint John the Divine*, are galvanizing to read. He sought a very special fusion between certain Eastern occult forms of knowledge and the apocalyptic tradition in Christian Gnosticism; and the fact that Steiner saw Russia as a bridge between the two must have appealed to Kandinsky. Then again, Steiner was interested in colour symbolism (Blavatsky was not). Colour had fascinated Kandinsky since childhood; now it had become his supreme obsession.

From the start Kandinsky had given music supremacy over painting. In 1911 he wrote, 'After music painting may well be the second of the arts unthinkable without construction . . . thus painting will attain the higher levels of pure art upon which music has already stood for several centuries.'[12] Here Kandinsky was acknowledging a debt to one of his greatest mentors, Schopenhauer, who had himself stated, 'to become like music is the aim of art'.[13] Kandinsky was aware of Hegel's ideas and deeply interested in what Hegel had to say about the role of imitation in art, but for him Schopenhauer was ultimately to play the same pivotal background role that Hegel had provided for Mondrian and Malevich. The ghost of Schopenhauer and particularly of his *The World as Will and Representation* (1818) hovers over the pages of *On the Spiritual in Art*. Representation is equated by Schopenhauer with ideals, morals and reason, but he places Will, which is associated with emotions and strivings, above it. Kandinsky was also deeply immersed in Goethe, and Goethe's *Farbenlehre* was to have a deep effect on his own views of the metaphysical and associational properties of colour, though he rejected some of the colour symbolism of both Goethe and Steiner in favour of interpretations of his own: red, for example, he saw as spiritual, reflecting perhaps his memories of the 'red' or icon corners of provincial Russian dwellings.

In the years succeeding 1908 the musicalization of painting through colour became a driving force in Kandinsky's aesthetics. Again he was summing up and redefining basically nineteenth-century attitudes, in a sense tying the emancipation of Fauve colour backwards in time. Baudelaire himself had spoken of the musical properties of colour; and by the end of the nineteenth century the idea of music being supreme among the arts because of its abstract, non-imitative qualities had become widespread. Kandinsky's contacts with music were very direct, and he was a fine amateur musician. To take a single example: Scriabin's *Prometheus* (1910–11), which made use of a colour organ, had thrilled him and he praised Scriabin's search 'for equivalent tones in colour and music'.[14] Soon he came to find Scriabin's music not sufficiently rigorous and, for him, 'too beautiful'.[15] His own music of the spheres was to be of sterner stuff.

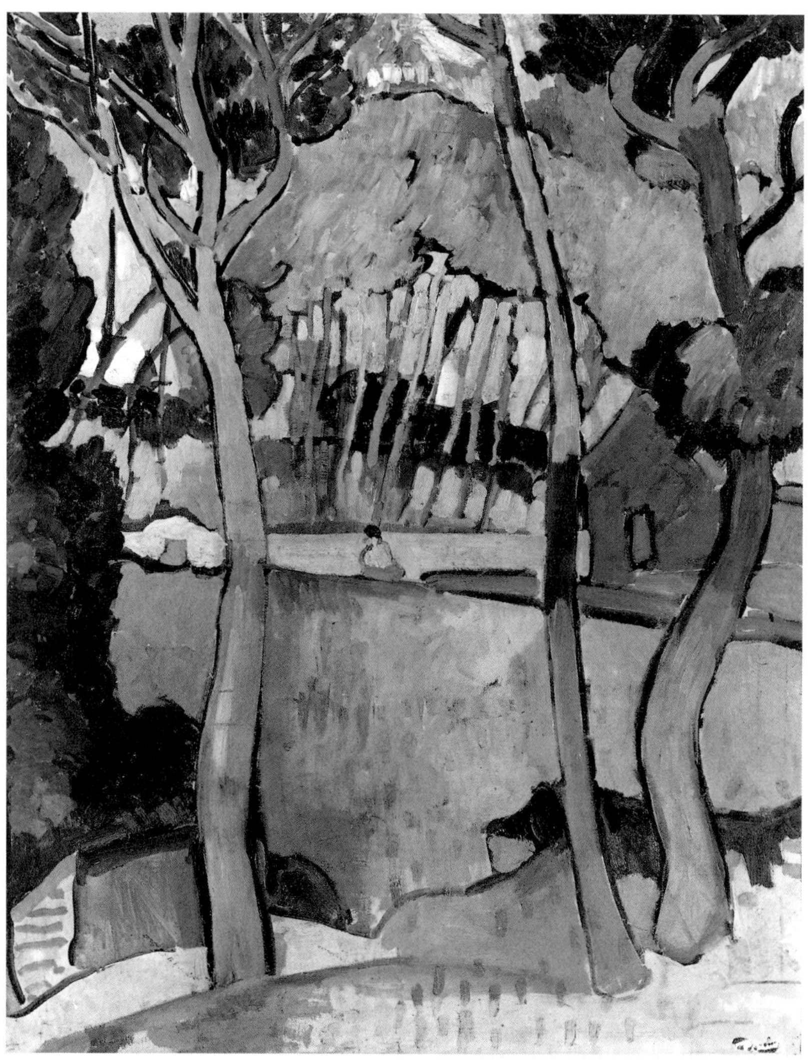

56 André Derain, *Trois Arbres, L'Estaque,* oil on canvas, 1906.

Although it was not until the publication of *On the Spiritual in Art* that Kandinsky elaborated on the three categories into which he was dividing his pictorial output, he was rehearsing them by 1909. His *Impressions* he described as direct
impressions of external nature, his *Improvisations* as 'impressions of an internal 58
nature, chiefly unconscious'[16] and spontaneously conceived. But his *Compositions* meant most to him, and for him the word 'composition' came to take on a talisman-like quality.[17] The *Compositions* were elaborated over a long period; as he notes, 'Here reason, the conscious, the deliberate, and purposeful play a preponderant role.' Then he adds an all-important caveat: 'Except that I always decide in favour of feeling rather than calculation';[18] and he insists that the *Compositions* are the result of 'inner necessity', a ubiquitous expression at that time. The *Compositions* convey 'the inseparable, indispensable, unavoidable combination of the internal and the external element, that is of content and form.'[19]

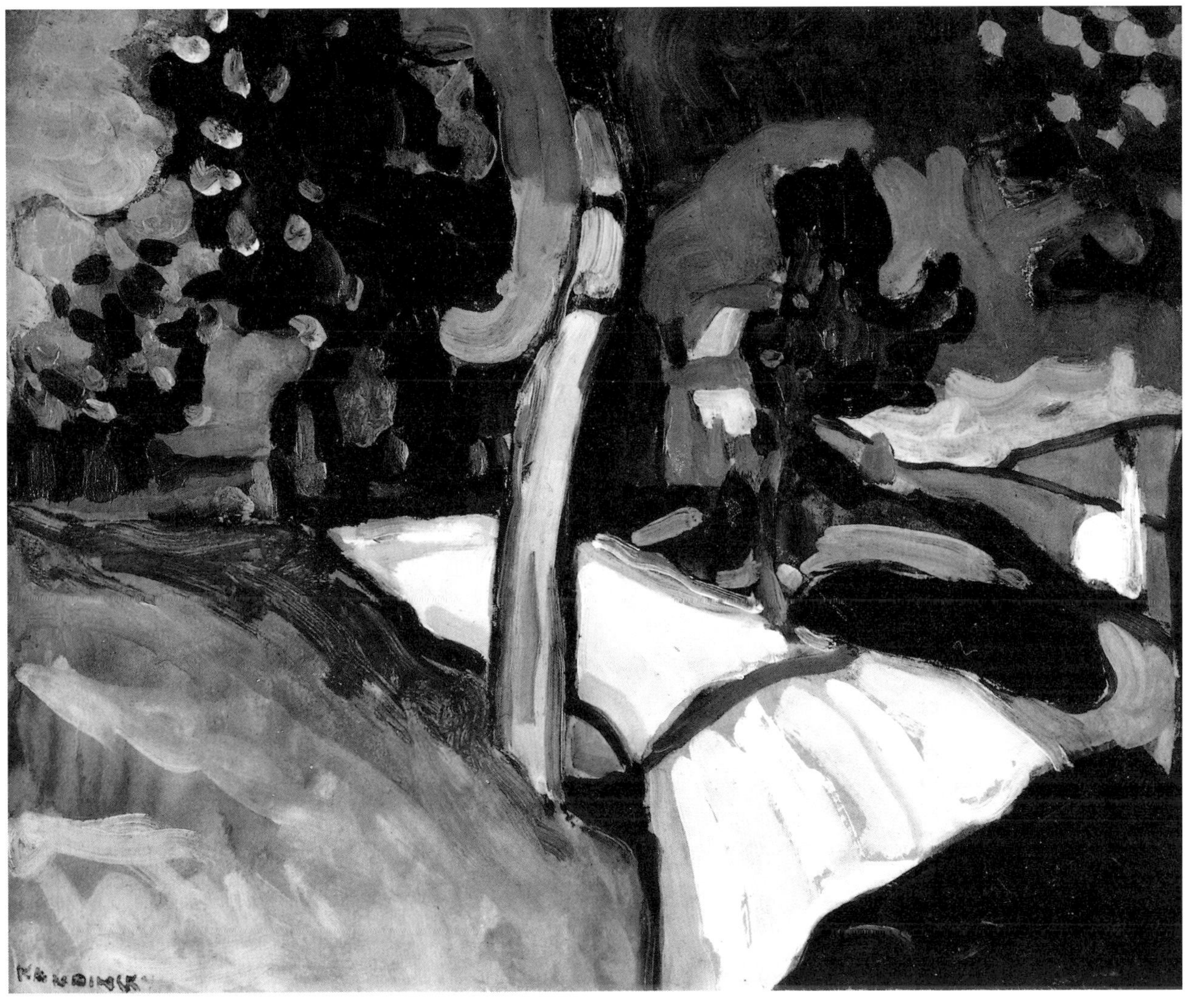

57 Kandinsky, *Murnau: Kohlbruberstrasse*, oil on cardboard, 1908.

Kandinsky's *Compositions*, and indeed *On the Spiritual in Art* itself, raise the whole question of how the artist wanted his paintings to be viewed. His consciousness of the role of the spectator is one of the factors that separates him sharply from Mondrian and Malevich; and this in itself underlines the romanticism of his vision. Mondrian saw the emergence of abstract art as a slow but inevitable process, and he believed that society would eventually accept it and so reap the rewards of living a better, purer life. Malevich certainly came to think in terms of revolution and of the reform of life, but the the headlong speed with which his art had moved left him with an indissoluble dilemma. On the one hand, painting had pointed the way forwards, but it had also had its day; on the other hand, could it be revived in a new guise to play a cardinal role in a reformed universe? He saw his potential public not as spectators of art at all but as travellers in a new, space age. Kandinsky, for all that he was a visionary and a utopian, saw the apocalypse as looming on the horizon, and once suggested 'maybe by the year 2000'.[20] In the years between 1909 and 1914 he was tortured by the question of how abstract abstract could be. Contrasts, even contradictions, were fundamental to his aesthetic. Yet a certain confusion now clouds the mind of this most intelligent of men. When reading his published statements of the time, it is sometimes difficult for us today to distinguish between what he felt his art should be aiming for, and, on the other hand, how it should be looked at.

There are, or were, ten *Compositions*, of which seven are still extant. Numbers I, II and III were destroyed, but the sketch in oils for the second, dating from 1910 (or very late in 1909), gives us a good idea of what that work might have looked like. Kandinsky felt it was a key work in his development. It is colouristically more sumptuous than anything he had yet produced; and although in *On the Spiritual in Art* he speaks at length of the component parts of painting, he also makes it clear that colour is the principal conveyor of the 'inner necessity'. He talks not just about the sounds but also about the scents that emanate from colour. He writes, 'Colour is the keyboard, the eye is the hammer. The soul is the piano with its many strings.'[21] The *Sketch for Composition II* shows how Matisse's *Le Bonheur de* 59, 60
vivre of 1905–6, which broke new territory in the history of colour, and which Kandinsky had seen in Paris, continued to haunt his visual memory.

A comparison between the two works is deeply revealing. If the colour in Matisse's masterpiece is both highly abstracted and vaporous, it remains adjectival in that it qualifies and reinforces subject-matter. In the sketch for *Composition II* colour is used in a more material fashion insofar as it is more thickly applied. Because of the painting's density and even greater divorce from nature or perceived reality, Kandinsky's blues, his reds, his yellows, are becoming nouns, objects, substances in their own right: blue is blue, red is red, yellow is yellow. In the painting by Matisse the subject is a vehicle for formalistic experiment. In the sketch by Kandinsky form and content, while they reinforce each other, co-exist; they go hand in hand, together yet apart. In the Matisse the compositional arrangement is traditional and echoes most closely seventeenth-century variants of Renaissance prototypes, although traditional perspectival devices are subverted, given tension, by distortions of scale. Kandinsky emphasized the importance that *Composition II* held for him when he said, 'In *Composition II* one can see the free use of colour without regard to perspective.'[22]

Kandinsky also insisted that if his intensified colours all appeared to hover on the same pictorial plane, their *inner*, psychological weights were very different, and that this spiritual depth or layering more than compensated for the abandonment of conventional perspectival effects. This implies space of a new kind. Kandinsky also said, '. . . the collaboration of different spheres entered into my pictures of its own accord. By this means I avoided flatness.'[23] The use of the phrase 'different spheres' suggests in turn that the new space will be a cosmic space. Kandinsky's contacts with French Symbolism must have made him aware of the emphasis that Gauguin and its younger practitioners were placing on the necessity of declaring the integrity of the picture plane. Like all good paintings, *Composition II* respects the picture plane; but the pocketing of space, both visually and psychologically, suggests, too, a space that can engulf us. To this extent the picture plane now carries with it implications of concavity: as our eyes penetrate into individual areas, compartments of visual activity, others swim out to the periphery or sides of our field of vision.

58 Kandinsky, *Improvisation 9*, oil on canvas, 1910.

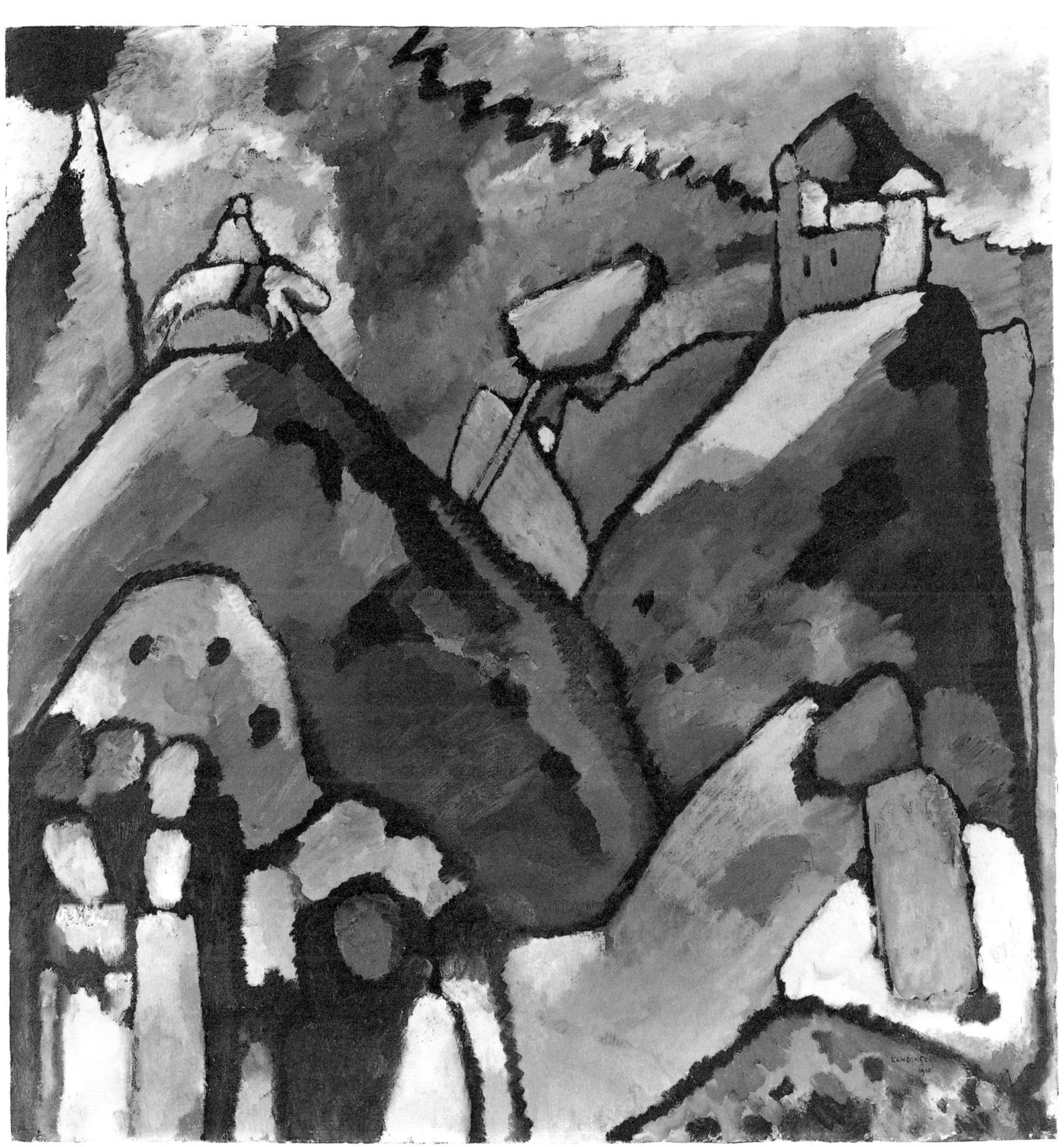

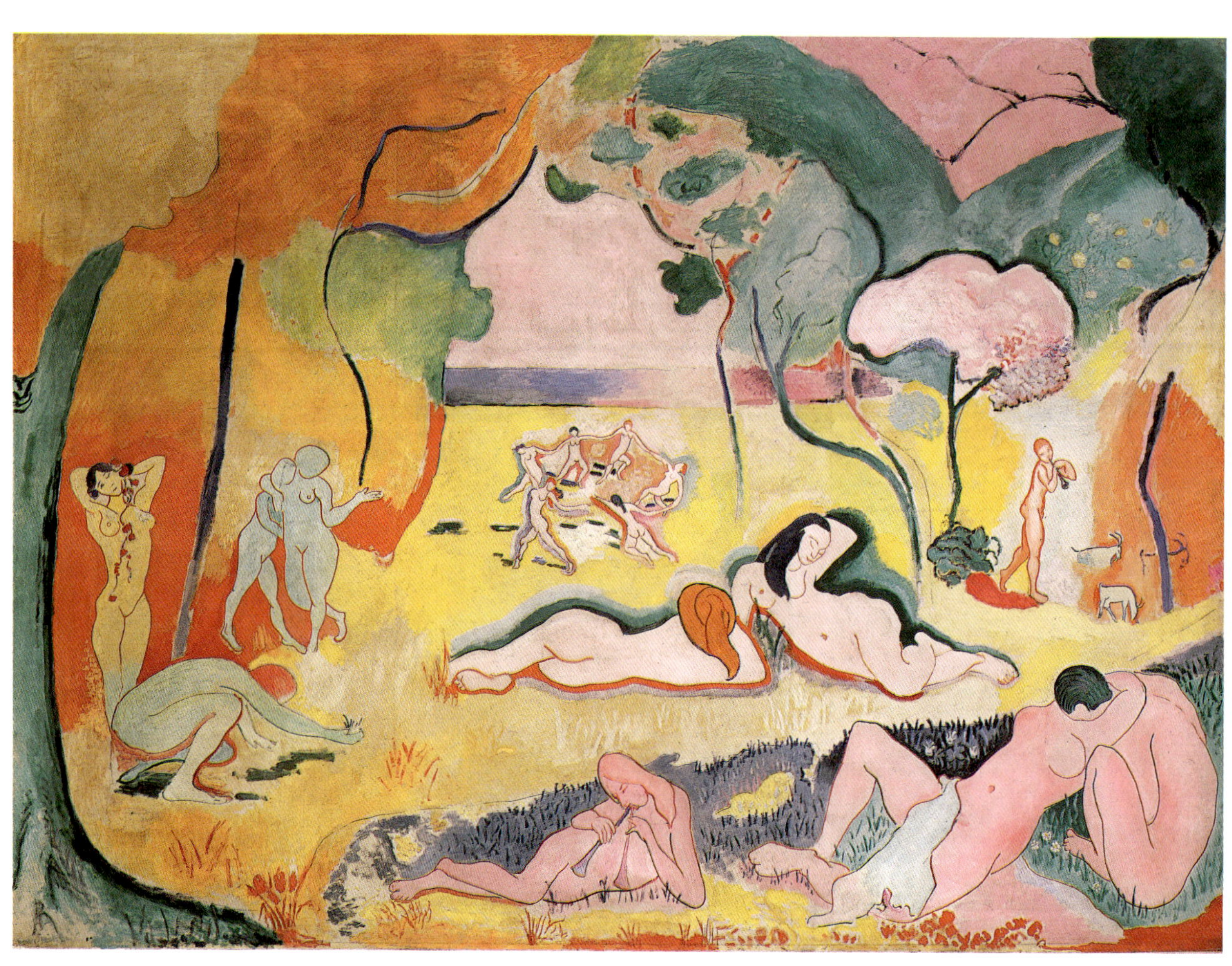

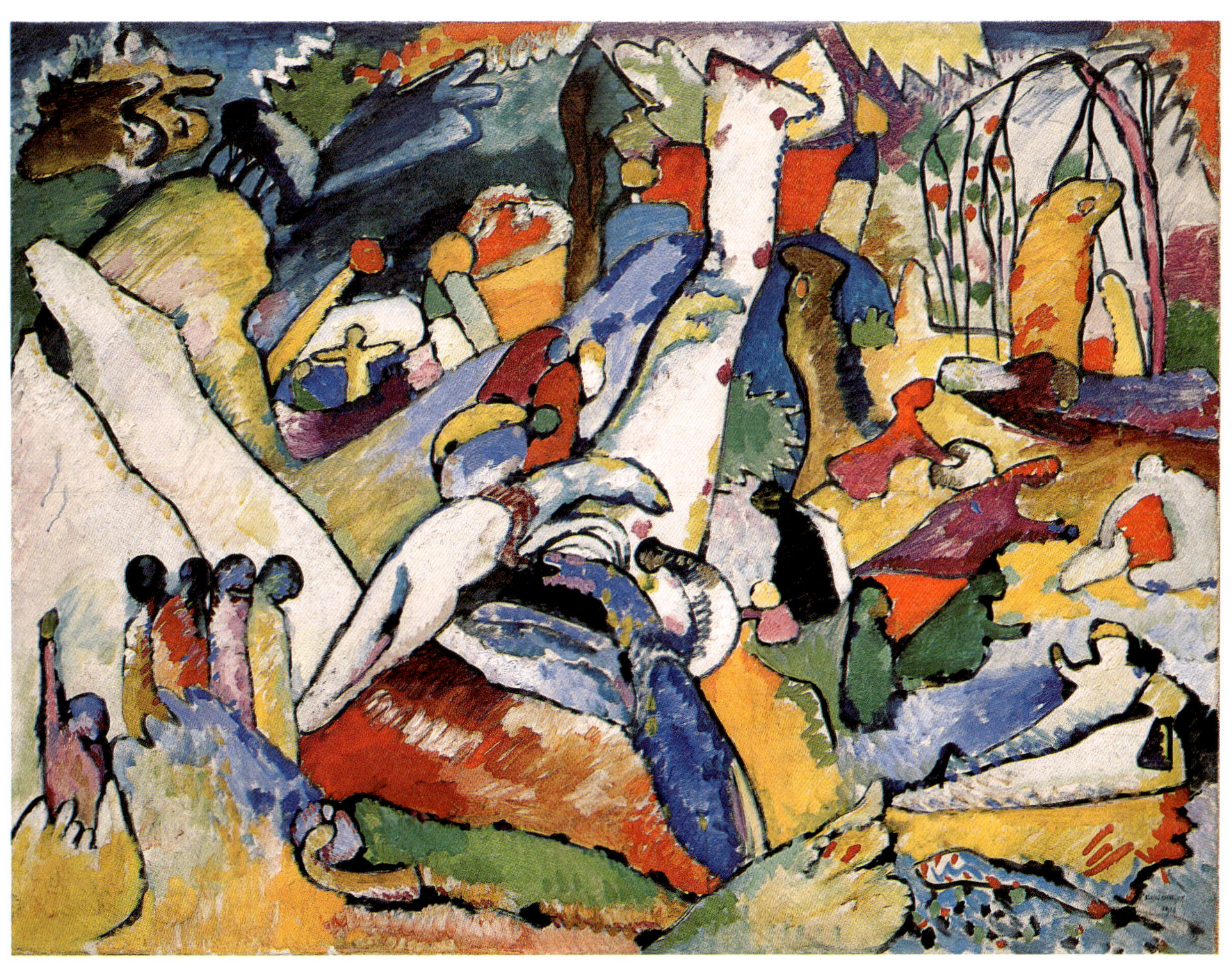

59 Henri Matisse,
Le Bonheur de vivre,
oil on canvas, 1905–6.

60 Kandinsky, *Sketch for Composition II,*
oil on canvas, 1909–10.

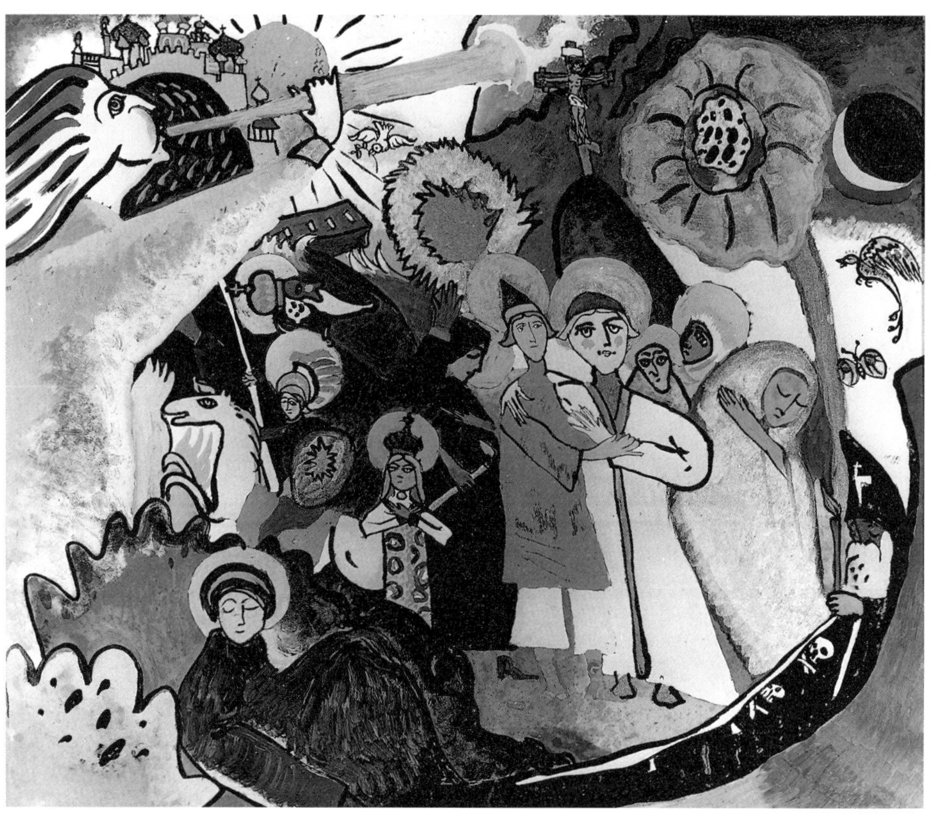

61 Kandinsky, *All Saints I*, painting on glass, 1911.

In *Composition II* the imagery is still relatively easy to read in terms of isolated elements: the leaping horseman at the fulcrum of the composition, the solemn group of figures to the bottom left, the reclining figures to the right, and so forth. But the fact that Kandinsky scholars have been able to place such totally different interpretations upon this and subsequent pre-war *Compositions* perhaps in itself confirms that, by using a plethora of disparate, often deliberately ambiguous iconographic sources, Kandinsky was now already working towards cancelling out or at least veiling his imagery. Given his fear that art of a non-referential nature might too easily slide into decoration, it is not surprising that, as he worked towards the abolition of recognizable images, he was also rejecting much of his earlier iconography – gone are the fairy-tales and romances of earlier times. Simultaneously he was widening his range by exploring a wealth of religious iconography, both Christian and pagan, in such a way that when we look at his paintings, even if we cannot 'read' them in terms of subject-matter, we are still aware of the fact that we are looking at works of profound cosmic significance, at works that are *about* something.

If it is in Kandinsky's *Compositions* that we can best chart the great trajectory that his art was following, we must not forget that these paintings were being informed by his more experimental works that were feeding them. Among these were his reverse paintings on glass, inspired by a folk tradition that was particularly prevalent in Bavaria around the Murnau region. The paintings on glass

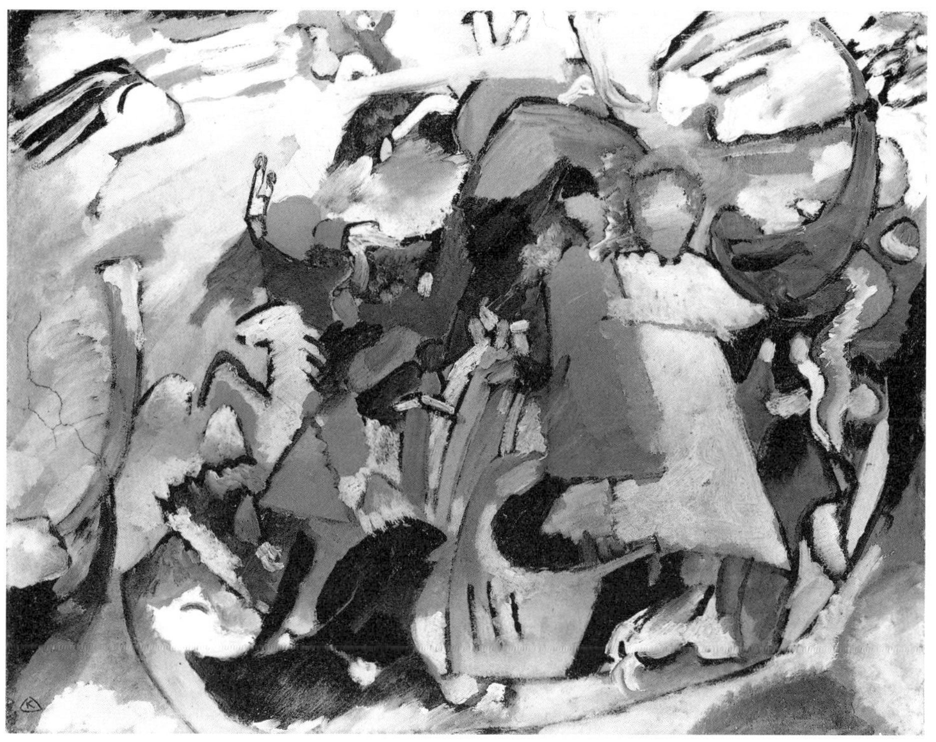

62 Kandinsky, *All Saints I*, oil on cardboard, 1911.

further sharpened his appreciation of folk art, but they also had an effect on his technique. In a sense the artist painting on glass is working blind from behind his support, since it is only when the glass support has been turned around that the
61 artist can see what has been achieved. In *All Saints I* of 1911 some of the line is surprisingly thin and crisp but at other moments it thickens and blurs slightly, the result of pressure being applied from behind rather than from in front. Similarly, when coloured pigment is being applied smoothly and flatly, it transposes onto the reverse side of the glass panel fairly predictably, but when applied thickly or in a broken technique, it looks smudgy when the glass support is reversed. Kandinsky had the extraordinary ability to conceive of finished canvases entirely in his mind and often to retain such mental images for years at a time. *Composition II* was the outcome of a vision he had had during a bout of typhoid fever at least five years earlier. But he was now also coming increasingly to welcome the element of chance, of the unexpected, in his work. The paintings on glass helped here; and Kandinsky came to insist that while he was at work, all the verbal, literary rationale underlying each individual painting evaporated or was transcended by pure feeling which took control of him so completely that many works dating from this period were executed by him while in an almost trance-like state. The influence of Kandinsky's glass painting on the mainstream of his production speaks for itself
62 when we compare *All Saints I* with its counterpart, painted in oil on cardboard and almost certainly later.

Composition IV of 1911 was regarded by Kandinsky as an advance over *Com-* 63
position II in that he felt it was 'more powerful . . . at the same time harder inwardly, clearer'.[24] Imagery is still reconstructible. At the centre of the composition stand three Cossacks, identified by their red headdresses, holding lances. To their right (the viewer's left), above a rainbow-like arch, are two leaping horsemen, jousting. To the right of the composition stand two groups of paired figures. The left-hand side of the painting in particular illustrates Kandinsky's attempts to endow line with the same degree of abstraction as he had found for colour. Despite the fact that Mondrian had found his way into abstraction largely through a notational use of line, it is much harder to abstract line than it is to abstract colour, because line, even when it has ceased to circumscribe and define objects, takes on a hieroglyphic, script-like character that demands to be 'read'. Line always carries or implies meaning in a way that colour patches do not. In this connection it has been suggested that Kandinsky sought the aid of the stick figures and markings of Lapp shamans' drums, which set out to create diagrams of the universe and its forces.[25] Wagner and his Valhalla has also been evoked in connection with this painting,[26] but in this context another composer, Arnold Schoenberg, seems even more relevant.

In January 1911, Kandinsky attended a concert at which he heard Schoenberg's *Second String Quartet* played as an accompaniment to words by Stefan George, a poet whose work meant much to the painter. The event is commemorated in
Impression III (Concert). The painter and the composer now began a correspon- 64
dence,[27] and their ensuing friendship was to become a cornerstone of Kandinsky's life and aesthetic. There is no doubt that Schoenberg propelled Kandinsky towards further abstraction at several different levels. Kandinsky acknowledges a debt when, in *On the Spiritual in Art*, he discusses Schoenberg's *Theory of Harmony*.[28] Schoenberg's rejection of melodic and thematic repetition in favour of an unbroken flow of sound in a musical continuum in which every phrase is equally developmental, and his insistence on dissonance, which was one of the characteristic features of atonal music as a whole – all these factors were to be fundamental to Kandinsky during the next years. They led not so much to a rejection of Wagner but to the conviction that even this musical giant's towering achievement might be superseded. Kandinsky came to feel that the attempt to find a pictorial equivalent to the lushness of Wagner's spellbinding thematic repetition and the embroidery of his motifs might reinforce a tendency towards the decorative which he so feared. Schoenberg's example, on the other hand, reinforced Kandinsky's apprehension of the possibility of a pictorial world in a constant state of strife and flux and change.

Composition V, again of 1911, was to become Kandinsky's most controversial 66
painting. It was rejected for exhibition in the NKV (The New Artists' Association) on the technical ground that it was too big. All Kandinsky's pre-war *Compositions* were large. The first measured approximately 4 ft x 4 ft 6 in. and thereafter they got steadily bigger. *Composition V* is mural-sized, over 6 ft x 9 ft, but one cannot help suspecting that the true issue at stake was its degree of abstraction. Kandinsky resigned from the association and countered by setting up the Blaue Reiter exhibiting society. Its first exhibition opened a few months after the NKV's, and the *Blaue Reiter Almanac* came out in May 1912, just after the second edition of *On the Spiritual in Art*. It cemented Kandinsky's position as leader of the Munich avant-garde. The scope of the Blaue Reiter group was international and its breadth of vision still astounds: nevertheless its members comprised a relatively small intellec-

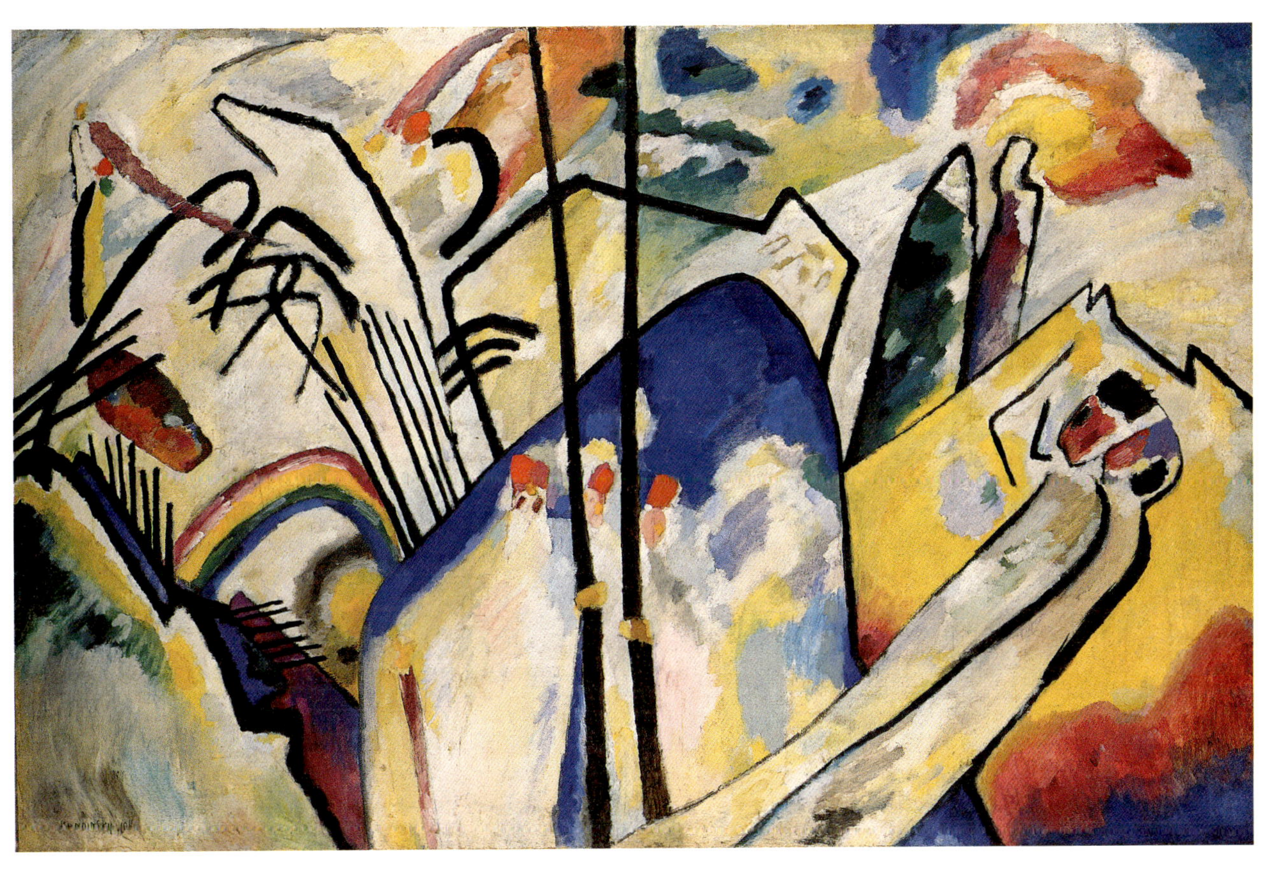

63 Kandinsky,
Composition IV,
oil on canvas, 1911.

tual élite. The *Almanac* raises another interesting point. It illustrates a vast wealth of apparently disparate images, ranging from contemporary German, Russian and French art to undatable votive pieces and other folk art, and back to medieval and pre-Columbian art. Oceanic and African and other tribal art bulk large.

Although so-called 'primitive' art had been of vital significance to many young artists of the twentieth-century avant-garde, in particular, in Germany, to Die Brücke (formed in 1905), it is significant that it had little to offer emergent European abstraction, and this despite the fact that both Mondrian and Malevich had reached abstraction through their immersion in Cubism, which had relied on tribal art as one of its two major sources of inspiration. Kandinsky spoke of the 'shattering impression' made upon him by 'African art',[29] but basically its formal implications touched him little. He predicted, wrongly, that the impact of tribal art on the twentieth-century avant-garde would be of short duration. He felt that his own propensity towards the 'concealed' saved him from the harmful side of folk art; certainly the direct statement was never for him. The wealth of illustrations in the *Almanac* can perhaps best be viewed as unified by a desire to search out the magical, healing properties in the art of all cultures and ages; of the *Almanac* Kandinsky wrote, 'we have hopes for so much that is healing in it'.[30]

Composition V was the most abstract in appearance of the series to date; and yet 66
in a lecture delivered in Cologne in 1914 Kandinsky referred specifically to biblical sources of inspiration: 'I calmly chose the Resurrection as the theme of *Composition V* and the Deluge for the sixth.'[31] And it is possible that the controversy that had surrounded the painting impelled him to affirm verbally that his art had content of cosmic implications. Yet the fact remains that the only two surviving sketches for the work are purely diagrammatic notations of compositional 65
arrangements and that scholars have had to turn to other related works to reveal the hidden iconography of the picture: the angels sounding trumpets, the citadel above the dominant trumpet form, the red-tipped, tube-like candles carried by the faithful, below them the dead rising, and the boat with oars to the lower left. In his Cologne lecture Kandinsky also stated that his ultimate goal was 'to create pure painting'.[32] Surely here he has virtually achieved that aim. The space has become turbulent, shifting and now truly and deeply pocketed, allowing him to create various centres of interest. It is the panoramic, encircling space that had been suggested to him in the 'red' or icon corners of houses in the Vologda region all those years ago, a space in which we can be present and lose ourselves completely. But how does Kandinsky want the spectator to respond to the picture's content? Because he was asking himself this question he forces it in upon us also. Despite their extraordinary beauty and presence, these *Compositions* remain, to some at least, problematic pictures. Kandinsky needed an ambitious theme to carry or provoke the supreme ambitions he held for his painting. He felt that the residual perfume of his abstracted images would engage the viewer, but ideally only at a subconscious level, and thus help each viewer to recognize in this painting not a particular subject, but the fact that he or she was being transported by it into a transcendental world, into a sphere of a higher spiritual order.

Much later, in the 1930s, when abstract art had become accepted, Kandinsky would insist again and again (he makes nine references to this) that it was he who had invented abstract art and that he had painted his first abstract canvas in 1911.[33] The work in question is almost certainly *Picture with a Circle*.[34] He tells 67
us that at the time he was dissatisfied with it, and perhaps this was because he

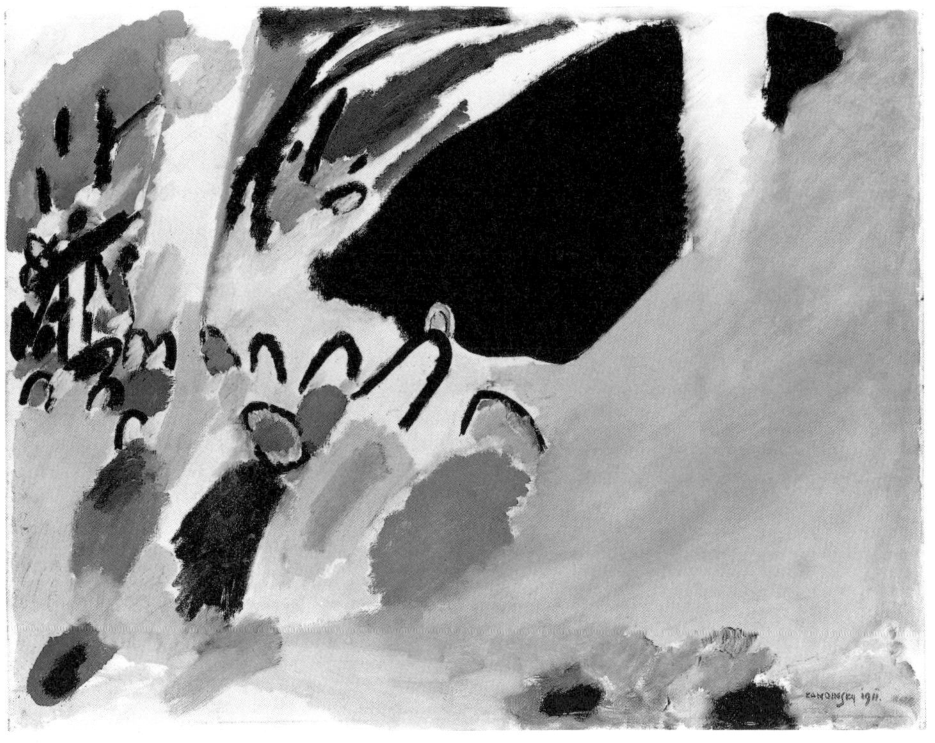

64 Kandinsky, *Impression III (Concert)*, oil on canvas, 1911.

thought he was moving too fast. Certainly the picture looks forward not only to Arshile Gorky but to Rothko, and hence to many aspects of American Abstract Expressionism of the 1940s. It is a perfect demonstration of the simultaneous divorce and alliance of line from what Kandinsky himself would have called his 'colouristic smudges'. The picture has a strongly subaqueous quality, and to my knowledge no Kandinsky scholar has been able to ascribe to it convincingly even a hidden or veiled iconography. Between 1912 and 1914 Kandinsky was producing paintings to which he gave titles referring only to colours and forms. Others like
68 *Small Pleasures* of 1913 make overt use of recognizable imagery. Clearly Kandinsky was consciously playing off different *kinds* of paintings one against another. This raises an interesting question. Might not the fact that we need the commentaries of a handful of Kandinsky specialists to tell us that not one of Kandinsky's canvases executed immediately before 1914 is in reality an abstraction at all mean that in effect that is precisely what some of them are, or were, in intent?

69 *Composition VI* of 1913, based on the theme of the Deluge (Genesis 7–8), is a work about which Kandinsky wrote extensively and lucidly,[35] and the studies and diagrams that lead up to it represent very graphically the dichotomy of his thought, of which he himself was aware. If Mondrian's self-knowledge is one of the things that makes the purity of his vision so moving, Kandinsky's self-awareness, his ability to analyze his every motive and his every move, are qualities that make him paradoxically possibly the most complex of all great twentieth-century artists. Some of the studies for *Composition VI* show easily recognizable images of figures and animals in lightning and rain proceeding towards the ark. Other more diagrammatic studies which contain written notations are purely abstract. Kandinsky

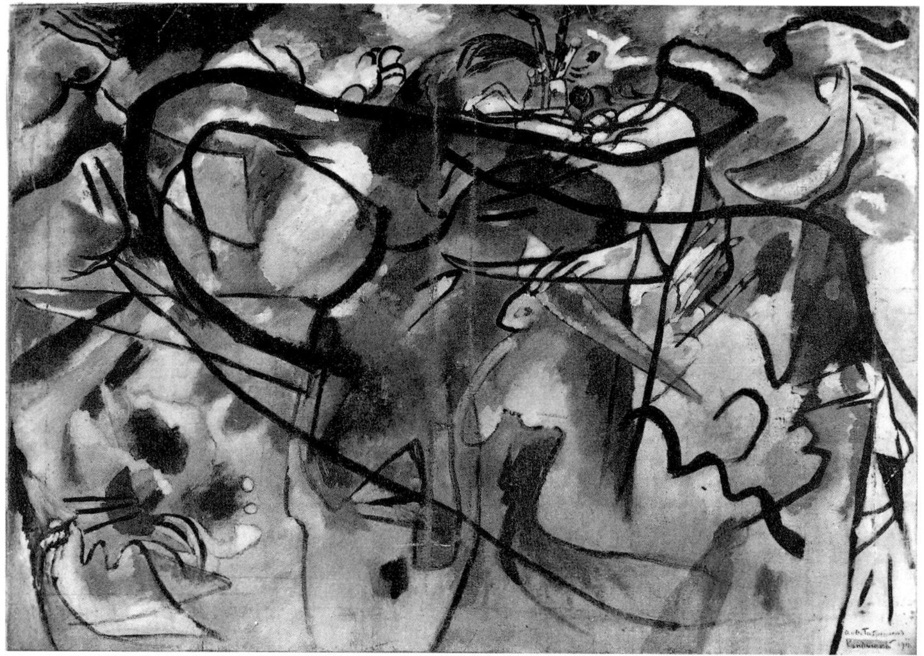

states that he carried a mental picture of the work around for a year and a half and that it had its starting-point in a glass painting, now lost. But when he came to execute the painting, he admits, he experienced enormous difficulties. This was because on the one hand, when he tried to clarify what he calls 'my image of the picture' – and it is revealing that he talks of the totality of the composition as his 'image' – by means of 'corporeal forms', the results were confusion. On the other hand, he notes that 'I sought to achieve the impression by purely abstract means. But it didn't work.' He goes on to say: 'This happened because I was still obedient to the expression of the Deluge, instead of heeding the expression of the word 'Deluge'. In other words, for his major works Kandinsky sometimes picks up a theme or themes, transposes them in his mind's eye into pictorial terms, and subsequently – when actually at work before his easel – seeks as it were to detonate his picture into the sort of life he wishes for it by finding a *resonance* of his original thematic starting-point. This process took place most effectively when he was working in a state of semi-trance; and this in turn often occurred most effectively in the final studies for the *Compositions*. In the concluding or definitive statements more conscious procedures reassert themselves with, at times, a renewed recognition of the original thematic starting-point.

The large study *Improvisation Deluge* has been analyzed extensively in terms of 70
hidden imagery, but is more abstract than the finished work (to take a single motif, the ark-like form at the lower left in the study is more easily identifiable as a boat in the final version). In his own analysis of the picture Kandinsky talks of the dramatic quality of the linear elements in the painting and how he used colour to mitigate them. He talks for example of making 'a whole fugue out of flecks of different shades of pink'. Once again he makes it clear that it is colour that abstracts,

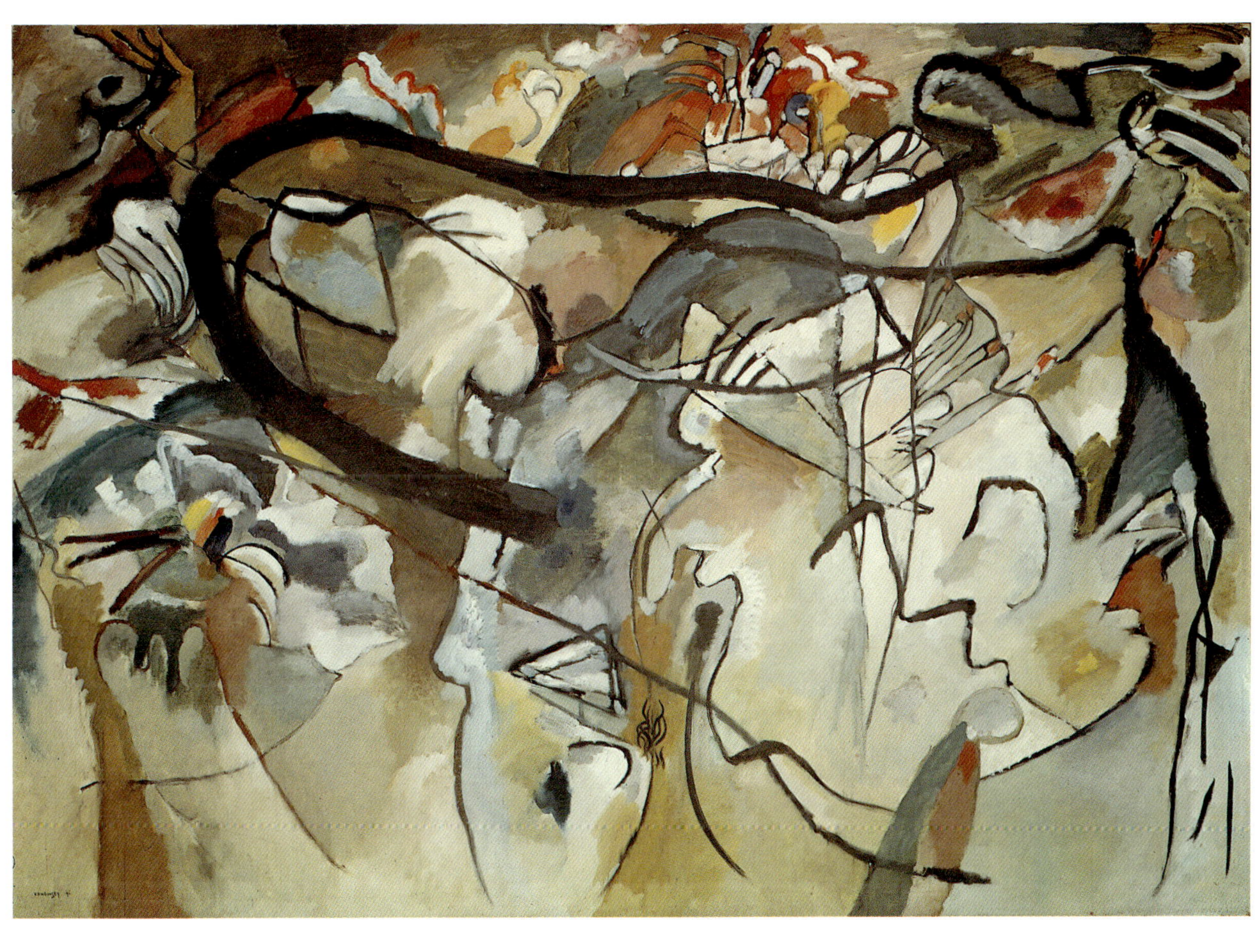

65 Kandinsky, *Sketch for Composition V*, oil on canvas, 1911.

66 Kandinsky, *Composition V*, oil on canvas, 1911.

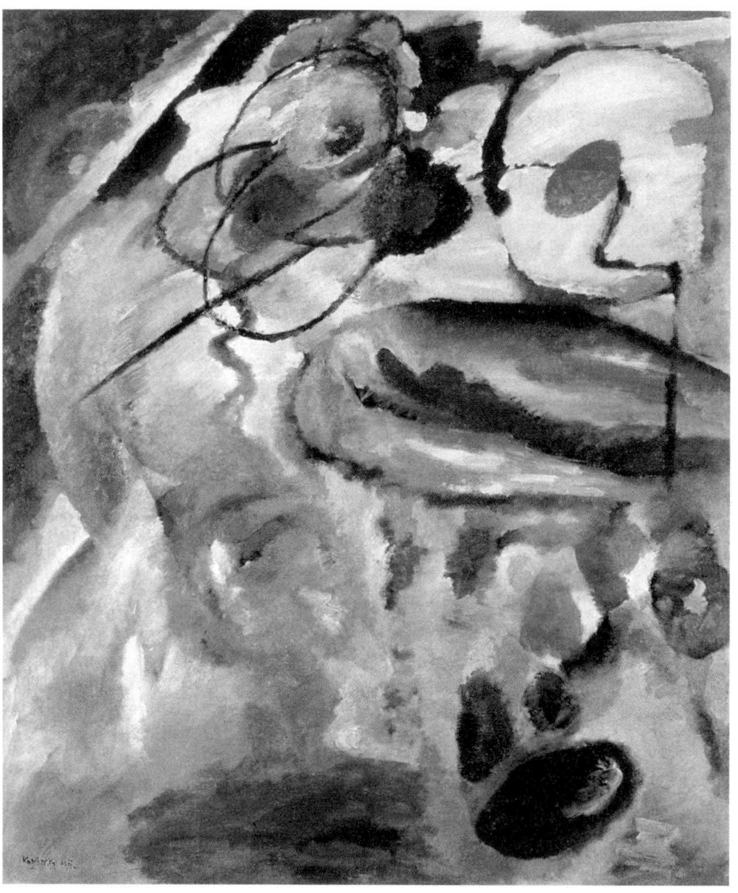

67 Kandinsky, *Picture with a Circle*, oil on canvas, 1911.

musicalizes and integrates the picture within the context of a sensation of cataclysm. A comparison between the late study and the finished picture is instructive at another level. Although both paintings are profoundly spatial, in the case of the study the viewer's eye is led restlessly in and out of depth: the space is at once impacted and claustrophobic. In the final pictorial symphony there is an increased contrast between light and dark, giving the eye of the beholder a greater chance to absorb the work's significance. Here Kandinsky has succeeded in achieving the cosmic, infinite space which he had been seeking; the dark forms that overwhelm the left two-thirds of the composition and the more open area on the right serve to relieve the brooding atmosphere while at the same time enhancing it. Yet the percussive, musical orchestration of both the colours and the lines also generates feelings of expectation. If the Deluge is indeed upon us, beyond it lies the promise of a new world.

Black, when orchestrated with bright colours, as opposed to being used as a neutral background, Kandinsky saw as being negative and despondent ('. . . Black has an inner sound of nothingness bereft of possibilities.'). White, on the other hand, haunted him just as it did all the early abstractionists. He saw it as being imbued with silence ('. . . white also affects our psyche like a great silence, which

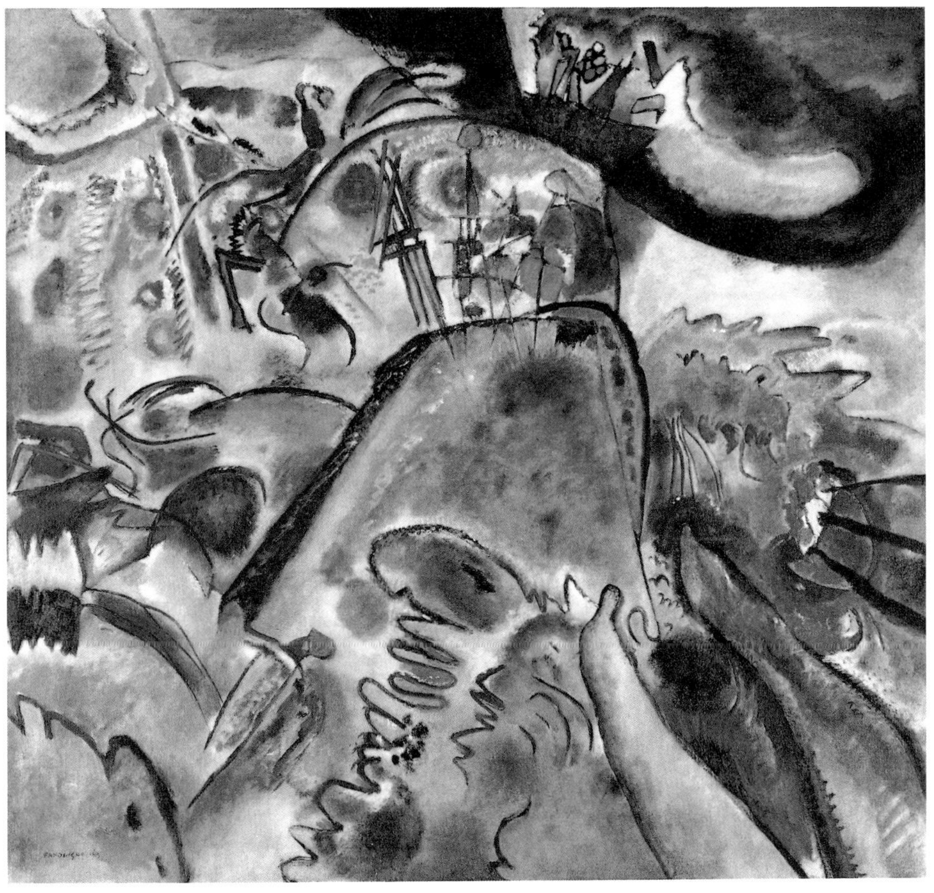

68 Kandinsky, *Small Pleasures*, oil on canvas, 1913.

for us is absolute')[36] and hence used it warily when he sought to imbue his paintings with the sound and clash of colours; he also saw it as being expectant, as did Malevich, and this once more helps to place his work in opposition to Mondrian's, for it was when the whites totally superseded the expectant greys in Mondrian's
71 palette that his art moved into a new phase. *Painting with a White Border*, again dating from 1913, was regarded by Kandinsky as an impression of Moscow, yet in his lengthy contemporary description of the picture[37] he talks of only one specific motif – the *troika* or three-horse sled seen at the top left. Apart from this, his analysis of the work is in purely formalistic terms. It is of significance that, when discussing a work that does not achieve the significance of one of his *Compositions*, Kandinsky does not feel he has to justify its existence by reference to some universally significant subject-matter. The blue forms to the centre right, allied to a white lance-like shape which is the fulcrum of the composition, may recall, irresistibly, earlier images of St George, yet these he refers to simply as 'broad brush-strokes'. The truth is that as he succeeded from time to time in divorcing himself from legible imagery, the literary sources upon which he had drawn to give his ever more abstract paintings substrata of meaning often forced themselves back irresistibly through his subconscious. In other words, there exists a continuous

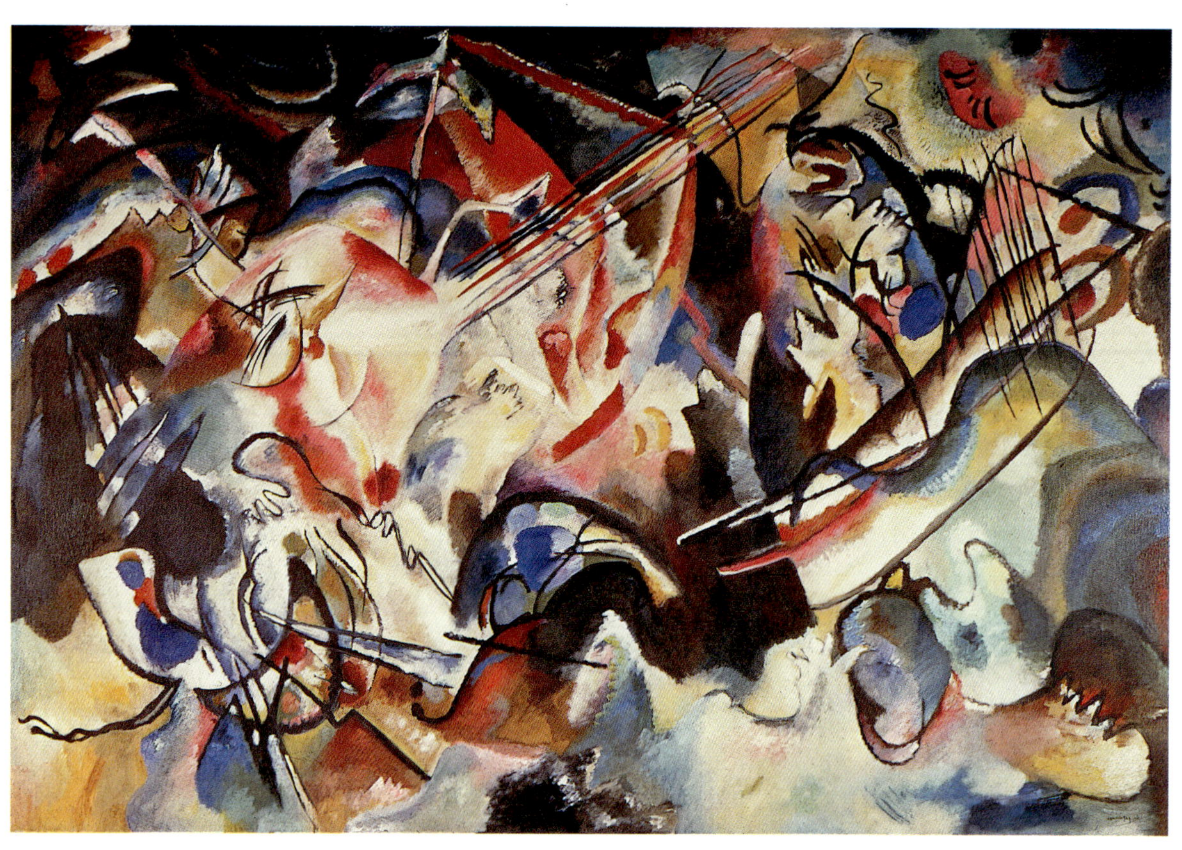

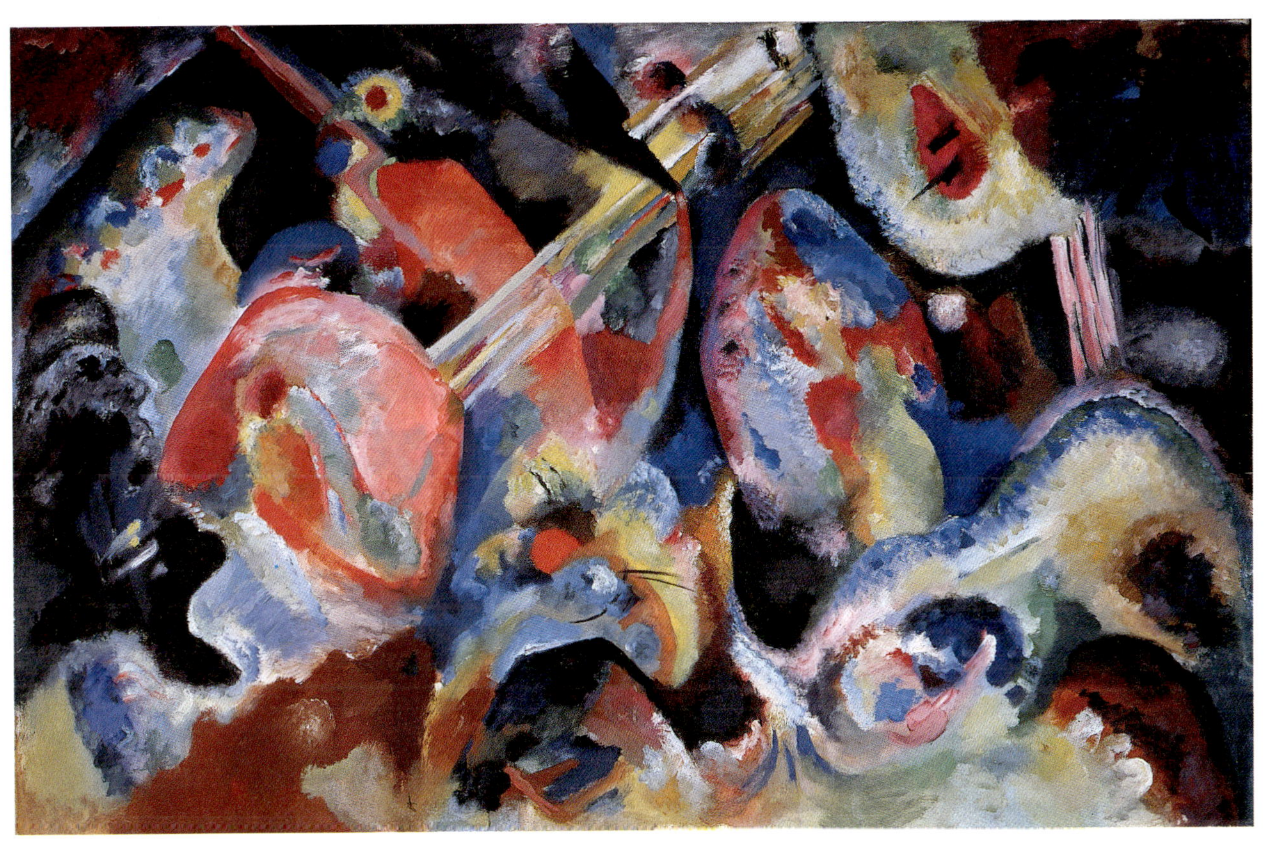

69 Kandinsky, *Composition VI*, oil on canvas, 1913.

70 Kandinsky, *Improvisation Deluge*, oil on canvas, 1913.

dialogue, a duality in these works between abstract forms, which he was increasingly courting, and the iconography that had originally invoked them. Years later, in 1937, but long before the flood of literature about his imagery had engulfed his work, Kandinsky had come to see that some viewers were able to recognize more in his pictures than he himself had intended. This impelled him to insist that 'the content of painting is painting'.[38]

Composition VII (1913), the last in the great pre-war series, was the largest of all 72 (measuring approximately 6 ft 6 in. x 10 ft). It was painted very quickly, possibly because it had been preceded by over thirty preparatory works in different media. It is possible to explore and speculate on the imagery contained in some of them, but most of the linear notations are now diagrammatic or fizzy; some are almost psychedelic in feeling, as are many of their coloured counterparts. The iconography of the great picture derives ultimately most strongly perhaps from the Last Judgment; but other motifs referring to the Deluge and the Garden of Love also intrude. Surely we are now faced by a work in which the plethora of motifs and iconographic references have in effect cancelled each other out. Kandinsky himself felt no need to comment upon or to elucidate verbally the meaning of this picture. Any attempt to 'read' the painting as a whole or to dissect its component parts too specifically or literally would be to distort its author's intent, and also to deprive ourselves of a transcendental visual experience. One of the strongest legacies of Kandinsky's Russian heritage was his belief in the apocalypse, and beyond it a vision of a truer, better and happier world. *Composition VII* is an apotheosis. It embodies strife and chaos, but transcends them and the message it conveys is one of optimistic radiance. It is the most truly enveloping of all Kandinsky's paintings and because of its scale the combination and subordination of pocketed space and detail to an overall pictorial surge are quite simply overwhelming. Its effect has become not so much panoramic as cycloramic. The picture envelops and enfolds the viewer.

In the second 1912 edition of *On the Spiritual in Art* Kandinsky had flatly declared that 'nothing is absolute'.[39] He had insisted on a need for content not derived from the external world, while also insisting that the time was not yet quite ripe for a purely abstract art: 'Today we are still firmly bound to the outward appearance of nature and must draw our forms from it.'[40] But in notes made in 1914 for proposed changes in a new edition of the book he deliberately omits this passage in order to promote the idea of a purely abstract art.[41] In the course of his Cologne lecture of this same year, when discussing his recent painting, he says, 'In general I already knew quite definitely that I would conquer absolute painting.'[42] Kandinsky's absolute is a Romantic concept and hence a fluctuating absolute and one involving a contradiction in terms. Despite the total originality of his vision and of the means he had by now found of giving them expression, Kandinsky's great pre-war *Compositions* remain tinged by a certain residual nineteenth-century aestheticism in a way that the first abstractions of Mondrian and Malevich were not.

Mondrian's capacity for self-renewal was one of his greatest gifts, but his development was internalized to a unique degree. There is a sense in which Malevich burnt himself out, temporarily at least, a few years after his move into total abstraction, when the *Black Square* had turned itself into *White Square on White*. Countless among his successors were to experience the dilemmas he subsequently faced. However, Kandinsky's abstraction is also unique in that, during the remain-

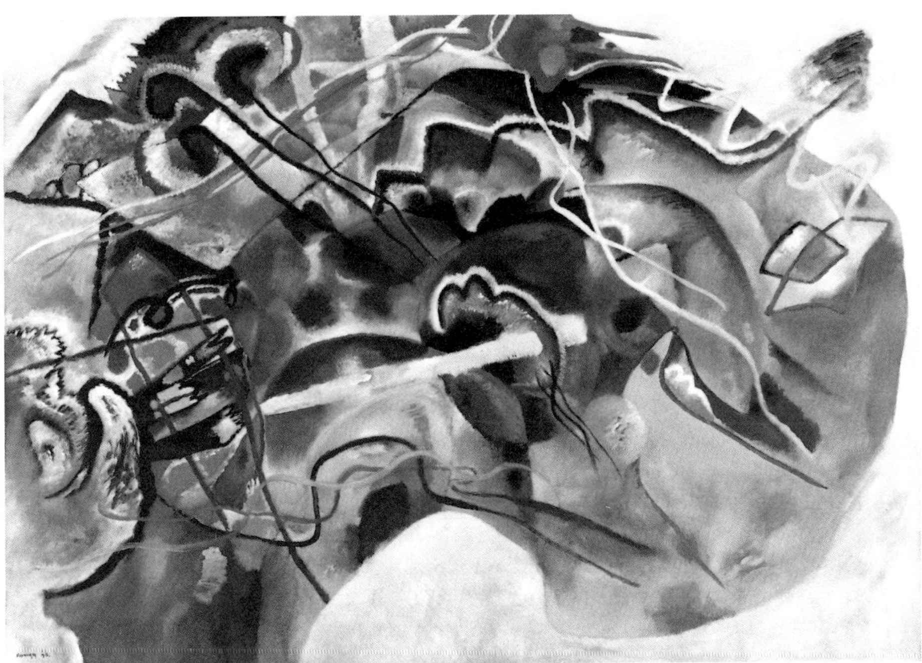

71 Kandinsky, *Painting with a White Border*, oil on canvas, 1913.

ing thirty years of his career, he found an astonishing way of allowing it to change direction, or of successfully adapting his art, his abstraction, to changing intellectual and artistic situations, even though the last one he experienced – Surrealism – was basically hostile to abstraction as an idiom.

In 1914, after the outbreak of war, Kandinsky returned to Moscow. Although he was not especially interested in politics, he did believe in social change, and certainly in the creation of a better and fairer society; but it was inevitable that he would eventually get caught up in the climate of revolutionary fervour. Yet (and this says much about a man who was by now in his fifties) the seven years he spent in Russia are in a sense a transitional period within his art. His production declined and some of the work of these years is not altogether felicitous. But he was looking and learning. Although he cannot have totally identified with Malevich's thought-processes, he did learn from him and even more from Rodchenko, who in certain respects, and as a Constructivist, viewed himself as Malevich's rival. At the same time Kandinsky recognized, right from the start, and more clear-headedly than most, that Constructivism was in certain respects touched by and allied to the Positivist and Materialistic tendencies against which all three of the great heroes of early abstraction had been in revolt. Through his experience of Russian revolutionary art Kandinsky absorbed, at many removes, some of the legacy of Cubism. He had been aware of Cubism's significance ever since his first encounters with it, but basically he was unsympathetic to it, and this attitude was one of the factors that distinguished his aesthetic from that of Malevich and Mondrian. His pre-1914 work had deliberately ignored Cubism, and his verbal disassociation from it was to be a leitmotif of his writings, right to the end of his days. This helps to account for his ambivalent feelings towards the art of the nineteenth century and subsequently

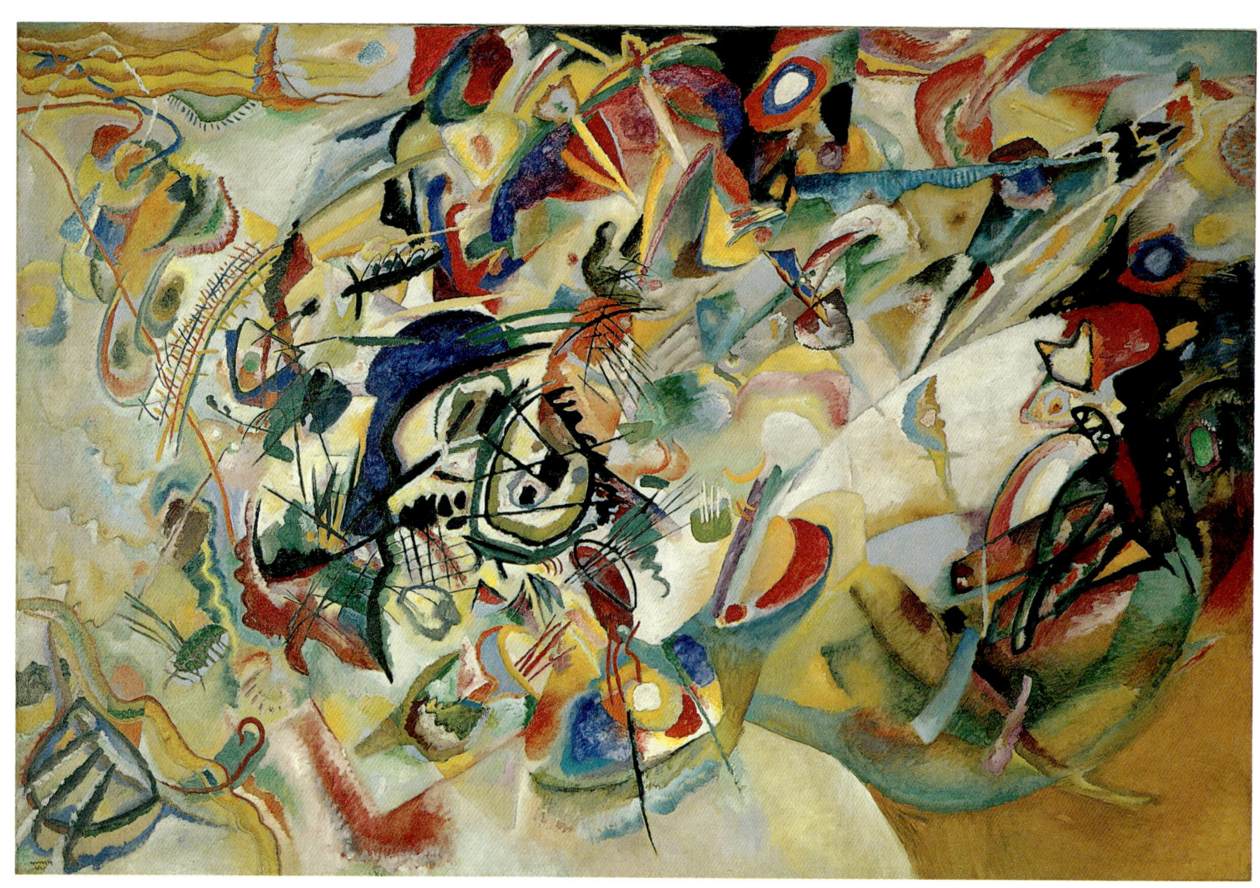

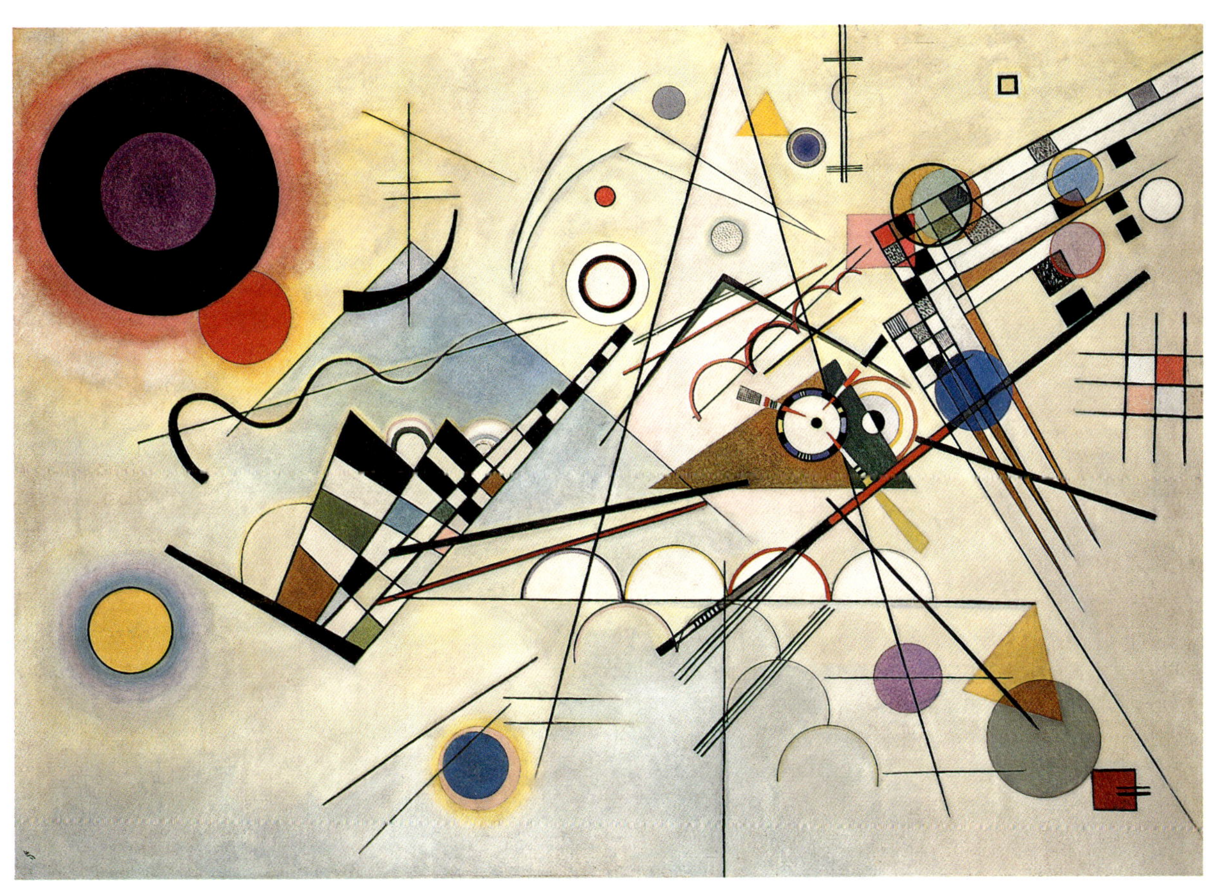

72 Kandinsky,
Composition VII,
oil on canvas, 1913.

73 Kandinsky,
Composition VIII,
oil on canvas, 1923.

towards the very twentieth-century modernism which he himself had done so much to foster.

Late in 1921 Kandinsky returned to Germany, having accepted appointment to a professorship at the newly founded Bauhaus. In 1925 he moved with the school from Weimar to Dessau and then briefly to Berlin before the institute was closed down completely in 1933. Russian influence within the Bauhaus was significant and Kandinsky was one of the moving spirits in the construction of what was known as 'the international house of art' and also as 'The Great Utopia'.[43] The Russian sojourn had altered his own art dramatically. It had converted him to geometry and the use of geometrical forms, which he had originally condemned. This in turn fostered the intellectually analytical and scientific side of his nature. The Bauhaus also released and capitalized on the pedagogical side of his make-up which found is fullest expression in his second-most famous book, *Point and Line to Plane*, published in 1926. This shows his debt to perceptual psychology of both the nineteenth and the twentieth centuries and a new interest in science and technology – subjects which had always interested him but which because of his Symbolist background and formation he had previously felt he had to distrust. On the other hand, he threw away nothing of his artistic heritage and continued to preach the doctrine of 'inner necessity' and intuition, and thus felt that the 'Great Synthesis' which he had always longed for had at last been achieved. In 1922 he was able to declare that: 'the irreconcilable is reconciled and . . . the epoch of the Great Spiritual has begun'.[44] There is a sense in which he had reached a second absolute.

What this represented in terms of his art is best exemplified by *Composition* 73
VIII, of 1923, which he recognized to be one of the highpoints of his achievement. In it the experience of revolutionary Russian art has been fully digested and assimilated and married to the richness and complexity of his pre-war Munich triumphs. The clarity of the geometry speaks for itself, as does the dynamic use of contrasts and pictorial counterpoint, which are now used more self-consciously but also more skilfully than ever before. Kandinsky had now fallen in love with the circle as a motif which, he admitted, had replaced the horse as a symbolic touchstone in his art.[45] He felt the circle had cosmic implications and his interest in astronomy has been confirmed by recent scholarship.[46] He also felt that pictorially the circle was 'a precise but inexhaustible variable' and 'the synthesis of the greatest oppositions'.[47] Those who are so minded can still detect in *Composition VIII* a boat, a lance-bearing horseman, and what they will; and by allowing for such interpretations Kandinsky is yet again, although probably unconsciously, presenting us with his Symbolist credentials. But to seek such interpretations is to deprive oneself of experiencing to the full the way in which a two-dimensional surface can suggest infinite space, which is a space of the spirit as much as that of the eye. The space of Kandinsky's pre-1914 *Compositions* had been treated in a truly original fashion and was cosmic in its implications, although it could also be argued that in another sense it was still an extension of the space of much traditional Mannerist and Baroque art, put to new ends. In Russia he had learned how a flat white surface can be made to read as, or at least to symbolize infinite space, and yet be a space that advances towards the viewer from the picture plane. With the experience of his last great pre-war *Compositions* behind him, he was able to make that space more palpable, more perceptible to the eye than the space of Malevich and his followers, which was more conceptual in its appeal.

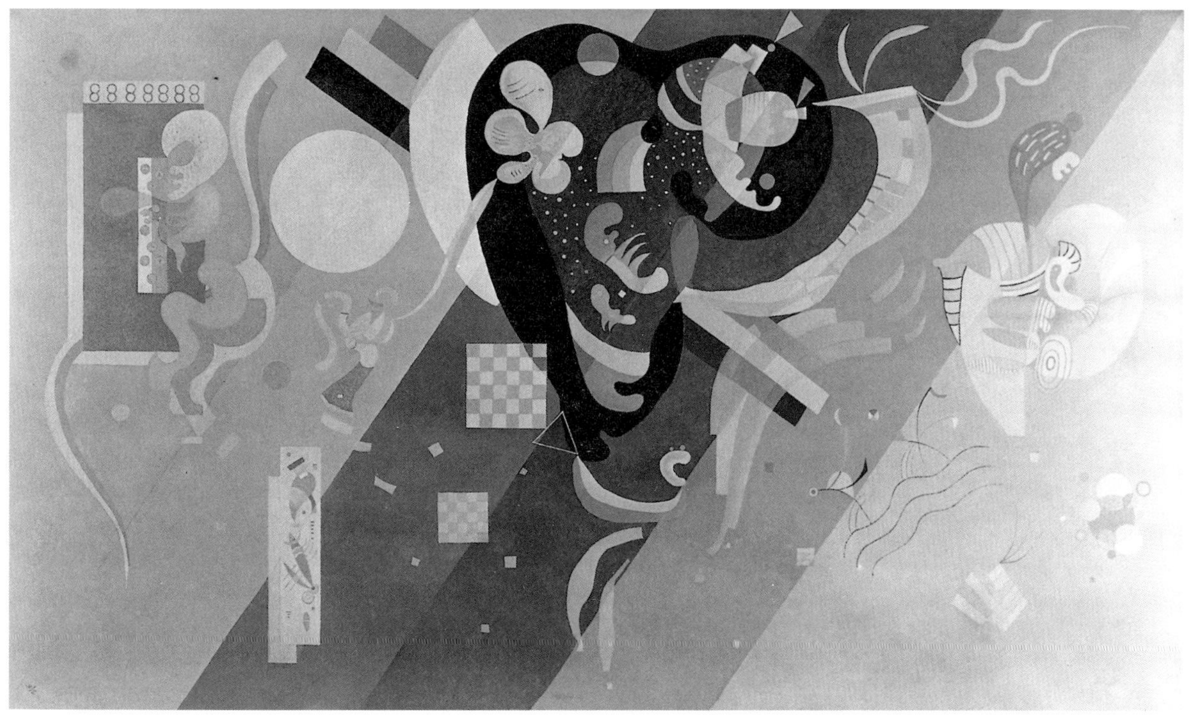

74 Kandinsky, *Composition IX*, oil on canvas, 1936.

Kandinsky had originally sensed the potential of a purely abstract art through his belief in the 'musicalization' of painting, although he had insisted from the start that he had no desire to paint musical pictures. He had soon come to feel that the achievements of painting could surpass those of music, in part because the visual arts largely dispensed with the temporal element built into the process of listening to sequential sounds or melodies. In doing so he was bringing to fruition a long line of enquiry going back more than a century. He continued to believe that colours and now forms and lines could evoke sounds. The circle, however, he saw as a silent shape. One of the most profound changes in his art after 1914 lay in the fact that, although he remained a supreme colourist, he no longer accorded colour pictorial supremacy. In the 1920s he was acknowledging the importance of silence in art, and this accounts perhaps for the quality of distillation that now creeps into his art for the first time. He declared that viewers must appreciate his own growing ability to hear a sound in the midst of silence. He goes further when he says: 'It happens that at times silence speaks louder than noise, that muteness acquires a sharp eloquence.'[48] And a little later on: 'My "secret" is purely and simply that I have over the years acquired . . . the happy ability to rid myself (and therefore my painting) of "background noise".'[49] In 1938, when looking back over his career, he said, 'In 1914 . . . a "great calm" began to hover before me. Nowadays this calm "Yes" holds its own even in the most complicated pictures.'[50] Well, yes and no.

In 1933, with the final closure of the Bauhaus and the worsening situation in the German art world under the Nazis, Kandinsky moved for a final time to Paris. The 1930s were by and large a difficult time aesthetically – in many ways this was from a visual point of view the most restless decade of the first half of the century, and as

a result possibly not a propitious time for abstract art. Kandinsky's own final, Paris decade (he died in 1944), poses certain visual problems which have yet to be critically overcome. As it had done early in the century, France forced in upon him an awareness of his Russianness and he now found himself both an international and also a stateless artist. In one of his last and most revealing statements, made in 1937, he said, 'Thus, next to the "real" world, art puts a new world that in its externals has nothing to do with reality. Internally, however, it is subject to the general laws of the "cosmic world". Thus a new "world of art" is placed next to the "world of nature" . . . a world that is just as real.'[51] There is a sense in which 74
his art reflects the restlessness of the times. Synthesis had always been his goal and he now achieved it in a new way, but one that exposed clearly the contradictions which had always been inherent and indeed central to both his character and his art. Line and colour now find an exact equivalence in his painting. Large, bold, compositional effects and structural devices are played off against an obsessive concern with detail. Kandinsky had never turned his back completely on nature as Mondrian had done, and he now came to feel that works of art are produced 'by following the laws of nature that govern the universe as a whole'.[52] He came from a Romantic and Symbolist tradition and yet he was now putting nature under the microscope in a quasi-scientific, almost clinical, way to discover its secrets. Already at the Bauhaus he was consulting biological dictionaries, and during his final Paris years he was investigating images from books and articles on natural history, zoology, and embryology. The images he was looking at – including extinct animals, amoebas, embryos, marine invertebrates, larvae and so forth (the list is endless) – account for the astonishing wealth and variety of smaller shapes in these pictures. The surgical precision of the rendering of shapes, images, is offset, but also sometimes vitiated by the use of increasingly sweet and decorative colour. These canvases baffle and tease the eye because of their superabundance. One is reminded of the fact that it was a superabundance of imagery that had helped Kandinsky to achieve his initial move into abstraction.

Ultimately Kandinsky remains not only one of the founder figures of twentieth-century modernism but also one of its great enigmas. In his writings he invites one into his mind only to shut one out again subsequently. In his pre-1914 paintings he had invented new concepts of space and had urged us to surrender ourselves to them. Subsequently his art had become steadily more remote; our gaze can engage with these pictures, but they are also 'out there', outside us. Although his eyes were directed towards the next millennium, Kandinsky's roots remained planted in the nineteenth-century. Because of this heritage it is in a sense ironic that Kandinsky was ultimately to be the most significant of the early European abstractionists in the context of the emergence of the second great wave of revolutionary abstraction that was to become one of America's greatest legacies to cultural history.

4
Pollock and the search for a symbol

Although the great pioneering European abstractionists reached such very different conclusions in their search for a visual reality that lay behind and beyond the world of tangible perception, and despite the fact that Malevich and Kandinsky were experiencing such a wide range of intellectual influences, the most immediate and compelling sources for the modernity of their vision were to a large extent shared and, viewed in retrospect, have about them an air of historical inevitability. The achievement of the great American abstractionists of the 1940s was more monolithic in that their visual achievements have more in common with each other than with those of their European forebears. This is not surprising since the American artists belonged to a single nation and thus shared a culturally more homogeneous background than did Mondrian, Malevich and Kandinsky, whose ideas were formed by the individual cultures of five European states: Holland, Russia, France, Germany and Italy. Nevertheless, the Americans were ultimately drawing on even wider and more divergent systems of ethnic and cultural sources, and this was in part at least because they were all touched in different ways by their experience of Surrealism, which had deliberately cast its cultural net so dizzyingly wide. The modernity of Surrealism was, so to speak, programmatically unlinear. In no case is the legacy of Surrealism clearer than in that of Jackson Pollock, whose career, in contradistinction to that of his colleagues in American art, was so meteoric. In this respect there are parallels with Malevich's headlong dive into the rapids of modernism; but Pollock's modernism was to be of a more complex and tangled nature.

Pollock grew up in Wyoming, and his family history and early upbringing are the stuff of the myth of the American West. Though patchily educated and rebellious, he found his vocation early on. Through some of his teachers he acquired an interest in Theosophy and other esoteric thought which, unbeknown to him then, had helped to form European abstraction. His first direct encounter with great art came in 1930, when, before moving east and to New York, he made a special trip to Cal-
75 ifornia to see José Clemente Orozco's freshly completed fresco *Prometheus* at Pomona College in Claremont. At a remove this work put him in touch with Italian Renaissance and Italian and Spanish Mannerist art, sources which at a submerged level were still informing his first great abstractions of the 1940s. These were

sources which early European abstractionists simply could not have accommodated. The public quality of Mexican mural art and its scale and social content were to affect Pollock deeply. One work by Orozco in particular, the cupola from the Hospicio Cabañas in Guadalajara (1938–39), which contained what was 76
arguably Orozco's greatest cycle, was to haunt Pollock for the rest of his life, although he knew it only through reproductions. Even today there is still a tendency in Pollock studies to see the influence of the great European modernists as superseding and replacing that of the Mexicans; this was not the case, however, and a lot of the dating of Pollock's early work needs revision. *The Flame*, for 77
example, is generally dated between 1934 and 1938 but cannot in fact have been painted before 1939 and more likely dates from the early 1940s.[1] Flame for Pollock, through Orozco's art, becomes a purifying and cleansing element; here it flickers and consumes the multi-figure composition that underlies it. In America, as in Europe, the elements were to be a key source for the move into abstraction.

On arriving in New York, Pollock enrolled at the Art Students League under Thomas Hart Benton. More than any other artist of his generation Benton reflected the cross-currents that were informing American art throughout the 1930s. During this period he emerged as leader of the Regionalist School that advocated a return to rural American virtues and subject-matter. Benton was a muralist and had studied the Mexicans. He was now also detaching himself from an earlier interest in European modernism that nevertheless continued to plague him. He believed in the social function of art and, like so many of his generation, he was influenced by the philosophy of John Dewey who saw art as a 'mode of communication between man and his environment'.[2] Benton also felt that the creation of a collective social psyche could generate new and specifically American art forms. Pollock came to reject virtually everything that Benton stood for, claiming later that the only earlier American artist who meant anything to him was Albert Pinkham Ryder (1847–1917), a painter noted for his visionary and poetic imagination. But it was during his years with Benton that Pollock began to widen his intellectual horizons and to absorb what a leading American art historian of the younger generation has characterized as the 'Modern Man' ethos.[3] Despite the reactionary quality of much of Benton's output, he was intellectually part of a group of progressive liberal historians and social scientists.

75 José Clemente Orozco, *Prometheus*, fresco, Pomona College, Claremont, California, 1936.

76 José Clemente Orozco, *Man in Flames*, cupola decoration, Hospicio Cabañas, Guadalajara, Mexico, 1938–9.

Modern Man literature originated in America in the 1920s with such works as James Harvey Robinson's *Mind in the Making* of 1921. It called for modern man's intellectual regeneration in the face of changing values and new sources of knowledge, and Pollock copied out passages of it. A highlight came with the publication in 1949 by Joseph Campbell, the foremost American mythologist of his time, of *Hero with a Thousand Faces*, a copy of which Pollock owned. Although Modern Man literature was diverse, many of its writers were psychologists or were interested in psychology; all were touched by the enormous vogue for anthropology emphasized by the teaching of Franz Boas at Columbia University. Many were Jungians or at least subscribed to the idea that Jungian thought superseded that of the cooler, more analytical doctrines of Freud. Like Jung himself, Modern Man writers and thinkers were concerned, through anthropology, with prehistoric and tribal art and the patterns of behaviour which governed it, and above all with man's ability to communicate, through art, across the ages. This was the theme, for example, of Harvey Ferguson's *Modern Man: His Belief and Behaviour*, published in 1936. Although Pollock was not a great reader, he had a true respect for learning and,

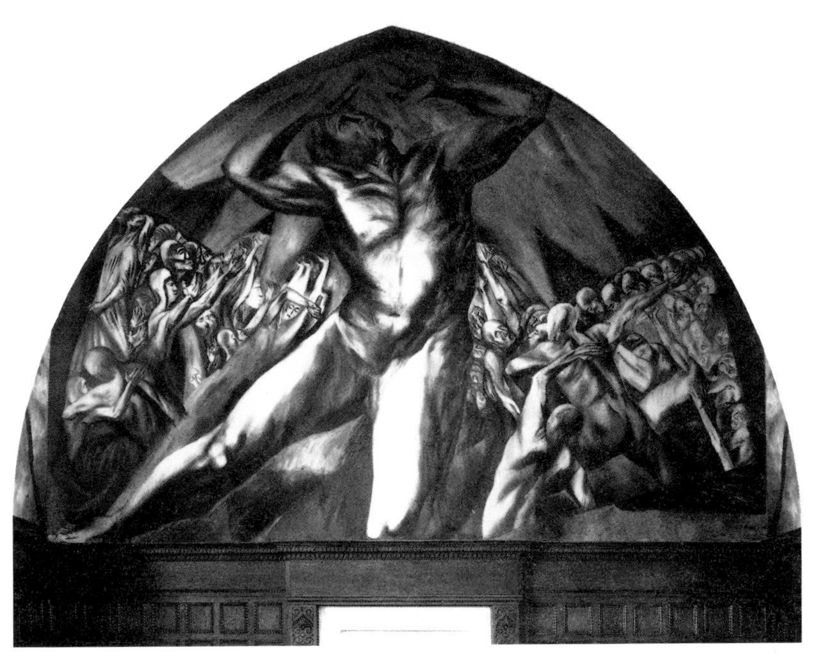

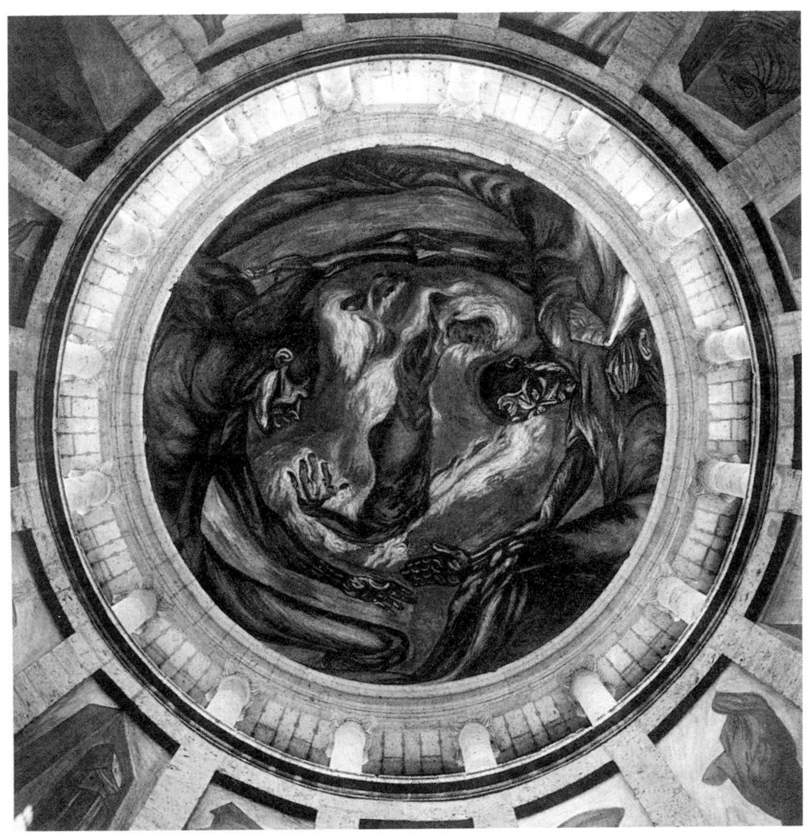

like a high percentage of artists, he picked up his ideas intuitively from the general cultural climate in which he lived. He thus came to the conviction that if art was about communication it was also about self-discovery. The European abstractionists had taken it for granted that they had something to communicate, although Malevich saw himself as talking to the future and Mondrian felt it might be some time before his message was fully understood, while Kandinsky awaited both the apocalypse and the next millennium. The need for communication in new, emergent American art was much more consciously and aggressively felt, and it was linked to an unusual and indeed unprecedented search for individual and personal identity. Literature on the subject is now fairly extensive, and yet the dichotomy between the search for self and the longing to identify with an absolute – the greater than the self – has yet to be satisfactorily accounted for. Although the Abstract Expressionists, as they were to become known, saw their art as arching backwards into time immemorial, they also saw themselves as belonging to the here and now in a more self-conscious way than their European forerunners.

It was through Benton and his circle that Pollock first made contact with New York's Jungian community. His interest in Jung was quickened when he met John Graham, a Russian émigré painter and theorist. Pollock had read Graham's article 'Picasso and Primitive Art', which had appeared in the *Magazine of Art* in 1937,[4] and had sought Graham out. Graham was a walking encyclopaedia of Jungianism, shamanism, ritualistic art and magic in general; and Pollock later claimed that Graham was the one person who knew what his art was truly about.[5] The year 1937 also saw the publication of Graham's *Systems and Dialectics*.[6] Its Jungian bias is demonstrated by his statement that 'In general races and nations develop culture in proportion as they have free access to the racial past according to folklore.'[7] Graham also writes: ' . . . a painting is a self-sufficient phenomenon and does not have to rely on nature . . . there are men with absolute eyes who can evaluate every form in nature, understand its language, represent it, transpose and re-evaluate it absolutely.'[8] Soon Pollock was forced to seek psychiatric treatment for the alcoholism that had plagued him since his youth. Between 1939 and 1942 he underwent psychotherapy under two committed Jungian analysts.

During the late 1930s and in the very early 1940s Orozco was still the major influence on Pollock's paintings; Pollock studied his work in reproductions and was consulting the murals of 1932 at Dartmouth College in Hanover, New Hampshire, which he visited in 1937. Pollock was particularly fixated on the *Sacrifice* 78
panel, the most frequently reproduced work of the series. 'Sacrifice', it is worth noting, is also the title of the last chapter of Jung's *Psychology of the Unconscious* (1913),[9] and it becomes a recurring theme in Pollock's work at the time. 79

Drawings and more casual jottings dating from *c.*1937 confirm that Pollock was also making contact with the graphic idiom developed by Picasso in connection with his studies for *Guernica* of 1937 – the painting itself was shown at the Valentine Gallery in 1939, causing wider comment than any modern work exhibited in America since Whistler's *Portrait of the Artist's Mother* (1871) had toured the country during the Depression. Pollock was also now looking at Picasso's related etching *The Dream and Lie of Franco*. The great Picasso retrospective which opened at the Museum of Modern Art late in 1939 made an overwhelming impact on him. The influence of Orozco and Picasso can be seen in equal measure in *Birth*, 80
on which he probably worked between 1940 and 1941. It is in his attempt to resolve the clash and collision between Mexican and indigenous native American

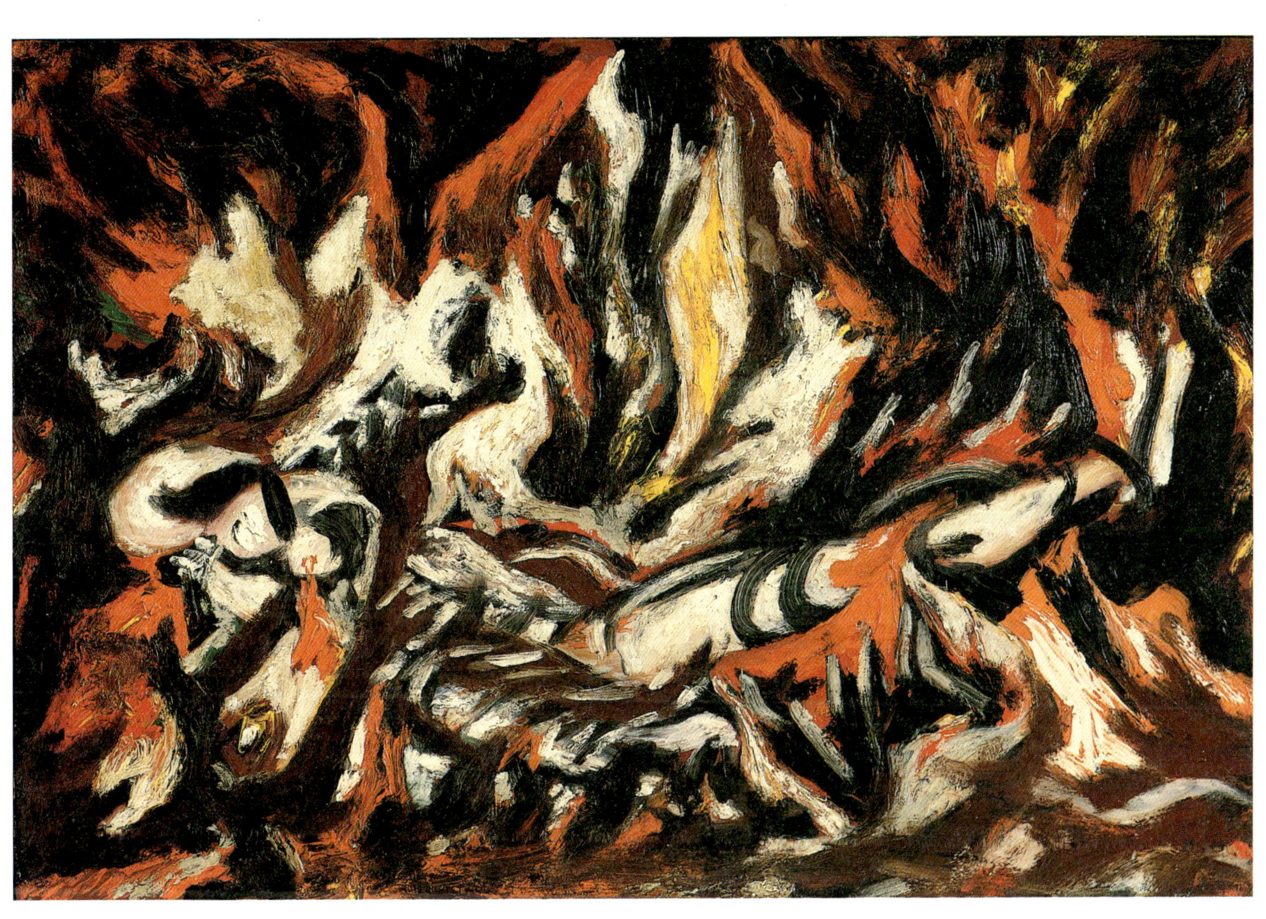

77 Pollock, *The Flame*, oil on canvas, *c.* 1940.

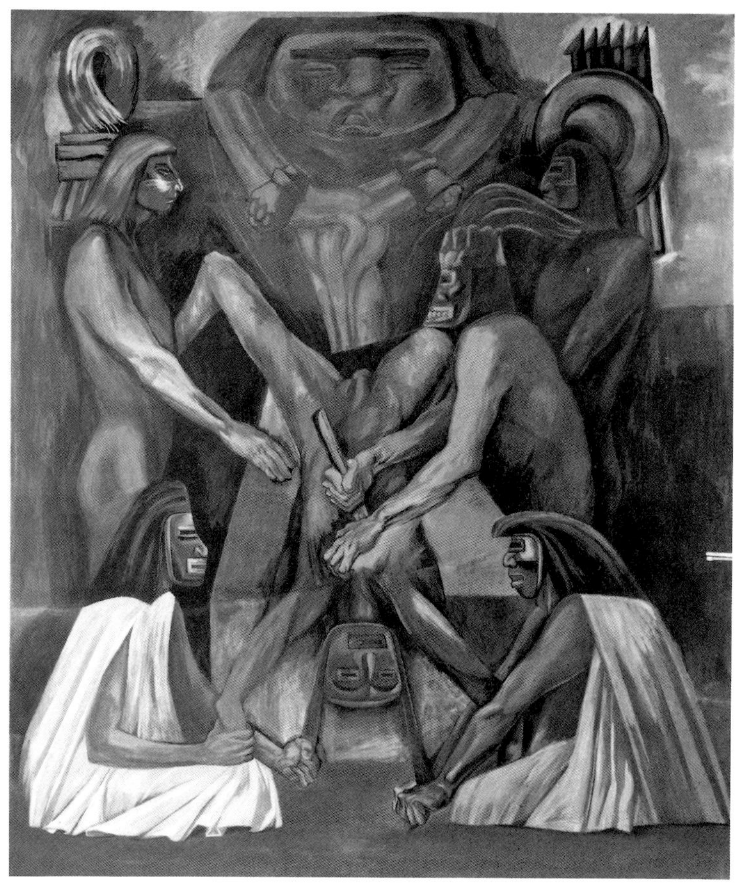

78 José Clemente Orozco, *Ancient Human Sacrifice*, mural painting, Dartmouth College, New Hampshire, 1932–4.

79 Pollock, *Untitled (Naked Man with Knife)*, oil on canvas, c. 1938–41.

art with the mainstream of European modernism that Pollock emerges as the most significant figure in experimental American art. It was again after his contact with Graham that Pollock seriously turned his attention to North American Indian art, which so intrigued the Surrealists. This manifests itself most overtly in his canvases of 1942 and the immediately succeeding years; these works are larger than any he had hitherto produced. Pollock owned publications on American anthropology and on regional ethnographic surveys, and he was as deeply influenced by the factual photographs and diagrams that were reproduced in them as by the artifacts he could see in New York at the Hay Foundation (The Museum of American Indian Art), which contained the best collection in the world of British Columbian, Alaskan, pre-Columbian and American Indian art. Pollock must surely have seen the exhibition 'Indian Art of the United States' mounted at the Museum of Modern Art in 1941; this marked the popular acceptance of Indian artifacts as art rather than as ethnological curiosities. Graham also quickened Pollock's interest in the Surrealists' belief in psychic automatism and in the cult of a spontaneous, free-flowing line. Graham, though not a profound thinker, was right for Pollock because he was simultaneously an intellectual agitator and a condenser of ideas, and this appealed to the impetuosity of Pollock's nature.

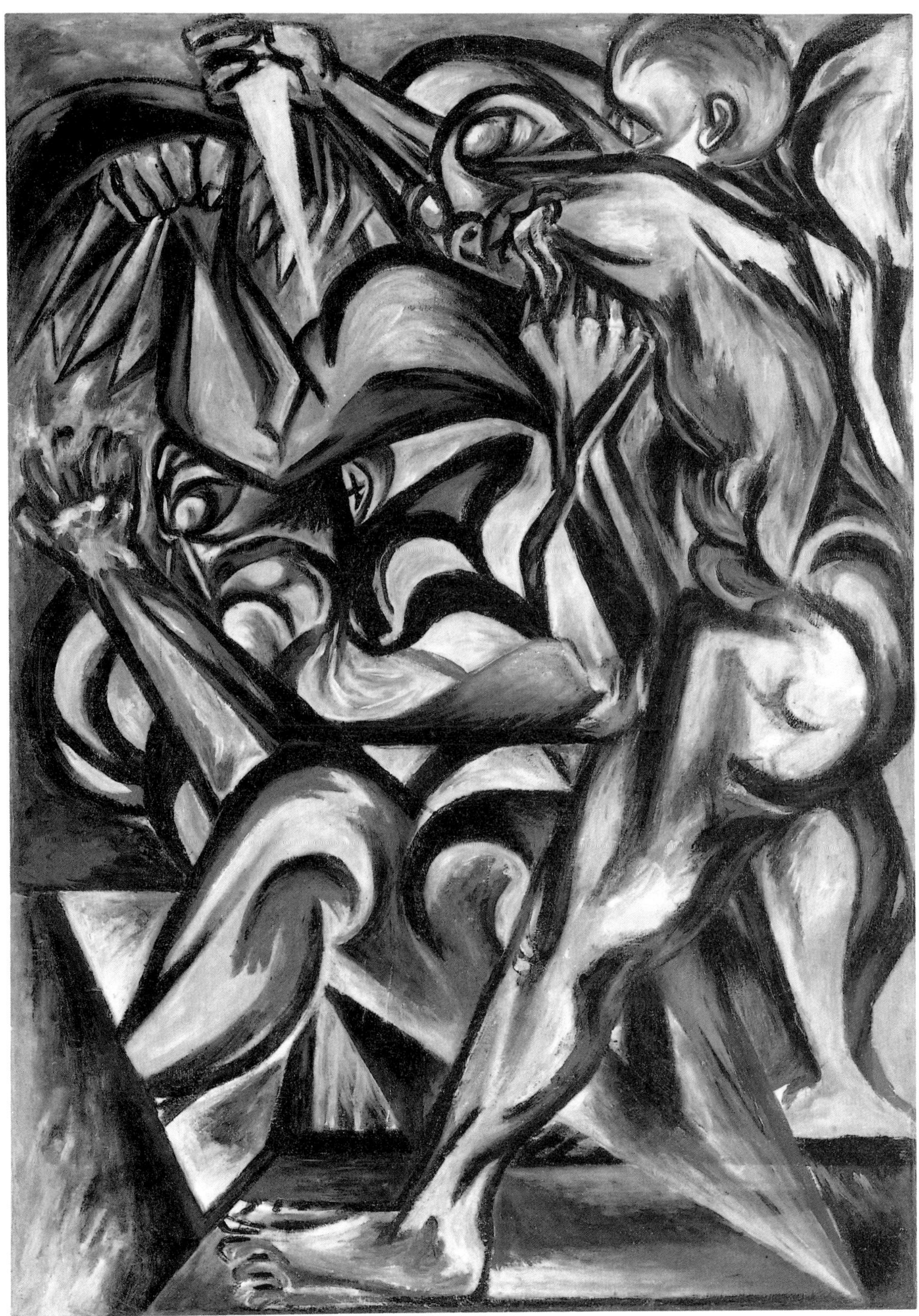

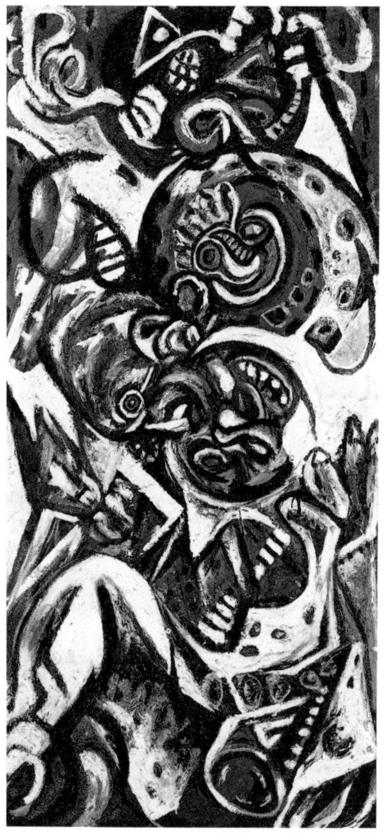

80 Pollock, *Birth*, oil on canvas, *c.* 1938–41.

81 Pollock, *Moon Woman Cuts the Circle*, oil on canvas, *c.* 1943.

Moon Woman Cuts the Circle, of *c.* 1943, is one of the works that demonstrate 81
most overtly Pollock's debt to American Indian art and to the myth and ritual which inspired it. Here is a brief passage from a *Treaty on Navajo Sand Painting* (1916), a study which Pollock could not have read but which indicates how deeply he was intuitively identifying with his sources: 'red, the colour of flesh and blood, hence signifying plentiful meat and life, is also the colour of danger, war and sorcery. Being therefore dangerous it can also protect from danger . . . for the attraction of good, red is placed on the outside of the red and blue body of the encircling rainbow guardians and towards the outside in other motifs containing it.'[10] Similarly, many of the images illustrated in the 1952 edition of Jung's *Symbols of Transformation* (earlier editions had been sparsely illustrated) seem very relevant to works executed by Pollock in the previous decade; but then it was through his interest in Jung that Pollock began searching out archetypal images. The Haida tattoo of the woman in the moon used by Jung, for example, relates indirectly to *Moon Woman Cuts the Circle*. He also discussed the Hiawatha legend at length. Hiawatha, for Jung an archetype of the mythical hero, had a grandmother who had lived in the moon;[11] and for Jung the Moon Woman becomes a metaphor for the anima, the female principle, counterpart of the male animus. He also equates the anima with the unconscious. Pollock may not have actually read all that much Jung, just as Mondrian may well never have read his way through the entire Blavatsky text that meant

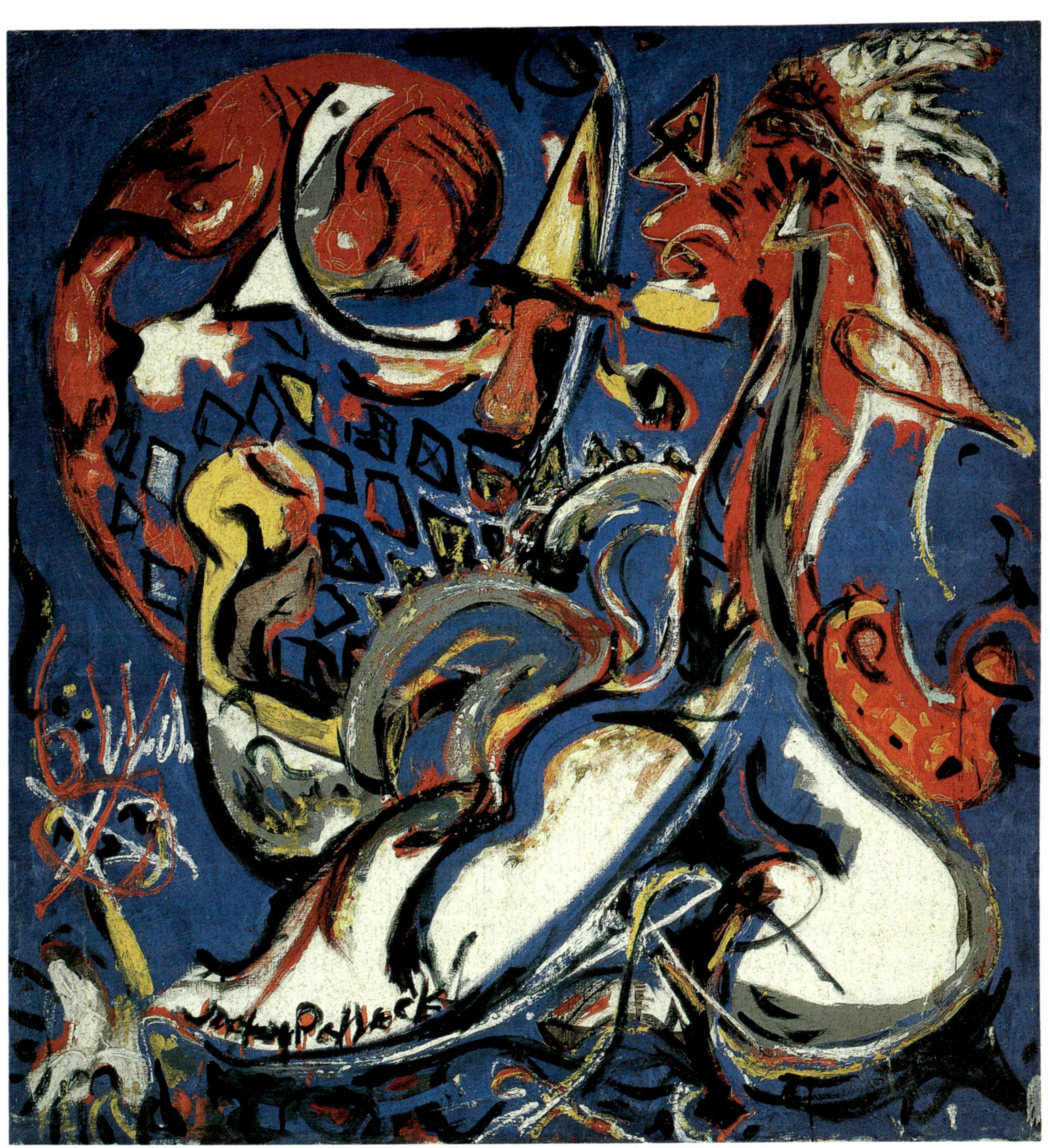

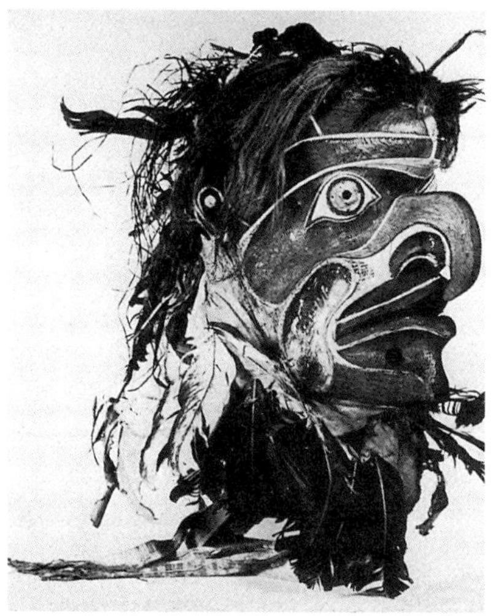

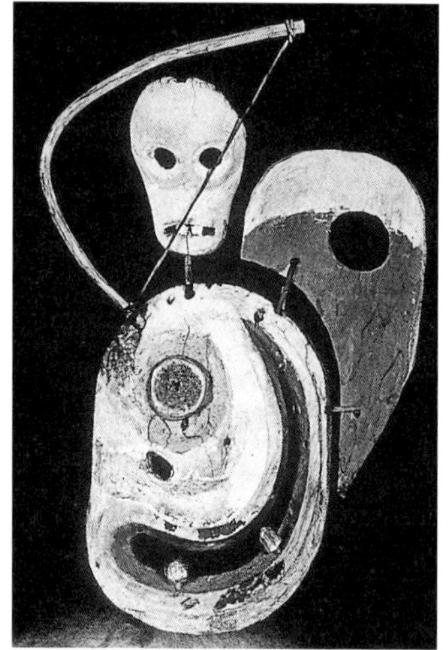

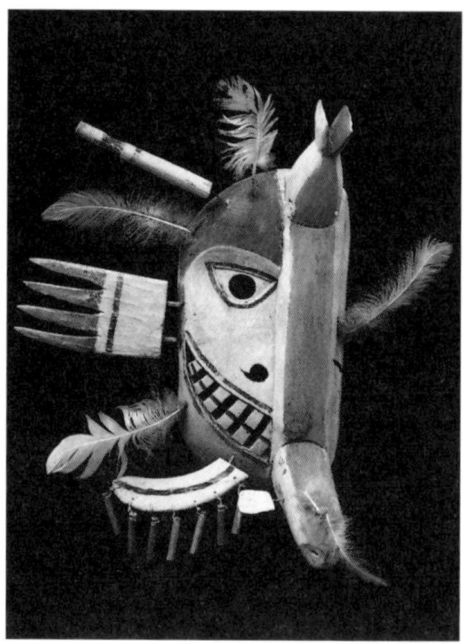

82 Kwakiutl mask.

83 Inuit mask from the Lower Yukon area.

84 Yu'pil grinning mask with divided countenance from Alaska.

so much to him (see p. 15). But there is no doubt that as Pollock progressed in his own therapy he was delving, with the help of his analysts, ever deeper into Jungian thought and trying to cultivate associational procedures, although one of his analysts tells us that he had difficulties in doing so.[12]

During 1943, and largely through these associational procedures, Pollock's work became increasingly broad in scope and ever more richly layered in imagery. In keeping with Jungian principles his interest in the myth and culture of early civilizations grew ever wider, and the forms he used to illustrate it were borrowed from a multiplicity of sources ranging from ancient Assyrian, Egyptian, Maya and other pre-Columbian art, through and up to contemporary work by the Surrealists,
many of whom were now active in America. *Male and Female in Search of a* 85
Symbol owes a debt to both Inuit and Hopi art, and clearly Pollock has at the same 82–84
time been consulting Miró's art of the 1920s. But what makes this such a key work 90
in Pollock's œuvre is that the glyphs that fill the space between the figures are derived from the symbols or conventions used to denote speech in countless codices and artifacts of the distant past. As Pollock roamed the museums and browsed through anthropological publications, he must surely have become obsessed by these mysterious symbols from the past which he sensed were speaking to him; and he must then have felt within him the desperate need to communicate in turn through his own canvases with all art, past and present – to identify with the very idea of art itself. In the process of doing so he must have felt that he was on the threshold of creating a pictorial *lingua franca*.

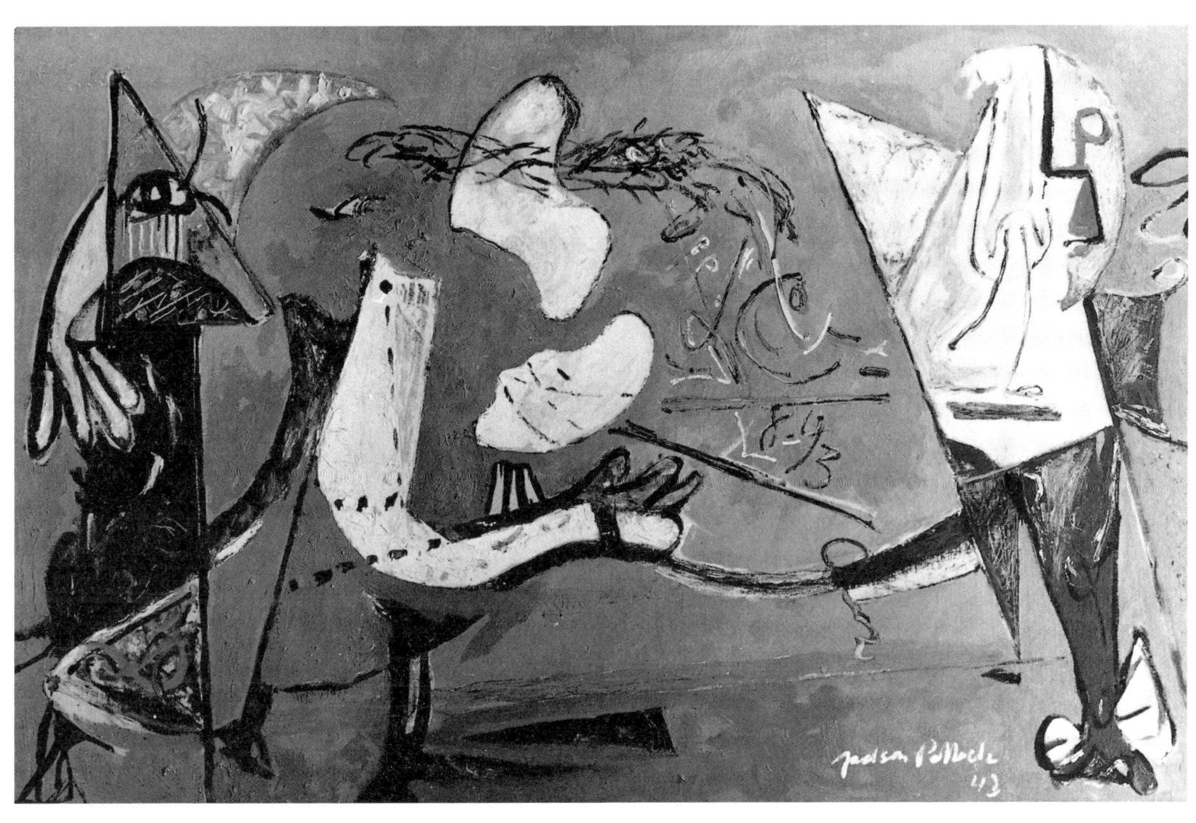

85 Pollock, *Male and Female in Search of a Symbol*, oil on canvas, 1943.

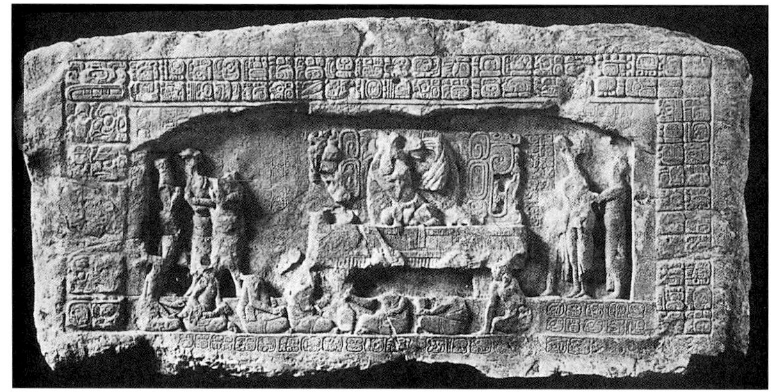

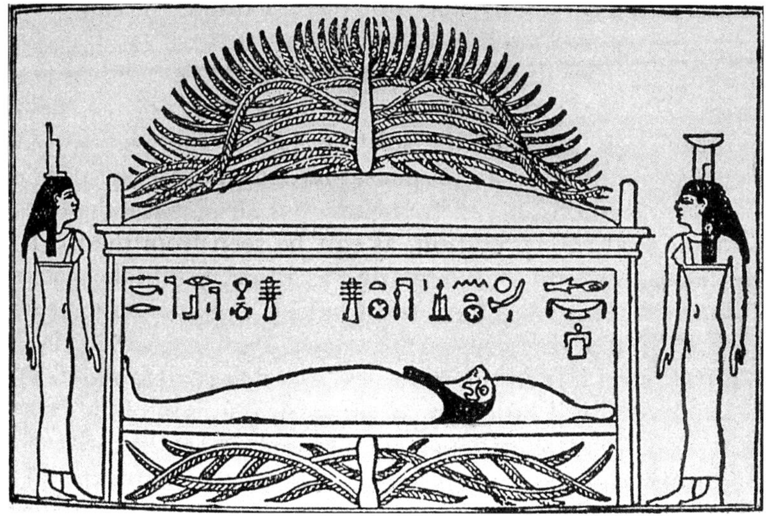

86 Maya relief from Piedras Negras, Guatemala, late eighth century.

87 'Osiris in the Cedar Coffin', drawing after an ancient Egyptian relief at Dendera.

The most majestic of all the canvases shown in Pollock's first one-man exhibition at Peggy Guggenheim's gallery 'Art of This Century' late in 1943, *Guardians of the Secret*, obviously has its sources in ceremonial, commemorative bas-reliefs found in civilizations scattered all over the world. Its composition, for example, resembles a Maya relief, from Piedras Negras in Guatemala, shown at the Museum of Modern Art in 1933 in the exhibition 'American Sources for Modern Art'. It is also instructive to see it placed next to a diagram of an Egyptian relief depicting Osiris in the Cedar Coffin, as illustrated in the 1952 edition of *Symbols of Transformation*. In the same chapter in which he discusses the Hiawatha myth Jung writes: 'Snakes and dogs are guardians of the treasure. . . . The sacred cave in the temple at Cos consisted of a rectangular pit covered by a stone slab with a square hole in it'.[13] Jung interprets the secret so jealously guarded as the unconscious; and the underworld and ordeals of death he sees as symbolic of the shadow world every human being is subjected to in the recesses of the mind. The sojourn of the Hero in the underworld Jung interprets as his delving into his own unconscious and the dredging up of hidden sources of action.

88 86 87

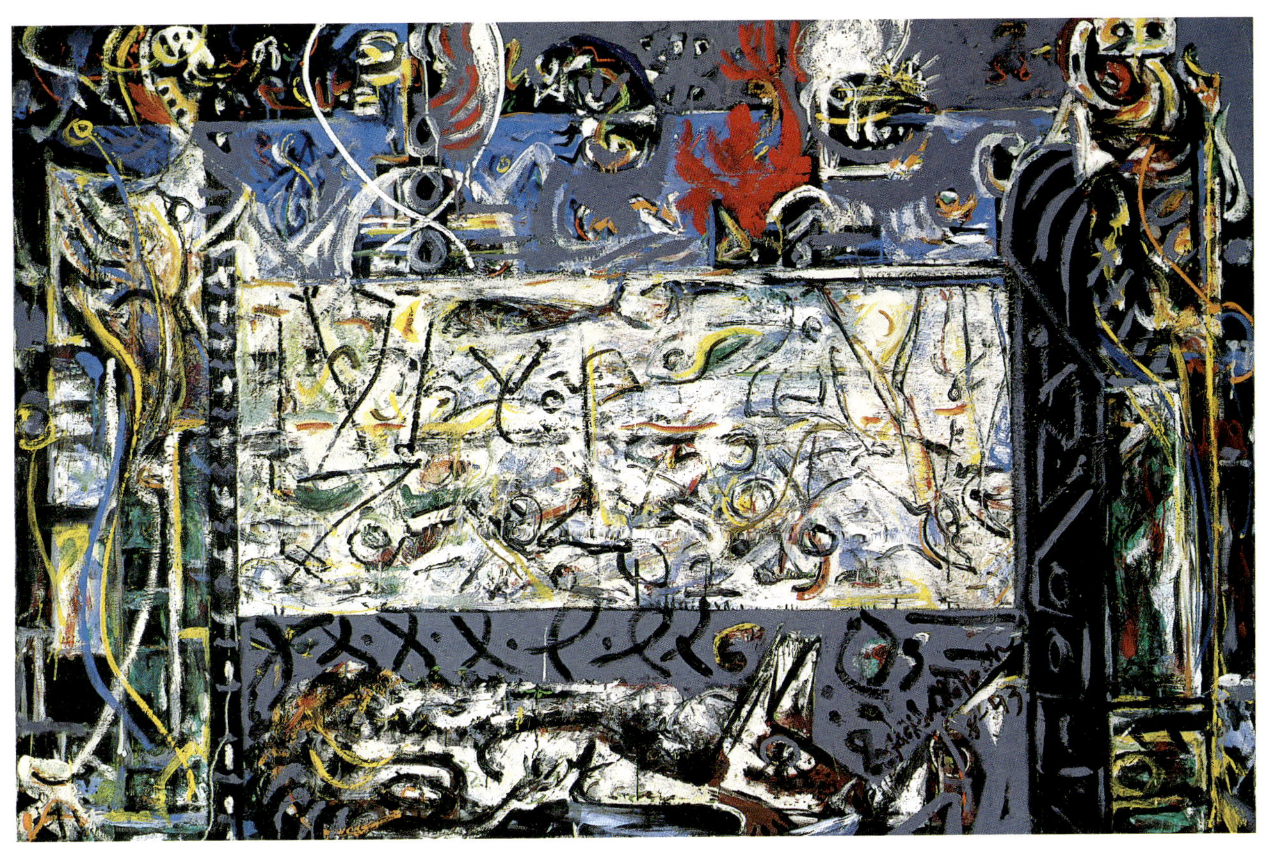

88 Pollock, *Guardians of the Secret*, oil on canvas, 1943.

There is no doubt that Pollock was by now trying to paint from the unconscious, although as the Surrealists had learned in the 1920s this is something that is extremely hard to do. Painting a stream-of-consciousness picture is rather like writing a stream-of-consciousness sonnet – one keeps running up against the restrictions of one's format. And as several critics have remarked, these paintings of Pollock's are not so much *from* the unconscious as *about* it. On the other hand, Pollock's technique was becoming increasingly bold and unorthodox. His imagery has become so rich that he is also now at times forced to block parts of it out for the sake of pictorial clarity and eloquence – the blue grey areas around the central tablet in *Guardians of the Secret*, for example, were originally lavishly embellished. The central part of the tablet itself, scored with brush-marks, is the most commanding and mysterious part of the picture and it foretells future developments in Pollock's art. Soon he was to move up into the secret place itself, into a realm where the physical gesture with paint and the pictorial symbol become synonymous. In *Pasiphaë*, a slightly later painting, the guardians or sentinel figures are 89
paired and the central rectangle is replaced by the recumbent figure. The entire surface of the painting is now encrusted with energetic, very physical markings. These do not only participate in rendering iconography, but also simultaneously assert themselves as expressive gestures or symbols in their own right. What Jungianism ultimately offered Pollock at this moment in his career was the concept of symbolization as a language of the unconscious.

This raises the nature of Pollock's relationship and debt to Surrealism. Although during the 1930s American artists were exposed to virtually the whole gamut of Surrealist art, there was an aspect of the American psyche that was deeply resistant to the Surrealist ethos, not least because, although the Surrealists had set out to reform life by breaking down taboos and intellectual and moral values of all kinds, Surrealism was ultimately an élitist movement, composed of a clique of like-minded intellectuals who were out to shock themselves and each other: one must be aware of the pinnacles of Western culture before one can delight in knocking them down or turning them on their heads. Then again, Surrealism retained a strongly anti-aesthetic bias at all times. The American artists who came to prominence in the 1940s had from the start been absorbed in the problems of the creation of high art. The Surrealists had used art to attack contemporary society. The Americans, and Pollock in particular, became concerned quite simply with acting out art itself. For the Surrealists art was a technique for living, for the Americans it became, temporarily at least, a way of life.

Then the obsession with sexuality which was one of Surrealism's most obsessional features was foreign to the American ethos of the time. It was this more than any other single factor that distinguished the Surrealists' interest in anthropology and primitive art and cultures from that of the American anthropologists whose work was of particular interest to artists. The Surrealists saw so-called primitive art as being drenched with sexuality and sexual metaphor in a way that most American anthropologists did not. (A more Freudian-inspired and more sexually oriented anthropology was practised by figures such as Mabel Dodge and Margaret Mead.) The Surrealists revered Freud because he associated creativity with the forces of the libido, whereas Jung saw art as dealing in symbols which interlocked in every age and cultural manifestation; he felt that the value of understanding these symbols might lie in their healing power and hence might redirect modern life. The orthodox Surrealists, although they used Jung, ultimately

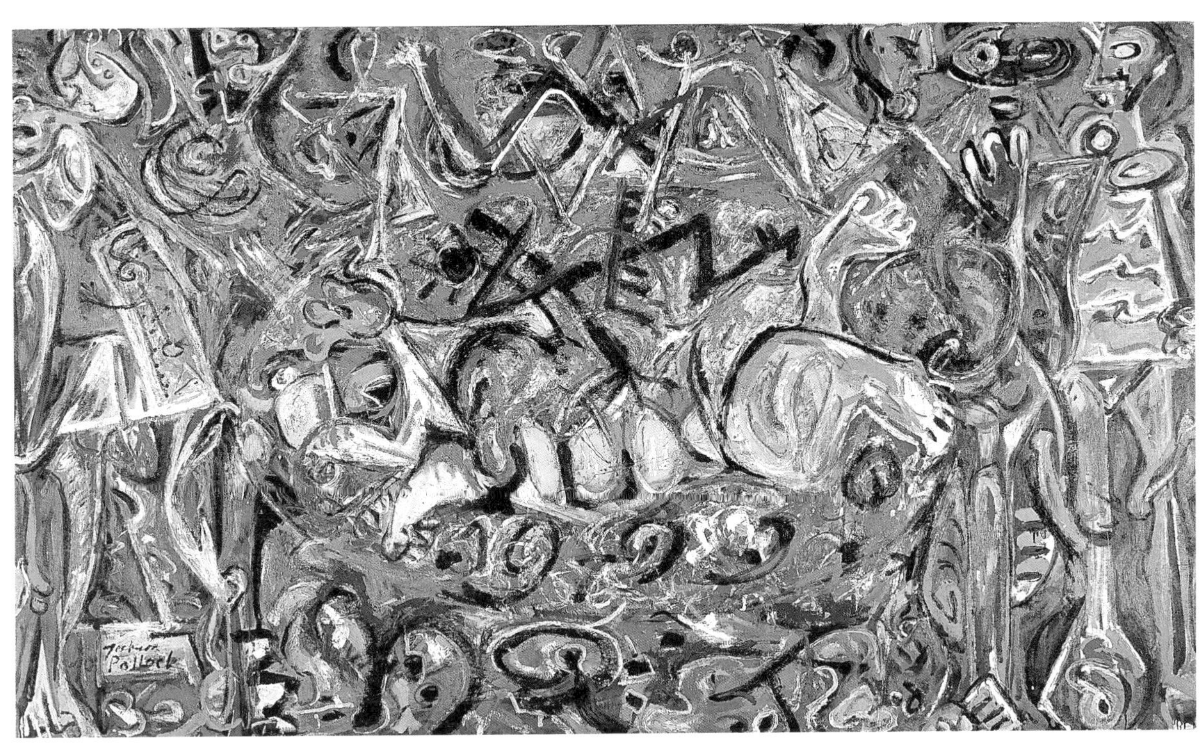

89 Pollock, *Pasiphaë*,
oil on canvas, 1943.

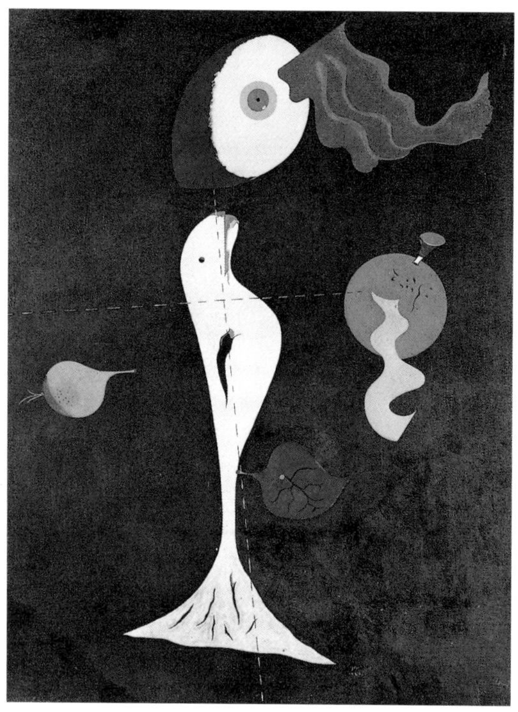

90 Joan Miró, *Nude*, oil on canvas, 1926.

distrusted him. Similarly, although they originally rejected myth, they then flirted with it, only to denounce it again.

Nevertheless, the influx of Surrealist expatriates was of incalculable importance to American intellectual and artistic life. For example, the French painter André Masson, whom Pollock met in 1943, was to be a considerable force in his art. In the same year John Graham organized an exhibition juxtaposing great names in French art with emergent American talents, including Pollock. Miró, the European artist most admired by Pollock after Picasso, was given the accolade of a major retrospective at the Museum of Modern Art in 1941; it was to affect Pollock deeply. Miró was one of the stars of Surrealism, but, unlike his more doctrinaire colleagues, he was also one of nature's Surrealists. Hence, again, he was right for Pollock. Pollock was not an intellectual. His reactions were visceral and he did his learning visually, setting it against the context of abstract ideas that were provided for him and not out of them. Miró, while he had been cultivating associational procedures, had gone back to prehistoric cave painting, and he had learned how to use the symbolic, calligraphic diagrams of Neolithic art in such a way as to conduct through them a dialogue with his artistic mentors of all periods. In other words, Miró's painting *speaks* to other painting of both the past and the present through 90
the symbolic diagrams. His example helped Pollock to reconcile the conflicting sources he had been consulting and thus to further layer his work unselfconsciously; this is one of the reasons why Pollock responded so immediately to carved and incised Indian rock art which superimposed artistic activity from different prehistoric and historic periods.

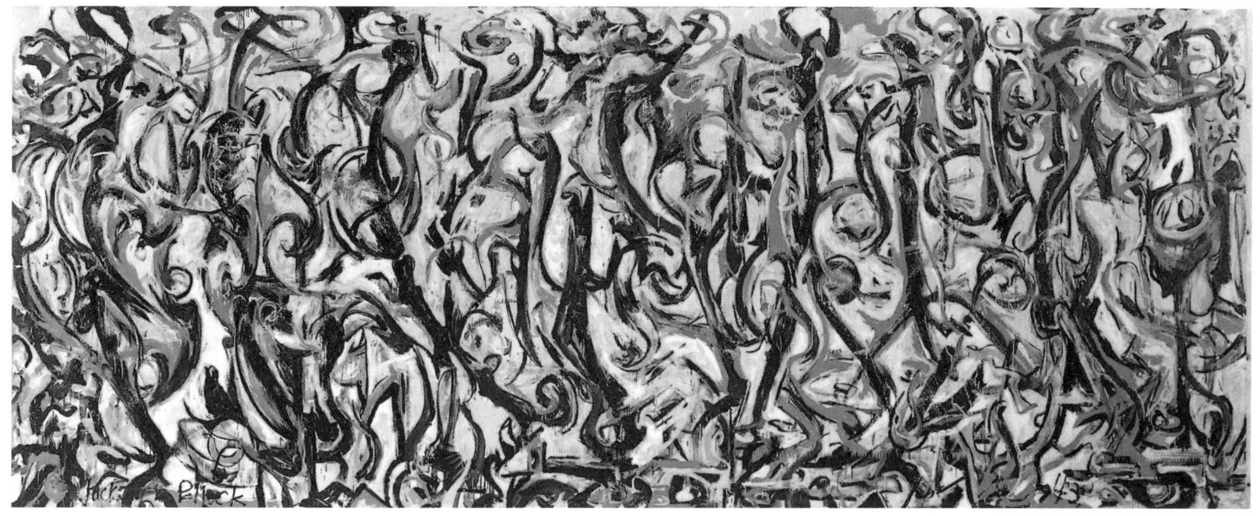

91 Pollock, *Mural*, oil on canvas, 1943.

91 The large *Mural* commissioned from Pollock by Peggy Guggenheim for her home in Manhattan in 1943 and speedily executed by him either at the end of that year, or right at the beginning of 1944, marks a turning-point in his art. This canvas is Pollock's most integrated work to date. Perhaps it is not surprising that while Pollock was working in so concentrated a manner, and in a semi-automatic technique, memories of his encounters with Mexican mural painting should have risen from the depths of his subconscious. If one can imagine for oneself one of the more impacted and frieze-like of Orozco's frescoes – *The Rebellion of Man*, of 1936, for example, from the theatre of the University of Guadalajara – viewed through 10 ft of clear, undulating water, it would be very like the Pollock *Mural*. This is Pollock's last farewell to the greatest mentor of his early youth. One of the most distinctive features of Orozco's style was the way in which his figures wear their white skeletal structures imprinted on their bodies. The sensation of the fusion of internal and external body imagery in the Pollock contributes to the ambiguity of figure to ground that is so cardinal to his move into abstraction. Here the figures are rendered calligraphically, but now more *as* calligraphy than *by* calligraphy. The painting measures some 8 ft x 20 ft and its scale is crucial to the development of American abstraction in the late 1940s and 1950s. It is also significant that it was executed in Pollock's relatively small studio (a partition wall between two rooms had to be removed to accommodate it) and was designed to be viewed at relatively close quarters in Peggy Guggenheim's home. This is environmental art, large-scale painting seen from close up. As one looks at the picture, one can easily imagine Pollock measuring himself up to each of its rhythmic component parts as he ranged

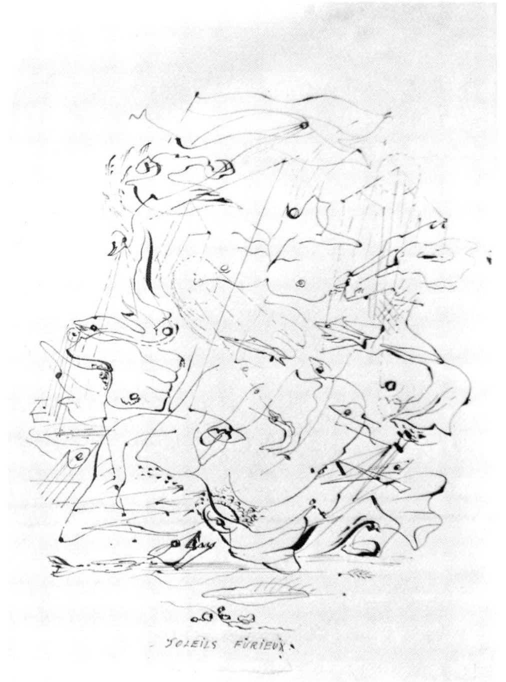

92 André Masson, *Furious Suns*, pen and ink, 1925.

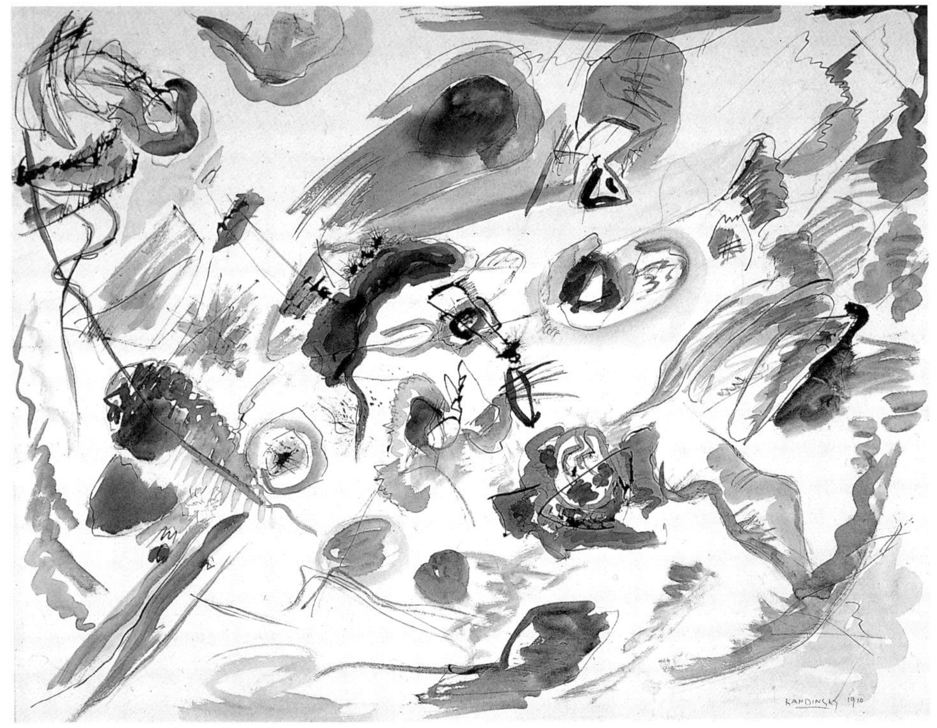

93 Vasily Kandinsky, *Study for Composition VII*, watercolour and India ink on paper, 1913.

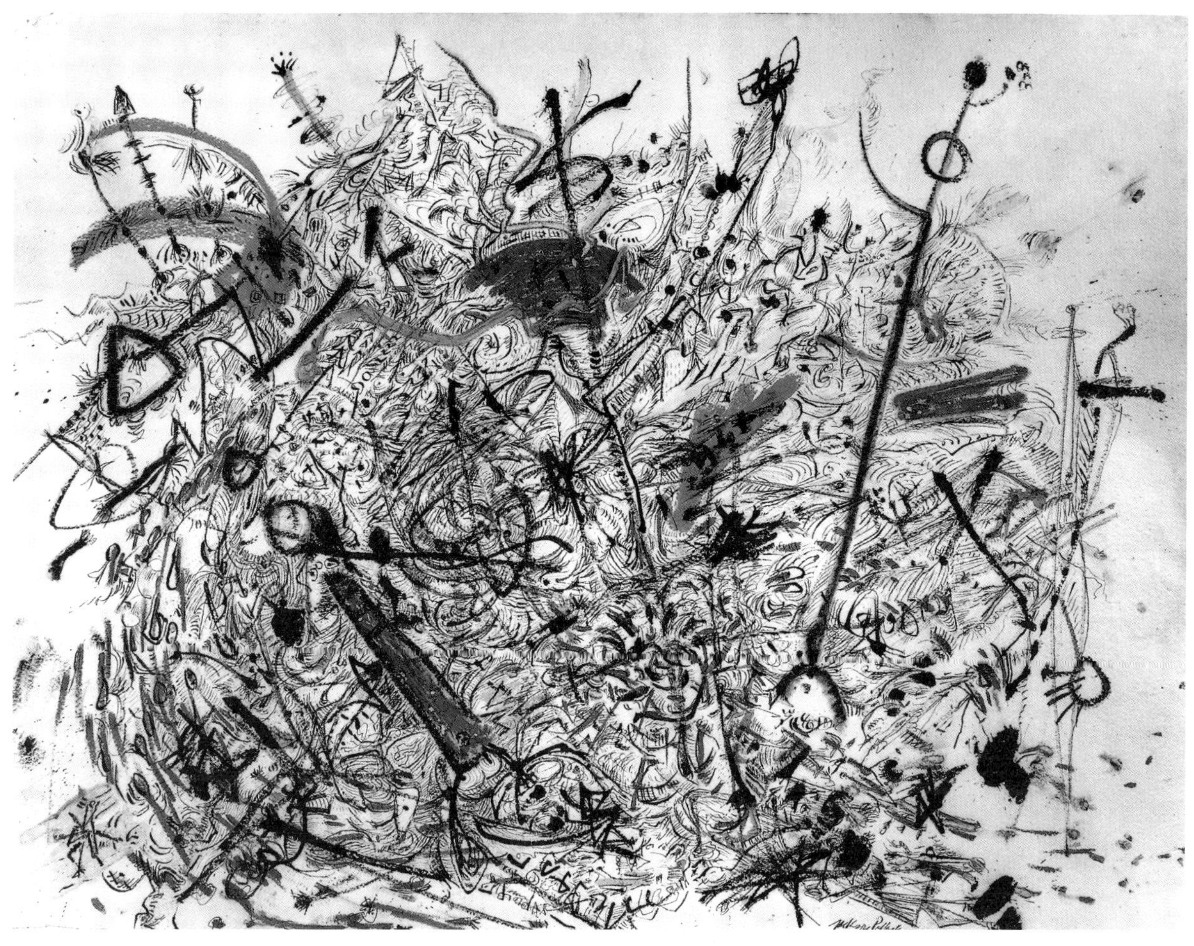

94 Pollock, *Drawing*, wash, pen and black and coloured inks, pastel, gouache and wash on paper, *c.* 1946.

back and forth across the painted surface, and the viewer experiences an overwhelming sensation of the physical act of painting, of mark-making that matches the scale of the human body. As in the case of Kandinsky, Pollock's imagery is so rich, so all-consuming that its component parts have begun to cancel themselves out in favour of the overall surge.

94 Pollock's most truly automatic works are perhaps a series of relatively small drawings produced between late 1943 and 1946. A comparison with André
92 Masson's early experiments in automatism of 1924 is telling. In these sketches by Masson the emergent imagery (hands, breasts, feet and so forth) is fairly predictable. The more abstract and emblematic nodal or focal points in Pollock's works have about them a feeling that is more truly atavistic and mysterious. These smaller works are important in Pollock's move into an ever freer, more gestural
93 manner. Some of them possess a dappled quality that is reminiscent of Kandinsky's first abstractions, where drawn and coloured forms float against an indeterminate field; in 1943 Pollock worked briefly as a custodian at the Museum of Non Objective Art in New York (subsequently to become the Solomon R. Guggenheim Museum), fabulously rich as it was in its holdings of Kandinsky's art.

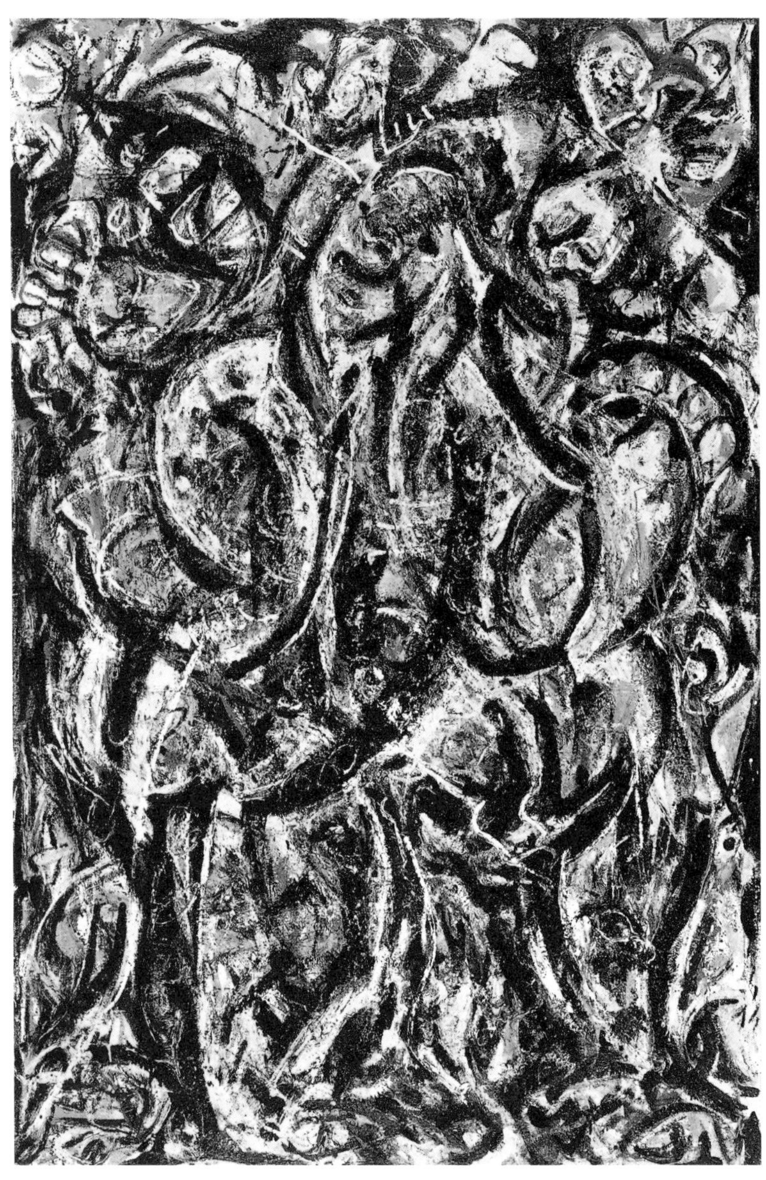

95 Pollock, *Gothic*, oil on canvas, 1944.

Gothic of 1944, a work of commanding scale, still has figurative overtones. Basi- 95
cally it is a three-figure composition, but it is easy to see why it appeared to many contemporary viewers as totally abstract. A large percentage of the paintings of 1944 through to 1946 have immediately recognizable figurative elements, and their titles, although invariably conceived after the pictures themselves had been painted, confirm the Jungian content. Simultaneously, however, a second strain in Pollock's work begins to manifest itself, characterized by what he and many contemporary New York painters would have called a more 'all-over' feel. *Eyes in the* 96
Heat of 1946, for example, is built up in heavy impasto applied in short rhythmic strokes; it still contains suggestions of hermetic symbolic imagery. However, with

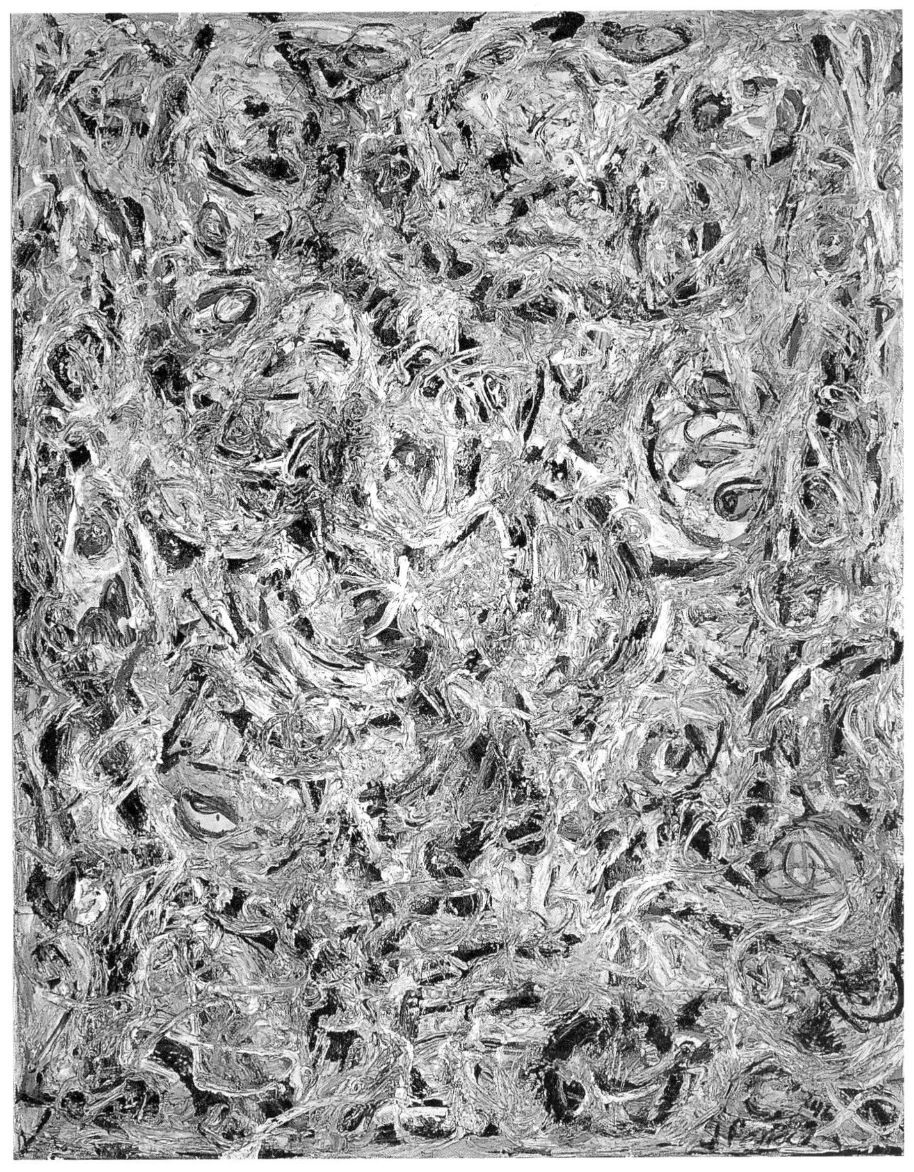

96 Pollock, *Eyes in the Heat*, oil (and enamel?) on canvas, 1946.

the first poured or dripped paintings of 1947 all hints of earlier imagery are not so much dismissed as subsumed into the inner life of the pictures themselves, into their webbed, multi-layered ebb and flow. Clearly, as the 1940s progressed, Pollock was moving away from his earlier Jungian view of the unconscious being made manifest and brought into play with the forces of contemporary and everyday life through the use of symbols. There is a sense in which Jungian symbols (and indeed Freud's own theory) are based on metaphors for the ongoing forces that prompt or compel us to endure, to cope with life, and – in the case of artists – to allow them to produce art, to express themselves. From a Jungian angle they thus act as seers who help to reveal the processes of the hidden unconscious, yet simultaneously to ally it to the workings of the conscious mind. If Pollock still saw, and continued to see, his creative work as arising from the unconscious, he had also come to regard the result as proceeding from pure and spontaneous action.

In 1947, the year in which he moved into his fully developed 'dripped' or 'poured' technique, Pollock described his working method thus: 'My painting does not come from the easel. I hardly ever stretch my canvas before painting. I prefer to tack the unstretched canvas to the hard wall or on the floor. On the floor I am more at ease. I feel nearer, more a part of the painting since in this way I can walk around it, work from the four sides and literally be *in* the painting. . . . When I am in the painting I am not aware of what I am doing. It is only after a get acquainted period that I see what I have been about. I have no fear of making changes, destroying the image etc., because the painting has a life of its own. I try to let it come through. It is only when I lose contact with the painting that the result is a mess. Otherwise there is a pure harmony, an easy give and take, and the painting comes out well.'[14] Although the tone of the statement is matter-of-fact, the underlying assumptions are metaphysical and amount to an almost mystical view of painting as a rite or act of magic. Kandinsky had seen his role as shamanistic and believed that his own and certain other art had healing properties. Pollock saw his art at the time of his 'breakthrough' into abstraction as salvation. Although he would probably not have acknowledged it, what he was seeking was in part at least salvation for himself. Allied to this search was a desperate need to communicate, to use line and paint as script, as a universal message. For American abstractionists (and this divides them sharply from their European antecedents) salvation, both personal and in terms of the regeneration of art, had to come from within each individual artist.

It is notable that a high proportion of Pollock's first fully resolved dripped or poured paintings of 1947 – and these include some of the most exciting and successful of them – are upright in format and on a human scale (they average approximately 6 ft 6 in. x 3 ft 6 in.). It is in these pictures that we sense most strongly Pollock measuring himself up to a pictorial surface, his visceral identification with it. To this extent the canvas in turn confronts him with his own presence. Yet it also allows him to pass through it, as if through a mirror, into a realm where the self is transcended. Gesture, as translated into pictorial rhythm, now replaces – one might even say actually becomes – the hermetic symbol. The gesture was a grand one and to function at its most compelling it required a format as big as or bigger than the man who made it. The 'Guardians' who had stood over the jealously kept secret are no longer required because the secret is revealed as painting itself. The titles that Pollock bestows on these early abstractions are revealing. *Full Fathom Five* (a key picture for the artist, though relatively 97
small in scale) may well have been begun as a two-figure composition – and we know that many of Pollock's abstract works were begun with legible imagery – but, as the title suggests, the imagery has been buried, drowned, by the dense skeins of paint that flow back and forth, meshing and tangling as they do so across the pictorial support. The work is executed in oils, although the surface also incorporates unorthodox materials, buttons, keys, combs, cigarettes and so
forth, traces of human existence, of a life being lived through art. *Cathedral*, 98
which combines oil paint with more easily pourable aluminium paint, is a more nearly perfect painting, having about it a soaring quality that reminds one of Barnett Newman's famous statement about modern artists having to make cathedrals out of themselves.[15]

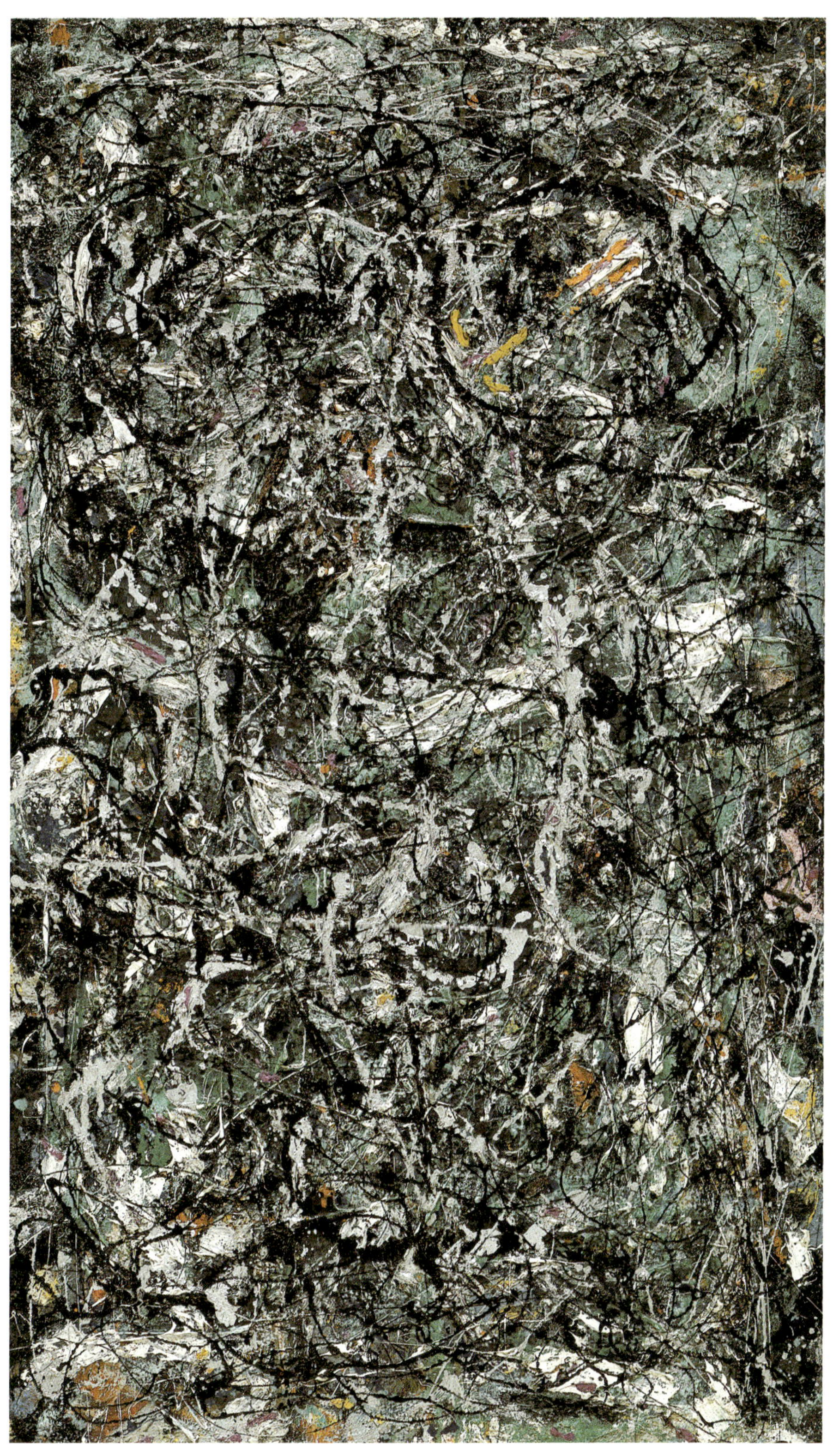

97 Pollock, *Full Fathom Five*, oil on canvas, 1947.

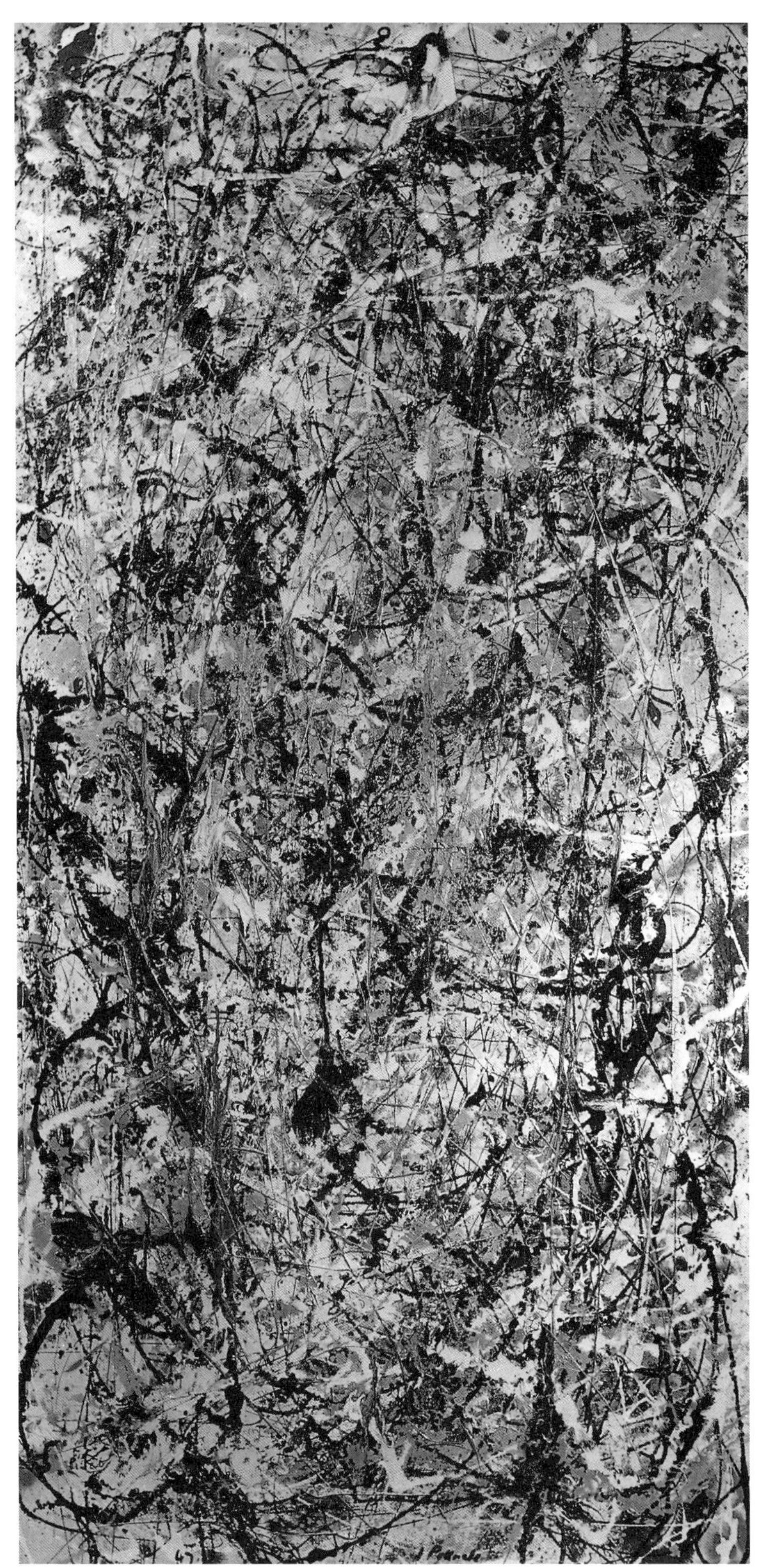

98 Pollock, *Cathedral*, oil and mixed media on canvas, 1947.

In latter years Pollock was somewhat distressed when the automatic aspect of his work was over-emphasized at the expense of its formal properties, and certainly as each painting progressed his working methods seem to have become slower and more deliberate, and the gestures, the mark-making more conscious, the dripped accents more refined and more sparingly applied. The artist's method of working on the floor obviously allowed for greater control in the application of ribbons of wet, runny paint. It also did away with the associations implicit in the artist's first mark. Faced with a bare, upright canvas, a painter's first instinct is generally either to trace a horizontal, which immediately implies a horizon, or else a vertical, which on a large canvas invokes body imagery or a subliminal human presence.

In October 1945 Pollock married his long-time friend and associate, the artist Lee Krasner. A trip they made the previous August, when they visited the then fairly remote area near the tip of Long Island, had resulted in her suggestion that they leave New York and buy or rent a house in the country. Pollock finally accepted the idea and, with the help of a grudging loan from Peggy Guggenheim, the couple bought a run-down farmhouse with barn on 5 acres of land about 7 miles from East Hampton on Long Island. They moved out of New York City in November 1945 and spent many months clearing and restoring the house. They also rebuilt the barn on a nearby site, so providing an unimpeded view of the sea from the house.

The barn itself was small but had a pitched roof; its walls were not especially high. It was at this point in Pollock's career that the lateral, horizontal expansion of his formats begins to assert itself. With the inevitable pull to the horizontal the analogies with landscape or with nature begin to force themselves in upon the spectator. He said, 'My concern is with the rhythms of nature . . . the way the ocean moves . . . I work from the inside out, like nature.'[16] It is within this context that Pollock had made his famous retort to the painter and teacher Hans Hoffman, who had suggested he should work more from nature; to which he replied, 'I *am* nature.'[17] We are reminded of the importance that water and the sea had for Mondrian during his own move into the realm of abstraction.

Contrary to much of what has been written about Pollock, he was an edge-conscious artist, and he would define the edges of his compositions with masking tape, even when working on the floor. But the carefully calculated movement of the skeins of paint extending off a picture's edges and back onto the canvas creates a sense of constant flux. Like nature, these paintings have in a sense no beginning and no end, and despite their formal beauty they are in a constant state of becoming. Faced with a Turner landscape, we are overcome by a feeling of awe because the artist's sensitivity to atmospheric effects and the power and beauty of his imagery force in upon us an imaginative transposition, with the result that we feel ourselves surrounded by the forces of nature that he depicts. When confronted by a large abstract canvas by Pollock, and this is where scale is all-important, one is taken over by it because the viewer is literally confronted by a painting that is also a pictorial arena in which the painter symbolically acts out the drama inherent in being a romantic artist involved in the creation of his own myth.

The most successful of the 'all-over' drip paintings – and the greatest of all Pollock's works – tread that balance, on a knife-edge, between configurations of paint that evoke or have analogies with the rhythms and forces of nature, but which also cause one to measure oneself up to them in such a way that one is always aware of the human scale and of oneself as a human presence in relation to

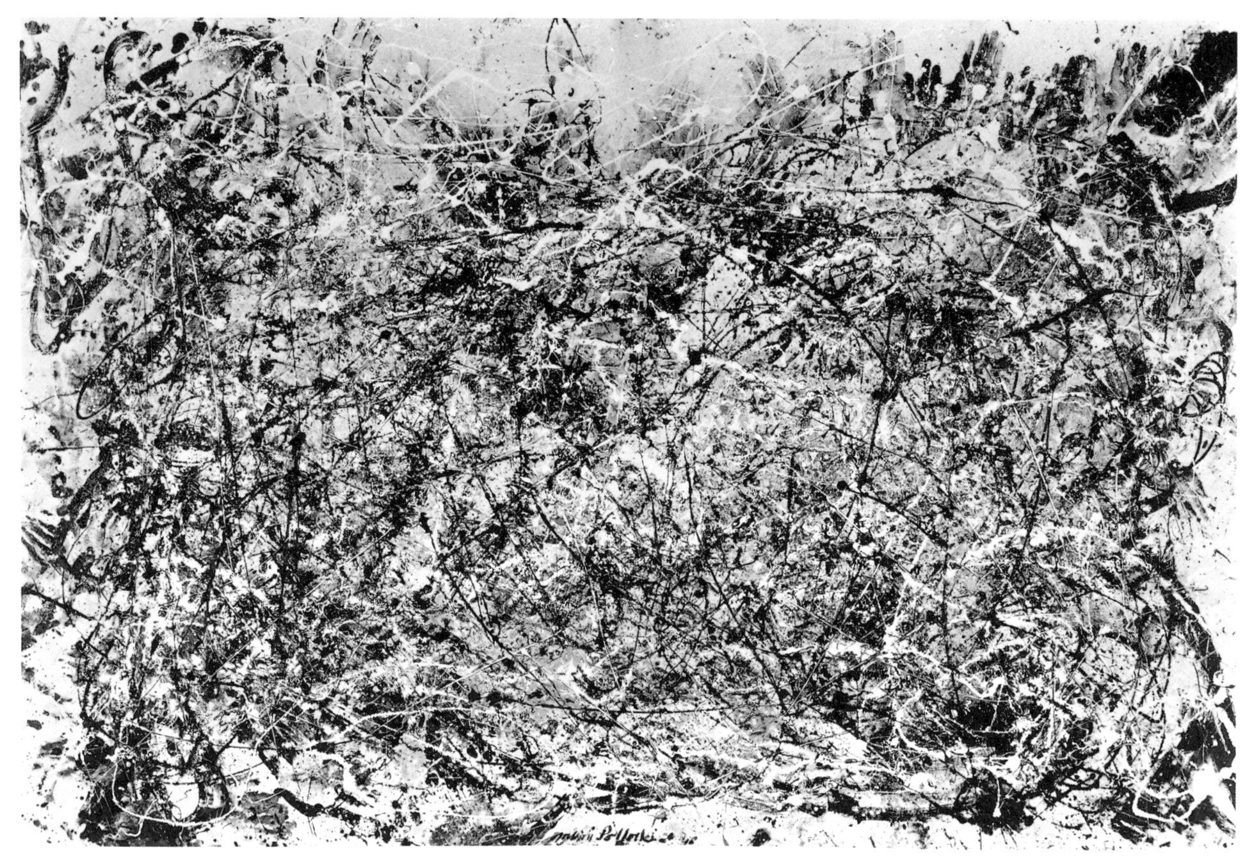

99 Pollock, *No. 1A*, oil and enamel on unprimed canvas, 1948.

them. Some of Pollock's earliest surviving works of the 1930s featured figures absorbed into landscape settings which sometimes appear to consume them. Subsequently he had become primarily a figure painter, and a painter of the human predicament in that he had embodied in his art the need for communication through increasingly abstract symbols which he hoped might have universal validity. Now he had found and realized himself most beautifully, most fully, most successfully, in works which invite analogies with the forces of nature but in which the human figure is present only by implication or totally absent. It is because of the equation or identification of body to paint surface in these paintings that, whatever their scale, they never dwarf us in the way that, for example, a thumb-sized watercolour notation of a storm at sea by Turner can.

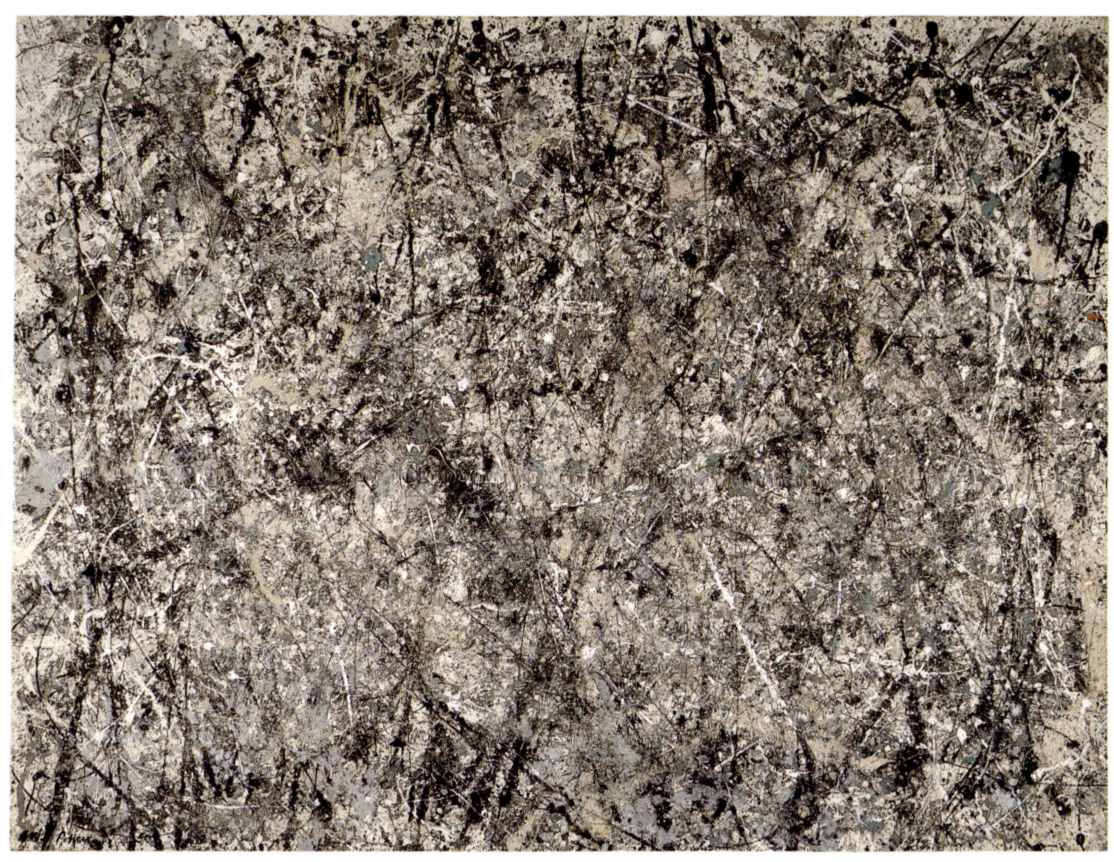

100 Pollock, *Lavender Mist,* oil and enamel and aluminium paint on canvas, 1950.

It has been suggested that whereas the atavistic, Jungian paintings executed between 1938 and 1946 are attempts to portray or symbolize the unconscious, the works which succeeded them become by contrast metaphors of the unconscious.[18] Yet the most purely abstract of Pollock's paintings produced between 1947 and 1951, and the subsequent reprises on them, are also layered with such a wealth of metaphor of so many different kinds – of the power and flux and surge and energy of nature, of the human body in relationship to it, and so forth – that the metaphors cancel each other out (in a reverse but analogous process to the way in
99 which the plethora of imagery in a Kandinsky cancels out figuration), so that we are left – how else can one put it – quite simply with abstract paintings. There is
100 even a sense in which Pollock was, in them, representing the unrepresentable.

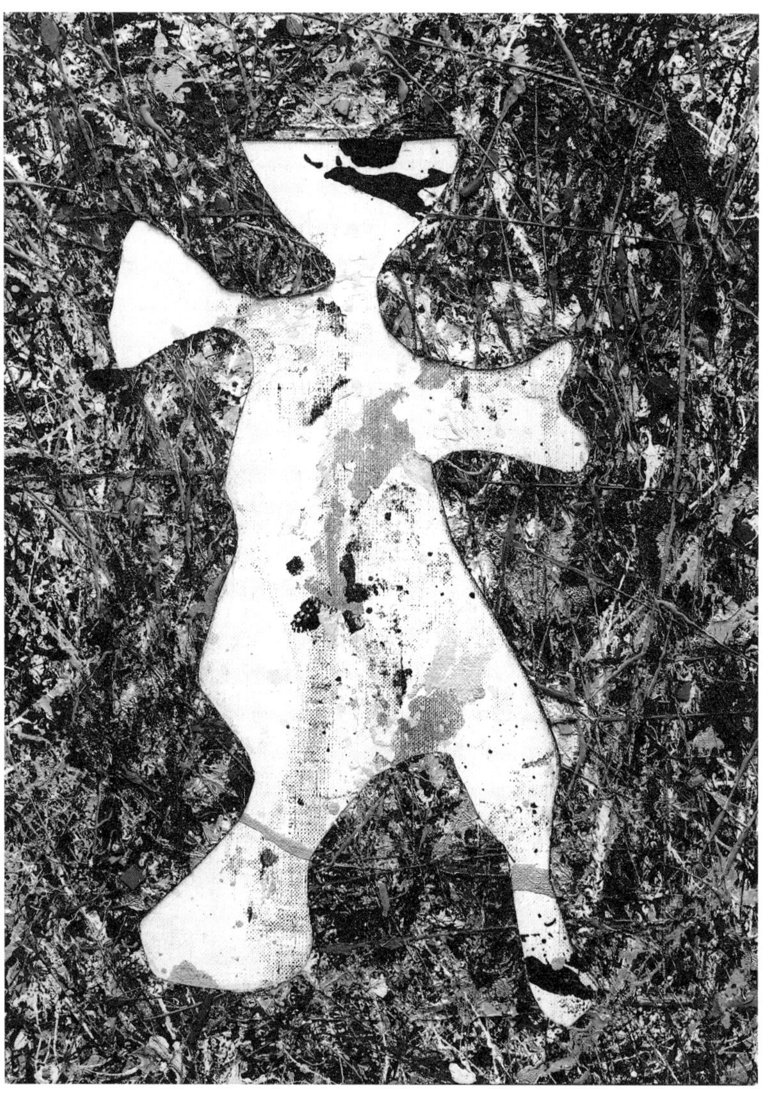

101 Pollock, *Cut Out*, oil on paper cut out over canvas, 1948.

Perhaps, in a very general way, this could be said of much of the most ambitious abstract art.

Pollock once declared flatly: 'Abstract painting is abstract. It confronts you.'[19] Yes, but he also said, 'I'm very representational some of the time and a little all of the time.' Even more revealingly, he remarked, 'When you're painting out of your unconscious, figures are bound to emerge.'[20] Insofar as it is possible to recreate imaginatively both the initial and the final dripping sessions or applications of paint, these tend to have been of a vertical emphasis. Thus with the benefit of hindsight one can relate them to or see them as evolving from the configurations of standing figures dating from the first half of the 1940s. Already in some of the paintings of 1948 and particularly in a few of 1949 (significantly it is those in which Pollock seems to have gone on working longest and in which the skeins of

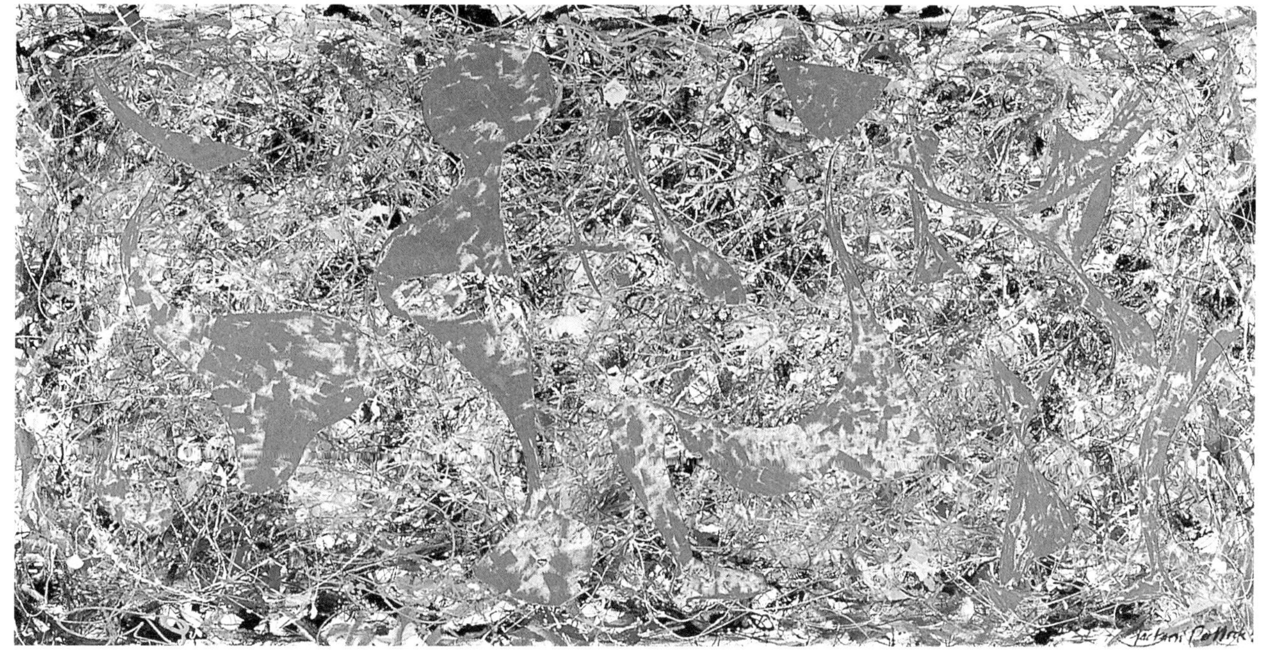

102 Pollock, *Out of the Web*, oil and enamel on masonite, cut-out, 1949.

paint become over-entangled and impacted) he seems to have felt that he had somehow lost the painting and to have experienced the need to reclaim it by scraping or cutting through to a few bolder, simpler forms or shapes. The results are invariably suggestive of body imagery and hence have the effect of reasserting once
101 more in a very palpable way the human presence. *Cut Out* of 1948 is the most
103 obvious and extreme example of this process. A comparison between *Autumn*
102 *Rhythm* (1950) and *Out of the Web* (1949) illustrates Pollock's working and
mental processes in an illuminating way. The rhythms in *Autumn Rhythm* are open and free; it is one of Pollock's most beautifully resolved compositions. The skeins of paint in *Out of the Web* have become coagulated, clotted, even as it were muscle-bound. The picture had become, in Pollock's own words, 'a mess'. He rescued it by introducing delicate suggestions of body imagery, achieved by cutting

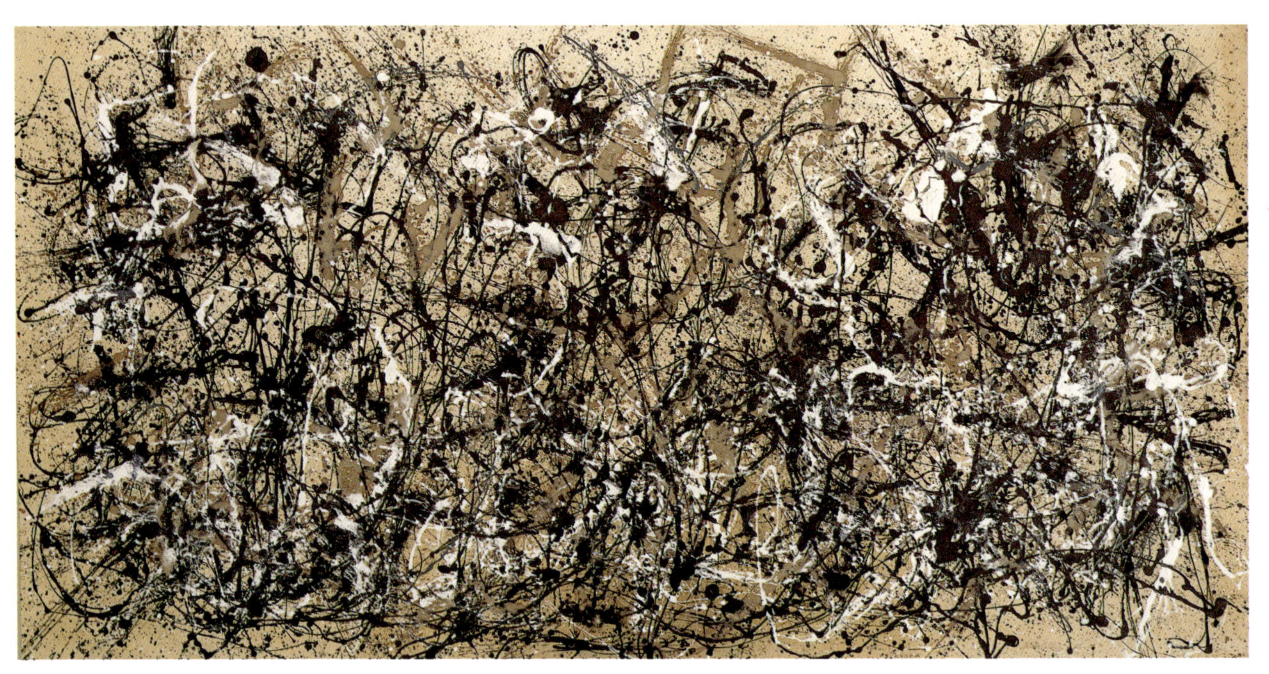

103 Pollock, *Autumn Rhythm*, oil on canvas, 1950.

or carving through to the support, in this case composition board. These configurations suggest those of the figures in *Search for a Symbol*. The skeined calligraphy, the symbols of communication which he had been seeking had at one point become ineloquent, mute. To reinstate their message, he was forced to reassert the presences which had initially evoked them.

In the early 1950s the figurative element reasserts itself in different ways. This is
104 apparent first of all, and perhaps most suggestively, in works such as *Echo* of 1951.
Here the configurations at the left in particular read as human presences, with the
lower extremities virtually duplicating the treatment of legs and feet developed in
the early 1940s. The work as a whole once again conveys that earlier sense of
ritual. In contrast to earlier works, however, the process has been reversed, in that
one senses not so much a progressive veiling or abstracting of imagery, but rather a
105 surfacing or re-emergence of it. Similarly in *Ocean Greyness* of 1953 atavistic
symbols no longer serve as a starting-point for evoking pictorial rhythms, as they
106 do, for example in *Composition with Masked Forms* of 1941, but rather seem to
swim up out of them. If the preceding great abstractions had stood in as metaphors
for the unconscious, and had hence evoked a partial descent into its mechanisms,
Pollock's work was now experiencing a move up from the unconscious into a
realm where controlled accident gives way to much more consciously manipulated
pictorial effects.

The figurative works of the 1950s are complemented by approximately the
107 same number of more purely abstract works, one of which, *Blue Poles* of 1952, is
a landmark in the history of abstraction and represents, the apogee of Pollock's
second and more consciously structured dripped manner. We have an eye-witness
account of the despair and frenzy that accompanied its creation,[21] yet the finished
work is characterized by a heightened sense of elegiac grandeur. By now Pollock
was almost certainly consulting the work of slightly older colleagues who had in
the previous five years flourished in the climate which he himself, more than other
single figure, had helped to create. Here the configurations of strongly articulated
uprights tipped off the strictly vertical suggest affinities with some of the most
heroic works of Barnett Newman. The element of cancellation that had characterized Pollock's art since the 1940s persists and is perhaps best and most
108 dramatically demonstrated by *The Deep*, a major work of 1953. This is a painting
that had been worked and built up in sooty blues and black until it became a
virtual monochrome. Pollock then worked inwards from the edges of the canvas
in white enamel, harking back to earlier practices, but simultaneously reversing
the processes used in works like *Out of the Web* and *Cut Out*, where imagery had
been retrieved not by painting back over and blocking out, but rather by arbitrar-
ily superimposing it or cutting through the surface to it. Imagery can itself be
abstract, witness the works of Mondrian which are images in their totality, and
the configurations of forms that grace Malevich's Suprematist canvases. The
image here achieved stands for and symbolizes more vividly than in any other
work by Pollock the unconscious itself. Again, the formal purity of the work and
the planar ambiguity – the darks clearly stand behind the whites, but the whites
also read as a foil to the central abstract imagery – call to mind the contemporary
work of Clyfford Still, with whom Pollock briefly felt himself in sympathy.

The story of the last three to four years of Pollock's life is, however, not just that of the oscillation between abstraction and the recovery or resurfacing of figurative imagery. Looking at these late canvases, one cannot escape an overwhelming

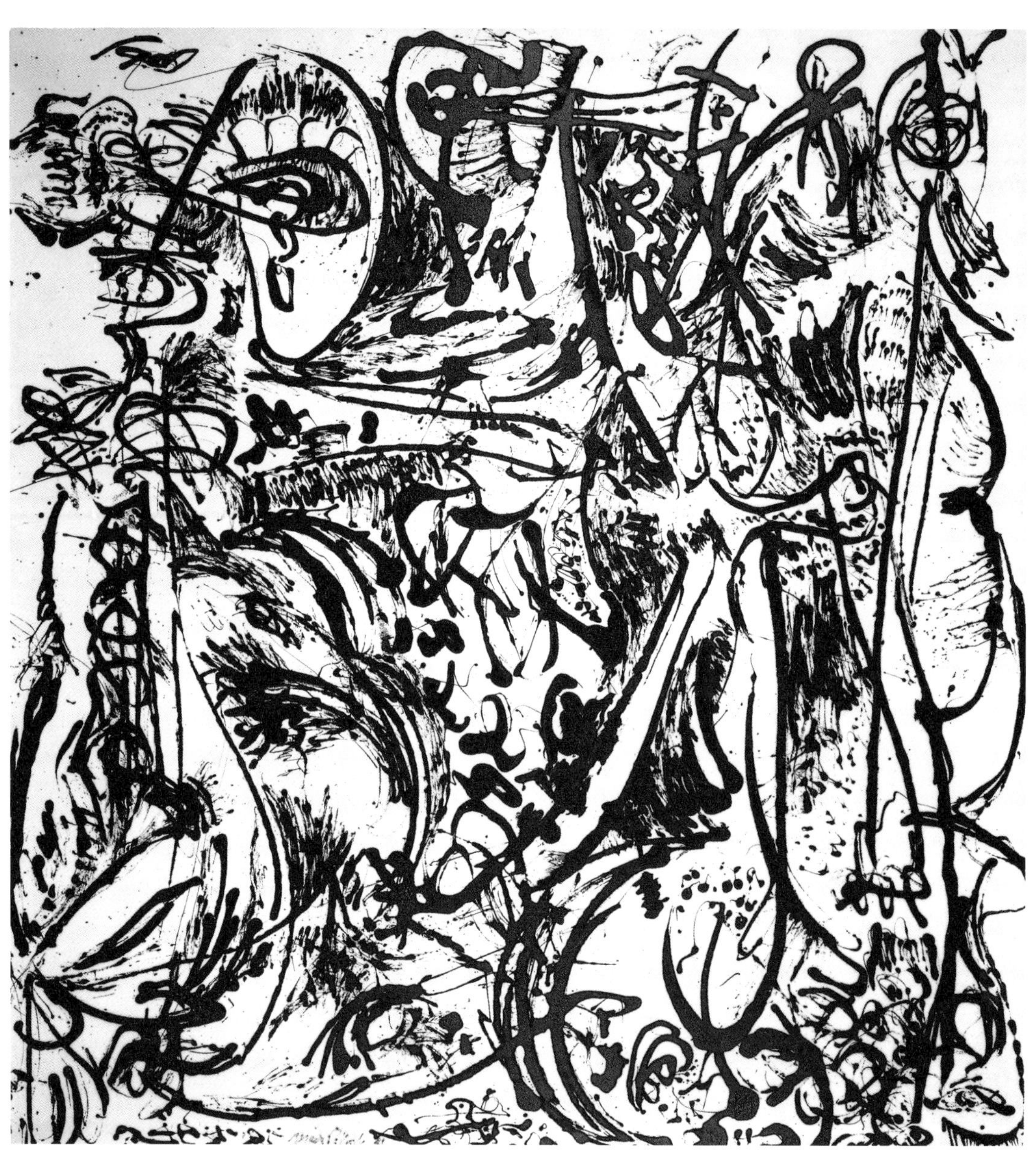

104 Pollock, *Echo*, enamel on unprimed canvas, 1951.

impression that Pollock was unconsciously, and once again symbolically, attempting to re-enact the pictorial events and sequences that had formed and marked his emergence first as a significant and then as a great painter in the years between 1942 and 1947. He was obviously aware of the fact that the greatest and most original of his works were the abstractions produced between 1947 and 1953. For Pollock there could be no absolutes because of the restlessness and instability of his temperament and vision. In a very different way from Mondrian, who had rejected the concept of an absolute, Pollock was nevertheless aware of it. He saw or sensed it as being embedded in the steady surge of creativity which had carried

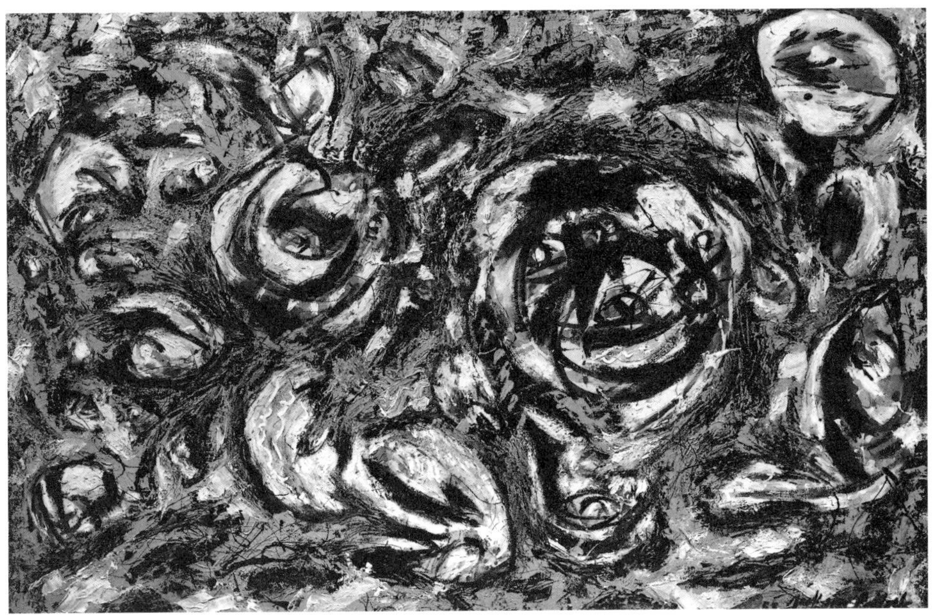

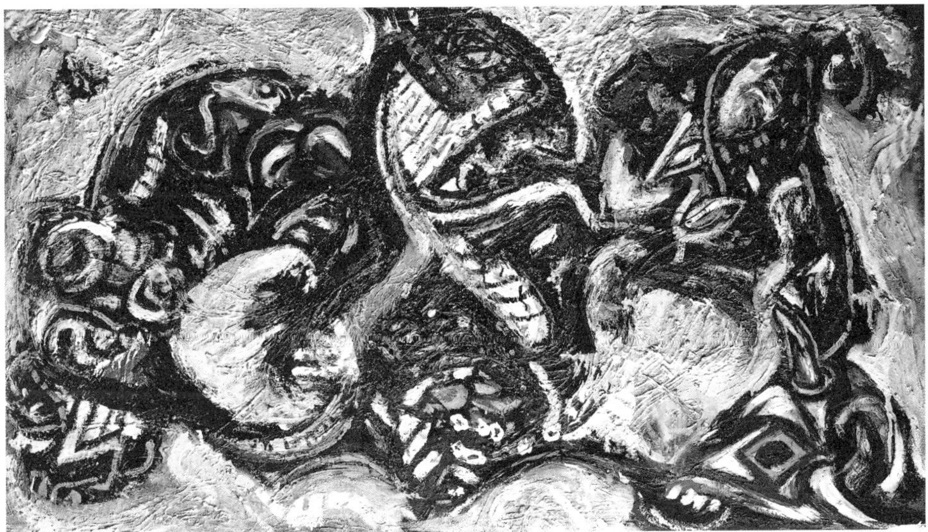

105 Pollock, *Ocean Greyness*, oil and duco on canvas, 1953.

106 Pollock, *Composition with Masked Forms*, oil on canvas, 1941.

art onwards since time immemorial. He must have known, if only subconsciously, that in his greatest works he had, so to speak, gone beyond himself, transcended his struggles. Despite their formal complexity, his best abstractions were distillations of his vision of painting as calligraphic messages or semaphores to the totality of art, to the greater than himself. Yet, like so many of his contemporaries in American art, he was obsessed with the idea of art as self-discovery. 'Painting is self-discovery', he declared. 'Every good artist paints what he is.'[22] And the facts of his private life would seem to bear out the assumption that, despite having found himself as a painter, he had not succeeded in finding himself as a person.

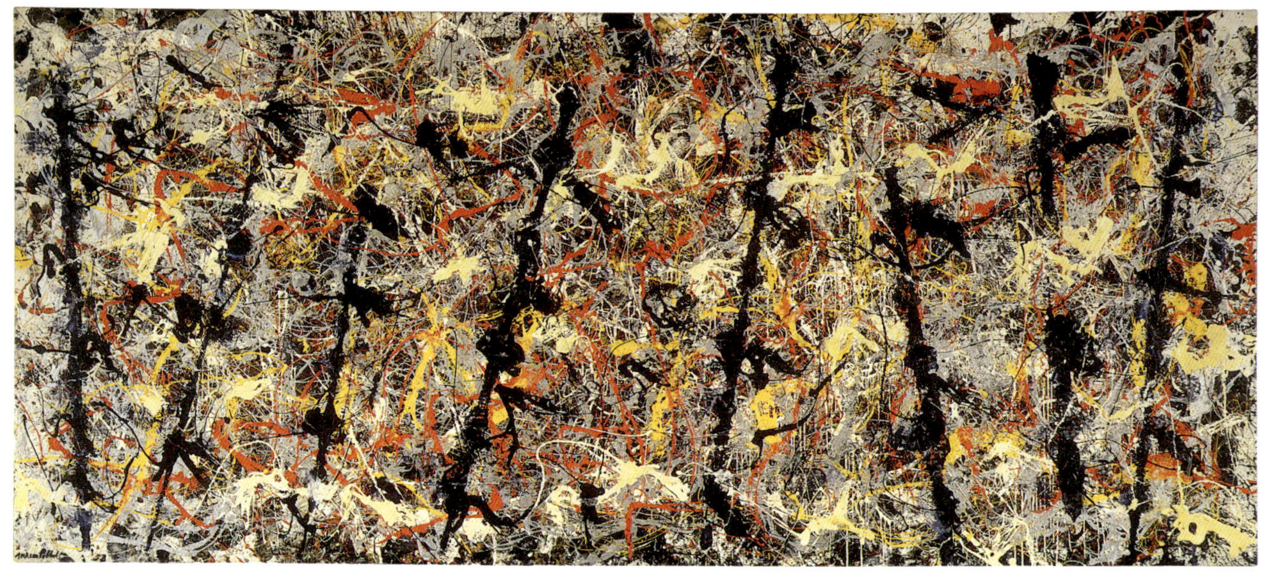

107 Pollock, *Blue Poles*, oil, enamel and aluminium paint with glass on canvas, 1952.

108 Pollock, *The Deep*, oil and enamel paint on canvas, 1953.

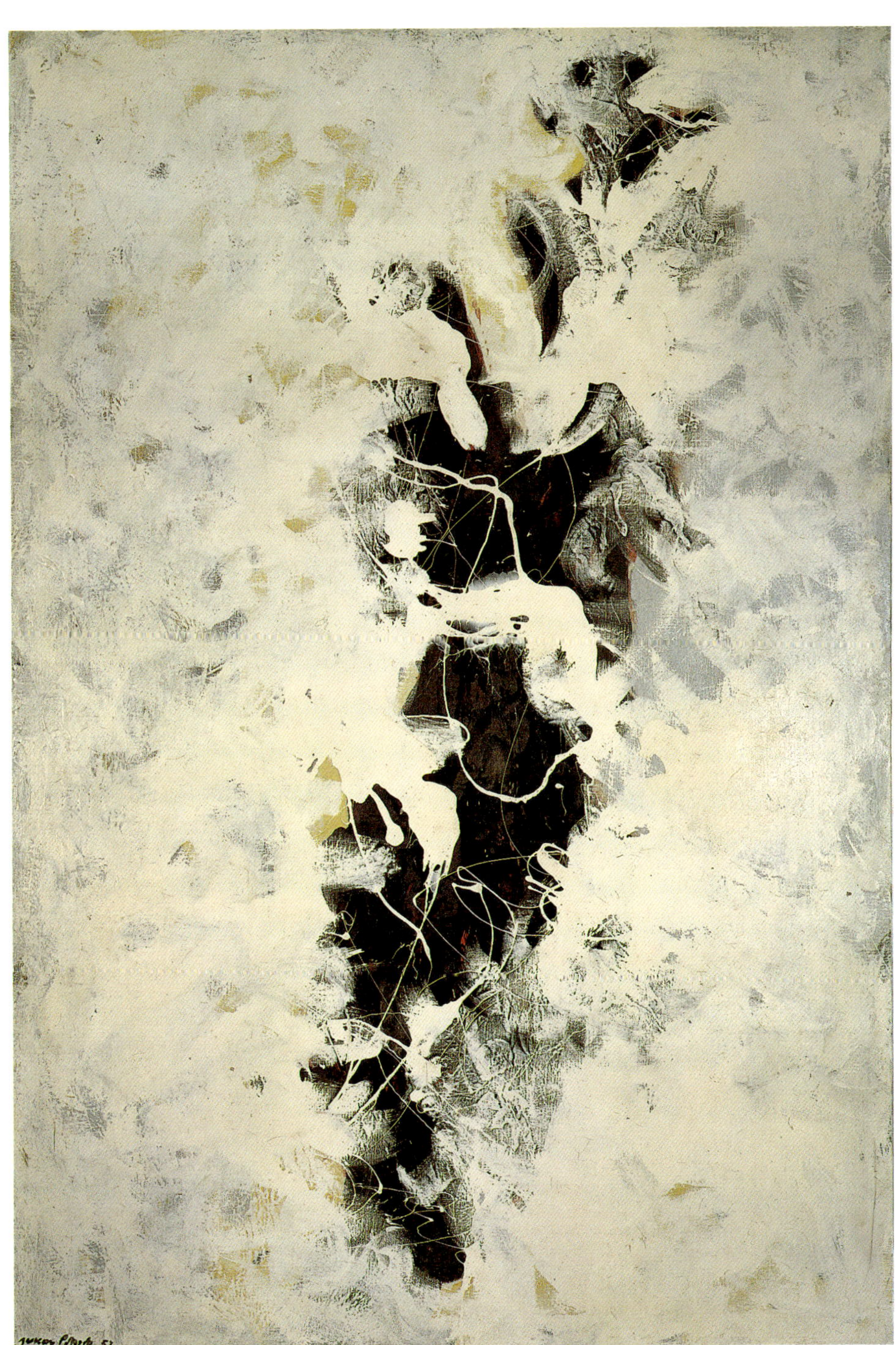

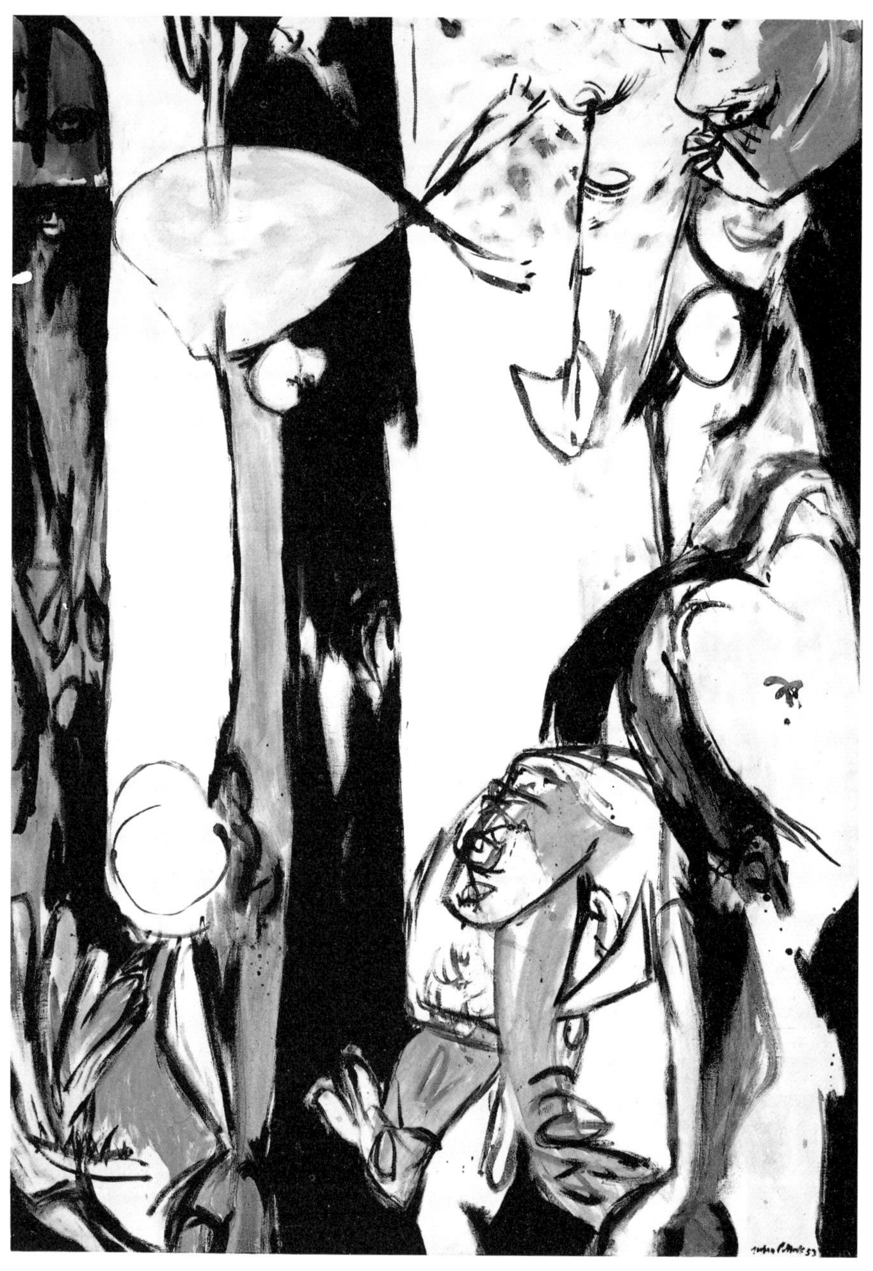

109 Pollock, *Easter and the Totem*, oil on canvas, 1953.

From 1953 onwards Pollock's output declines and indeed during 1954 he produced almost nothing. Despite his relative youth, certain works of Pollock's final years betray signs of fatigue and strain. *Easter and the Totem* of 1953, for example, 109
recalls his own work executed ten years earlier, which had been indebted to the compositional procedures of Synthetic Cubism, and now there are also references to those works by Matisse which had finally acknowledged such procedures. But the sense of excitement and discovery has evaporated. The feeling of insecurity

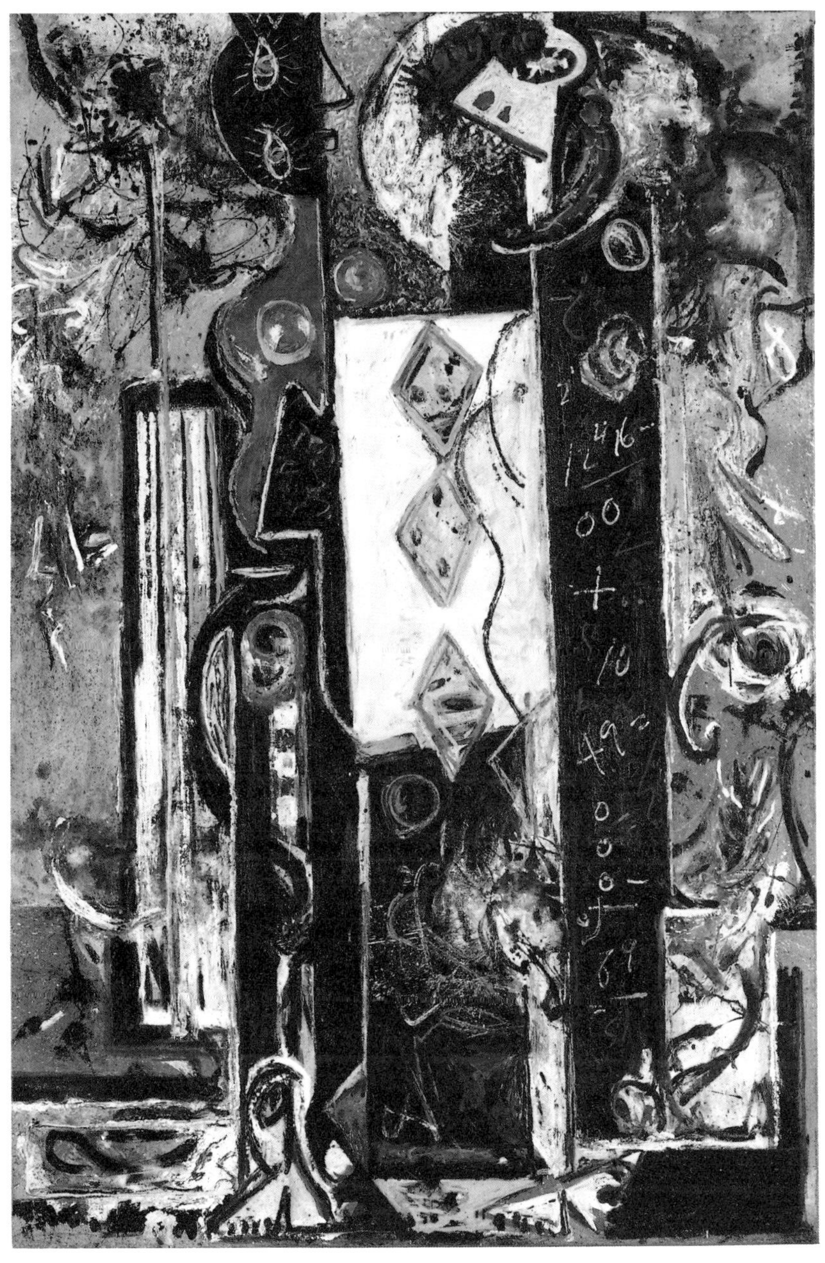

110 Pollock, *Male and Female*, oil on canvas, 1942.

sensed in many of the late paintings is evinced in some of his statements of the time. Pollock seems to have recognized that there were certain gaps, certain visual lacunae in his artistic self-education. Yet the consultations with Matisse, for
110 example, are faint-hearted. A comparison between *Easter and the Totem* and *Male and Female* of 1942 demonstrates that Pollock's rites of exorcism were losing some of their potency. A brief flurry of activity in 1955, which confirms and restates Pollock's personal commitment to gesture and through it to abstraction, produced

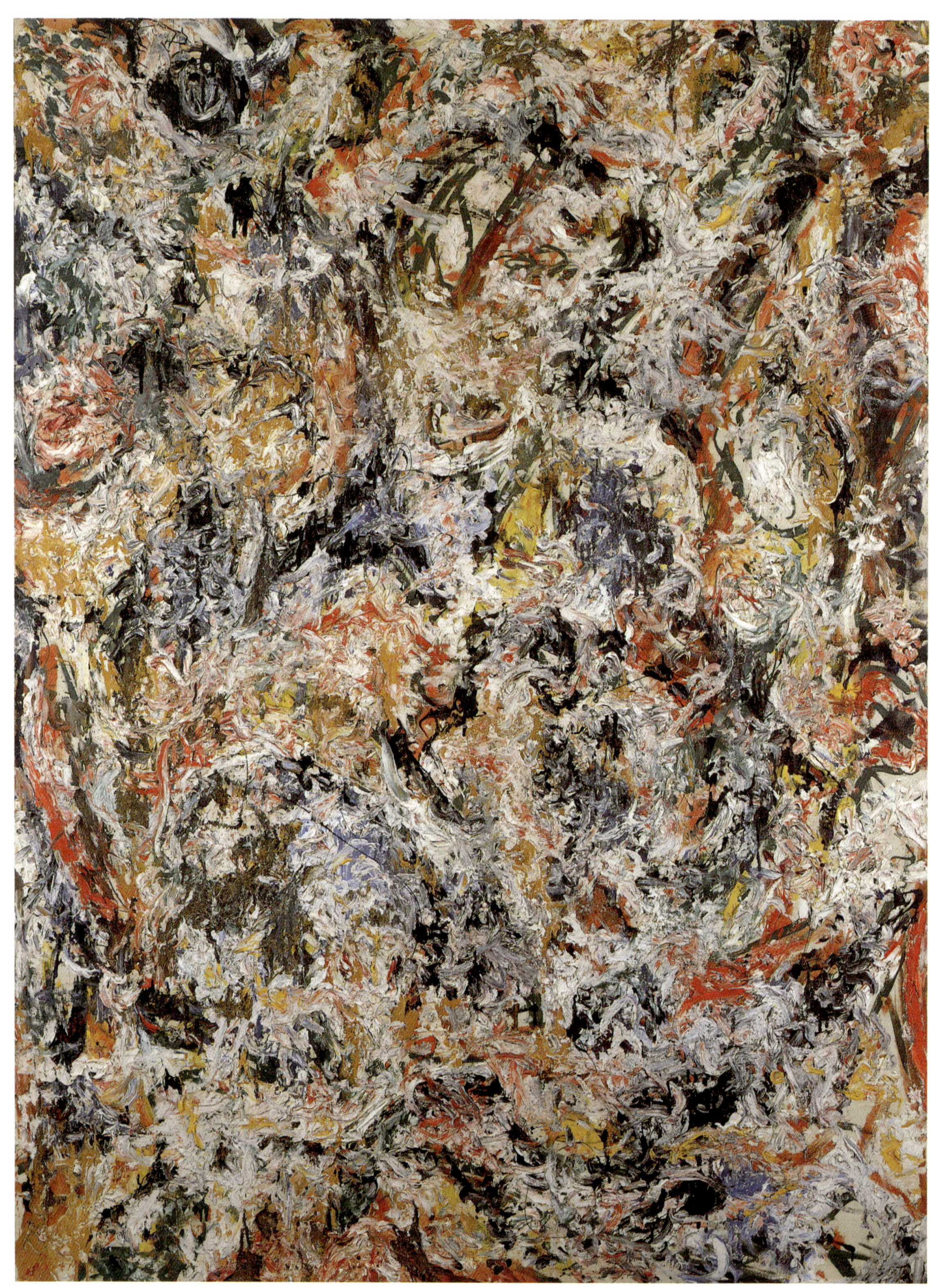

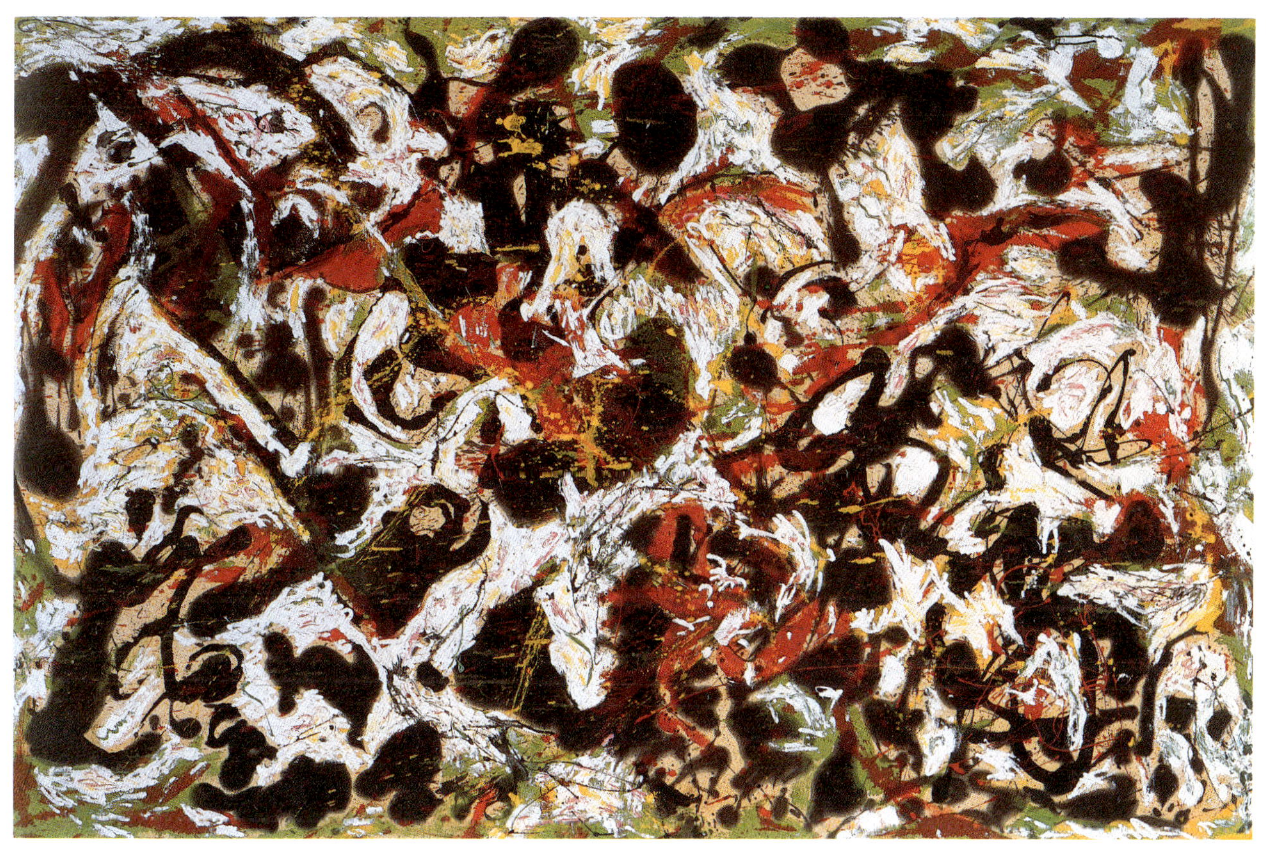

111 Pollock, *Scent*, oil on canvas, 1953–5.

112 Pollock, *Search*, oil and enamel paint on canvas, 1955.

works such as *Scent*, a latter-day and indeed beautifully fragrant if aesthetically 111
more self-conscious version of *Eyes in the Heat* of 1946. Most poignant, when we
remember the importance the artist sometimes attached to titles, is *Search*, also of 112
1955. This painting recalls in its colour harmonies the tortured but dynamically
charged *The Flame*, a work dating from some fifteen years earlier. Pollock's move 77
into abstraction between 1947 and 1949 had been liberating and exhilarating. The task of keeping this abstraction alive and charged with meaning had also put a terrible strain upon him as an artist, just as it would upon countless of his lesser successors. His untimely death in a road accident while drunk in 1956 can be regarded as a virtual act of self-immolation. Earlier in the year, the Museum of Modern Art had honoured Pollock by asking him to inaugurate a series of solo exhibitions to be called *Work in Progress*. When the exhibition opened in December, Pollock was no longer alive to witness the lessons to be learned from it.

5

Newman, Rothko, Still and the reductive image

Barnett Newman, Mark Rothko and Clyfford Still were all born between 1903 and 1905; they were thus some ten years older than Pollock, and they achieved their fully mature, abstract idioms more or less simultaneously and immediately after their junior's 'breakthrough' years. This reinforces the point that most of the great revolutionary, pioneering abstractionists found their way into abstraction relatively late in their careers. In the case of the Americans this is doubly remarkable since, by the time they hit their respective strides, abstraction had been recognized as a viable pictorial language for over thirty years. Clement Greenberg, who was to become the most influential formalist critic of his age (and who for that reason is now much decried), maintained that in New York studios in the second half of the 1930s abstraction was the burning issue.[1] A. E. Gallatin opened his Museum of Living Art in 1933 with an exhibition entitled 'The Evolution of Abstract Art'. In 1936 Alfred Barr mounted his legendary 'Cubism and Abstract Art' at the Museum of Modern Art in New York. That same year the American Abstract Artists Association was founded. Several of the thirty-nine artists who participated in its first exhibition had belonged to the earlier Abstraction Création group which had strong links with Paris. The arrival of Mondrian in New York in 1940 was a major event; he was by now a mythical figure to other artists – but he had trodden his path so single-mindedly that, although he had followers, no heir to his position had emerged. To even the most informed American artists, Malevich was little more than a name. And despite the steady influx of leading Bauhaus figures throughout the 1930s, the climate of abstraction in America, as in Europe, was tepid. Spirituality had become at this time almost a derisive term. Much of the abstraction being produced on both continents was either of a somewhat academic nature or had fallen into the decorative mode that was so much feared by Kandinsky.

The careers of Newman, Rothko and Still raise another point of general interest in the evolution of abstract art: they were none of them naturally talented, as Pollock had been, and for that matter neither were Mondrian and Malevich. It says a lot about the nature of abstraction that it was the vision of these artists and not their natural gifts that enabled them to turn themselves into great artists. They believed above all else that abstract art could speak of new and profound pictorial

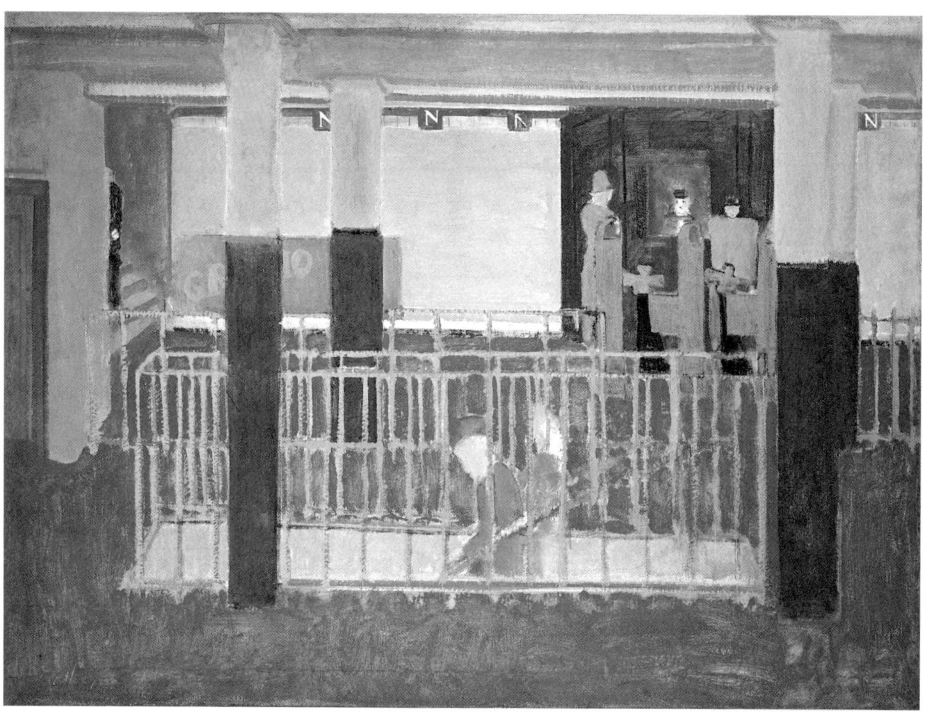

113 Mark Rothko, *Subway Scene*, oil on canvas (hardboard), 1938.

truths. The case of Pollock is somewhat different. It was through his use of abstraction that he succeeded in changing, or at least modifying, the face of much succeeding art, and this he recognized, although while he had followers he had no successors. The purity of the disciplines of abstraction, however, he found too constricting. Rothko, too, spoke often of making no distinction between abstraction and representational painting – but within the context of his own work his example belies his words. A great wealth of scholarship on American art of the 1940s has been unleashed during the past two decades; yet two artists, Newman and Still, continue to present us with problems, in that their artistic origins remain veiled in a certain amount of mystery. None of Newman's very early work appears to have survived. Still was prolific but only a fraction of the works that were in his studio at the time of his death in 1980 have been exhibited.[2]

Rothko, on the other hand, we can now see more or less whole; and it is in a sense paradoxical that an artist who produced works of such mystery – and they are mysterious if only in the sense that it is almost impossible to analyze why they exert such an extraordinary spell on the beholder – should be at the same time one of the great abstractionists in whose art it is possible to chart the slide from representation into abstraction with clarity. This analysis is possible partly at least because Rothko was honest in acknowledging his sources, both visually and verbally. The *Subway* paintings of *c.* 1936–8, to one of which he later attached 113
importance,[3] convey the mood of the Depression years. They are melancholy; the figures within them are wraith-like and make no contact with each other. They are organized in terms of compositions that are markedly governed by verticals and

horizontals which, as they intersect, form a kind of grid encapsulating spatial cells. Compositionally, and thematically insofar as they represent the descent into a Stygian, subterranean world, they look forward to the darkly elegiac but slightly
114 menacing mood of Rothko's penultimate manner.

None of the three American painters under consideration here was a theorist, even in the retrospective fashion that Mondrian, Malevich and, to a lesser extent, Kandinsky all were. Newman, Rothko and Still were more deeply cultured than Pollock, and all were more articulate. Newman, the most vocal, was that peculiarly American phenomenon, a latter-day oracle. In his utterances Still was the most Delphic and certainly the most abrasive. In the 1940s Rothko wrote revealingly about the processes of the new art, although it is significant that after he had achieved a fully emotive visual language he ceased to express himself in print and regretted ever having done so.

All three men were intellectuals, but promoted an art that was not. In view of this bias, it is doubly remarkable that up till the late 1940s their views about the direction that a new American art should follow, and the destination they had marked out for it, were in advance of their practice. Their European progenitors were all, in different ways, visionaries and had dreamed of an art of the future; their theory, however, was mostly at the service of visual discoveries already made. The Americans saw themselves as the art of the future before they had yet got to it. They were beating on the doors of a visual territory as yet undiscovered. This situation came about, in part at least, because of the fact that they found a lot of the abstract art to which they were exposed insufficiently eloquent. Then, although two of them (Newman and Still) came to express hostility to the premises of Surrealism, the Americans – because of their own cultural and geographic situation – found themselves profiting from the intellectually liberating properties of Surrealism in a more down-to-earth and visceral fashion than European artists of their own generation. It was because of this that, while capitalizing on its heritage, the Americans were able to distance themselves from the more esoteric aspects of Surrealism, from its game-playing, from its somewhat incestuous ultra-sophistication that went hand in hand with a slightly infantile desire to shock not simply the intellectual community at large, but rather themselves and each other. There is a very real sense in which the Surrealists represented the culmination of a European romantic sensibility which spans over a century and a half, while the Americans represent a reappraisal of those sensibilities and their most fundamental tenets. The Surrealist expatriates formed in many ways an enclosed community; but the febrile intellectual climate they engendered, which was ultimately to be their greatest contribution to cultural history, was of inestimable importance to emergent American art. 'We are the mind's agitators', the Surrealists had proclaimed;[4] and so they were.

The most revealing document for an understanding of the somewhat fragile but potentially explosive situation in New York in the early 1940s is the letter written to the *New York Times*, published on 13 June 1943; signed by Rothko and his friend Adolph Gottlieb, the letter is a reply to a critic who had expressed bafflement at their work.[5] In fact the letter was originally written by Rothko and was then modified by Gottlieb with the help of Newman. Gottlieb was at this point an intimate friend of Rothko's and one of the most seminal figures on the New York art scene; he was possessed of a rigorous and objective mind, and – more than any other figure of his group and generation with the exception of Newman, but

114 Mark Rothko, *Black on Maroon,* oil on canvas (hardboard), 1958.

before him – saw that both Surrealism and abstraction pointed the way forward, but that neither movement was totally fulfilling current artistic needs and expectations. As late as 1947, Clement Greenberg was referring to Gottlieb as 'perhaps 115
the leading exponent of a new and indigenous school of symbolism . . . ' which includes, he goes on to say, Rothko, Still and Newman.[6]

The letter makes five points, and it is worth quoting them in full, not just for the elements that are, in a sense, simplistic and that many European artists, and in particular the Surrealists, would simply not have troubled to voice (and this applies to Clauses 1 and 2), but above all for subsequent proclamations that are prophetic:

1) 'To us art is an adventure into an unknown world which can be explored only by those willing to take risks.'
2) 'This world of the imagination is fancy-free and violently opposed to reason.'
3) 'It is our function as artists to make the spectator see our way, not his.' (and this is startling because not one of the pioneering European abstractionists would have made such a suggestion so aggressively).

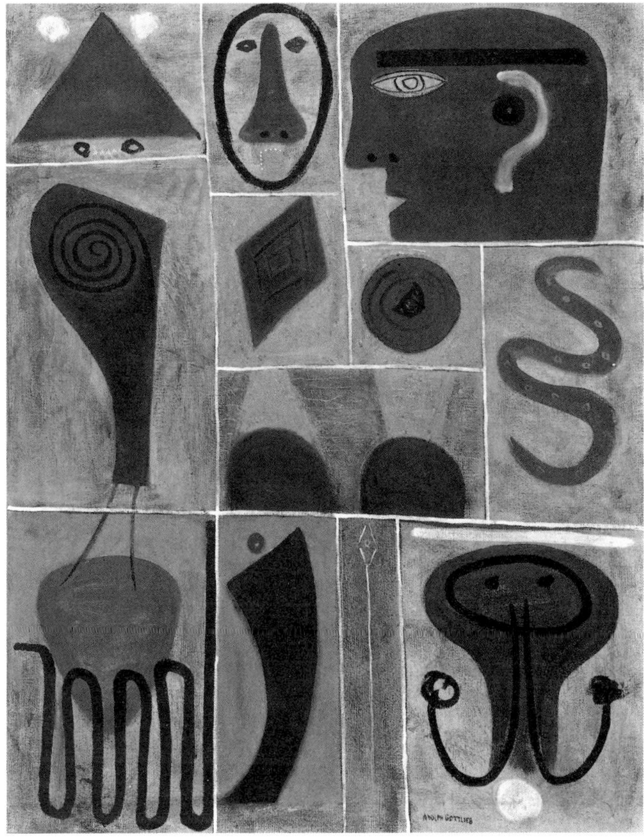

115 Adolph Gottlieb, *The Voyager's Return*, oil on canvas, 1946.

4) And now that we are on to anti-Surrealist and potentially original territory: 'We favour the simple expression of the complex thought. We are for the large shape because it has the impact of the unequivocal. We are for flat forms because they destroy illusion and reveal truth.'
5) 'It is a widely accepted notion among painters that it does not matter what one paints so long as it is well painted. This is the essence of academicism. There is no such thing as good painting about nothing. We assert that the subject matter is crucial and that only that subject matter is valid which is tragic and timeless. That is why we profess spiritual kinship with primitive and archaic art.'

What emerges from the letter is, in the first place, an acceptance of the liberating properties of the Surrealist ethos combined with a rejection of absolutely everything that they stood for visually; this is coupled with an acknowledgment of some of the formalist conclusions reached by international abstraction of the 1930s, while at the same time recognizing the necessity to imbue it with a new or renewed cosmic significance. Mondrian had sought to eliminate the tragic from art; the

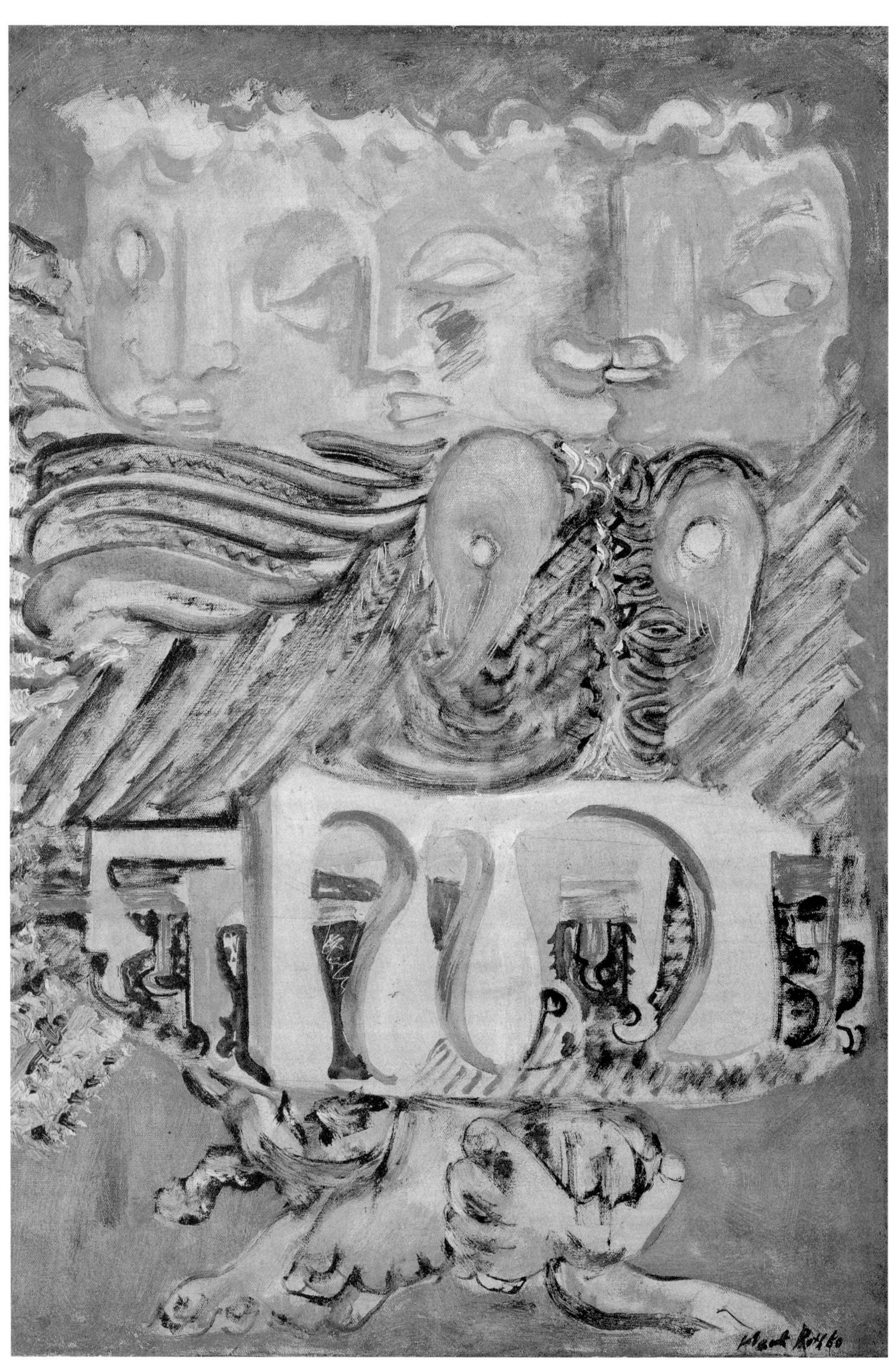

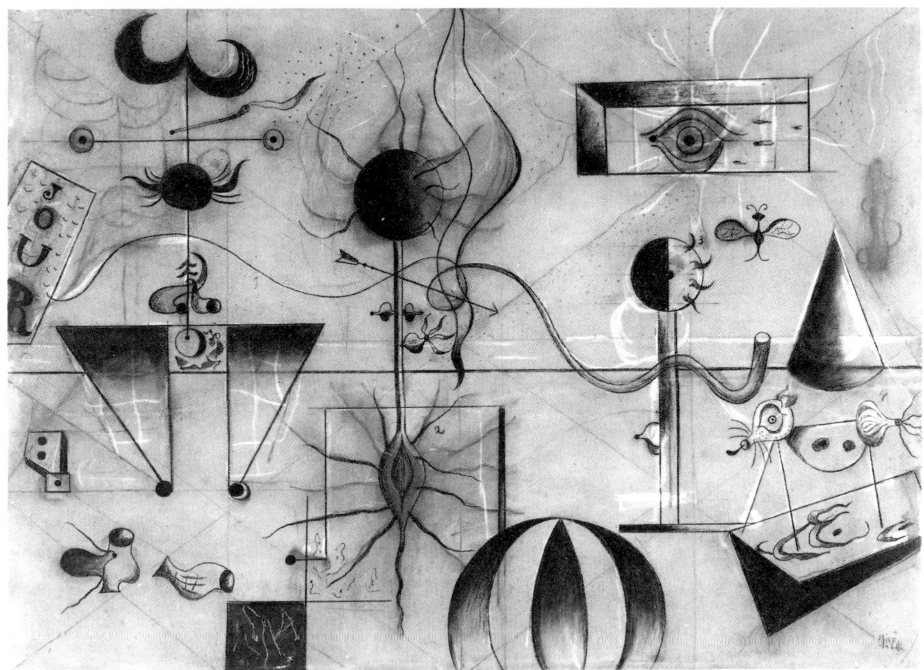

Americans – ironically, in the face of what subsequently became of so much American art – were out to cultivate it.

116 In the light of the claims made in the letter Rothko's *Omen of the Eagle* of 1942, one of the works which had indirectly provoked it, comes as a total anticlimax. Yet it is also one of the most revealing of Rothko's mythologizing works. While studying in high school Rothko had read the Greeks and had developed in particular an admiration for Herodotus. This painting, he tells us, was inspired by Aeschylus' *Oresteia* trilogy. However, he also emphasized the point that the picture does not illustrate any particular incident in the drama but 'is concerned with the Spirit of Myth which is generic to all myth at all times'.[7] The picture demands to be read from the top down in strata, layers, both visually and psychologically, and this lends the work an archaeological quality which sets it apart from Surrealist antecedents. Each horizontal band declares a separate stylistic source. At the top are heads referring to masks of Greek tragedy. Underneath are bird-like heads found so often in Surrealist paintings of the 1920s and 1930s, here embedded in wing forms probably derived from Mesopotamian reliefs. Below are forms which are phallic but which also have architectural connotations. And it was Rothko's profound and enduring interest in the architecture of the past that was one of the factors that separated him so sharply from even his closest colleagues. The tangle of feet below again declares an allegiance to Surrealist sources; the foot, for
117 example, was an obsessive concern of Miró, the Surrealist for whom Rothko was to entertain the most lasting admiration.

However, the real importance of *Omen of the Eagle*, inadequate as a work of art though the painting may be, is that it puts us very directly in touch with what was

116 Mark Rothko, *Omen of the Eagle*, oil and graphite on canvas, 1942.

117 Joan Miró, *The Family*, vine charcoal, white pastel and red conté on oatmeal paper, 1924.

to be, without question, the most important and enduring of Rothko's intellectual sources. In the 1930s he had discovered Nietzsche's *Birth of Tragedy*; he revisited the work at intervals throughout his life, and towards the end of it he was planning an essay on his debt to this great thinker. It was a debt that was in fact shared by many of his closest colleagues but felt so deeply only by Still. This early treatise by Nietzsche was to be of seminal importance to Rothko. In its attempt to contact the complex structure of Hellenistic thought and ritual in forms that might make it seem relevant to contemporary society, *Omen of the Eagle* is a Nietzschean picture. Despite the uplifting radiance evident in so much of his work, Rothko was by nature basically a pessimist, and the pessimistic currents of thought prevalent in the 1940s, culminating in the interest in Existentialism that touched so many American intellectuals late in the decade, coincided with his nature; Kierkegaard in particular held him in thrall. This intellectual climate lent depth to Rothko's own creative processes while helping to subvert him emotionally. His identification with Nietzsche, at a deep and intuitive level, sustained him, on the other hand, to the very end. Ultimately Nietzsche accorded the Greek Dionysiac and tragic mode supremacy; but its counterpart, the radiant Apollonian solution, was also to elevate him as it did Rothko.

The *Birth of Tragedy* is centred on Greek art (its alternative title was *Hellenism and Pessimism*), and Nietzsche suggests that it was through the sublimation of art that the Greeks, who felt so acutely a sense of helplessness in the face of the forces of nature, history and destruction, yet achieved survival. Rothko's haunting of the Near Eastern and Greco-Roman rooms of the Metropolitan Museum was a source of inspiration to him because through them he could absorb some of the intangible ethos of a spirit that had been conjured up by his greatest intellectual mentor. Yet there was torment in his exaltation, a torment which Nietzsche would have understood. Although Rothko rejected Orthodox Judaism, it was a complementary and – even if only at a subconscious level – quite obviously a deep and central part of his cultural heritage, and one which, because of its edicts on certain forms of representation, helped propel him towards abstraction. Again, it added to his intellectual unrest. Despite its prophetic grandeur, Nietzsche's thought is a deeply wounded thought. So it was to be with Rothko's art; his painting is wounded painting. Ultimately both men, Nietzsche and Rothko, would succumb to the Furies which they had sought to exorcise.

Rothko now began to look more closely at Surrealist art and to instruct himself not only in its outward pictorial manifestations, but also in terms of the journey inwards and downwards which Surrealism's psychoanalytic bias had encouraged. Rothko had a knowledge of both Freud and Jung, and indeed by now their ideas had seeped so deeply into the general cultural ethos that it would have been impossible at the time for any alert intellectual in New York to ignore them. Rothko's delving into his own psyche reinforced the archeologizing tendency in his work in another sense. He was now also going 'underground' in that he was consulting textbook diagrams of geographical, and, above all, palaeontological, layering and cell development. In this his work had certain parallels with Kandinsky's final Paris period; but Rothko was not interested either in patterning and multiplication or in putting things under the microscope, as were Kandinsky and, subsequently, Newman. Rather he was after reduction and isolation, into a movement backwards, into archaeological origins. His search for the primeval, like that of his closest associates, was not – as in the case of Pollock – involved primar-

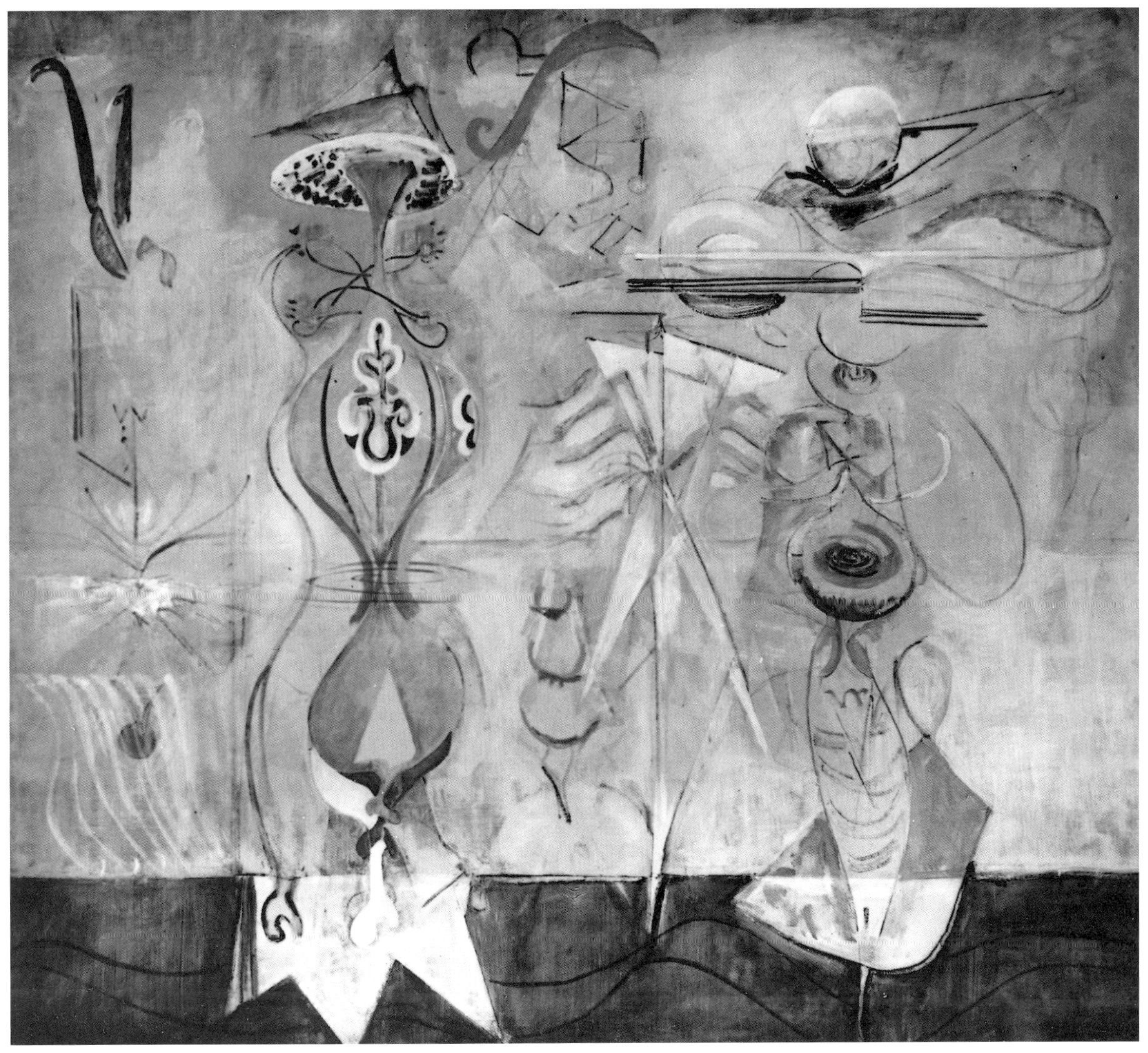

118 Mark Rothko, *Slow Swirl at the Edge of the Sea*, oil on canvas, 1944.

ily with discovering a pictorial *lingua franca* that would unite all artists across the frontiers of space and time, but rather with a process of a scraping bare, with an attempted new beginning. This quality of scraping bare is reinforced in his choice at this time of watercolour and gouache as mediums, of wet techniques in which the paint dries in such a way as to allow the luminosity of the ground or support to be always apparent.

118 In a seminal work dating from 1944, entitled *Slow Swirl at the Edge of the Sea*, two hybrid figures – male and female – are rendered by configurations which had been largely pioneered by Miró, and which subsequently had become universal coinage in Surrealist parlance, although in Surrealist art such composite figures are invariably loaded with an eroticism that is notably absent in Rothko's figures. His presences do not so much face each other, but rather confront the viewer very

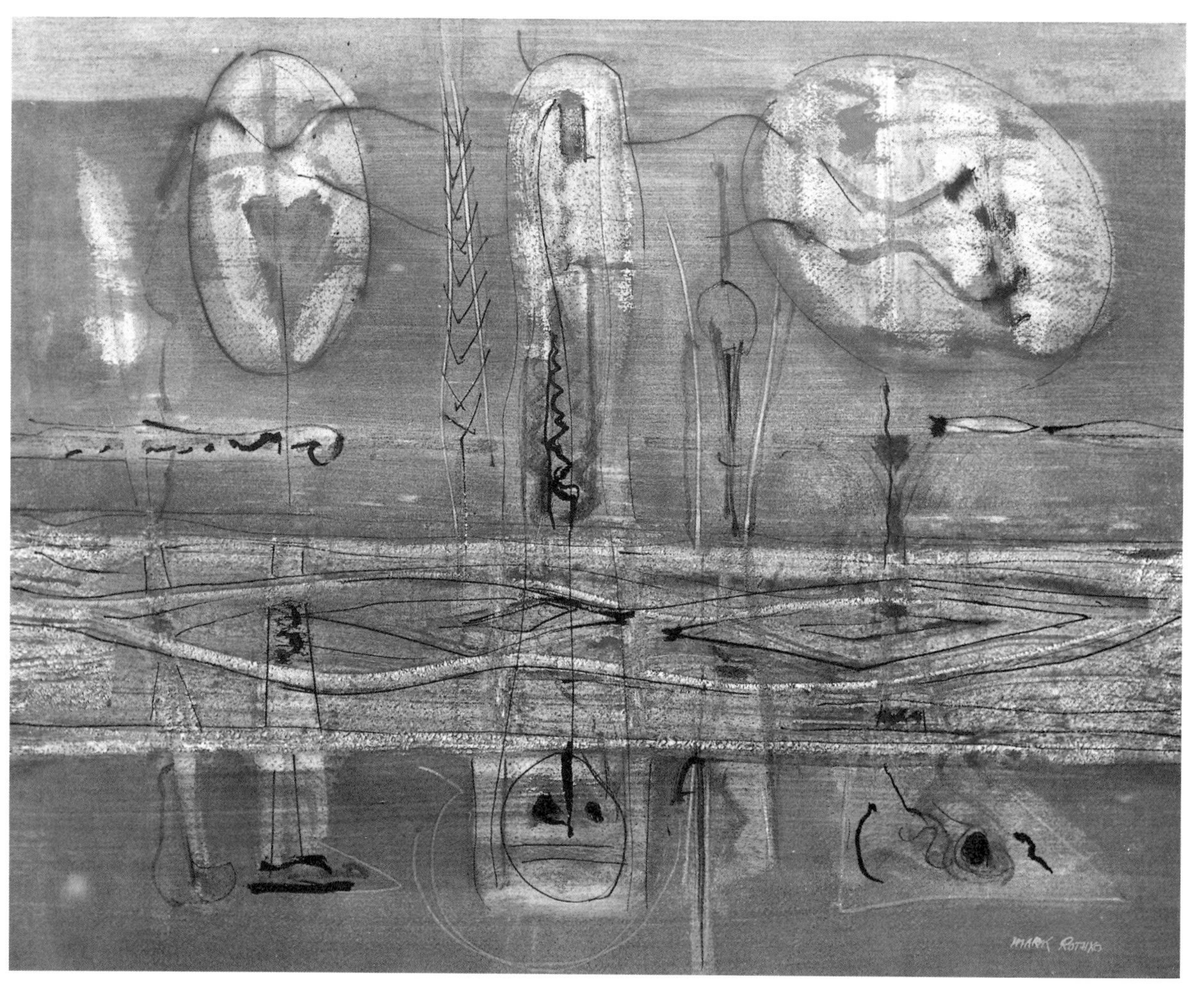

119 Mark Rothko, *Entombment 1*, gouache on paper, 1946.

directly. The spaces between them and around them are activated by totemic, Miróesque markings, and figures and space seem to partake of the same washed substance or ether. Despite Rothko's interest in the primordial, his art of the time has about it a quality of fastidiousness and delicacy that sets it apart from that of his contemporaries.

119 Some of Rothko's configurations, those of *Entombment I* of 1946, for example, remind one of his admiration for Klee, master of the miniature and – double irony – the least single-minded of all the great twentieth-century artists. *Entombment I* also invites comparison with the archeologizing, stratified landscapes that Max Ernst was producing in the mid-1930s. Whereas the Ernst scenes look lunar and fanciful, the Rothko, despite its petrified fragility, appears to be speaking of the human condition, of endurance in the face of imponderable forces.The sensation of stratification has now been shifted to the areas behind the hybrid, composite presences which are rendered graphically, by linear devices. The banded backgrounds are markedly horizontal in their axes, while the presences line up in vertical rhythms, so giving rise to a sense of the ubiquitous post-Cubist twentieth-century grid attempting to assert itself. The horizontal banding also becomes increasingly watery or submarine, hence the lower extremities of the hybrid figures seem to mirror and reflect their upper ones. As in the slightly earlier, overtly archaizing works, the areas between these extremities seem oddly compressed and uncomfortable if we attempt to read them in terms of body imagery. The sensation of tension at mid-canvas persists and is deliberately cultivated by Rothko in his first fully mature abstractions.

Rothko was represented at the exhibition entitled 'The Ideographic Picture', organized by Newman, which opened on 20 January 1947. It seems to have been soon or even immediately after this that he came to believe that even unspecific references to natural forms were detrimental to what he now had to say. With his first *Multiforms*[8] of this year the waters of abstraction flood over his compositions, although in them
120 he abandons the use of watercolour for wet, runny oils. The *Multiforms* are larger in format than most of what he had produced hitherto. In them there still remains some of the sensation of smaller forms reflecting larger ones, and some of the sensation of banding lingers on, although the relationship of images or presences to ground has become increasingly equivocal. The subliminal grids in earlier works had often acted as box-like devices which contain suggestions of imagery. Now it is as if these boxes or compartments had been sealed or lidded and embedded in what might be described as liquid geometry.

These are reductive works in that recognizable imagery has been suppressed, although the pictorial surface is still very broken and active. Henceforth the development of Rothko's art was to be concerned with enlarging and simplifying his forms while reducing detail or incident to scrubby, brushy paint effects at the edges of individual shapes and between them.

In his essay 'The Romantics Were Prompted', printed in the winter 1947–8 issue of *Possibilities I*, Rothko wrote of his own new shapes: '. . . they are unique elements in a unique situation. They are organisms with volition and a passion for self-assertion. They move with internal freedom, and without need to conform with or to violate what is probable in the familiar world. They have no direct association with any particular visual experience, but in them one recognizes the principles and passion of organisms.' The new formal innovations and a note of assertiveness, even the occa-
121 sional hint of menace in his work at this time speak of the advent of a new and disturbing presence in Rothko's art and life.

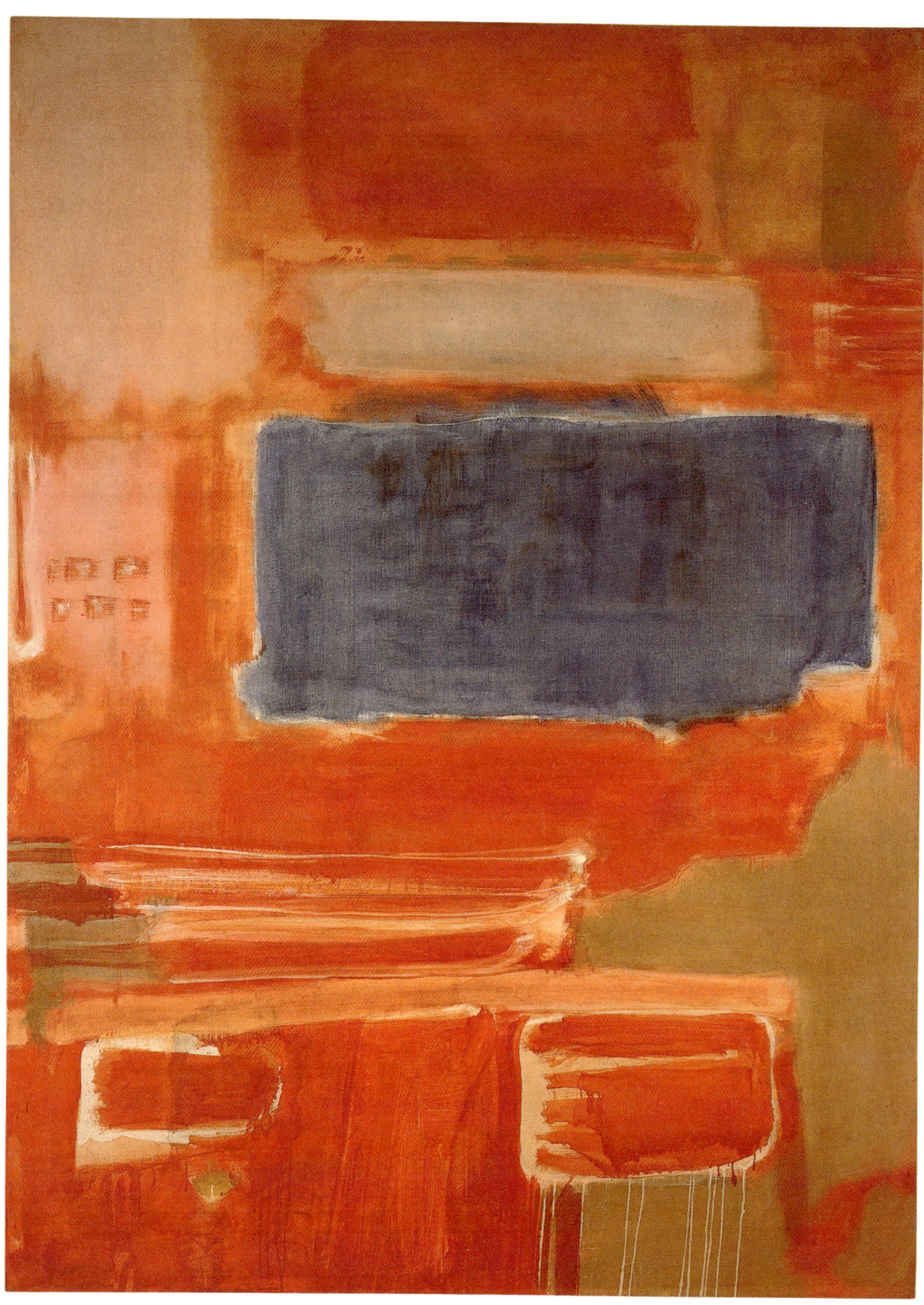

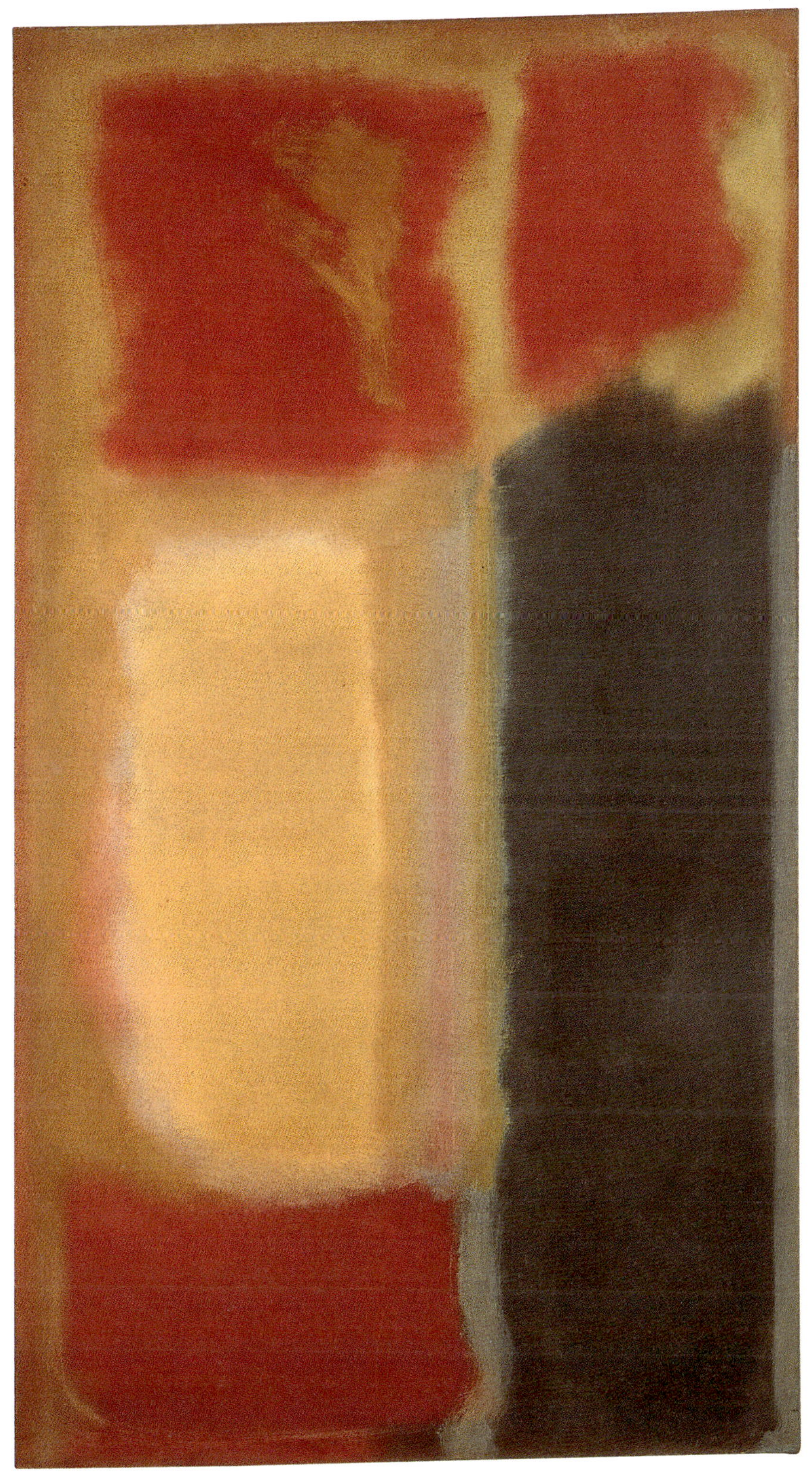

120 Mark Rothko, *Untitled (Multiform)*, oil on canvas, 1948.

121 Mark Rothko, *Number 15*, oil on canvas, 1948.

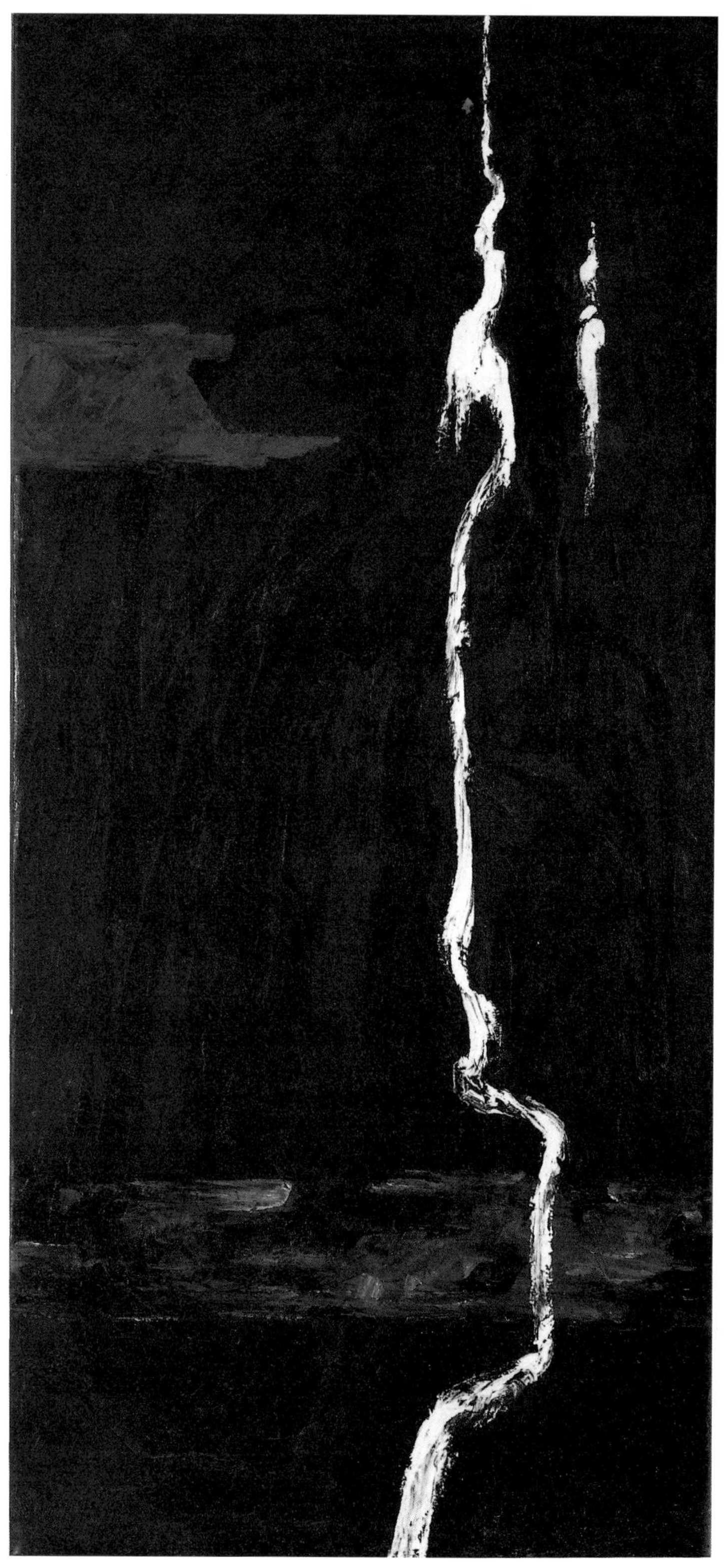

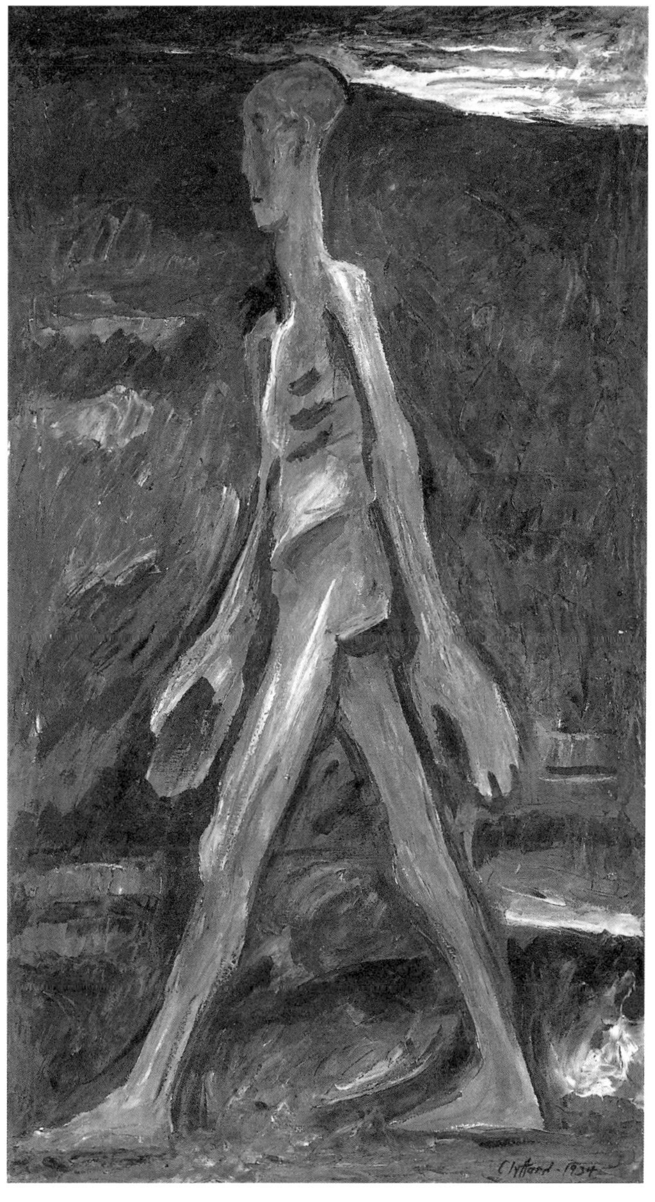

Clyfford Still was born in North Dakota and grew up in Canada (in Alberta)
and on the west coast of the USA (he was educated at Washington State College,
Pullman). He made his first trip to New York in 1925, and enrolled in the Art Students League but left, he tells us, after only forty-five minutes; and such behaviour
would certainly have been characteristic for him. He headed back West. Most of
122 the 1940s were spent in California. He made several more visits to New York and
knew what was going on in artistic circles there; he then went to live there for nine
months in 1945–6 and again for an extended but broken period from 1950 to
1961. Although by the early 1940s New York had eclipsed Paris as the capital of

122 Clyfford Still, *1944-G*, oil on canvas, 1944.

123 Clyfford Still, *Untitled* (formerly *Striding Man*), oil on canvas, 1934.

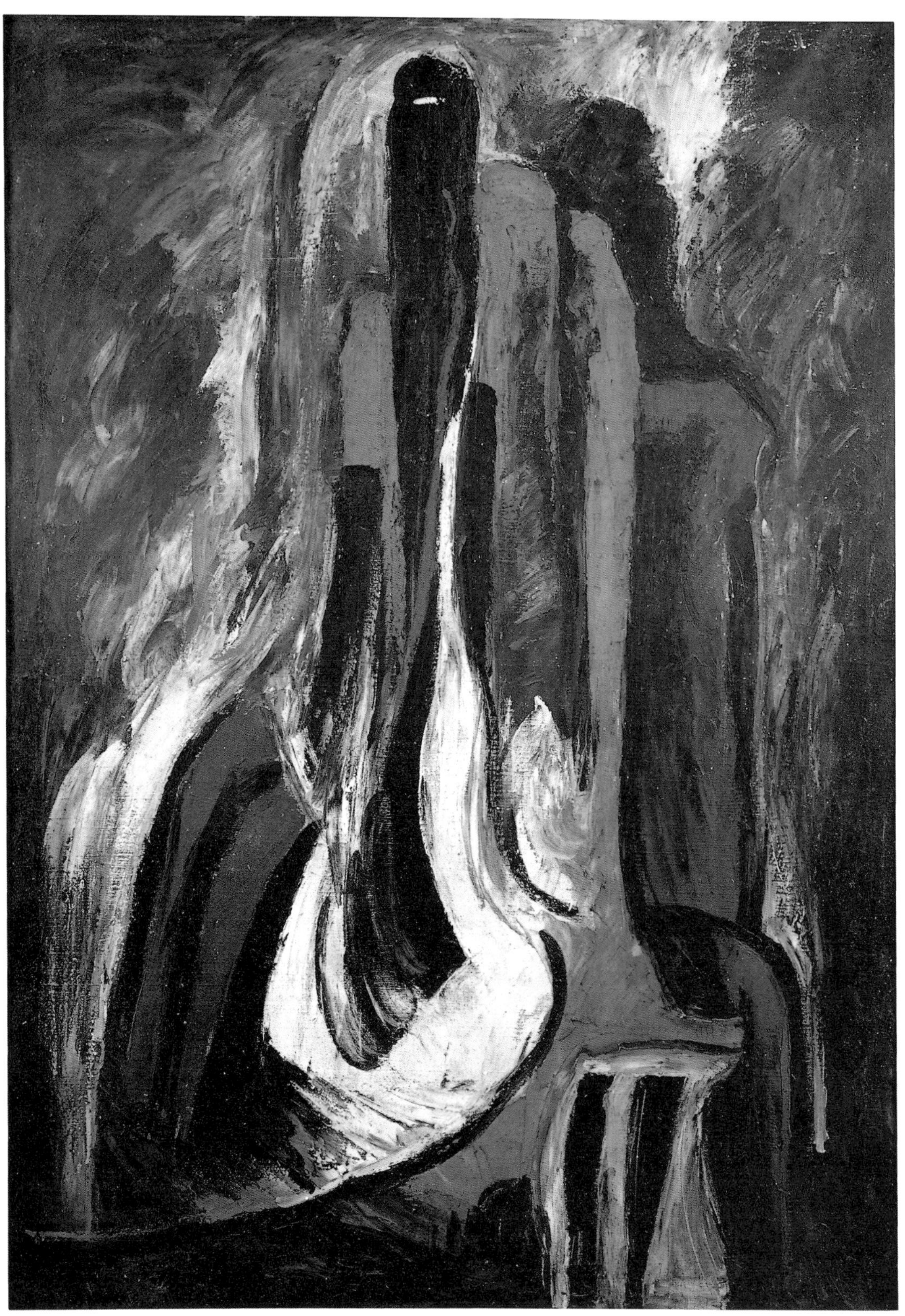

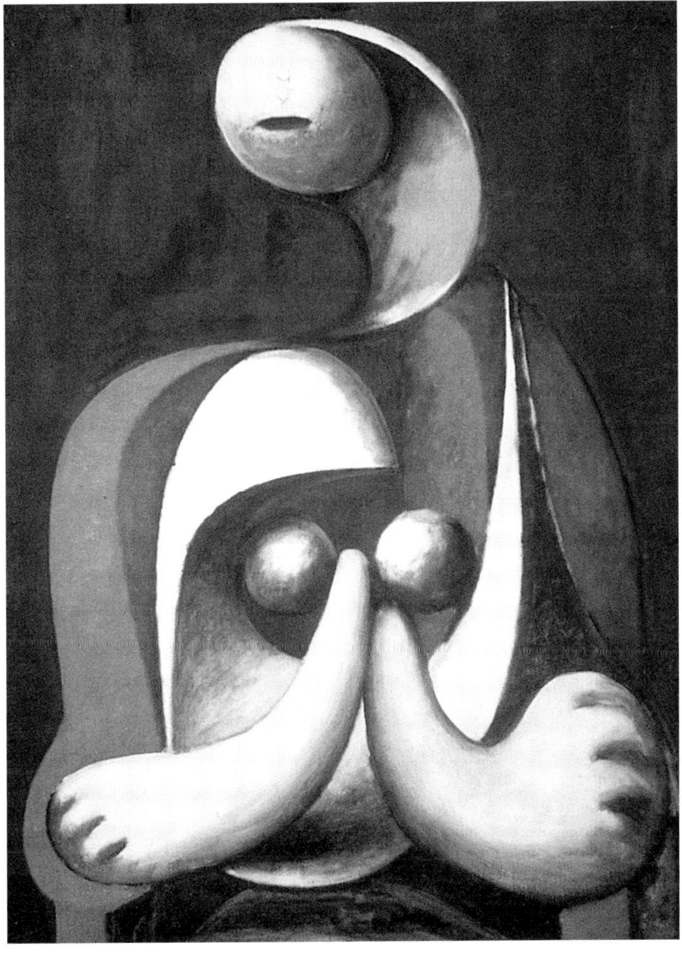

124 Clyfford Still, *1937–38-A*, oil on canvas, 1938.

125 Picasso, *Woman Seated in a Red Armchair*, oil on canvas, 1932.

the avant-garde pictorial world, it is worth emphasizing that the two most visually inventive and complex of the painters who were helping to bring this about, Pollock and Still, grew up in the vast elsewhere. As he would have wished, Still remains an enigmatic figure. From time to time reproductions of very early paintings surface in a mysterious fashion; these are baffling in that the works are difficult to date and it is hard to find direct antecedents for their aggressively savage, almost caricatural imagery. The artist's own dating of his subsequent work is often open to challenge and he also later suppressed titles given to earlier and transitional works, titles that might have helped us to feel our way into his creative thinking.

123 Still's *Striding Man*, for example, is now designated *Untitled (PH-323)*. Presumably it is one of the works of 1934–5 which the artist himself described as 'bordering on the Tragic'.[9] The word 'tragic' evokes once more the spectre of Nietzsche, whose influence was as important for Still as it was for Rothko, although while Rothko was fixated on *The Birth of Tragedy* (the only work of Nietzsche's to which Newman was prepared to give the time of day), Still appears to have been more influenced by Nietzsche's later, blacker and more apocalyptic

and aphoristic pronouncements. They inform and colour his own very personal
prose style. A note made by Nietzsche in 1888 resonates in the mind when one
looks at Still's early work: 'Truth is ugly. We possess *art* lest we perish of the
truth . . .'.[10] In *The Twilight of Idols*, of 1889, Nietzsche sees any possible salvation as arising from '[being] without fear in the face of the fearful . . . possessing
courage and freedom of feeling before a powerful enemy, before a powerful
calamity'.[11] Certainly Still came to regard all his erstwhile colleagues as powerful
enemies and their work as a calamity. The bony, stick-like figure asserting his
presence by striding out over a scorched landscape again puts us in mind of Nietzsche's Zarathustra, similarly claiming his identity: 'A man's stride betrays
whether he has found his way: behold me walking.'[12] Also significant for future
developments in Still's art are the exaggeratedly large hands and the way in which
the bone structure in the pelvic area is conveyed by black gashes. The deeply
atavistic quality of this work provides a further reminder that like so many of his
colleagues, but possibly to an even greater degree, Still was steeped in Sir James
Frazer's anthropological study *The Golden Bough*, first published in 1890 and
reissued in an abridged edition in 1922.

Still also tells us that over succeeding years he worked his way through the
Bauhaus, Dada, Surrealism and Cubism, listing them in that order.[13] There are
intimations of Synthetic Cubist substructures in some of the works of the second
half of the 1930s and certainly Surrealism comes through in a deliberately savage
way in the 1940s. But canvases of these early years which have survived, or which
the public have been allowed to see, are more remarkable for their startling originality than because of their derivations. Occasionally one senses behind Still's
apparitions the presences of Picasso's figure pieces of the 1930s; the configurations of a work like *1937–38-A* for example, call to mind those of Picasso's 124
Woman Seated in a Red Armchair of 1932, although the resemblances may be 125
fortuitous and the work by Picasso is one that Still could have known only in
reproduction. Yet the question of Still's sources is all-important to an understanding of his art, if only for negative reasons. This brings us to another way into
abstraction, one that was unique to himself. Not only was Still approaching his
sources in a spirit of aggression, but he was also consciously seeking to obliterate
all allegiance to them and to a European tradition of art, not so much because he
was out to cover the traces, so to speak, but because he felt he could find his true
self only by metaphorically destroying his mentors. Later on, he succeeded in producing some of the most transcendental and awe-inspiring images of the modern
era, but his early abstraction was also one born out of rage, even out of hatred for
all art other than his own.

On the visual evidence, by the mid-1930s Still was already studying American
Indian art. This was to be his prime weapon in the war he had declared on the
European tradition. His '*No. 2*' of 1936–7 shows a standing figure rendered by 127
thin, flickering white outlines which describe or suggest component parts of the
body embedded back into each other and then back further again into a slab-like
surround thrown into relief by a turbulent halo of white impasto. A large white
hand appears to grasp an unidentified object. In *1938-N No. 1* the internal struc- 128
ture of a seated or standing(?) figure is again described by a stele-like presence
rendered in muddy dark tones; the lower white, claw form represents an outsize
hand or possibly the interior, skeletal structure of the body. These configurations
are paired to an irregular but pronouncedly upright form which rears up from the

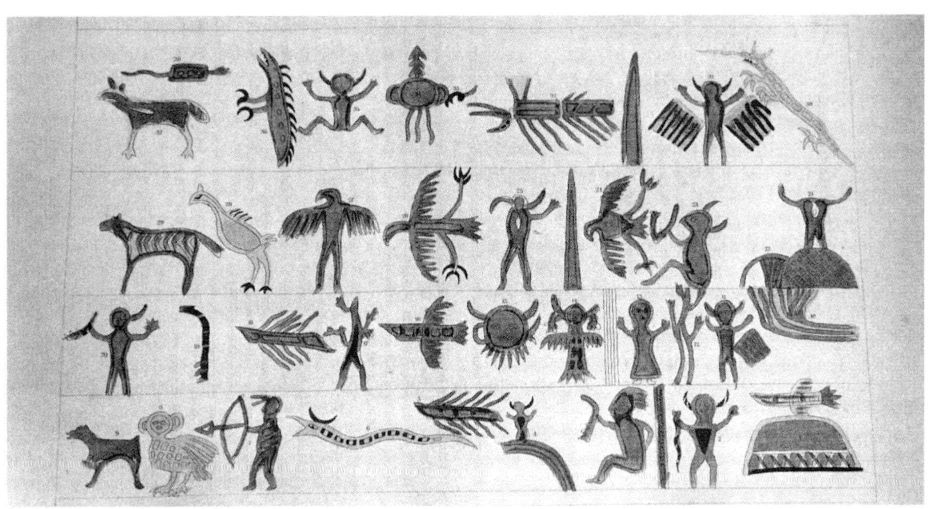

126 Shaman Mnemonic System of the Grand Medicine Society, published 1853.

bottom of the canvas, ending in a crook at the top. This shape or image is a recurrent one in Still's work and has been explained in a relatively recent publication by
126 Stephen Polcari, who illustrates a diagram of the 'Shaman Mnemonic System of the Grand Medicine Society', published in 1853 by the U.S. Bureau of Indian Affairs,[14] although Polcari does not suggest that Still was looking at this particular set of images (there were other similar diagrams and artifacts which he easily could have consulted). The white form in this painting and similar forms in other works by Still are surely derived from the shaman's staff or wand. The feathered and flanged forms ascribed to both figures and animals, the repeated bending and twisted linear rivulets and the way in which the reductive images sometimes carry their outlines within themselves rather than on their outer contours – all these features are relevant to Still's emergent vocabulary of forms.

A contemporary or slightly earlier untitled picture reads rather like a close-up of
130 *1938-N No. 1*, with the shaman's staff to the right, a mysterious central form, again almost certainly of shamanistic origin, with a cluster of forms representing what appears to be a hand to the left. These works are of cardinal importance in Still's evolution because in them the human form and the attributes of magic and exorcism that it wields become increasingly intertwined and formally interchangeable. The human presence – the seer, the shaman or, perhaps, the artist himself – has now become confounded with his own instrument of change and transformation. This becomes very apparent, for example, in a later work,
131 *1945-H*, in which it becomes virtually impossible to distinguish body imagery from the magical attributes associated with it. Kandinsky's interest in shamanism had led him to the conviction that art could have a palliative, curative function.

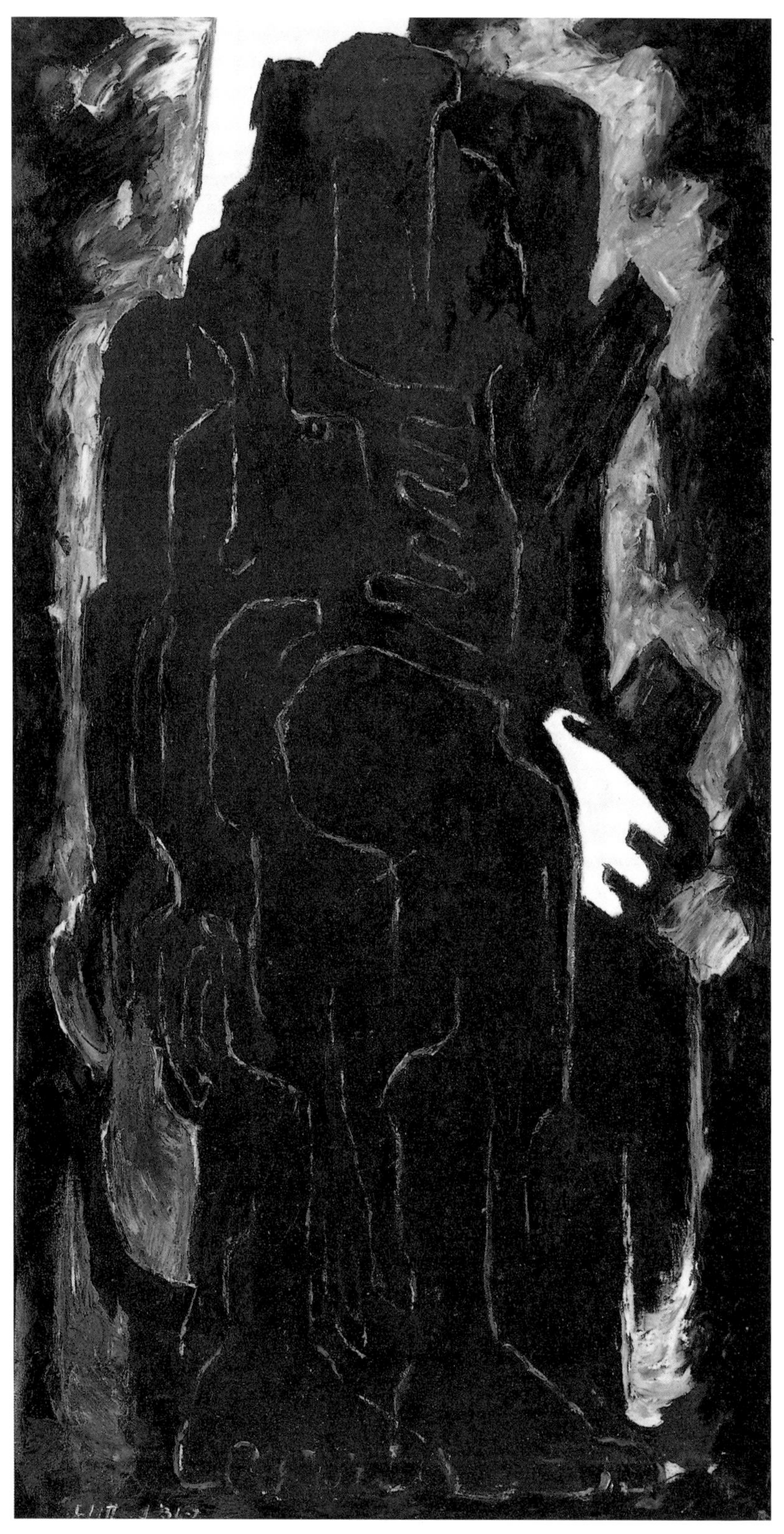

127 Clyfford Still, *1936–7 No. 2*, oil on canvas, 1936–7.

128 Clyfford Still, *1938-N No. 1*, oil on canvas, 1938.

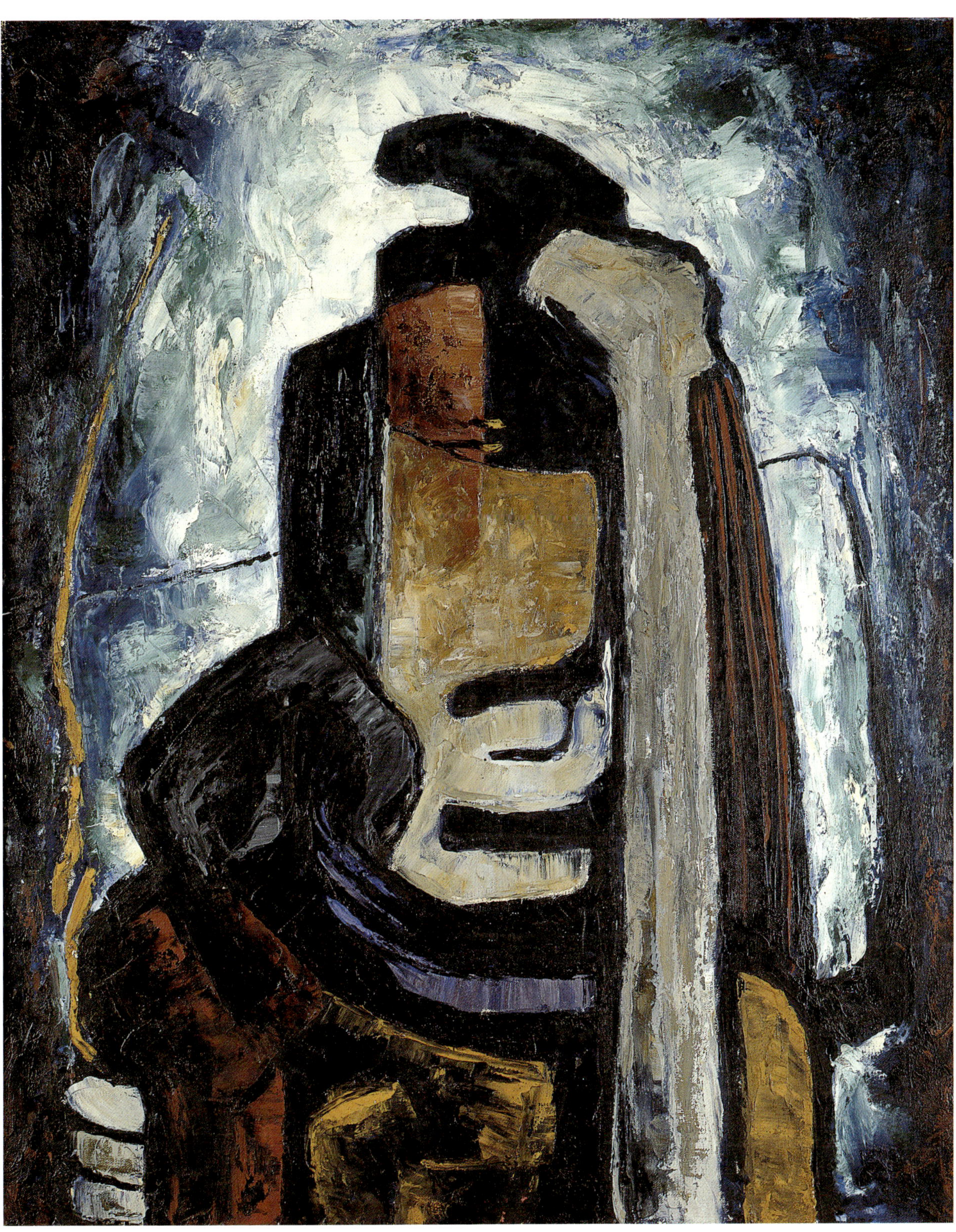

Pollock had worked himself, very physically, into a shamanistic stance partly at least in an attempt to exorcise his own demons. Still used his understanding of shamanism to exorcise all other art. There is a very real sense in which it propelled him into total abstraction.

One of Still's most overtly shamanistic paintings, *Untitled*, of 1936, depicts the 132
head and shoulders of a figure, themselves rendered in the forms of a crook or staff, clutching in an exaggeratedly large hand a phallic attribute. It provides
perhaps a clue to the genesis of *1941–2-C*, which shows an upright tomb-like or 133
stele form, totally abstract in appearance, against a cindery background and streaked by rivulets of blood-red. Perhaps Still is here telling us that man has
become his own monument. 'I paint only myself, not nature',[15] he declared. The 134
dominant shape or presence recalls the rock formations in Böcklin's *Island of the Dead* of 1880, possibly the most reproduced work of its day, as well as being on view in the Metropolitan Museum, New York. There may well be no direct influence or even connection between the two works, but a certain affinity of mood does serve to place Still in a tradition of the more disturbing, 'Sturm und Drang', aspect of Northern Romanticism. This image of Still's remains one of the most enigmatic in all twentieth-century art; it marks a turning-point in his art and perhaps accounts for the fact that he saw 1941 as a year of particular importance in his development.

Another strongly shamanistic work, *1943-J*, introduces a new and in a sense 129
prophetic note of ambiguity into Still's painting. In this work the dominant, stele-like presence remains centralized but is also allowed to bleed off the left-hand side of the canvas, with the result that the relationship between the imagery and the background becomes somewhat equivocal.

Although Still was later to disclaim any affinities with Surrealism, the years 1945 and 1946 mark his closest contact with the movement. In 1946 he was given a solo exhibition at Peggy Guggenheim's 'Art of This Century' Gallery and this obviously involved his making visits to the gallery. The skeins of rope-like substance in Still's
canvas of 1946 shown as *Self Portrait* in his exhibition there clearly owe much to a 136
group of paintings executed by Max Ernst in 1927, in which the first configurations were achieved by throwing string dipped into paint onto the horizontally
placed canvas. One of these, *Le Baiser*, hung for a time behind Peggy Guggenheim's 135
desk in the part of the gallery which housed the bulk of her own private or permanent collection. A comparison between the two paintings reinforces the impression that the jagged white vertical lines that traverse Still's canvases, both previously and subsequently, represent some sort of *élan vital*, the inner core or spirit of the human spirit. Still himself talked of the linear elements in his pictures as 'skeletal lines' and 'life lines'.[16]

Another canvas, dating from 1945, which featured in the exhibition evokes 138
Ernst's *Forest* and *Horde* paintings of the mid-1920s. All these works partake of a 137
dark, primeval quality, although the Still is more deeply atavistic, even apocalyptic. The confrontations also serve to emphasize the fact that whereas the relationship of image to ground in the Ernst paintings is conventional and traditional, in the Still it has become ambiguous and mysterious. Rothko produced an introduction to the catalogue in which he asserted that Still's 'paintings are of the earth, the Damned and the Recreated'. Although Still later repudiated Rothko's words, he could presumably have done so at the time, had he felt that they were seriously misrepresenting him.

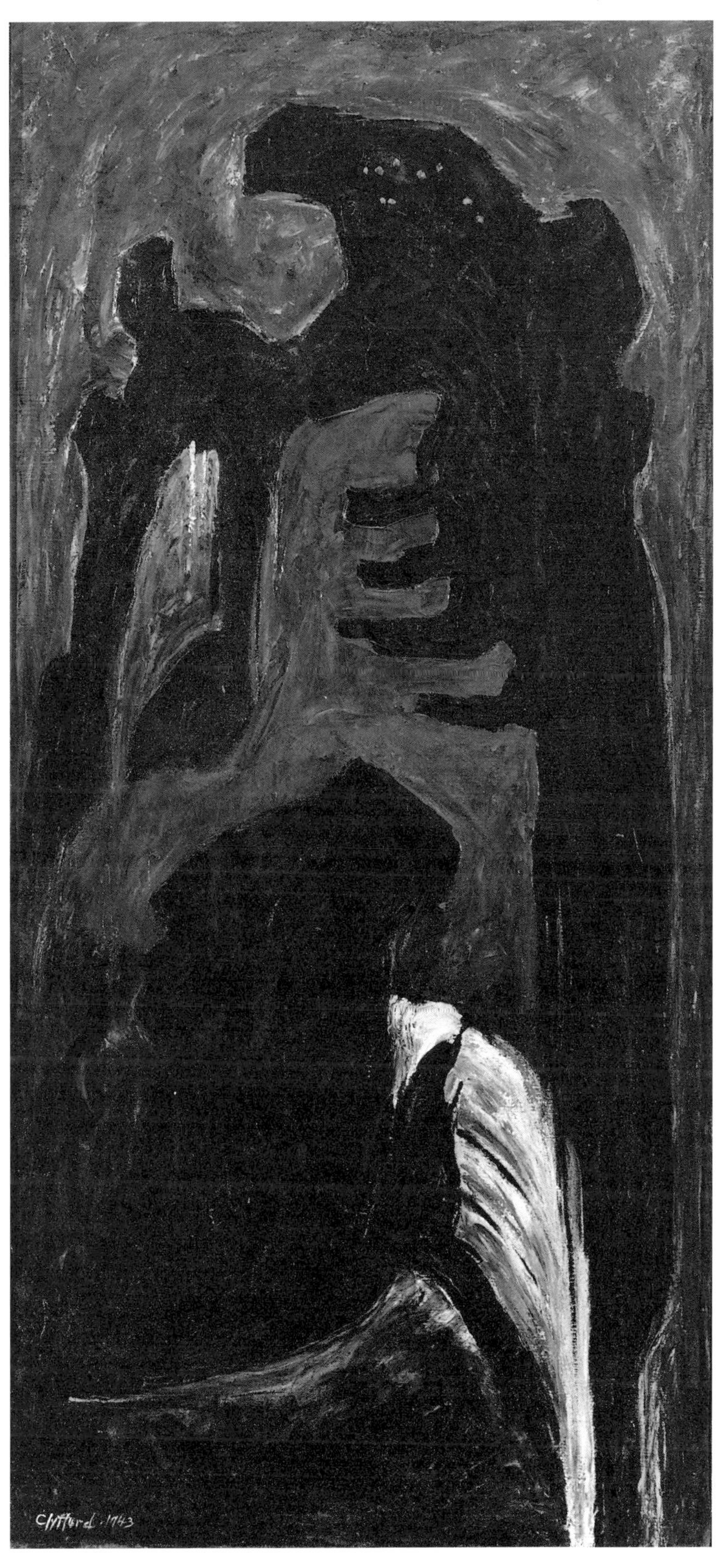

129 Clyfford Still, *1943-J*, oil on canvas, 1943.

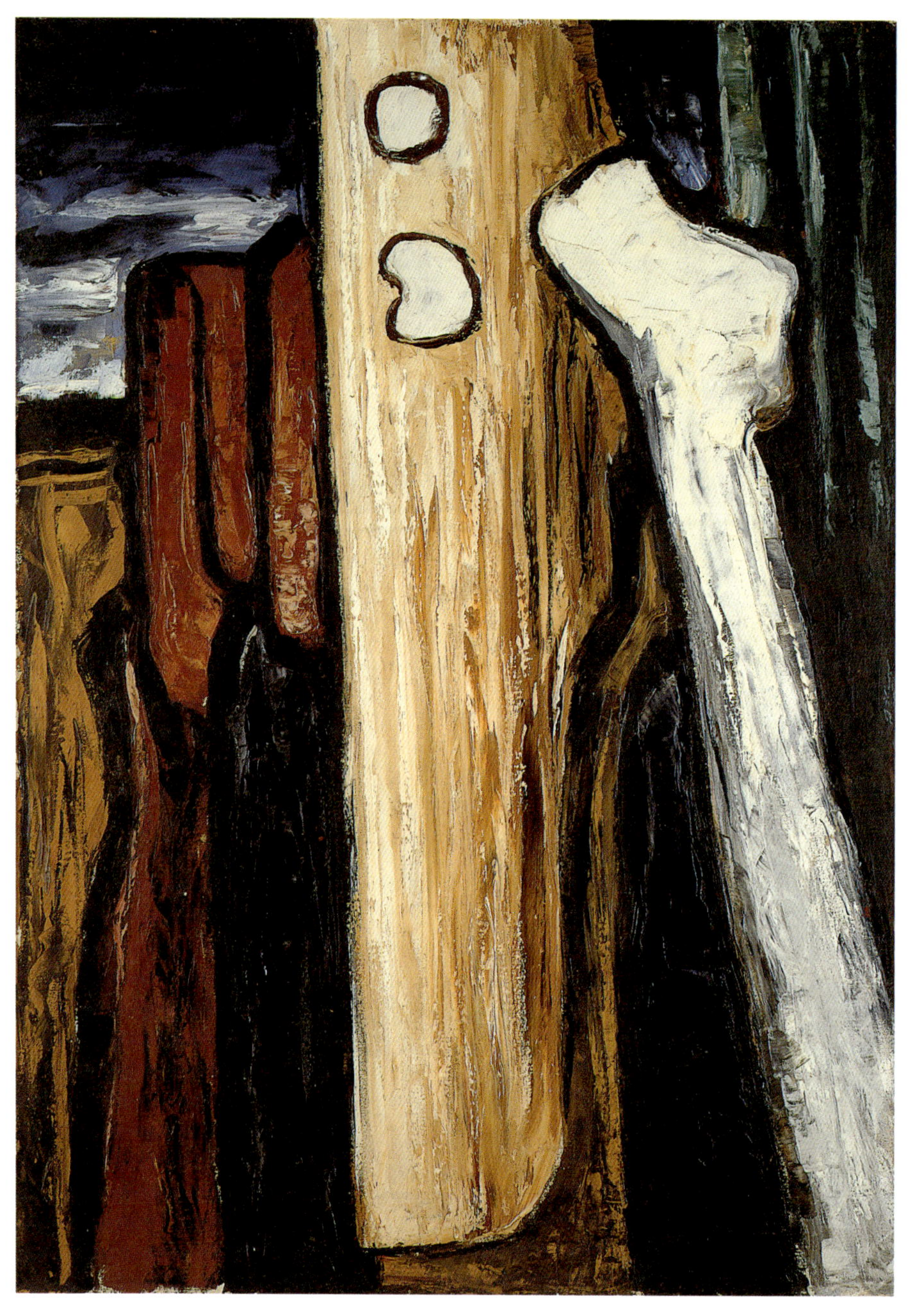

130 Clyfford Still, *Untitled 1937*, oil on canvas, 1937.

131 Clyfford Still, *1945-H*, oil on canvas, 1945.

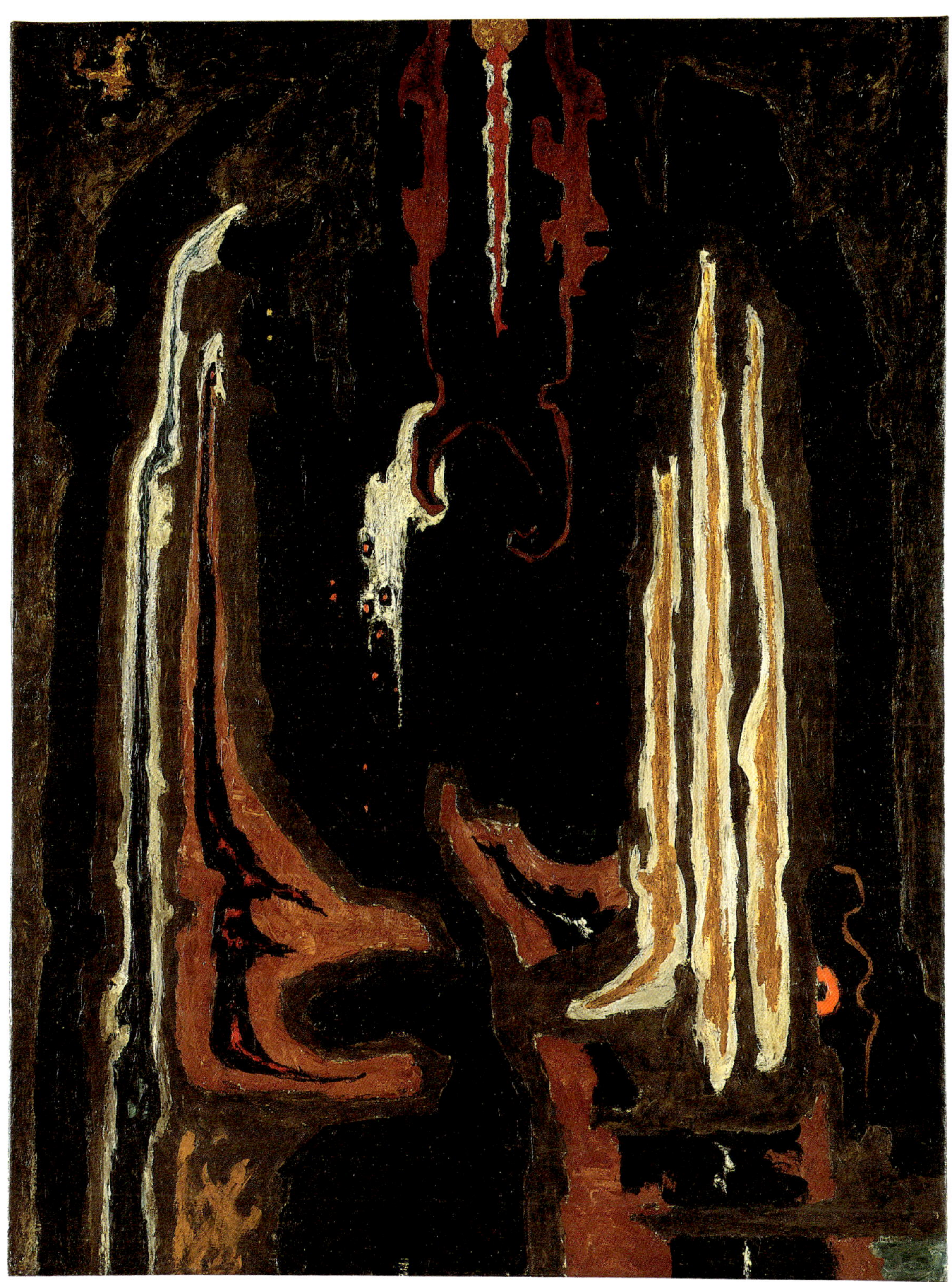

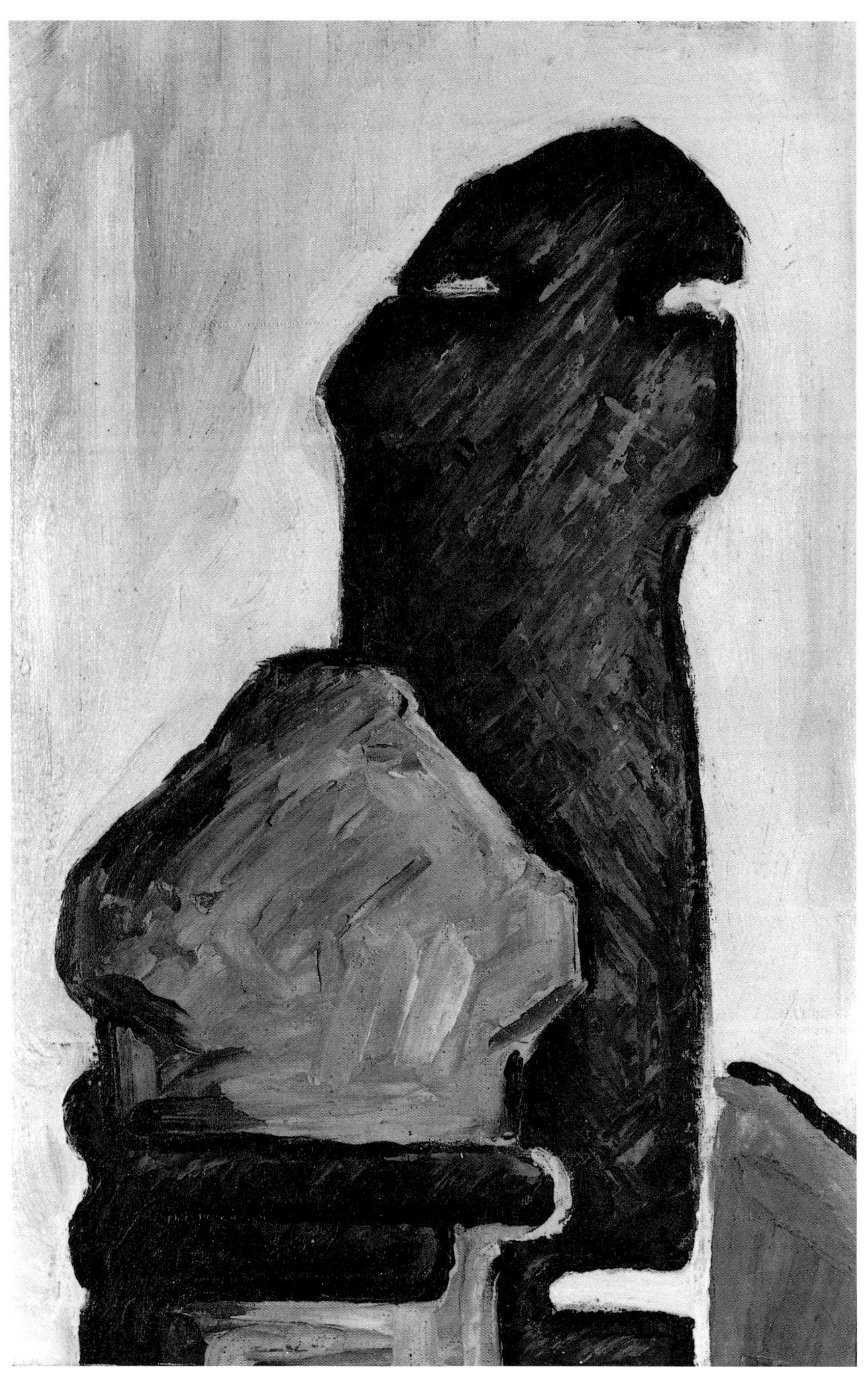

132 Clyfford Still, *Untitled, 1936*, oil on burlap, 1936.

133 Clyfford Still, *1941–2-C*, oil on canvas, 1942.

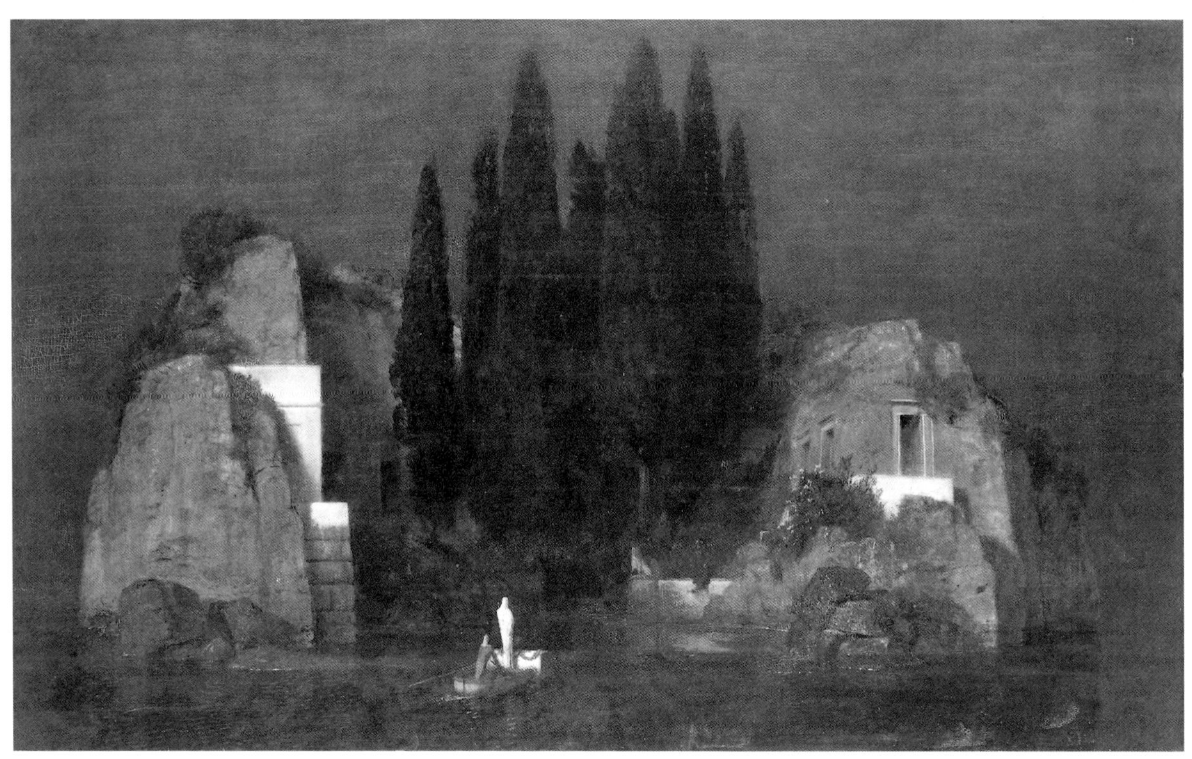

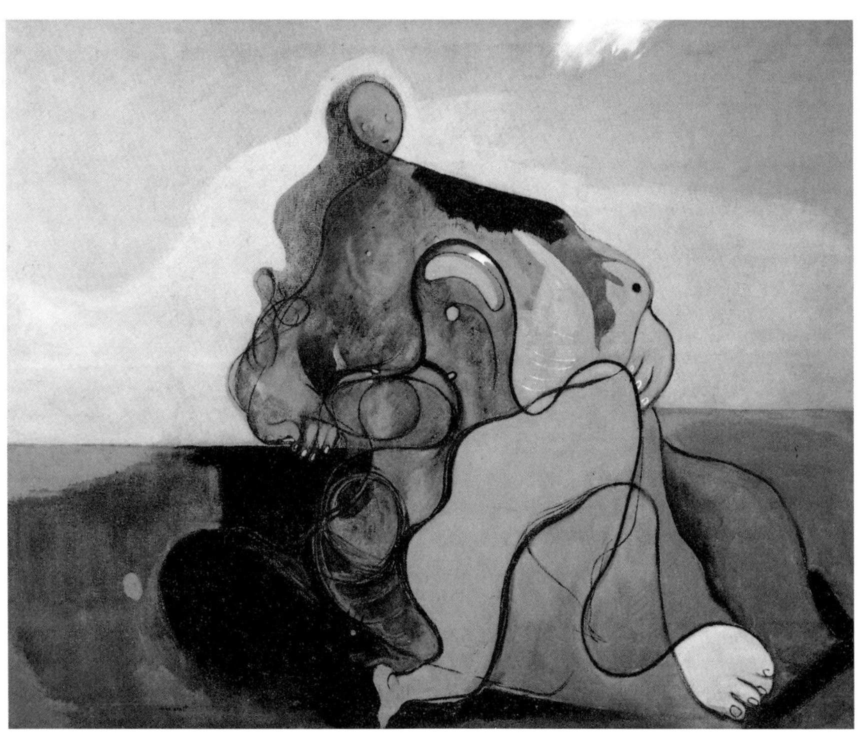

134 Arnold Böcklin, *Island of the Dead*, oil on wood, 1880.

135 Max Ernst, *Le Baiser*, oil on canvas, 1927.

136 Clyfford Still, *Untitled (Self-Portrait)*, oil on canvas, 1946.

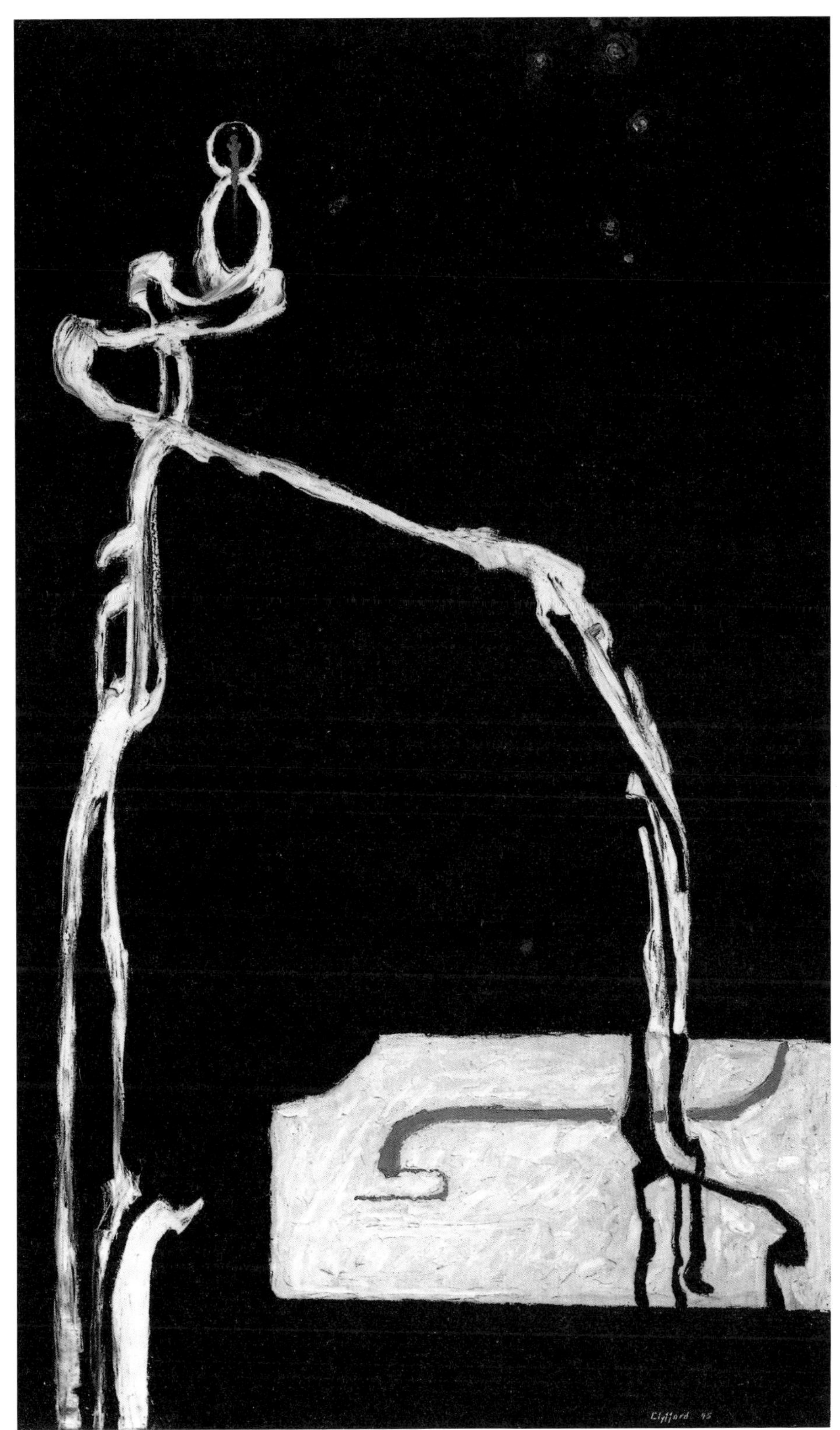
Clyfford 45

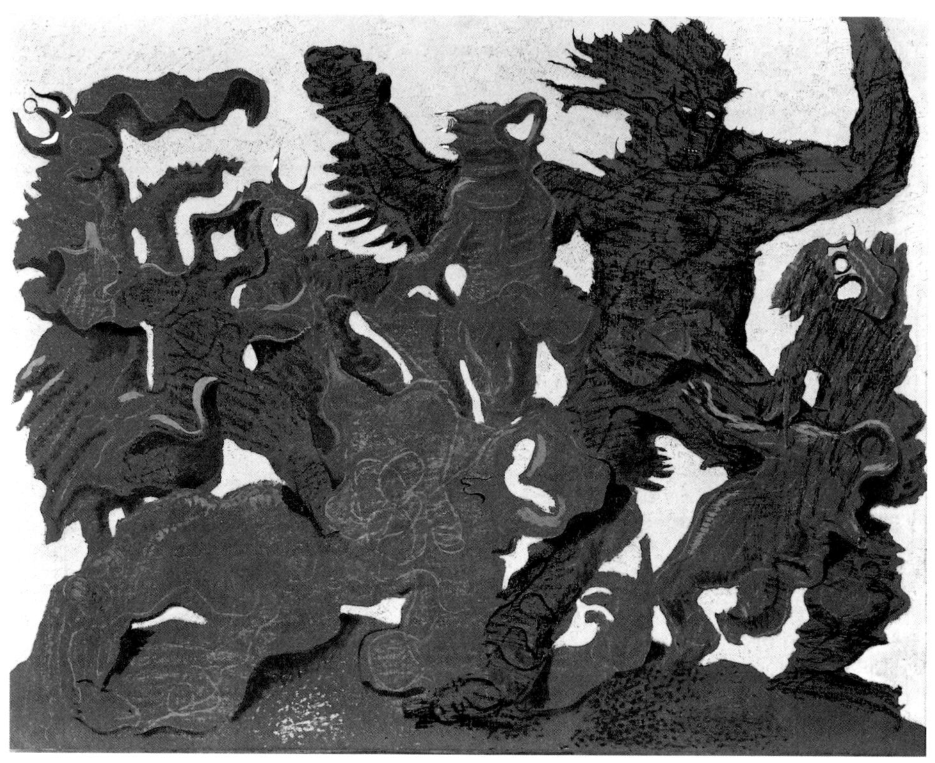

137 Max Ernst, *The Horde*, oil on canvas, 1927.

138 Clyfford Still, *Untitled 1945*, oil on canvas, 1945.

Still was also learning from Miró, spatially a subtler and more experimental artist than Ernst. Predictably, he was drawn to Miró's moodiest, blackest, nocturnal works of the 1920s, like, for example, *Dog Barking at the Moon* of 1926. In 139
Still's *1945-K* the humanoid presence posed on the white ledge to the right 140
appears to have been derived directly from the ubiquitous shamanistic staff or drumstick. The dominant red vertical, which reads almost as an ascending river or canyon of blood, forces the viewer's eye ruthlessly up the surface of the canvas and foretells the sensations of visual vertigo that Still's later work so often induces. The picture is a reworking of *Untitled 1937*. Indeed, Still is the most self-referential of the great American abstractionists, constantly looking back into himself and renewing and revitalizing old configurations and themes.

The same compositional forms, transposed or reshuffled, are to be found in *Sep-* 141
tember 1946; but now it is as if Still was moving up into his art. If Kandinsky had distinguished two main ways into abstraction, 'veiling' and 'stripping bare', one might add a third, 'moving up and in'. Here it is as if Still has entered his own compositions, focusing on or allowing certain areas or configurations to become the picture's subject-matter. For example, the red force or presence seen in the earlier work seems now to have moved to the right, becoming more tenuous and confounded with the drumstick or staff. The white ledge-like form is allowed to flow up onto the surface at the top right, so that the spatial ambiguities in Still's work are becoming ever more important and deliberate in their manipulation. Are the

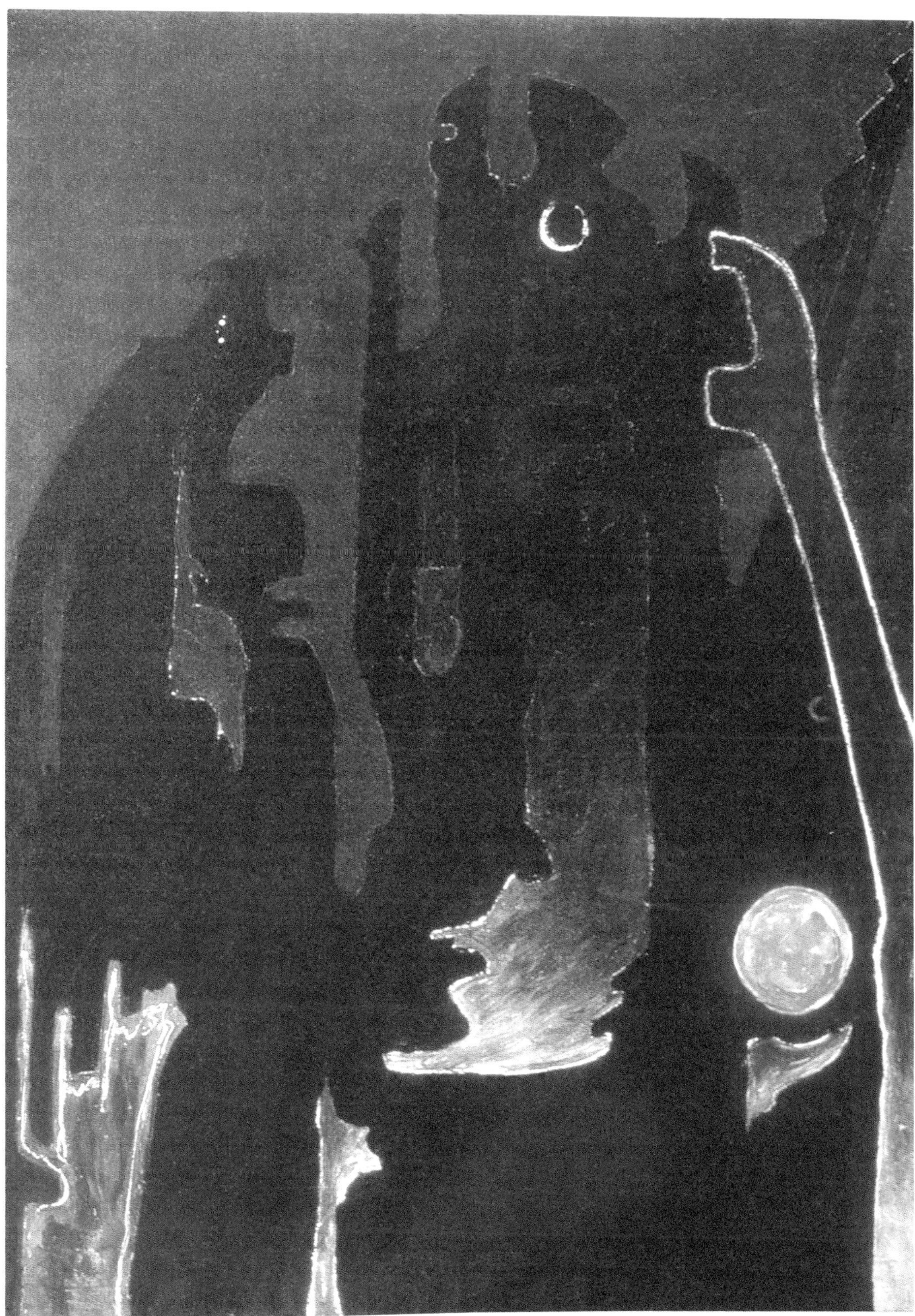

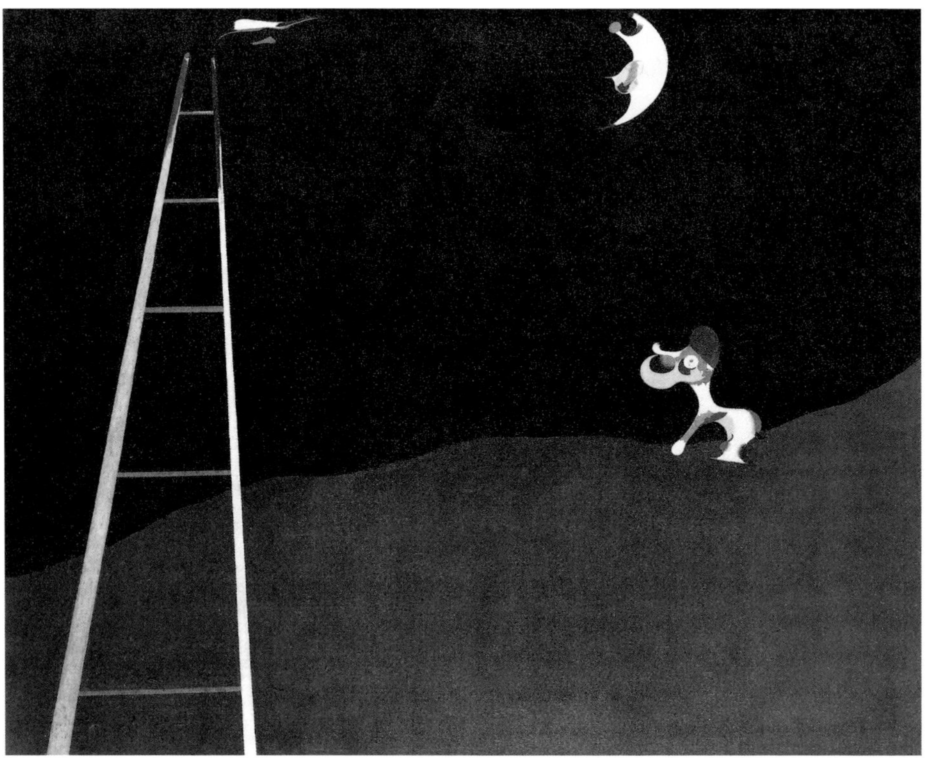

139 Joan Miró, *Dog Barking at the Moon*, oil on canvas, 1926.

140 Clyfford Still, *1945-K*, oil on canvas, 1945.

green-black cracks embedded into the whites or have they been superimposed onto them? Technical analysis of the painting can answer such questions, but at first glance, and for the unaided eye, it is impossible to say.

The new painterly freedom that begins to inform Still's work in 1946 must surely owe much to an exposure to Kandinsky. But, once again, it is as if Still has moved up into a part of Kandinsky; and whereas in Kandinsky drawing, or linear definition, and colour still exist largely independently of each other or co-exist and reinforce each other, in Still they have become confounded, synonymous. Similarly, the spatial ambiguities present in Kandinsky's work have here become starker, so that although Still's work is imbued with depth it is also much flatter. In Still's work, henceforth, the imagery of preceding years becomes increasingly sublimated or sacrificed to the independent life of the canvas, a self-subsisting entity. In the work he produced in 1946 it is still possible to look for reminiscences of earlier motifs. In 1947, however, more or less at the same moment that Pollock achieves his fully developed dripped or poured manner, Still moves into total abstraction, though he himself would undoubtedly have claimed to have done so much earlier.

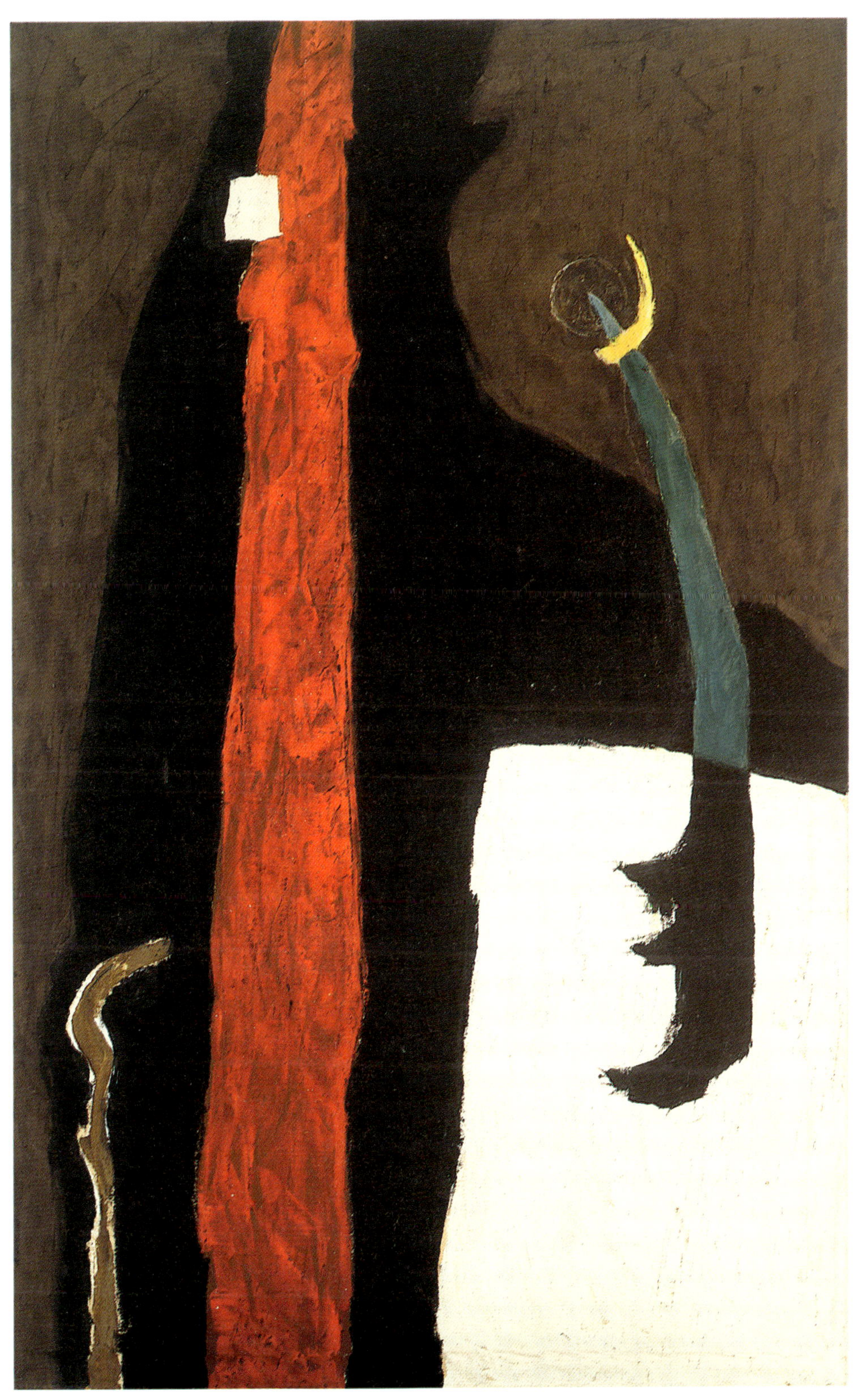

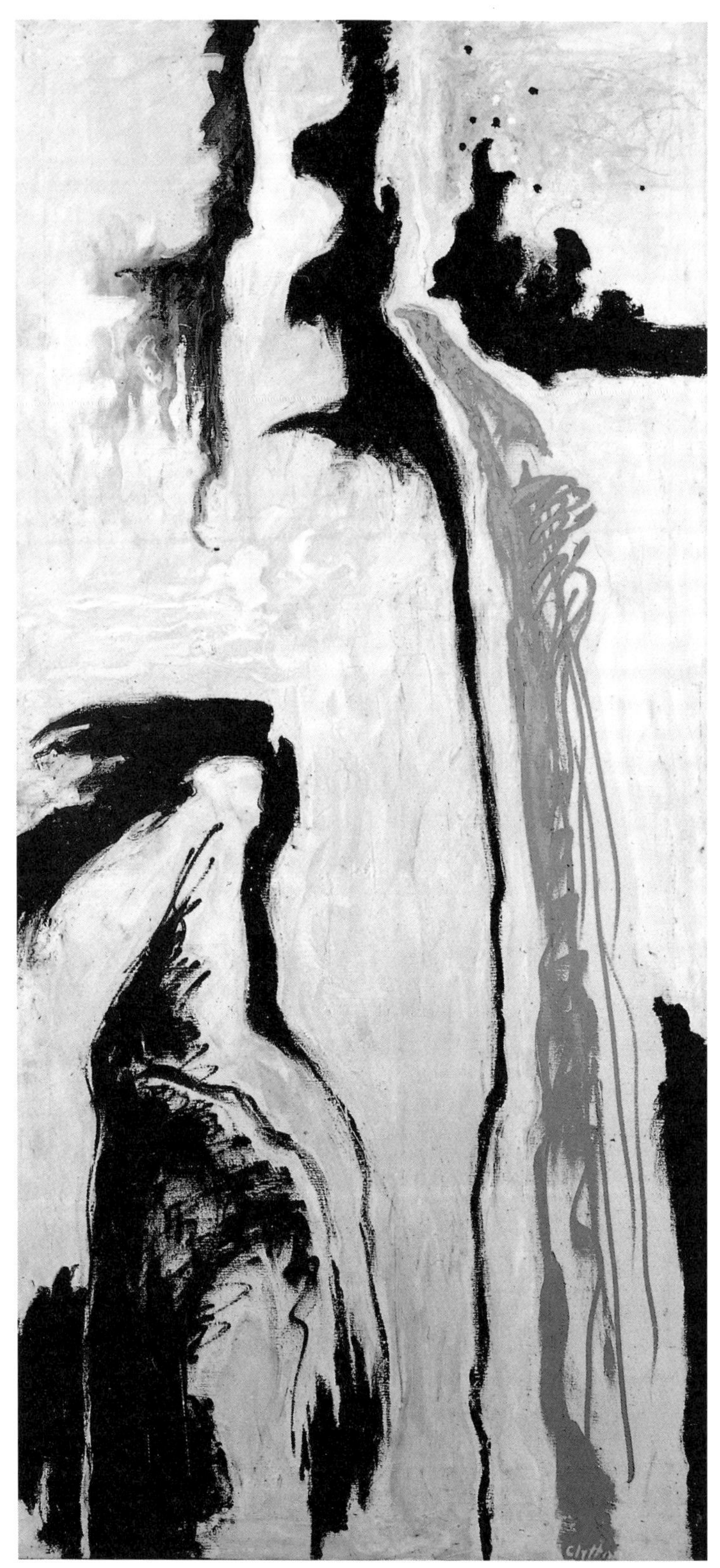

141 Clyfford Still, *September 1946*, oil on canvas, 1946.

In the mid-1940s, when Rothko and Clyfford Still were consolidating their positions as artists, Barnett Newman remained better known as a writer and critic. This situation accounts, in part at least, for the fact that he was the last to gain recognition as a painter. Newman was an enormously charismatic figure and his writing is compelling and invigorating, although the messianic quality of his pronouncements is somewhat at odds with his nature; at times one even senses a touch of the dandy, a certain jauntiness, underlying his apocalyptic prose. Still was an earth-shaker, a sorcerer with more than a touch of blackness to his magic; his self-consciousness is betrayed by every phrase he uttered. Rothko, in turn, became increasingly aware of his image; far from relieving him of his anxieties, however, fame, when it came, served to enhance the genuinely tragic nature of his vision. Like Mondrian, whom he admired, Newman was basically an optimist.

One of the most revealing of Newman's critical essays was his review of The Museum of Modern Art's exhibition 'Art of the South Seas', mounted in 1946. Newman saw very clearly why the Surrealists were so addicted to this art form, but he felt they were looking at it in the wrong way, even from their own standpoint, in that they failed to interpret the meaning of its magical properties (and here Newman's debt to the American anthropologist and art historian Franz Boas is manifest). Newman writes, with genuine insight, '. . . instead of creating a magical world, the Surrealists succeeded only in illustrating it'.[17] He himself proposes a new, visionary art in which, as in primitive art, the artist must believe in the magic of his *act*. He remarks on the fact, deliberately ignored by the Surrealists, that so-called primitive art is often highly abstract in appearance, and he suggests that all its products are the result of terror of different forces. 'Modern man', he writes, 'living in times of the greatest terror the world has known . . . is his own terror.' And he says of the new American painting, '[its] techniques are the techniques of modern abstract art, but their roots lie in the same mythological subject matter that motivated the South Sea artists. They are thereby closer to him than to the traditional Surrealist.'

Newman's attempt to introduce a new way of looking at primitive art that would suggest a fresh beginning for modern art led him to write an essay, 'The First Man was an Artist', which appeared in *Tiger's Eye* in October 1947. He insists on the precedence of the aesthetic act over utilitarian considerations – a questionable, wildly romantic but deeply revealing assertion – stating that 'Speech was a poetic outcry rather than a demand for communication. Original man shouting his consonants did so in yells of awe and anger at his tragic state, at his own self-awareness and at his own helplessness before the void . . . man first built an idol of mud before he fashioned an axe. Man's hand traced the stick through the mud before he learned to throw the stick.' But Newman was an evolutionist, and to this extent a Darwinian, and when he came to trace his line down the empty canvas with a view to creating a new 'tabula rasa' for art, he did so with the advantage of insights gained from having cast his eye over three decades of highly sophisticated abstract art.

143 *Genetic Moment* of 1947 is, once again, at first sight a disappointment after the verbal pyrotechnics of the essay. On closer scrutiny, however, this painting goes further towards creating the desired 'tabula rasa' than one might at first suppose. One's first instinct might be, through art history, to try to relate the picture to Ernst's forest imagery. Yet the comparison serves to show rather how very far apart the works are, though unconscious echoes of Ernst may have conditioned

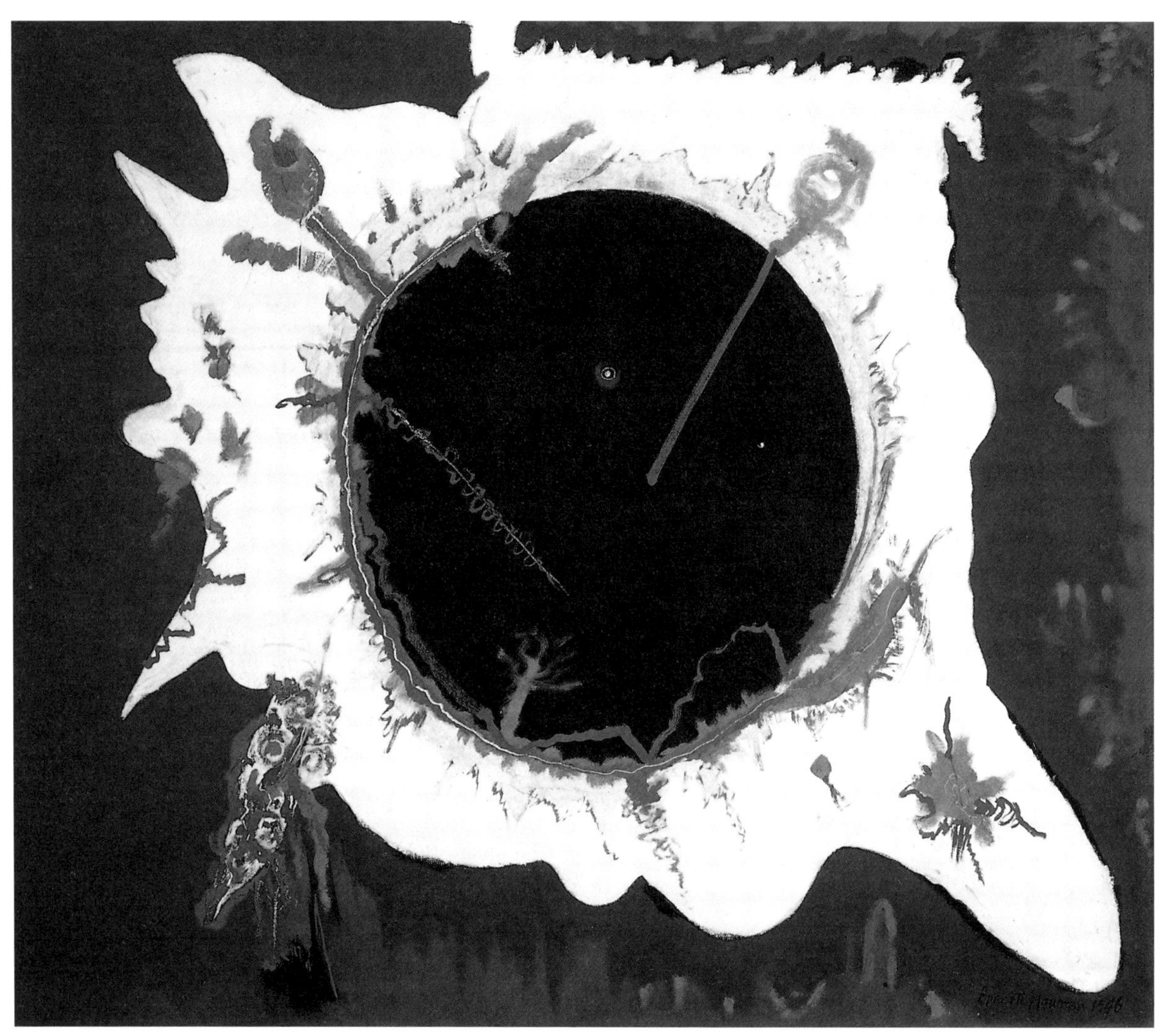

142 Barnett Newman, *Pagan Void*, oil on canvas, 1946.

143 Barnett Newman, *Genetic Moment*, oil on canvas, 1947.

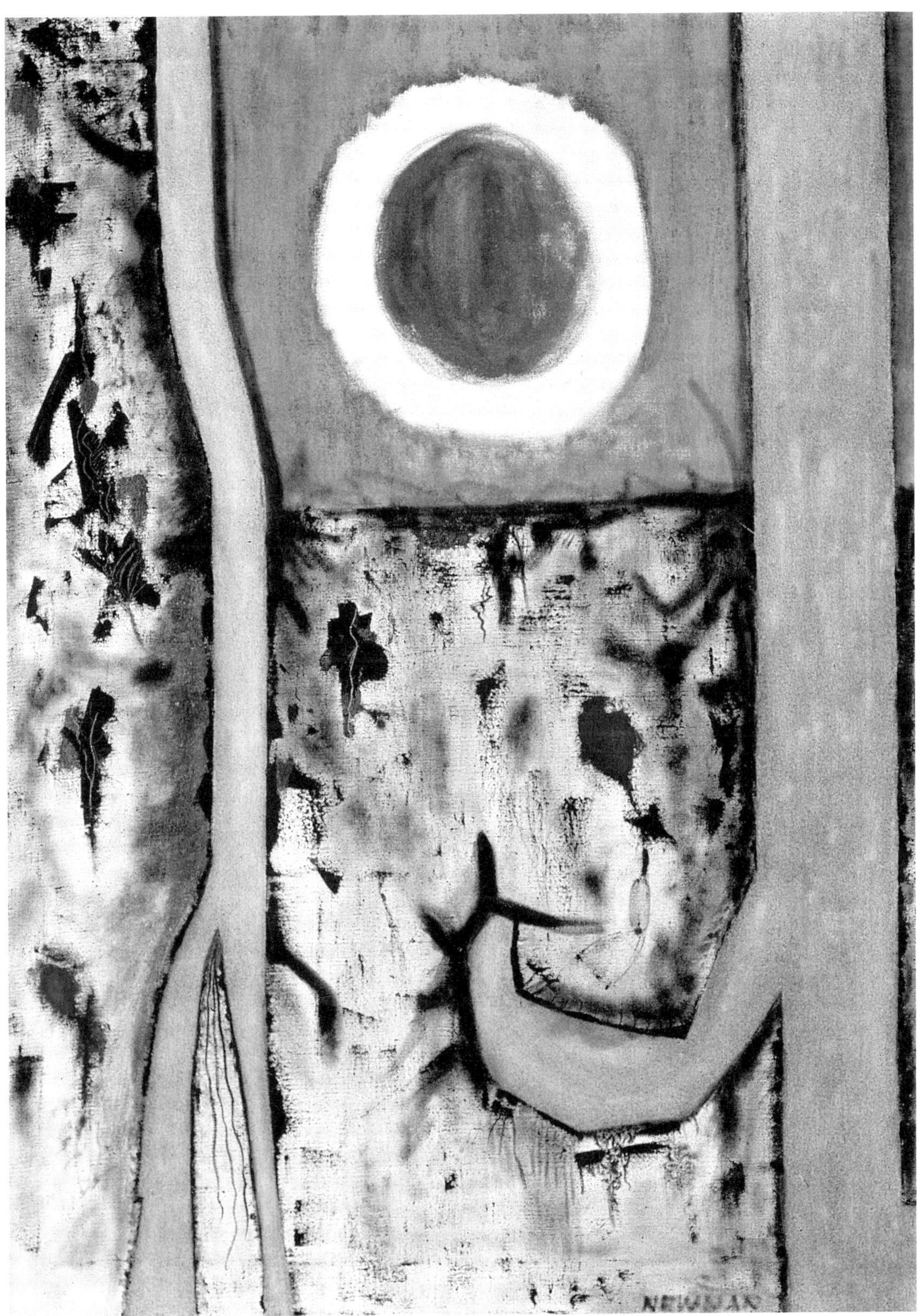
NEWMAN

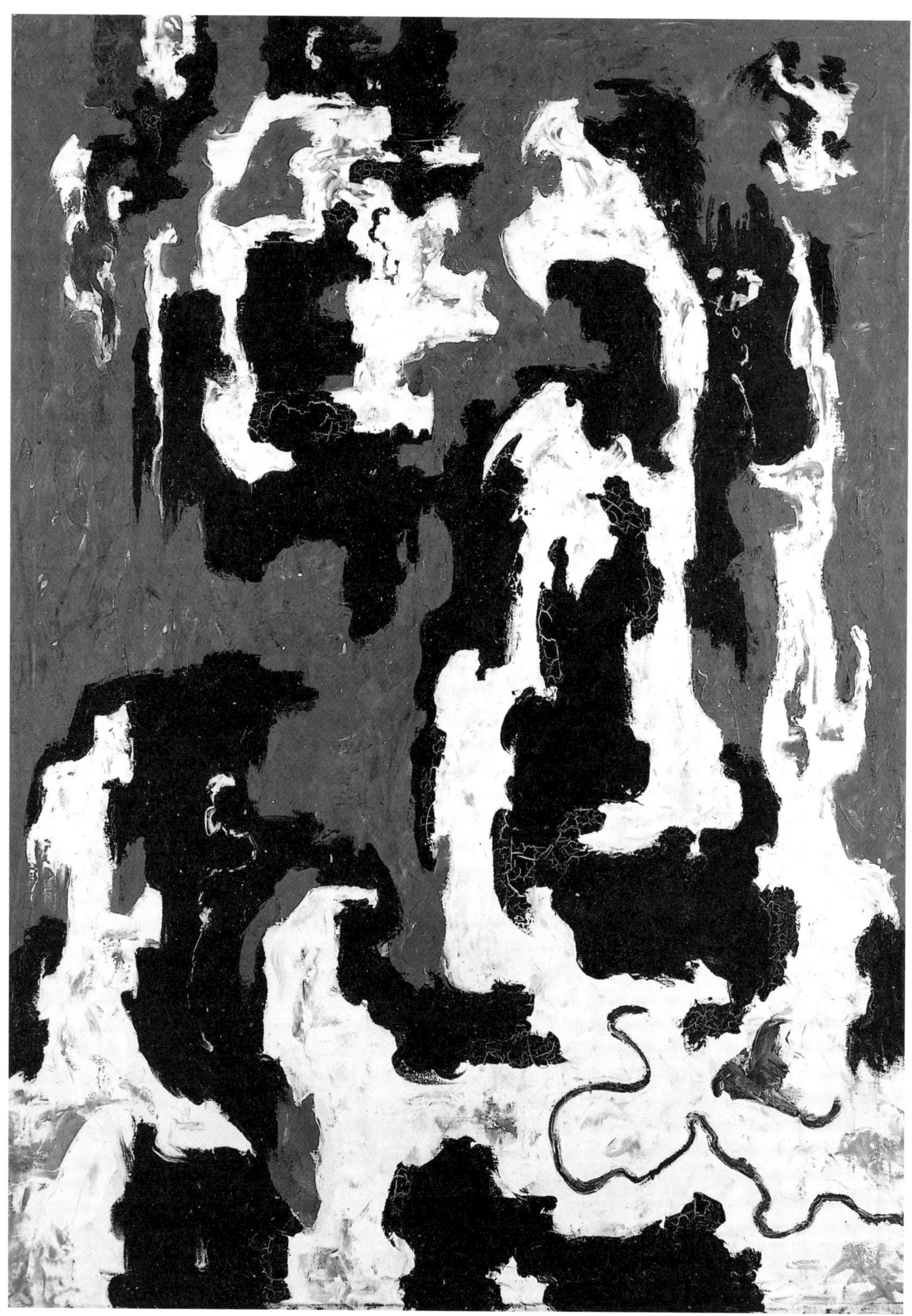

the disposition of Newman's imagery. Those elements which at first sight might read like tree-trunks in fact become the genetic emblems that the title suggests; the form at the left, slender and supple, splits at the base to reveal a triangle; the form on the right, broader and more solid, produces a phallic offshoot which reaches out to its female counterpart. Landscape connotations are negated by the fact that the potential horizon is omitted at the left, so that on close study the apparent solar form comes to read as an egg or enlarged cell between the two uprights. Smudgy dabs and strokes incised with sperm-like wriggles dapple the ground and reinforce the impression that what we are really looking at is a view of the origins of the species, seen, as it were, under a microscope. This sensation is generated
142 even more strongly in *Pagan Void* of 1946. Here surely it is of significance that in the early 1940s Newman had attended courses in both botany and geology at Cornell University.

143, 144 A comparison of *Genetic Moment* with a painting by Still executed in 1947 is revealing. Despite the dry, earthy quality of the palette and the cracked, caked quality of the pigment, the work by Still is more painterly and subtler in its ambiguous manipulation of space. The Newman by contrast looks diagrammatic. Despite the fact that the Still is more truly abstract (in the sense that there are fewer analyzable references to visual phenomena, whether seen in nature or viewed under the microscope), there yet remains in this and other contemporaneous works the sense of his fighting his way through and out of a lot of other painting towards something new. In Newman one senses the very rational scraping bare of the pictorial *status quo*.

In fact, in 1946 Newman was quite literally using scraping techniques, coupled with taking rubbings of textured surfaces pressed to the reverse side of the canvas. These techniques, 'grattage' and 'frottage', were dear to the Surrealists and Newman's brief adoption of them perhaps ultimately represents his greatest debt
145 to the expatriate French movement. *The Command*, of 1946, for example, reads almost as a textbook demonstration of them: 'grattage' or scraping to the left, 'frottage' or rubbing to the right. These two main compositional areas are separated by the white vertical of virgin or lightly stained canvas, achieved by the laying on of masking tape to isolate or separate the two larger areas awaiting the application of texture. Already the narrow vertical or ray was becoming a domi-
146 nant motif for Newman, as for example in *The Beginning*, also of 1946, but on stylistic grounds a slightly earlier work. Both these works, one representing the more traditionally painted kind and the other the formally experimental, are oddly unpictorial. Both of them clearly embody ideas, or perhaps more accurately, an idea – and Newman was single-minded as a painter – and they come across more as painted thought-processes than as inevitable configurations or meetings of visual forms.

The second half of 1947 saw relatively few new works from Newman; it was a period of cogitation. Revelation came on his forty-third birthday, 29 January 1948. On a relatively small canvas (27 x 16 in.), stained with Indian red, he placed an upright strip of masking tape, presumably preparatory to isolating left from right and giving them different textural effects. Instead, on an instinct, he coloured it orangey-scarlet. 'Suddenly I realized', he said, 'that I had been emptying space instead of filling it and that now my line suddenly came to life'.[18] The
147 result was to be *Onement 1*, and 'Onement' was to become a favourite title. In

144 Clyfford Still, *January 1947*, oil on canvas, 1947.

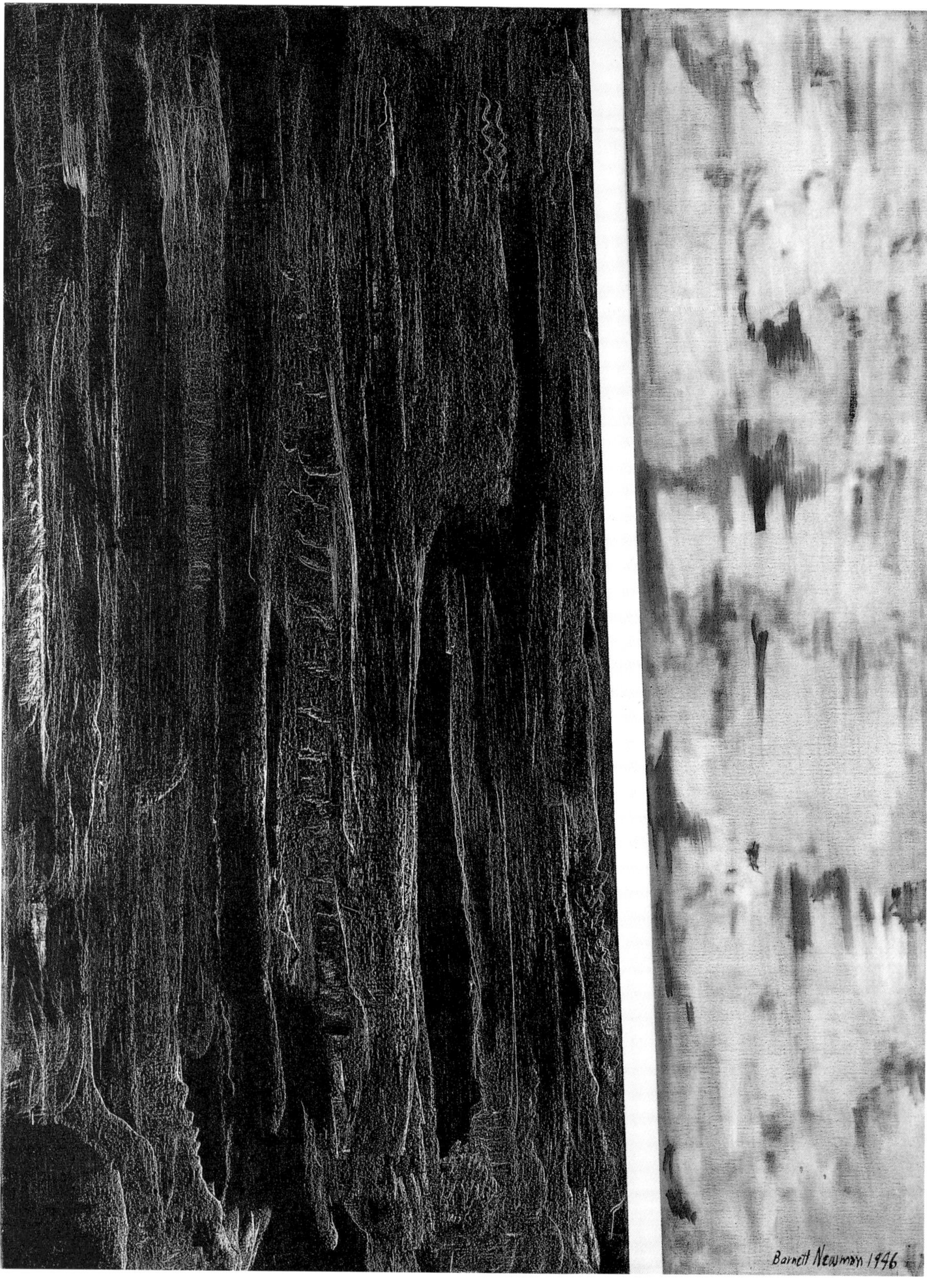
Barnett Newman 1946

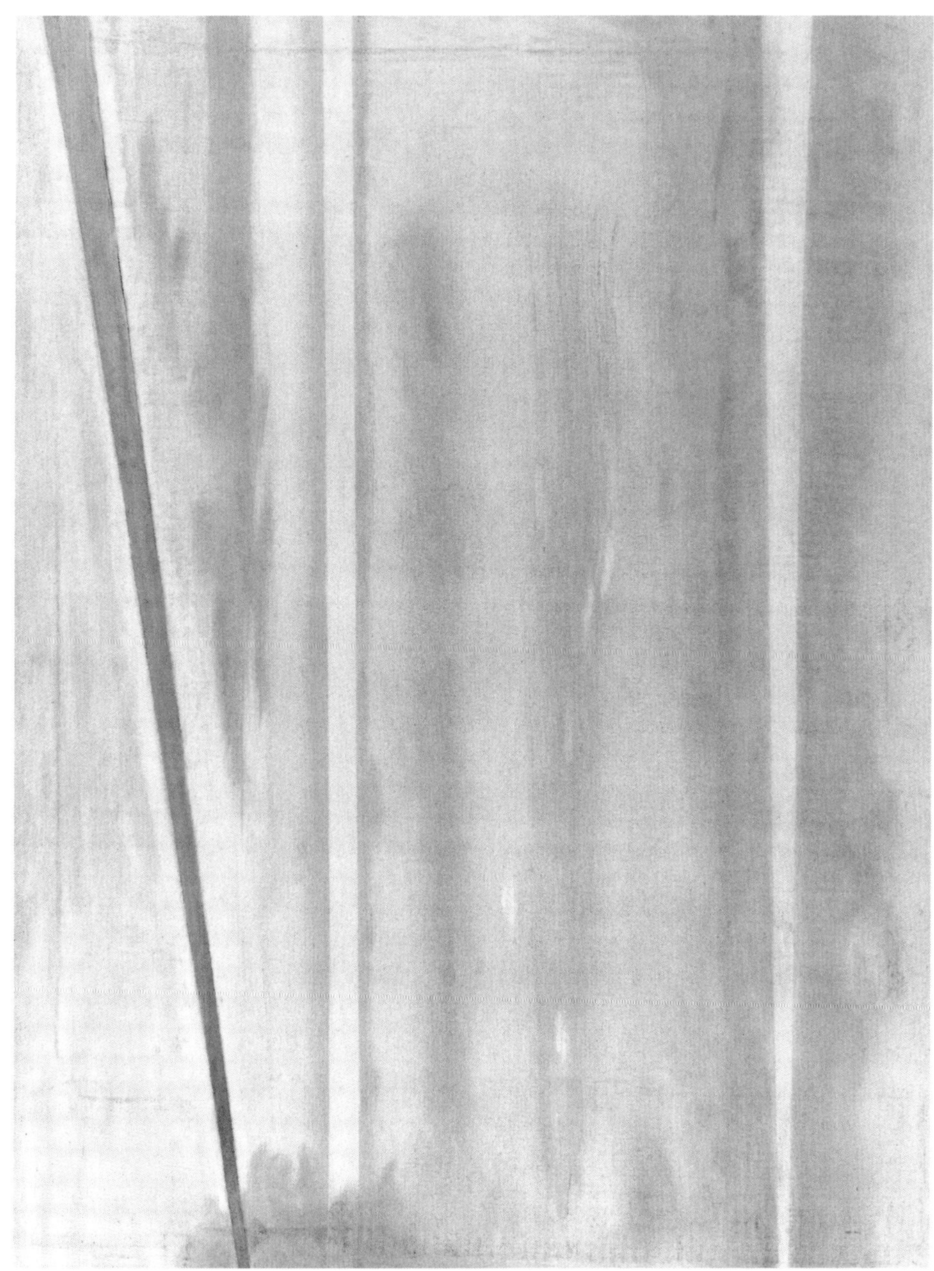

145 Barnett Newman, *The Command*, oil on canvas, 1946.

146 Barnett Newman, *The Beginning*, oil on canvas, 1946.

one sense the female and male elements of *Genetic Moment* have united and fused. In fact the revelation was twofold. In the first place Newman had created his 'tabula rasa', his drawing of a single line in the mud. In the works of Rothko and Still there had as yet been no question of absolutes, except in so far as they had reached up (or possibly 'downwards' might be a more telling way of describing the process) into total abstraction. In a very real sense Newman's 'tabula rasa' was his absolute. In the second place, as his own statement suggests, his revelation was a formal one in that he realized that the stripe was a two-edged line, pushing or splitting apart the areas on either side of it, yet simultaneously or conversely holding them together. These linear elements Newman referred to as his 'zips'. If we read his pictures upwards, the bands bond the adjacent areas together. As our eyes travel downwards again over the pictorial surface, the bands divide them or push them apart. There are relatively few individual works of art that can be said to have changed the course of art history: Titian's *Assunta*, Manet's *Déjeuner sur l'herbe* and Picasso's *Demoiselles d'Avignon* come immediately to mind. In the relatively brief time-span since the emergence of abstract art, its flow and development have been on the whole unaccentuated by particular works. But the implications of Newman's small, clumsy, but deeply numinous work, like those of Malevich's original *Black Square* of 1915, were to be incalculable. They are still reverberating in the work of some of the most exciting and visionary young talents at work today. The great European abstractionists had been imbued with the sense of art as the greater-than-the-self, and this feeling also informs much of Pollock's production. But Newman had, at a stroke, flung open the doors onto new territory. In 1947 he wrote: 'The American artists under discussion create a truly abstract world which can be discussed only in metaphysical terms. These artists are at home in the world of pure idea, in the meanings of abstract concepts, just as the European painter is at home in the world of cognitive objects and materials. And just as the European painter can transcend his objects to build a spiritual world, so the American transcends his abstract world to make that world real. To put it philosophically, the European is concerned with the transcendence of objects, the American is concerned with the transcendental experience.'[19] Or, to put it differently, the European abstractionists had been reaching out, looking over the horizon. The Americans, and above all Newman, were seizing the day.

6

Newman, Rothko, Still and the abstract sublime

When Barnett Newman produced *Onement 1* in 1948 and dragged his metaphorical stick through the metaphorical primeval mud, not only had he at a single
blow achieved the 'tabula rasa' which he had come to believe was essential to the
creation a totally new and quintessentially American abstract art, but he had also
found himself. 'The self, terrible and constant, is for me the subject matter of
painting',[1] he declared. It might perhaps be fair to say that the early European
abstractionists had achieved their absolutes, had purified and purged art, by in a
sense painting themselves out of their pictures, whereas the Americans were trying
to achieve some of the same ends by painting themselves totally into their canvases, by stepping up and into them, even in an odd way by becoming art. Prior to
producing *Onement 1*, when he had written about an emergent new art, Newman
had spoken of himself and his colleagues in the venture collectively; henceforth he
42 uses the first person singular. Malevich's *Black Square* had created its own 'tabula
rasa', but he and his followers also felt that if it pointed the way ahead, it simultaneously contained within itself the essence of the art of the past; and it was with
51 the *White Square on White* that he had touched upon the absolute, having in a
sense left art behind him. In Newman's case his *Onements* were the most reduc-
147 tive of all his pictorial statements. *Onement 1* was his absolute both in terms of its
content and of the forms that convey it. For him it was a rebirth and, more so than
in the case of any other abstract artist, in Newman's beginning was his end; henceforth he was basically playing variations on a single theme. He had fought his way
out of the historical continuum of art forms by stripping bare and at the same
time giving a philosophical structure to those forms. His problem now was to
prevent that historical continuum from closing back in on him and carrying his
work off in a direction of its own.

The title 'Onement' implies totality in reduction, wholeness and harmony, but also – as Newman pointed out in his choice of title – it refers to At-Onement, Atonement and the events of Yom Kippur, for the Kabbalists a time for meditation on the messianic secret, on the coming which symbolizes rebirth and the possibility of a new and radiant life. It is interesting to note that Joseph Campbell in his *Hero of a Thousand Faces*, a work certainly known to Newman, spells 'atone-ment' as two words. Newman's erudition was formidable and he drew upon a

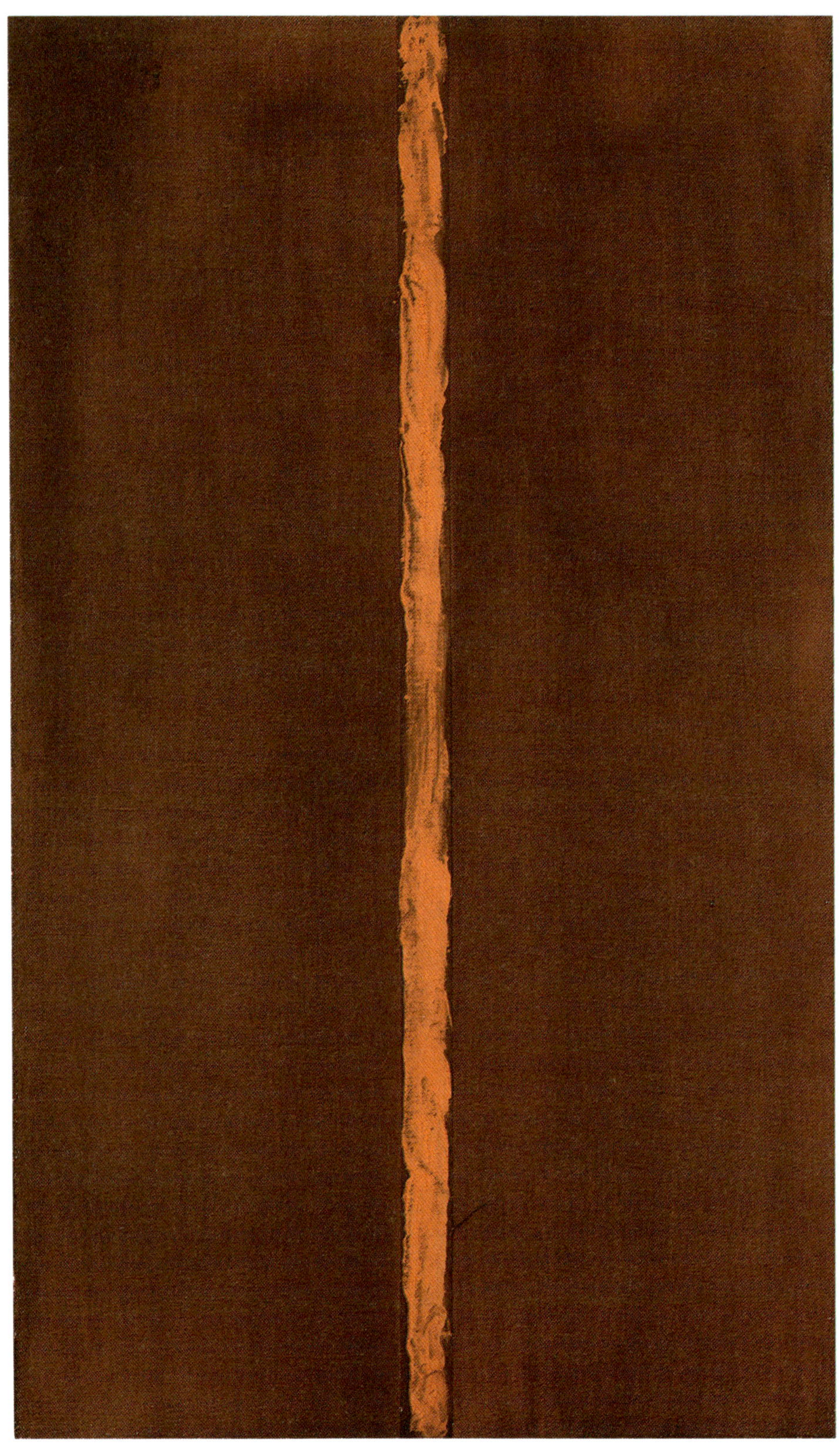

wide range of intellectual sources: Greek, Christian and above all Judaic. It was around 1946, that cardinal transitional year for American art, that Newman put aside classical myth (although he continued to to return to it for some of his titles) and turned to other sources: the Old Testament and – not surprisingly – in particular its first book, Genesis; the Talmud; and above all, as his friend and biographer Thomas Hess pointed out, 'that remarkable fusion of mysticism and logic that is known as the Kabbalah'.[2] Yet Newman's work cannot be too closely tied to Orthodox Judaism and it is dangerous to over-emphasize the Jewish heritage at the expense of the wider spectrum of intellectual stimulus which informed his work.

Newman turned to these sources, and in particular to the Judaic tradition, not so much for his subject-matter, or even strictly speaking for inspiration, but rather because he saw how such a system of thought could be used to infuse the art which he had envisaged for some years, but to which he sensed he was now about to give expression, with a sense of grandeur and emotive purpose. He had come to feel that an abstract shape could be 'a living thing, a vehicle for an abstract thought-complex, a carrier of awesome feelings . . . and therefore real'.[3] And whether the revelation of the effect of a single stripe on a coloured ground was primarily a technical and visual one, which he subsequently felt able to endow with great enough emotional and intellectual weight by secret, internal references to a body of visionary literature and thought, or whether his rediscovery of his Jewish heritage prepared the way for this vision is a question which I suspect even he himself could not have answered. With regard to Newman's *Onements*: in one of the two great Kabbalistic text books, Zohar, which in itself means 'Brightness', and which appeared in the twelfth century, we read: 'It is only when he is complete that a man is called "one" . . . when he is male together with female'.[4] The sixteenth-century Rabbi Isaac Luria informs us that the genetic moment corresponded with the appearance of a divine ray of light. And one of the most distinguished commentators on Luria tells us that '. . . the first being which emanates from . . . the fullness of divine light was . . . Adam Kadman, the primordial man. Adam Kadman is nothing but a first configuration of the divine light which flows from the essence of the Hidden God into the primeval space of the Tsim-Tsum [the vacuum essential to the true act of creativity] – not indeed from all sides, but like a beam, in one direction only'.[5] Many of Newman's paintings feature stripes or zips which can be read as rays of light piercing through the coloured grounds.

Whatever the metaphysical implications of the upright band in *Onement 1*, it records very physically the painter's presence: it is the mark that stands both for him as a body and for that body's act. Newman had been moved by the Giacometti sculpture exhibition which he saw early in 1948 at the Pierre Matisse Gallery, presumably because of the way in which Giacometti's thin, strip-like figures were so imbued with presence and life. The most compressed of these presences (like the one reproduced on the cover of the catalogue) must have meant
148 most to him. *Man Pointing* of 1947, on the other hand, also in the exhibition, looks as if he might be about to perform Newman's act, to make the mark on Newman's pivotal canvas. It is instructive, too, to compare *Onement 1* with a
149 work dated by Still to 1945 in which he has rendered the human figure as a single twisting line accentuated by two red dots which read as eyes, or possibly breasts. Whereas the Newman confronts the viewer very symbolically, in the Still we feel

147 Barnett Newman, *Onement 1*, oil on canvas, 1948.

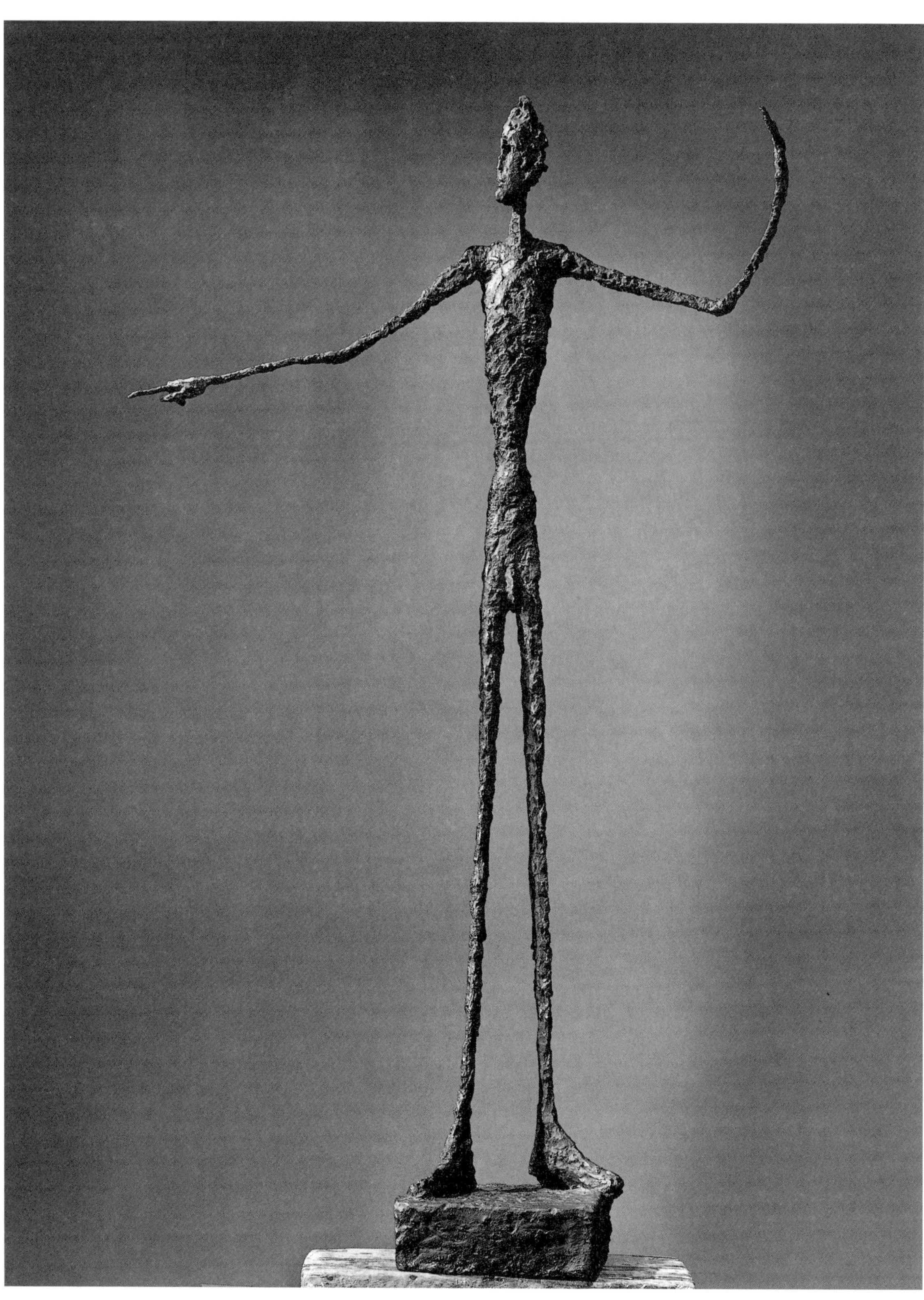

148 Alberto Giacometti, *Man Pointing*, bronze, 1947.

149 Clyfford Still, *July 1945-R*, oil on canvas, 1945.

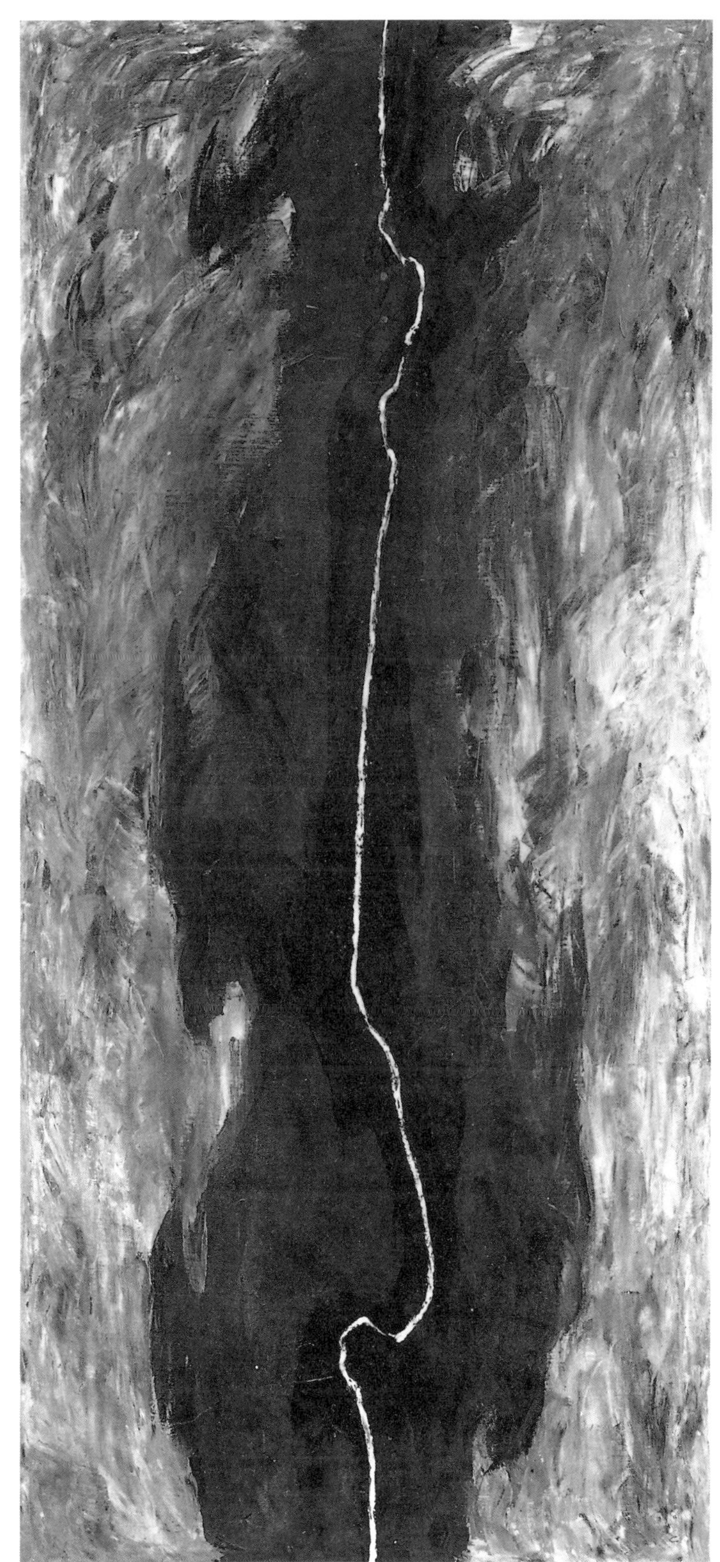

an invitation, which is simultaneously a threat, to move up into the dark central area of the canvas where we would feel ourselves simultaneously engulfed by a presence of our own height (the canvas is almost 6 ft high) and menaced by the ragged forces which move inwards from the sides of the picture.

It was in the mid-1940s that Still asserted himself as one of the most formally inventive artists of his generation. A work such as *January 1947*, for example, 144
forces one to modify or readjust critical terminology in order to discuss it. The painting has about it some of the same sensation of flux that characterizes Pollock's first 'drip' paintings and it evokes analogies with certain late works by Monet, in particular late works of the *Water Lilies* series, in that we have the sensation of looking up at the picture, reading the canvas vertically as it appears on the wall, and yet down onto it as though gazing into a pool of water. Monet's name had begun to occur in critical comment of the period.[6] In *January 1947* the white and black areas read partly as thickened linear rhythms, partly as shapes (although 'non-shapes' might describe them more accurately), while the act of deliberately running them off at the sides, coupled with the recurrent emergence of browns between them, defies any traditional figure-ground relationship. Greenberg was to remark: 'Still's paintings no longer divide into shapes, but into zones and areas and fields of colour.'[7]

A confrontation between contemporary canvases of Newman, Rothko and Still raises cardinal issues about the very nature of the new abstraction.The works look very different from each other and yet demonstrably share a common ethos. Without exception the great pioneering abstractionists – and the Americans were even more nakedly insistent upon this than the Europeans – believed that the *content* of their work was their prime concern and motivation. And yet as the alliances of the American painters in the pioneering years began to turn into rivalries in the late 1940s and increasingly in the 1950s, it was not the question of who had *said* what first in their pictures that became the obsessive and burning issue in the painters' minds, but rather primacy in the matter of formal innovation – who had done what first.

Inevitably as the visual idioms devised by the painters to strip pictorial language down to its essentials, to its purest expression, as this form of absolute was achieved, so its subsequent manifestations could for the most part only become increasingly self-referential. Mondrian's capacity for visual self-renewal within the context of reductive purity was greater than that of any other abstract artist, but there is no question that his work of the 1930s was more about itself, more about style, than his previous abstractions had been. It is consistent with the heroism of his vision that he had consistently sought to kick the ladder of his stylishness out from under himself, most notably when he was forced to flee Paris and particularly on his arrival in New York in 1940. Newman, more than any other artist, had sensed intuitively how to follow Mondrian's example. Latterly Mondrian had insisted upon the fact that the positive powers of destruction in art had never been sufficiently recognized. Now 'destruction' was becoming a favourite word and concept of Newman's within the context of his own work. Newman's manipulation of the destructive principle was much more self-conscious and certainly more programmatic than that of his mentor. Still's desire to destroy his progenitors was visceral. Rothko was more open to the past than either of them, but through his apprehension of their work he, too, increasingly transcended his visual origins.

It is now that the question of scale begins to loom large. The use of a large format had to a great extent been pioneered by Still; up to 1948 his canvases are on average larger than Pollock's. By the late 1940s Pollock recognized that his work was poised between easel painting and the mural,[8] and Newman and Still were working on approximately the same scale. The initial *Onement* had been relatively small. But by the early 1950s Newman had decided, in his own words, that 'scale equals feeling', and he now takes the lead in pushing scale to its limits. The issue of scale inevitably raises the concept of the sublime which became fundamental to revolutionary American abstraction.[9] The last great European painter to be preoccupied by the sublime was probably Delacroix. But the very nature of America's geography and its relative artistic isolation had kept issues related to the sublime very much alive and fundamental to much its nineteenth-century landscape painting. The sublime was revived as an issue in American painting of the 1940s, partly at least because the current passion for anthropology raised the question of man's relationship to his environment. In keeping with his Gothic cast of mind Still had been engrossed with ideas about the sublime since university days. Newman has left us with the cardinal document on the subject, his essay 'The Sublime is Now', delivered as a paper to a symposium on the subject and published in *Tiger's Eye* in December 1948.[10] In it Newman goes directly back to Longinus, who in the third century initiated the whole discourse on the sublime; and in this context it is worth remarking that Longinus' concern was primarily with rhetoric and that rhetoric touches Newman's discourse. Newman then moves on to Kant and Hegel, whose distinctions between the concept of ideal beauty and the exaltation occasioned by the sublime he finds confused, as indeed they were, although despite Newman's great clarity of mind he in turn misses the point that this confusion was fundamental to the very distinction these philosophers were making about the way we apprehend the beautiful and the sublime. Newman's own attempt to clarify the dilemma is as reductive as his contemporary painting and part of his principle of destruction: simply get rid of the whole concept of beauty, and in the process thus rejects European art that derives from classical or Renaissance traditions. The Gothic and the Baroque he puts slightly to one side.

Newman's strictures on Mondrian are of particular interest: 'even Mondrian... in his insistence on pure subject-matter succeeded only in raising the white plane and the rectangle into a realm of sublimity where the sublime paradoxically becomes an absolute of perfect sensation. The geometry swallowed up his metaphysics.' The concept of the sublime is one that touched Mondrian only indirectly, although the infinity of ocean and the starry firmament above it had helped propel him into abstraction. The sublime he would have associated with the tragic element in art that he was out to suppress. At a painterly level, however, Newman felt that the content of Mondrian's art had ultimately been obscured by style. Newman was not alone in associating the absolute with perfection, but if he was rejecting perfection when he created his 'tabula rasa', he also must surely have believed that in so doing he had created for himself a touchstone, a visual certainty or absolute from which a new art might then proceed with all its sublime imperfections.

Newman's essay is invigorating and challenging, but it is as important for what it implies as for what it says. Right at the beginning of it he states: 'The European artist has been continually involved in the moral struggle between notions of beauty and the desire for sublimity.' Kant felt that the apprehension of beauty was more easily reconcilable with concepts of morality than he was able positively to associate them with the thrill of sublimity. But by destroying or rejecting beauty Newman was not dismissing the idea of morality: on the contrary, he was implying that the very process of creating an original work of art is a morally affirmative act, and this is something that artists since time immemorial have at least instinctively believed. Newman concludes, 'the image we produce is the self-evident one of revelation, real and concrete, that can be understood by anyone who will look at it without the nostalgic glasses of history.'

Newman is particularly unkind about Burke, whose view of the sublime he sees as 'unsophisticated and primitive'. Despite this, he was nevertheless deeply indebted to him and to Burke's *Philosophical Inquiry into the Origin of our Ideas of the Sublime and Beautiful* (published in 1756) which, if it did not necessarily influence him in his choice of vast formats, must have confirmed his predilection for them. Burke felt that if an object is both simple and vast, the eye (and hence the mind) does not arrive readily at its bounds and has no rest since 'the image is everywhere the same'. He also states that, 'A species of greatness arises from [the creation] of the artificial infinite'; and he remarks furthermore that, 'A perpendicular has more force in forming the sublime than an inclined plane.'[11] In 1948, the year of his essay, Newman had taken a trip to Ohio, where he had experienced the sublime very physically. He was stunned by the presence he felt in the Indian mounds and by the openness and loneliness of their surroundings. He said, 'Here you get a sense of your own presence . . . I became involved with the idea of making the viewer present, the idea that *man is present*.'[12] Henceforth Newman's major concern was with creating in his paintings a sense of place. When we stand in front of a vast Newman, we get the sensation of being somewhere as much as of looking at something.

It was in 1949 and 1950 that the full force of Newman's talent began to make itself felt; during the latter year in particular a true monumentality begins to
inform his art, as for example in *Adam* of 1951–2. The composition reads like a 150
reversed and abstracted variant of that of *Genetic Moment* (1947), with the broader stripe standing again for the male principle and the more slender upright to the left for the female, although any such symbolism was by now probably unconscious. Adam, the Kabbalisitic interpretatation of the Book of Genesis tells us, was fashioned out of clay, and the background of the picture is a deep, rich earth; it is, however, dangerous to read any specific symbolism into these works. The titles always came after the painting process, and Newman stressed his intention to make the title 'a metaphor that describes my feelings when I did the
painting'.[13] *Eve*, of 1950, is more expansive, more welcoming. A dazzling field 151
of light cadmium moves across the canvas to meet the tight, darker band of alizarin that arrests its progress at the the right. Newman always insisted that his importance was as a draughtsman, and although the colour sensations he was evoking were original in that he presents us with saturated fields of single colours on a scale hitherto unencountered, already here one senses that the red is just as much a band pulled or extended outwards to become a vast upright as it is simply a larger contiguous shape to the vertical beside it. 'Instead of using outline, instead of making shapes or setting off space, my drawing *declares* the space',[14] Newman insisted. And of a vast, predominantly red canvas of 1968,
Anna's Light (measuring 9 ft x 20 ft), he remarked that he wanted to see how far 152

150 Barnett Newman, *Adam*, oil on canvas, 1951–2.

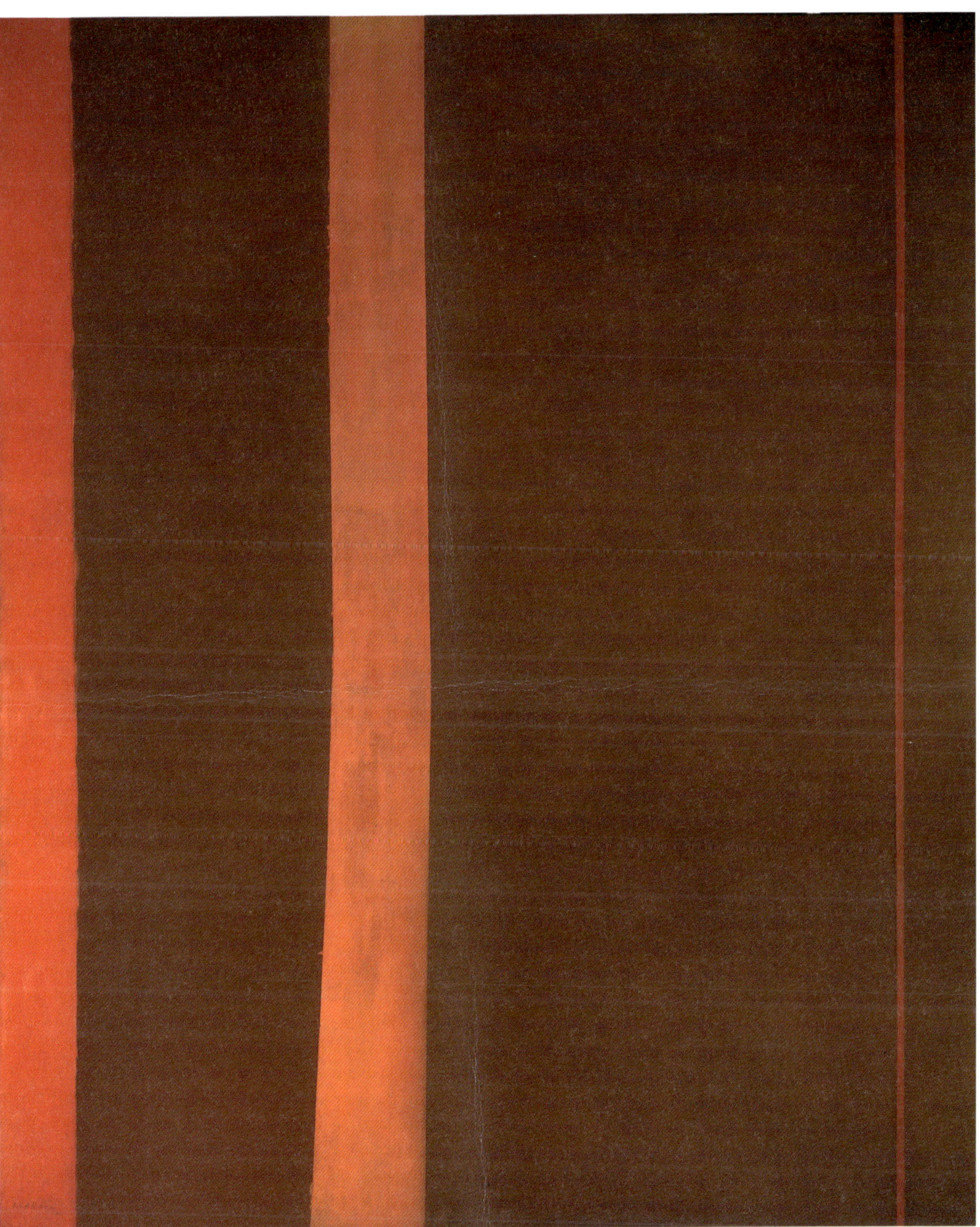

he could 'push red'.[15] In other words, the spectator is in effect looking at the widest red line ever to have been seen.

Newman had a tendency to work on pairs of canvases. This habit was not programmatic – and he insisted that each work was equally valid when seen separately. Rather the practice arose from the fact that when he was working on a particular canvas he became aware of the possibility of handling an identical format differently. Again here there are parallels with Mondrian, although Mondrian thought more in terms of series than of individual works. Once Mondrian had exhausted a series of possibilities within a group of pictures, he began the process over again in another. Newman likewise kept his art alive and avoided repetition by devising new individual constructs.The pair to *Adam*, in terms of
its being of almost identical size, is not *Eve*, but *Achilles* of 1952. It was perhaps 153
while working on this painting that Newman realized that the red form, broader than the areas to either side of it, had linear implications and could be read as a line expanded horizontally.

The grandest of Newman's paired canvases are undoubtedly *Vir Heroicus Sub-* 154
limis of 1950–1 and *Cathedra*, which belongs to the latter year. He had been 155
impressed by Pollock's *Number 1* of 1949 – it measures over 5 ft x 8 ft – when he had seen it at Betty Parsons' gallery the following year. Pollock had been the first to expand his canvases laterally, which was indeed the only way they could logically go after they had reached room or loft height. Newman, however, decided to push scale even further, stretching up the two 8 ft x 18 ft canvases. Eighteen was to become a standard unit for him and 'his number'. (Eighteen is what Marcel Duchamp would have described as 'mathematically agile': 18 inches = 1½ ft; 18 is also the product of 2 x 9, nine being at once an uneven number and one capable of multiple subdivision.) As Hess once again points out, the Shemoneh Esreh is the eighteenth and most important prayer in the three daily services in the Jewish temple and a number stressed in the Talmud.[16] *Vir Heroicus Sublimis* and *Cathedra* can be seen as iconographically complementary in that the title of the former suggests man's attempt to transcend his human limitations and hence his desire to act in a God-like way. *Cathedra* represents by implication the Chair or presence of the Divinity himself. Characteristically, Judaic and Christian references are fused. Speaking of *Cathedra*, Newman referred to Isaiah's vision: 'I saw the Lord sitting on a throne, high and lifted up, the train of his mantle filled the temple.'[17] Both works make use of what Hess calls Newman's 'hidden symmetry', which involved basically the deduction (or addition) of the width of a stripe or stripes from one unit which would otherwise be identical with another within the same painting, Yet again Mondrian had used similar devices to animate his first lozenge pictures. In *Vir Heroicus Sublimis* the pale, pinky-fawn zip to the extreme right was added later, after the work was provisionally finished, obviously to stop the painting drifting off too slackly to the side and to counteract or modify the insistence of the brightest 'zip' (second from the left). In *Cathedra* two 8-ft square areas are separated by a broad off-white band, but overall symmetry is avoided by the way in which a subsidiary pale-blue 'zip' passes through the right-hand square and the narrower area to the right of it, so suggesting that they share the same field.

Uriel of 1955 (of the same dimensions) marks a climax in Newman's fully 156
mature heroic manner, and there is a sense in which this painting unites the dual principles of *Vir Heroicus Sublimis* and *Cathedra* – the human struggle towards

151 Barnett Newman, *Eve*, oil on canvas, 1950.

152 Barnett Newman, *Anna's Light*, acrylic on canvas, 1968.

153 Barnett Newman, *Achilles*, oil on canvas, 1952.

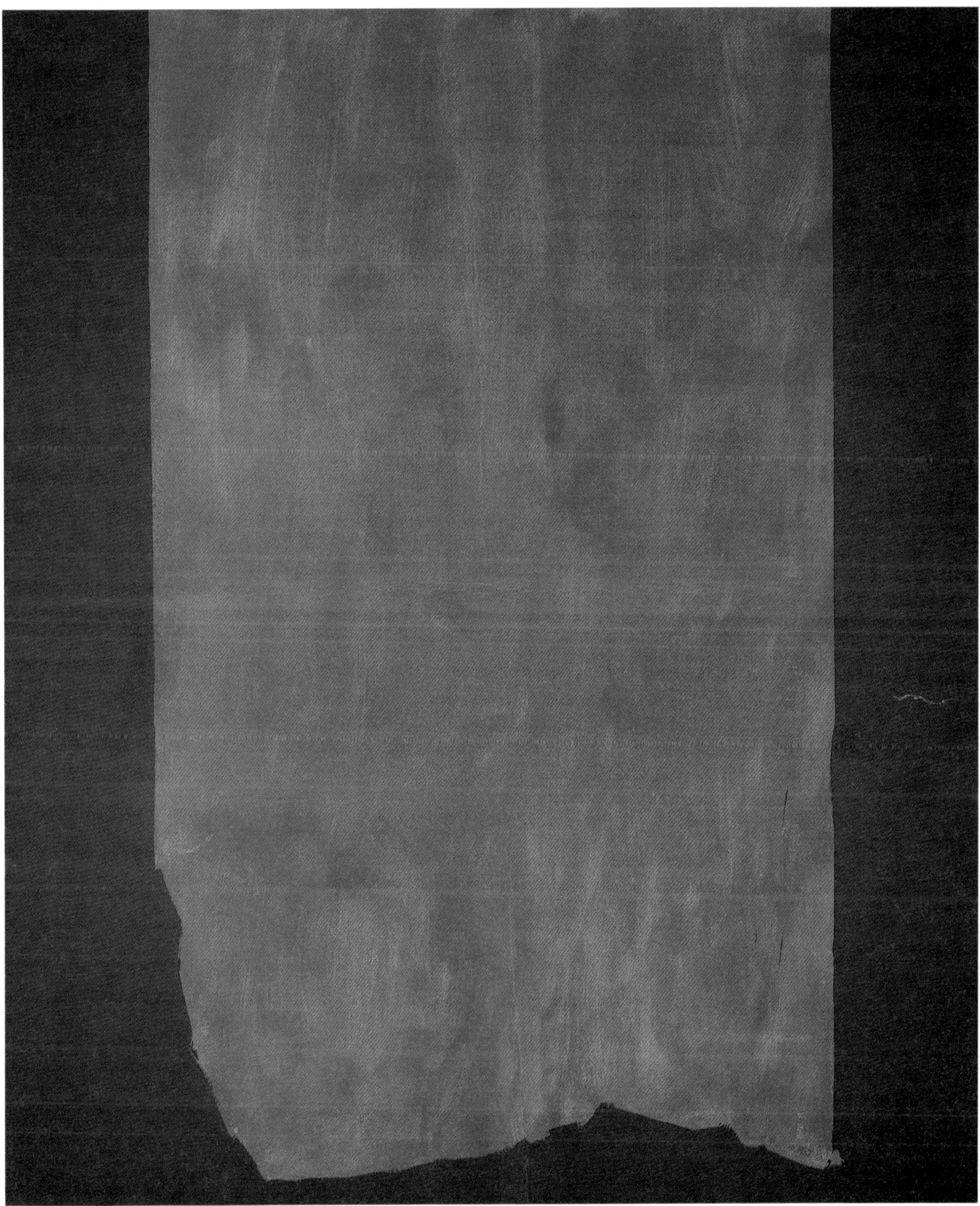

154 Barnett Newman, *Vir Heroicus Sublimis*, oil on canvas, 1950–1.

155 Barnett Newman, *Cathedra*, oil on canvas, 1951.

an unattainable perfectibility and the abstract perfection, in Newman's case, of some unspecified divinity. The title *Uriel* refers to the angel of light or 'Flame of God', who in the Torah performs the Promethean task of bringing the divine flame to earth. By now Newman was very much aware of providing contrast in his surfaces, using different kinds of paint or pigment, and already in *Cathedra* the blues had been subliminally mottled to avoid visual monotony. In *Uriel* the pale, celestial, almost eggshell blue advances from left to right, towards the earthier, muddier yet resonant brownish reds that Newman had used in *Adam*; it is brought up sharp by the darker zip, beyond which it emerges as a zip in its own right. Because it now occupies a narrow division between two darks, it reads as being brighter and lighter than the vast area to the left. It then bleeds through in a second, feathery zip that in turn transforms the left edge of the red-brown into a third zip. The work is a superb example of the combination of stunning simplicity with subtlety and ambiguity that had become the hallmark of Newman's art.

Still's absorption with the sublime was of a more intuitive and less analytical nature than that of Newman,[18] who tended to use his intellectual sources as platforms from which to launch a new kind of art, one which he first of all apprehended as being imminent and necessary, then formulated intellectually, illustrating it originally in a somewhat diagrammatic fashion, and to which he subsequently gave heroic expression. It was in a sense because of his great intellectual range that Newman was forced to become a synthesizer and, in the process, a

reductionist. Still, on the other hand, found in the ethos of the sublime confirmation of his own nature. He had rejected traditional concepts of beauty from the start, and long before Newman read and thought his way into doing so. Still was one of nature's anarchists, and it was the *status quo* of art that he was out to destroy. He rejoiced in the more disturbing and turbulent aspects of the sublime. Inevitably, because he was an artist of high stature he was to create a new kind of beauty – at times menacing, even crushing, at others of a radiant ferocity – that was at odds with, or which formed the counterpart to the magisterial serenity of Newman's art. If the concept of the artificial infinite is in different ways equally important for both artists, among other attributes ascribed to the sublime by the philosophers concerned with it, that of the terrible (and here again Burke is of particular relevance) struck a responsive chord in Still's psychological make-up. Unlike Newman's works, Still's are not analogies for places hitherto unimagined, nor do they serve as visual metaphors for the tragic, as are Rothko's. Rather they remained confrontations with demonic forces in which freedom or self-determination was the prize; and here the legacy of Nietzsche continues to shine forth. It might be fair to say that despite his sophistication, Still remains the most primordial of all twentieth-century painters.

Despite subsequent rifts, there is no doubt at all that during the second half of the 1940s and increasingly as the decade drew to a close, and then on into the early 1950s, Newman, Still and Rothko were drawing sustenance from each

156 Barnett Newman, *Uriel*, oil on canvas, 1955.

other's achievements and above all from the artistic climate which they were
mutually fostering, and which allowed their talents to flower further in such an
unforgettable way. In 1948, the year of Newman's first *Onement* painting, Still
157 had finished a virtually monochromatic painting, *1947–48-W No. 2*, begun the
previous year; this was a work to which he attached great importance. In it the
dark masses derived from his earlier body and shamanistic imagery soar up off the
top of the painting. The picture's metaphoric *élan vital* is rendered in upright
rivulets of blood red. But it is in 1949 and 1950 that Still's work opens up in
feeling and it is now that he emerges as a true colourist. He once stated: 'I never
wanted colour to be colour. I never wanted texture to be texture or images to
become shape. I wanted them all to fuse into a living spirit.'[19] But on another
occasion he confessed to having become a colourist.[20] When he did so, he was
acknowledging that, like all painters, he could not entirely escape his means.

158 In a resplendent, predominantly red work of 1949, coded simply *H*, Still makes
use of a more regularized, linear banding of yellow at the left, and this would
suggest that he was not unaware of developments in Newman's art. At a more
general level one senses the presence of Newman behind the new monumentality
which informs Still's work at this time and especially in the pregnant emptiness of
159 a yellow painting coded *November 1950* – a pivotal work in Still's development in
that it heralds a new spaciousness and fluency in his art. This was to go hand in
hand with an enhanced, oddly crusted luminosity which would become a hallmark of his subsequent art; here he may have learned a lesson from Rothko. This
luminosity informed even the darkest canvases of the 1950s, and Still's mastery of
the use of black was to become a unique feature of his work. Black he saw as
warm and generative.

It is deeply revealing of Still's art that in 1946 and 1947, when he was deliberately obscuring all distinction between forms derived from earlier images and the ground that contains them, the last residual or particularized shapes should have been those derived from the shaman's wand or staff. Now, having created his own kind of 'tabula rasa' with the monochromatic yellow painting of 1950, he marries a new breadth and expansiveness back onto his earlier concerns. Increasingly he simply leaves patches of canvas bare to read as colour and light, sometimes to act as haloes around jagged slabs of pigment. His vast, saturated fields once again take on a certain shape value, although his attitude to the picture edge is now much less self-conscious and liberated, with the result that the paintings seem more expansive. Small streaks of darker or contrasting colour flicker through the larger areas or fields, animating them. One might perhaps be justified in seeing them as subliminal acts of magic, messages, wafted from the shaman's wand: the totality of the pictorial surface or image and the act of magic or ritual are now confounded. The smaller colour accents work best when they are kept to a
minimum or when they become compositional entities in their own right. This can
160 be seen at work in the fluency and mastery of such a work as *L. No. 2* of 1951.
Here the central jagged yellow extends beyond the confines of upper and lower edges of the canvas, but the implication of yellow over white is denied by the more linear yellows at the sides which make the raw canvas and its white, plume-like personification (just off top centre, to the right) read as pictorial fields in their own right. At an intermediate level the smaller accents can be read as colour patches rather than as coloured accents or shapes and at this stage they can sometimes seem somewhat fussy and disruptive.

157 Clyfford Still, *1947–48-W No. 2*, oil on canvas, 1948.

158 Clyfford Still, *1949-H*, oil on canvas, 1949.

The work of the 1950s reaches one of its many climaxes in the masterpiece now in Buffalo, *1957-D No. 1*, one of the pinnacles of twentieth-century abstraction, 161
and possibly an unconscious answer to the monumentality of, for example, Newman's *Cathedra* or his *Uriel*. Still was, however increasingly detaching himself himself from developments in New York. Since 1952 he had either quarrelled with or divorced himself from all his erstwhile colleagues. When, after a long interval, he agreed once more to exhibit and to do a last brief teaching spell, he undertook these activities elsewhere.[21] Still vehemently rejected all landscape analogies with his art, and certainly any attempts to draw concrete parallels between his pictures and the landscapes of his formative years draw a blank. Yet his vision had been formed by the vastness and loneliness of the American and Canadian West, and one of the things that sets him apart from both Newman and Rothko is the essentially anti-urban quality of his art. There is a sense in which his pictures were, as he insisted, simply himself. Like Pollock, he *was* nature and his largest and most majestic canvases constitute the Grand Canyons of abstract painting. Certainly no other twentieth-century canvases can echo so dramatically the craving of earlier centuries for the sublime. Although as viewers we experience individual works by Still so physically, his idea of the sublime involves an ongoing, vertiginous sense of flux. When we stand in front of one of his works, our eyes are led so dizzyingly up the surface that we sometimes feel ourselves suspended over the top edge and about to fall off, only to begin the ascent once more – and, in contrast to Newman's paintings, Still's can never be read downwards as well. With Newman (although he did work occasionally in series, most notably in the *Stations of the Cross* of 1958–64) each picture is an individual entity, a separate world. Still's work on the other hand can best be appreciated as a continuum. He said, 'No painting stops with itself, is complete of itself. It is a continuum of previous paintings and is renewed in successive ones.'[22] Still's absolute, as he stressed, was quite simply himself, and it died with him. Newman's was a new beginning and then a succession of numinous places that he created. In them other artists found inspiration.

If Still attached particular importance to his painting *1947–48-W No. 2*, this was in part because Rothko, after seeing it in the summer of 1949 (when he was teaching for the second time at the California School of Fine Arts), borrowed the painting and took it back with him to New York. He lived with it for six years until Still called for its return after their relationship had become embittered. Clearly Still felt that his painting had conditioned Rothko's subsequent development. By 1949 Rothko had in fact achieved his own mature and totally personal 162
style, but Still had indeed played a part in its formation, both pictorially and psychologically. The subject of art and morality suffused the intellectual climate at the time. Still took a more belligerently moral attitude towards his own work than did any of his contemporaries. Rothko, a more vulnerable artist, sought in certain respects to emulate it. However, Rothko's *Untitled* of 1949 must surely illustrate 163
his response to the disturbing forces informing the painting by Still that he had taken into his home. In a letter of 20 April 1949, before Rothko's journey to the West, Still wrote to him: 'I await your arrival to announce the magnificent evil which our work must be to those who would suppress us.'[23]

The differences between these two paintings are as revealing as their similarities. Despite the fact that Still saw black as warm and affirmative, his surfaces are charred and cindery, while those of Rothko are soft and smoky. Still's contours

159 Clyfford Still, *November 1950*, oil on canvas, 1950.

160 Clyfford Still, *1951-L No. 2*, oil on canvas, 1951.

161 Clyfford Still, *1957-D No. 1*, oil on canvas, 1957.

are rough and jagged, like obsidian knives, and he defies a figure-ground relationship by running the blacks aggressively off all four edges of the canvas and picking up the whites in dots or small streaks within them. Rothko, although allowing the blacks to escape from the top of the canvas in a smudgy fashion, is still working – and continued to work – on a disguised, loose or subliminal grid. Like Still, he negates a traditional shape-to-ground relationship, albeit more tentatively, by allowing the blacks to flirt equivocally with the painting's edges; and his shapes, rather than the totality of the picture surface, remain its principal protagonists. In the painting by Still forces are on the move. In the Rothko presences hover; and although ultimately they derive from the grouped hybrids of previous years, they force us to confront and apprehend them so frontally and totally that we sense behind the interaction of soft shapes a single living spirit, a single entity. In 'The Romantics Were Prompted' Rothko had stated, 'For me the great achievements of the centuries in which the artist accepted the probable and the familiar as his subjects were the pictures of the single figure – alone in a moment of utter immobility.' Rothko insisted that the changes that came about within his individual pictures were the result of a desire to *clarify* content. Still, on the other hand, declared contemporaneously, 'I do not intend to oversimplify . . . I revel in the extra-complex.'[24] The smudgy contours in a Rothko, their slightly more tangible overlappings, odd coagulations of strokes and marks within large shapes – all of these read in his work as details within a gently pulsing whole; and he once said he felt his paint should appear to be 'breathed onto the canvas'.[25] Still's jagged, coruscating paint areas, often applied with long, supple spatulas, consume and cannibalize each other in an on-going dialogue.

As early as the mid-1930s Rothko had jotted down in his notebooks thoughts about the possibility of beginning works with pure colour; now, in the late 1940s, colour, applied in large, somewhat amorphous but commanding areas, was to be the prime vehicle of his art. Although Freud was thinking of a much earlier and very different art, as Rothko's biographer James E.B. Breslin has suggested, a sentence of his seems startlingly relevant to Rothko's aims: 'We cannot do justice to the particular nature of the psyche by linear contours . . . the diffuse colour fields of the modern painters would do better.'[26] In this connection it is instructive to revert very briefly to the transitional *Multiforms* executed between 1947 and 1949 (see p. 163). Rothko's essay 'The Romantics Were Prompted' confirms that he was still thinking in terms of shapes rather than in terms of colour. His work hitherto had been not highly coloured but rather delicately tinted, and in his work of 1947–8 he often tends to separate the elements with strongest colour contrasts by allowing the ground between them to come through as white outline; the effects achieved, though bold and direct, are somewhat inert.

Two things now happened. Rothko became aware of the fact that if flat forms or shapes embedded in aqueous space were to be his pictorial subjects, they must become visually more loaded, and that it was only through colour that this could be done. He now turned to Arshile Gorky, who had recently emerged as the greatest colourist on the American scene. 164 Rothko must have been fascinated by the way in which Gorky at times dispensed with outlines and achieved a shimmering luminosity by blurring the coloured edge so that it seemed to palpitate and throb. These effects are reinforced by the way in which Gorky surrounds his colour areas with a paler or darker nimbus. Through Gorky, Rothko was in turn absorbing from Kandinsky lessons in the abstract and emotive properties of colour divorced

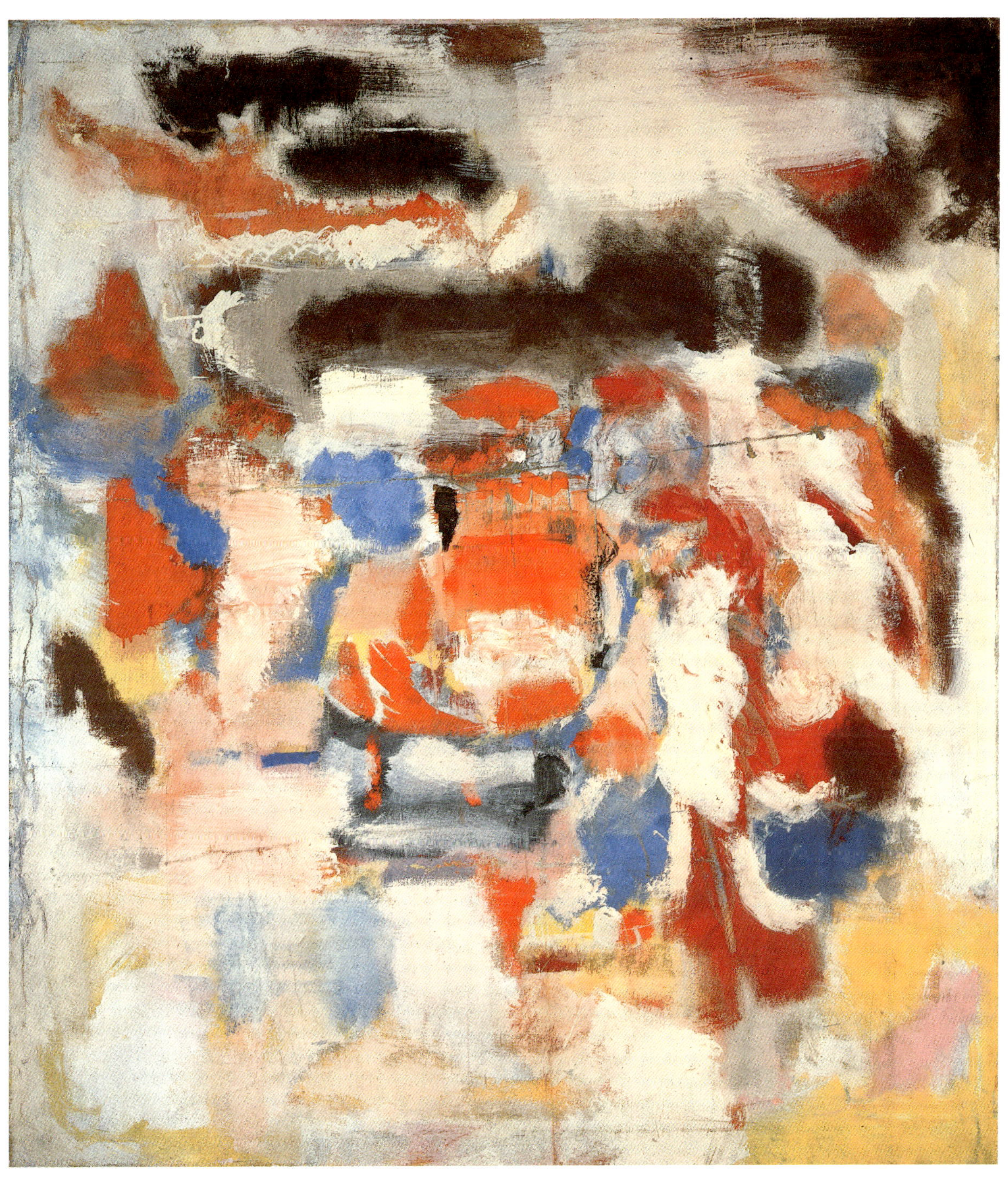

162 Mark Rothko, *Untitled 1948*, oil on canvas, 1948.

from the confines of lines or clearly delineated shapes. Secondly, like Still, but independently of him, Rothko proceeded to move up into his own pictures. By, so to speak, stepping up into them, he allowed their cumulative presence to cocoon or swathe him in the very matrix of pictorial matter. In 1949 he achieved his fully developed style and iconography: large, luminous rectangles, often only two of them, suspended one above another in floating space became the hallmark of his art. With canvases such as *Number 10* of 1950 he reached his own definition of 165
clarity which was to be 'the elimination of all obstacles between the painter and the idea and between the idea and the observer'.[27]

Rothko always insisted that he was 'no colourist',[28] a statement that is patently false and which was made, almost certainly, because he was reluctant to think that the beauty of his colour harmonies was vitiating their emotional charge, which he saw as being basically tragic. It is true that when we speak of the great colourists we tend to think of those artists who worked with a full palette, whereas in the case of Rothko he tended to work in individual paintings within gradations of some three to four hues. On the other hand, working with unusually large, saturated, flat planes of colour, Rothko has new lessons to teach us about its use.

There are many theories but no rules about colour. So-called 'hot colours' can be used in such a way that they look cool or even icy. Blues we tend to think of as spacious and restful, yet Matisse used to add small amounts of black to them to 'cool' them down. A confrontation between two complementary works by Rothko, *Green, Red on Orange* of 1951 and *Red, Dark Green, Green* of 1952, is 166, 167
instructive. Green tends generally speaking to be a pervasive, spreading colour, probably because of its association with renewal and growth in nature. Red by contrast is a more immediate and also a static colour. Most painters who use red in quantity tend to work around it; that it is to say, they go on changing the surrounding relationships rather than alter the original cadmium or vermilion hues. In the earlier work by Rothko the upper green area is smaller than the lower red one and floats above it, anchored by a darker fringe or banding at its lower edge, but at the same time expanding and spreading so that it gains equivalence with the larger, complementary red hue below. In the 1952 painting the relationships are reversed. But to support the heavier, more aggressive red the intermediate dark green – which represents what one might call in both works the 'area of suspense' and which Rothko himself would have called the 'element of violence' in his painting – has been thickened and widened, made more architectonic, girder-like.

There are dark Rothkos from the early 1950s and light ones from later in the decade, but the highest-keyed works tend generally speaking to lie in the first six years of the decade and many, like the exquisite *No.8* of 1952, are characterized 168
by an infinite variety of yellows, reinforced by apricot and orange hues. Even these works have about them a brooding, haunting air – and hence some of that tragic quality which Rothko felt to be the hallmark of his art. Yet these paintings also convey a feeling of liberation and exhilaration; and on visual grounds alone one senses that this period must have been the happiest in Rothko's entire life.

One of the characteristics of Rothko's work is how extraordinarily beautiful it makes the various shapes and even the dingiest garments of people standing in front of them appear. Newman had been been involved with the idea of 'making the spectator present'. In a different way, in Rothko's work the spectator becomes an integral part of the painting. And I myself am seized with the strange and irrational but overpowering sense that a Rothko, when not being looked at, somehow 169

163 Mark Rothko, *Untitled 1949*, oil on canvas, 1949.

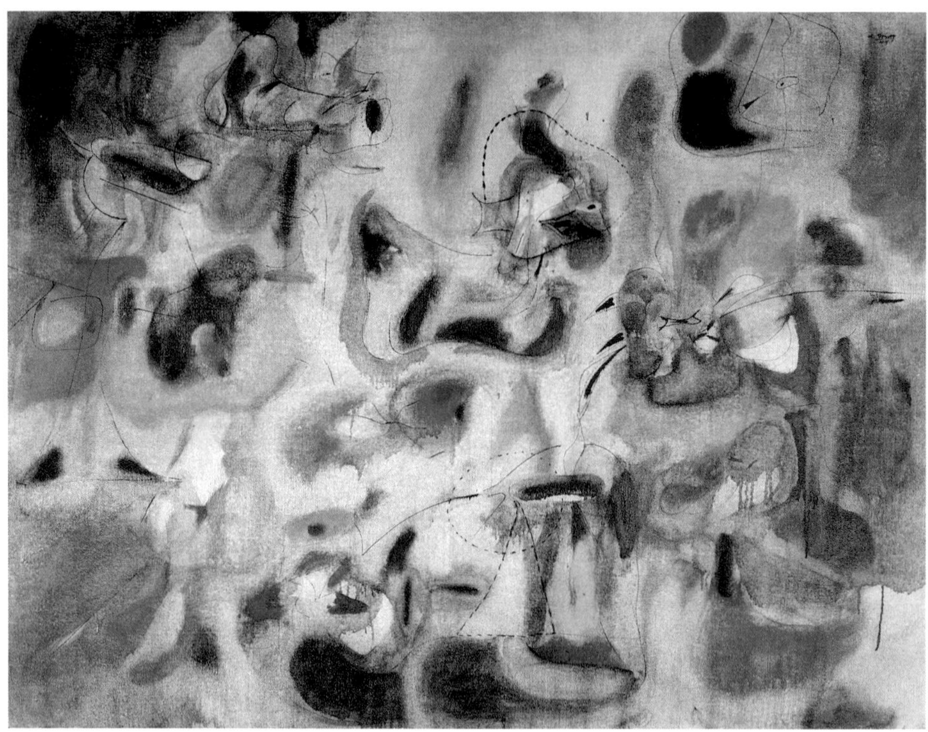

164 Arshile Gorky, *The Sun, the Dervish in the Tree*, oil on canvas, 1944.

165 Mark Rothko, *No. 10, 1950*, oil on canvas, 1950.

ceases to exist. In the case of optical painters such as Victor de Vasarely, Jesús Soto or Bridget Riley, we know that what we are are seeing or experiencing is something that is in fact taking place on a plane *between* the works and ourselves; and yet one can imagine that when the doors of the art galleries shut at night, the stripes or spots continue pulsing out into the darkness. The Rothkos, on the other hand, one imagines as remaining suspended in some nebulous half-world until the first visitor arrives to confront them the following morning. Possibly more any of the great abstractionists, and to an even greater degree than Kandinsky, Rothko was very conscious of the role of the spectator. Early in the 1950s he remarked, '. . . a picture lives by companionship, expanding and quickening in the eyes of the sensitive observer. It dies by the same token . . . How often it must be impaired by the eyes of the unfeeling and the cruelty of the impotent . . .'.[29]

Related to his apprehension about the viewer was his increasing obsession with how his pictures should be presented. Rothko liked his pictures to be hung near floor-level and, like Newman, he wanted his viewer to stand close to. He said, 'I paint very large pictures. I realise that historically the function of painting large pictures is something grandiose and pompous. The reason I paint them . . . is precisely because I want them to be very intimate and human, To paint a small picture is to place yourself outside your experience . . . to look at experience with a reducing glass. However when you paint the larger picture, you are in it. It isn't something you command.'[30] His statement stresses his own, gentler affiliation with the concept of the sublime.

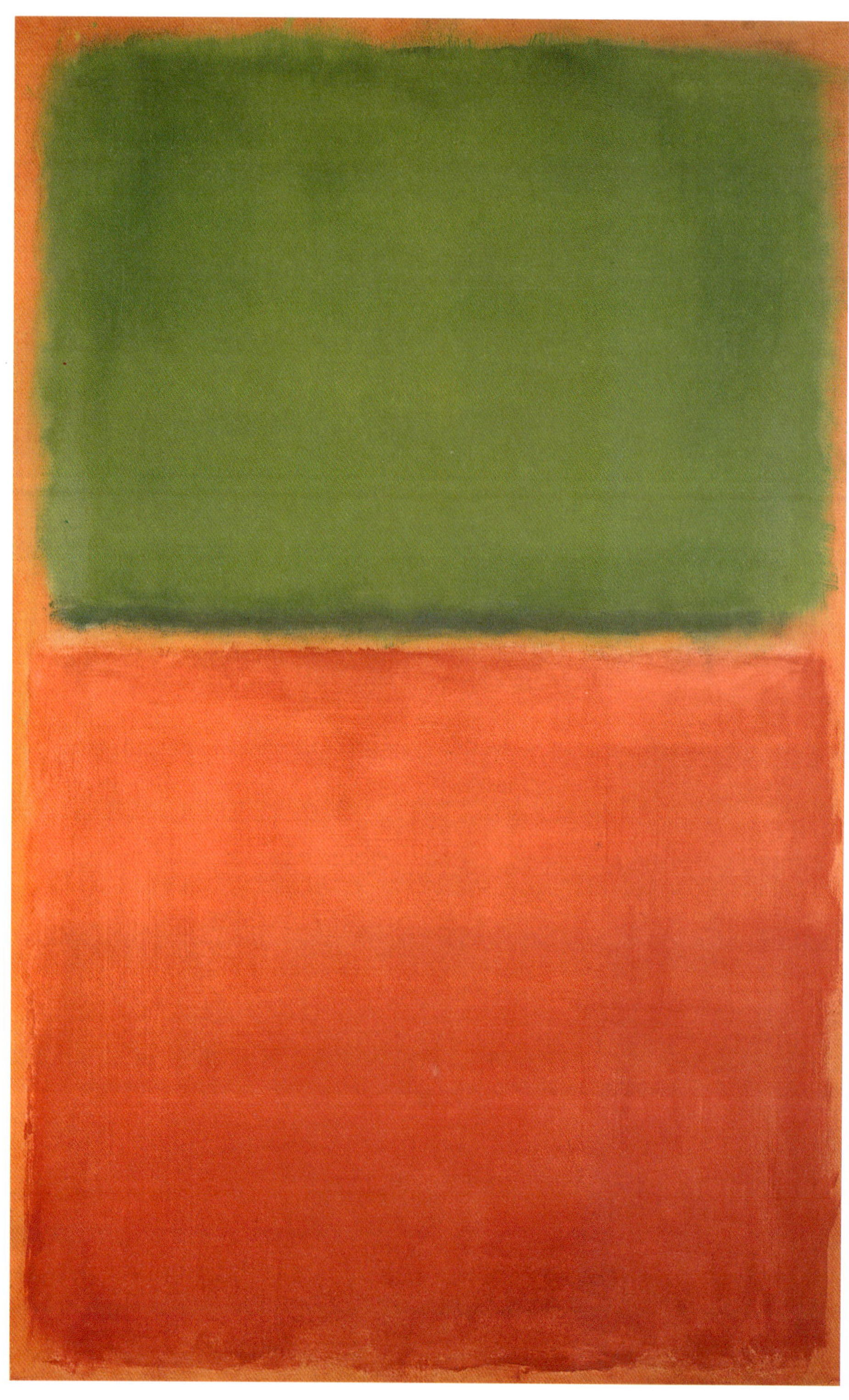

166 Mark Rothko, *Green, Red on Orange,* oil on canvas, 1951.

167 Mark Rothko, *Red, Dark Green, Green,* mixed media on canvas, 1952

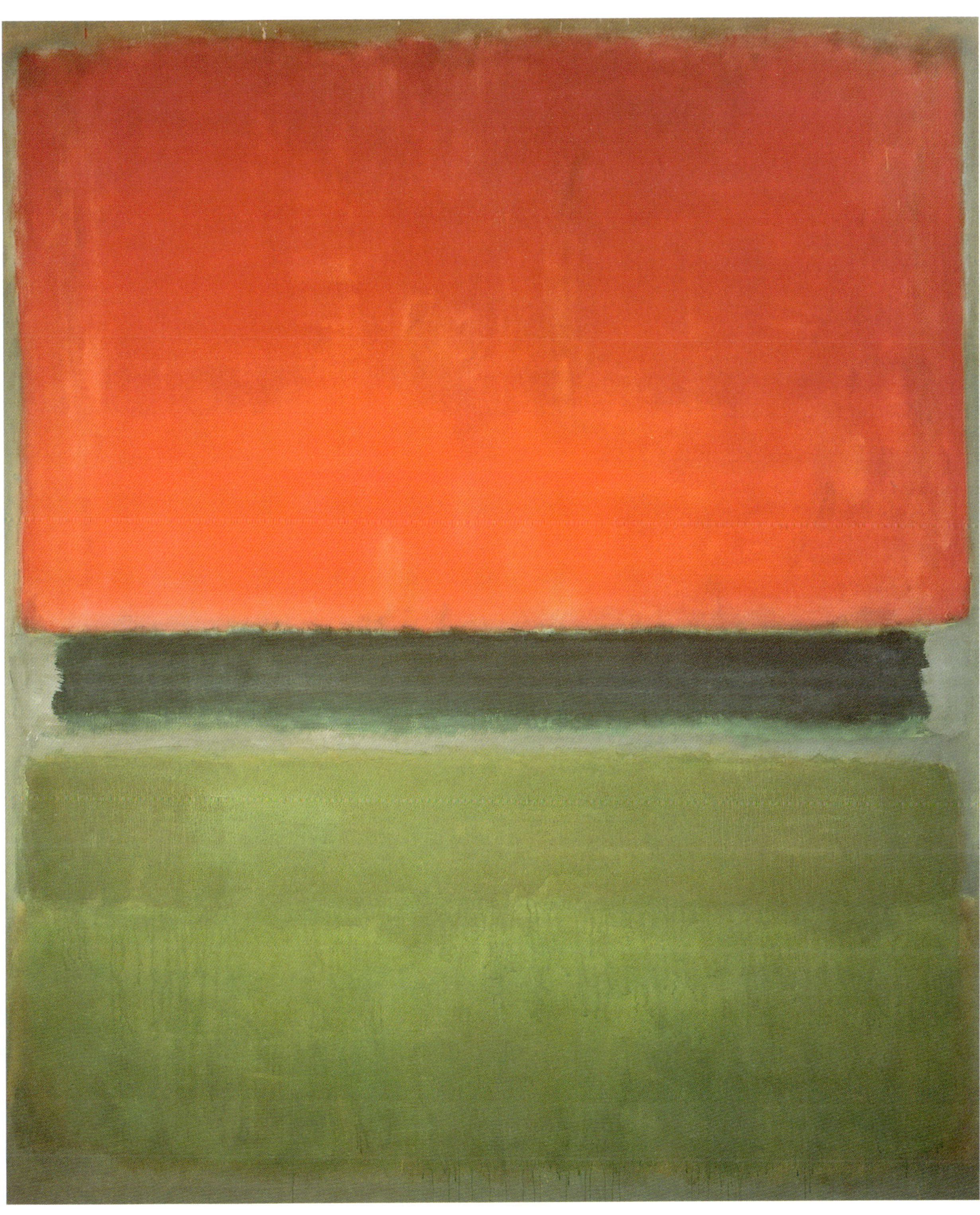

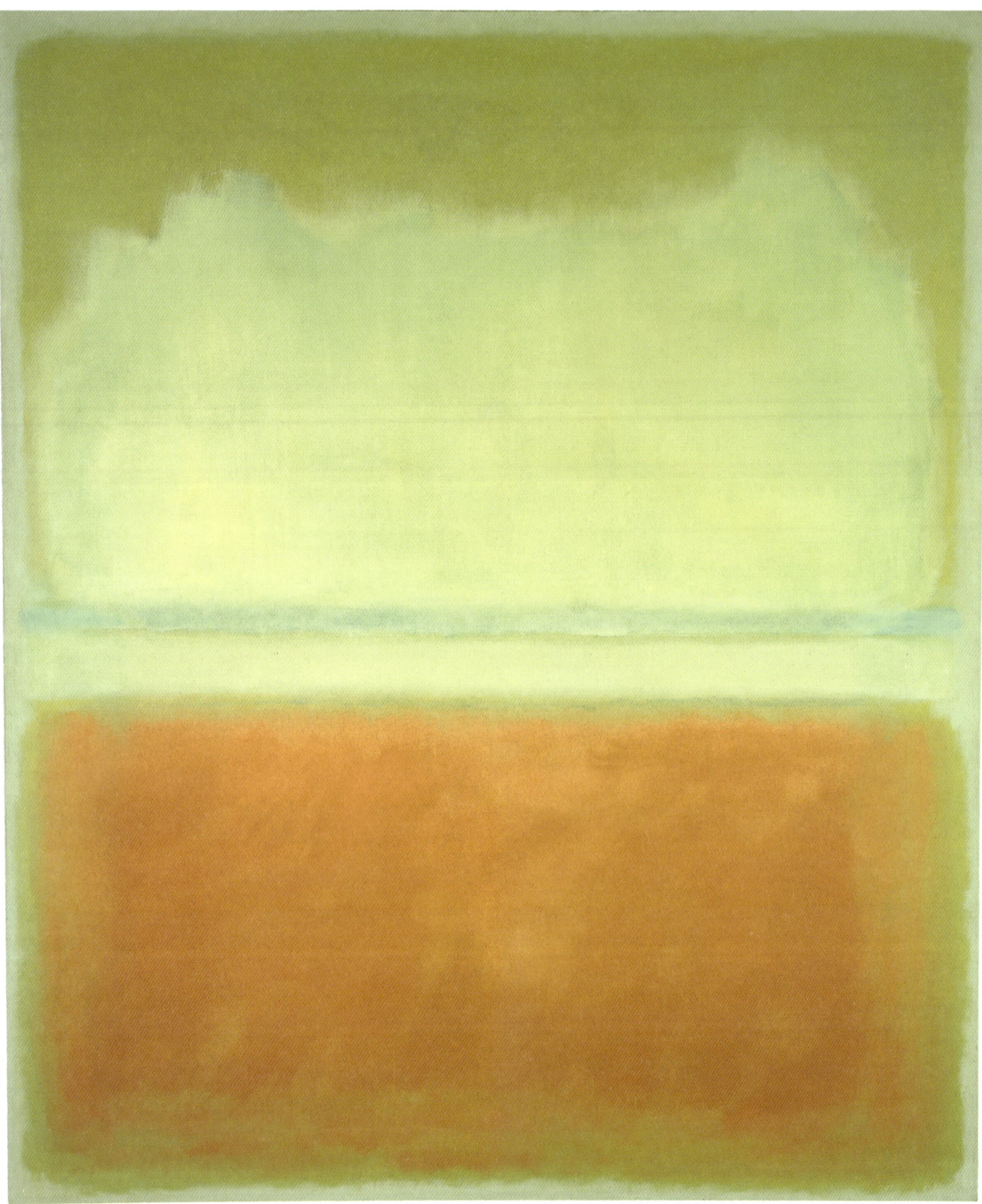

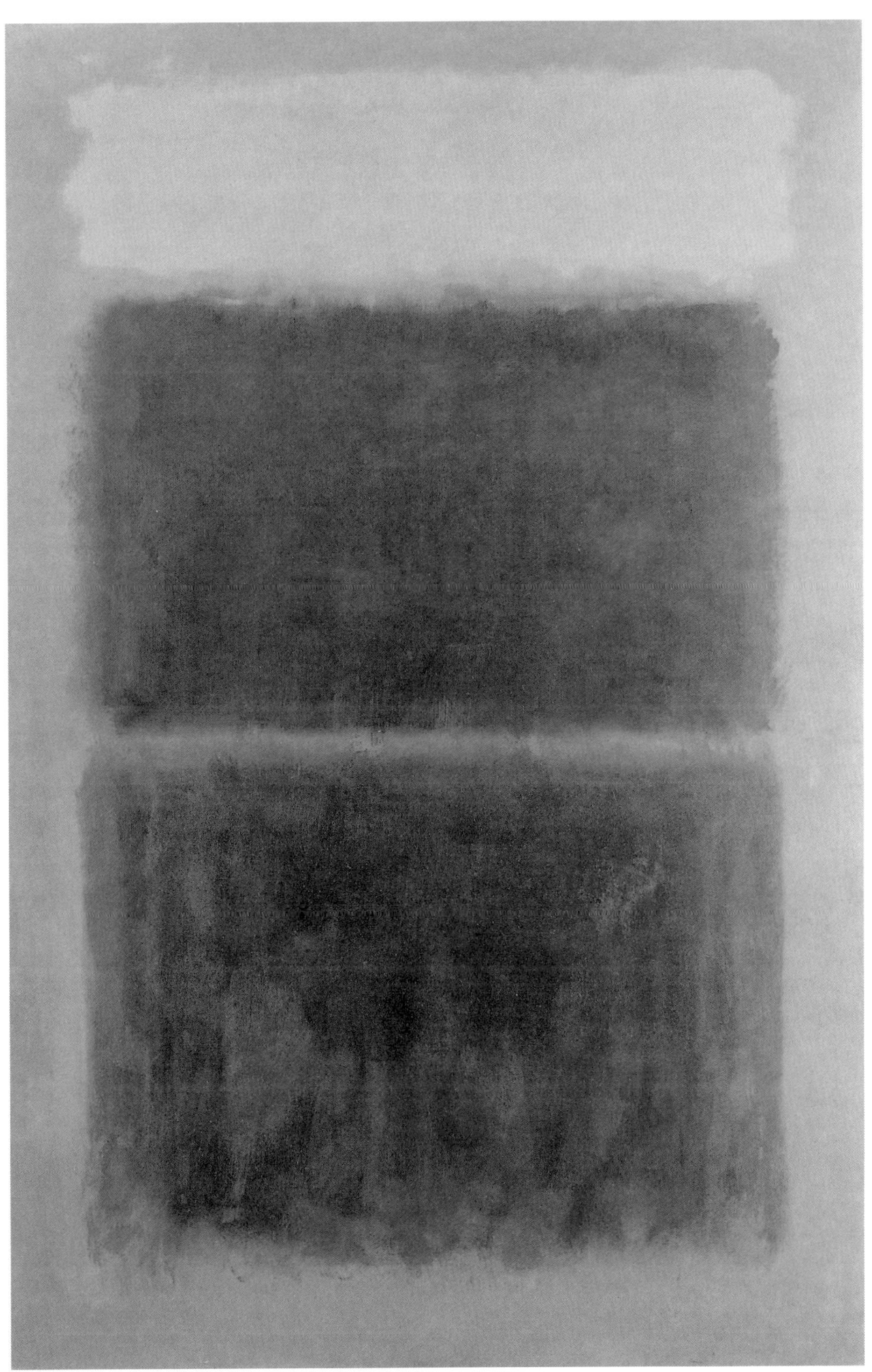

168 Mark Rothko, *Number 8*, oil on canvas, 1952.

169 Mark Rothko, *Light Red over Black*, oil on canvas, 1957.

Just as Rothko's trajectory into abstraction has with the benefit of time and scholarship become easier to talk about, so his fully mature style is more difficult to discuss than that of his closest contemporaries. If Newman's paintings can be apprehended as solitary encounters between the viewer and the viewed, their intellectual underpinnings nevertheless invite analysis. After we come to a partial understanding of Still's sources and his thought-processes, his works can be discussed in terms of formal originality and innovation. The spell that Rothko casts over us now is harder to convey. He came increasingly to dislike exhibiting his painting in the company of works by other artists, and his ideal would have been a series of environments peopled only by his own canvases. He also came to prefer his darker canvases; he was an admirer of Burke, who had advocated the use of dark hues in achieving sublime effects. He was distressed when visitors to the studio expressed a preference for the lighter ones; this surely was because he felt that the higher-keyed works were somehow 'easier' and hence less profound. This is not necessarily so, but from 1956 onwards the more sombre but equally luminous – one might even say effulgent – tonalities predominate. Some of them conform to the fully developed format arrived at in 1949; in others the shapes become more irregular and at times more distended, with resultant suggestions of doorways and frames leading to colour and depth beyond. He had come to think of his canvases, his images – and after he had achieved his fully mature abstraction it becomes possible to speak of the totality of his surfaces as his images – as a sequence of absolute inventions owing no debt to the past, including his own.

There is a sense in which by the the end of the 1950s both Rothko and Still had temporarily painted themselves out of history in a way that Newman and Pollock had not. During the years following Pollock's death in 1956 there were literally thousands of painters all over the world seeking to emulate his style. Newman had established himself as the most seminal artist for young, emergent American art. But if at that point in time Rothko and, to a lesser extent, Still were legends, nevertheless their work seemed to relate more exclusively to themselves. The stream of scholarship that continues to pour forth concerning them is indicative of the fact that history is closing back in upon them.[31]

In very different ways the subsequent careers of Rothko and Still demonstrate the personal and artistic problems arising out of the creation of aesthetic worlds which had become so completely self-referential. It could be argued that the largest percentage of great art produced since the Second World War has been in the field of abstraction. Rothko's art is some of the most life-enhancing of the modern age. Still's greatness is still insufficiently recognized. Yet Rothko's suicide in 1970, which had about it all the ritual and trappings of Greek tragedy, was the result, in part at least, of his own realization that he was repeating himself ever less cogently, that he had in effect painted himself into an impasse. This is a fate hinted at earlier in the career of Malevich, although abstraction was then in its infancy and its possibilities still seemed infinite. Rothko's predicament has subsequently been faced by a multitude of other abstract painters. And then Rothko himself paid the penalty of being a mystic in an age characterized by its lack of faith. Still, too, repeated himself, and indeed some of the late variants on earlier themes ring a little loud and hollow; increasingly, and perhaps inevitably, his reworkings of earlier themes simply became reworkings of compositional procedures. He was, however, sustained by a deep and justified faith in his own art and importance, backed by an undiminished fund of hatred for his colleagues in

170 Barnett Newman, *Who's Afraid of Red, Yellow and Blue I*, oil on canvas, 1966.

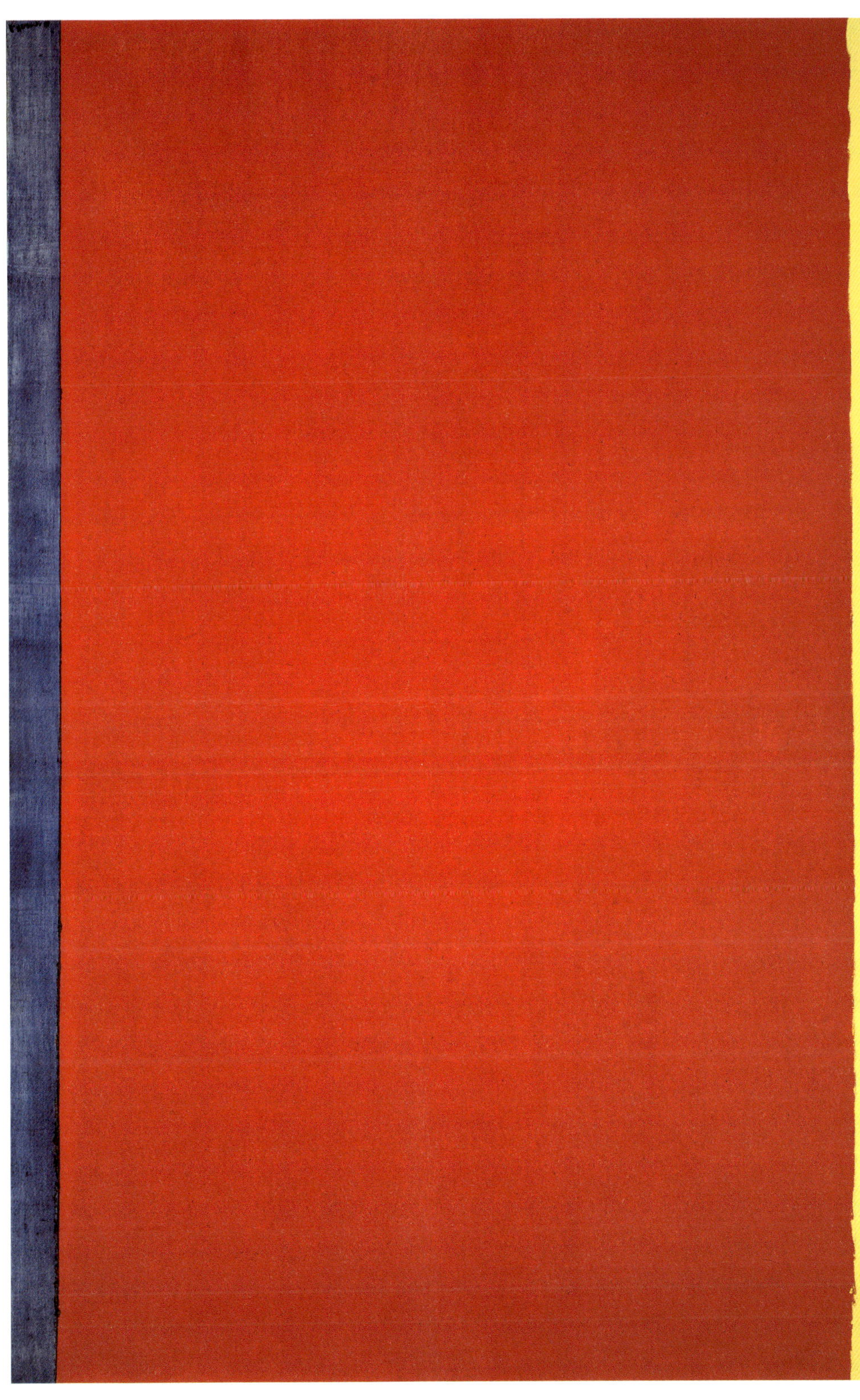

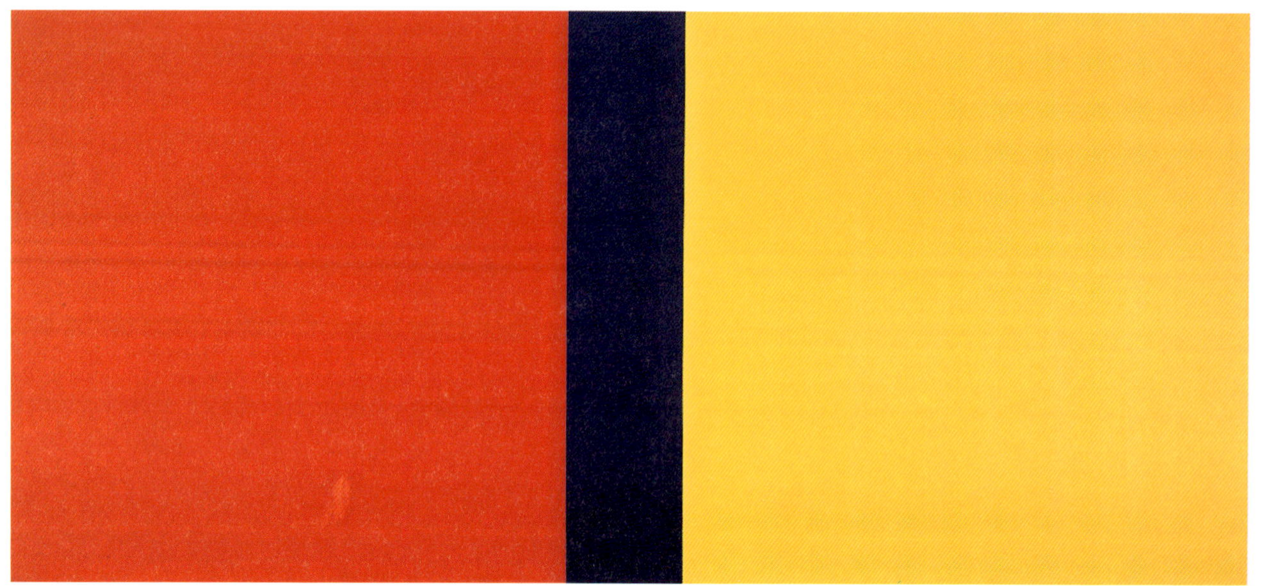

171 Barnett Newman, *Who's Afraid of Red, Yellow and Blue IV*, oil on canvas, 1969–70.

172 Barnett Newman, *Shining Forth (to George)*, oil on canvas, 1961.

the art world and even towards much of the art of the past – surely a terrible price to pay for sustained creativity, if indeed any price could be too high.

The case of Newman is somewhat different. Like Mondrian, he recognized the role of the destructive in art as a means of self-renewal, and for him each painting was a new beginning. He had attempted to divorce himself from a historical continuum but was eventually forced to acknowledge that to do this was an impossibility. In the mid-1960s he turned around in his tracks and confronted the history of abstract art head on. In 1966 he stretched up a large canvas to produce a work featuring a dominant red rectangle, which is introduced by a passive blue strip to the left, and which meets a more jagged yellow strip to the right, more active than itself. This was the first of his *Who's Afraid of Red, Yellow and Blue* 170 series. He said, 'I did have the desire that the painting be asymmetrical and that it create a space different from any I had ever done, sort of off-balance.'[32] The red came first and then he realized that the only colours (as opposed to the earlier bands of tonal contrast) that would work with it were yellow and blue. He goes on, 'I was now in confrontation with the dogma that colour must be reduced to the primaries, red, yellow and blue. Just as I had confronted other dogmatic posi-

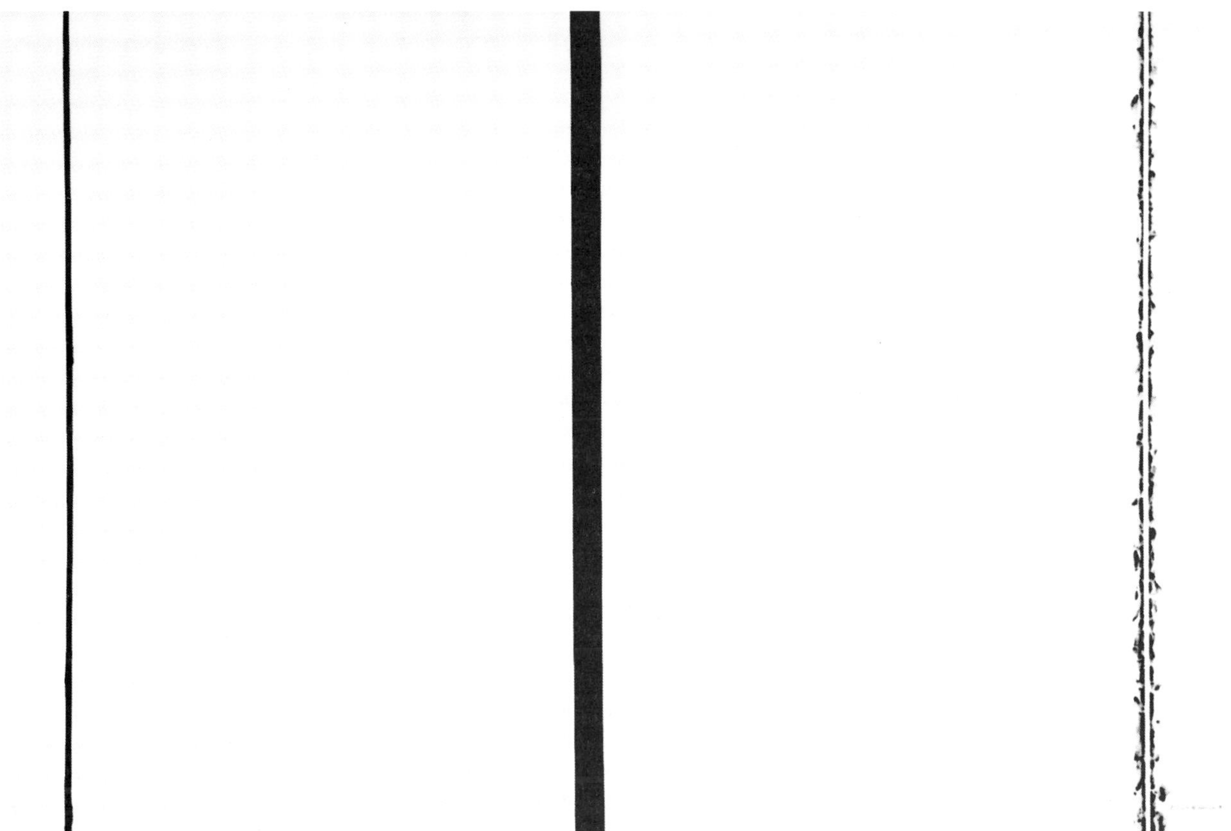

tions of the purists, neo-plasticists and other formalists, I was now in confrontation with their dogma, which had reduced red, yellow and blue into an idea-didact, or at best had made them picturesque . . . I had, therefore, the double incentive of using these colours to express what I wanted to do – of making these colours expressive rather than didactic. . . .'[33] It was a duel Newman fought bravely but not always successfully. The *Red, Yellow and Blue* paintings are the least resolved and least moving of all his major works. The colour equivalences of the side areas in these paintings are simply not exact and accurate enough to sustain those of the central areas; and when juxtaposed with the other two primaries his reds tend to sag and go brown (which reds are apt to do when applied to large surfaces). To balance the primary colours at full intensity or hue on such a large scale is a virtual impossibility. It is of significance that in the largest and cul-
171 minating work of the series, *No. IV* of 1969–70, Newman was forced back into symmetry and that the result smacks of bombast. To reinforce Newman's own
172 point that he was basically a draughtsman, one need only turn to *Shining Forth* of 1961, a work of comparable scale, executed in black and white, and one of the major masterpieces of twentieth-century art.

For all its anti-intellectual bias Newman's art was sustained by reference to systems of world thought that encourage critical analysis and he saw himself in continual confrontation with the art of both the recent and the more distant past. All these factors help to account for the fact that his art was to prove so seminal for that of others. The influence of Rothko was pervasive but oblique. He had imitators but no direct heirs, with the possible exception of Morris Louis, although Louis himself was more prepared to acknowledge a debt to Pollock. Still had neither. Despite the fact that that there have been substantial gifts of works by Still to major museums, as an artist he remains in a sense the great unseen.

The legacy of the greatest of American abstract painters was in one respect unfortunate. The use of a large format was essential to them; it matched their ambitions and they achieved them. But their paintings, when on view, cannibalize vast exhibition areas, whether public or private. They inspired others to produce many hundreds or thousands of canvases that were subsequently either destroyed or rolled up, languishing to this day in barns, lofts and studios the world over, most particularly in English-speaking countries. It is poignant to reflect that these paintings only saw the light of day or felt the contact of a human eye only while they were being painted. A vast proportion of abstract painting and sculpture produced during the 1960s, 1970s and 1980s was destined never to be seen. Over the past fifteen years many abstract painters have come to terms with expressing themselves in more modest formats. Profundity has been in short supply but it can and will reassert itself.

Notes on the text

1 Mondrian and the architecture of the future

1 *Natural Reality and Abstract Reality: An Essay in Trialogue Form* appeared originally in *De Stijl* in instalments, June 1919–July 1922. Passages quoted here are taken from a recent translation by Martin S. James, New York, 1995.

2 Op. cit., p. 31.

3 *The New Art –The New Life; The Collected Writings of Piet Mondrian*, edited and translated by Harry Holtzman and Martin S. James, Boston, 1986, and London, 1987, p. 14 (henceforth *Collected Writings*).

4 Carel Blotkamp, *Mondrian: The Art of Destruction*, London, 1994. p. 14.

5 *Collected Writings*, p. 169.

6 *Natural Reality and Abstract Reality* . . ., p. 55.

7 Blavatsky associated ovals with the concept of 'the cosmic egg'.

8 *An Abridgement of The Secret Doctrine*, ed. Elizabeth Preston and Christmas Humphreys, London (Theosophical Publishing House), 1966, p. 35.

9 *De Eenheid*, 6 November 1915.

10 *Collected Writings*, p. 42.

11 Ibid., p. 319.

12 Ibid., p. 28.

13 Ibid., p. 29.

14 Ibid., p. 14.

15 Ibid., p. 15.

16 *Natural Reality and Abstract Reality* . . ., op. cit., p. 35.

17 Letter to van Doesburg of 18 April 1919. Quoted in the catalogue to the Mondrian exhibition shared between the Haags Gemeentemuseum, the National Gallery of Art, Washington, D.C., and The Museum of Modern Art, New York, 1995–6, p. 190.

18 Loc. cit.

19 While in Paris, Mondrian had occupied a studio in the rue du Départ before leaving for Holland in 1914. In 1921 he moved back into a different studio in the same street and remained there until 1936.

20 *Natural Reality and Abstract Reality* . . ., op. cit., p. 81.

21 As early as 1917, Mondrian was insisting on the importance of a new kind of space in his work (see *Collected Writings*, p. 31).

22 In his theoretical writings Mondrian also refers to red as the most 'outward' of the three primary colours; see *Collected Writings*, p. 36.

23 See for example Yve-Alain Bois' essay 'The Iconoclast' in the Mondrian catalogue cited above (note 17).

24 *Collected Writings*, pp. 148–9.

25 In *i 10*, December 1927.

26 *Le Néo-Plasticisme: Aux hommes futurs*, Paris, 1920.

27 Hans L.C. Jaffé, *Mondrian*, London, 1970, p. 48.

28 *Collected Writings*, p. 48.

29 Ibid., p. 356.

30 Ibid., pp. 356–7.

31 Quoted in the Mondrian catalogue (see note 17), p. 293.

32 *L'Atelier de Mondrian*, catalogue to an exhibition of drawings held at the Staatsgalerie Stuttgart, 1980, p. 183.

2 Malevich and the ascent into ether

1 See in particular John Milner, *Kazimir Malevich and the Art of Geometry*, New Haven, 1966, to which I am much indebted.

2 The general consensus among Malevich scholars is that the artist never went to France. On purely visual grounds, however, I am tempted to think that he may have made this visit to Paris.

3 *From Cubism to Suprematism,The New Realism in Painting*, subsequently reissued as *From Cubism and Futurism to Suprematism. The New Realism in Painting*, 1916.

4 *On the New Systems in Art*, 1919. Malevich's misunderstanding of Cubism is underlined in the initial manifesto when he writes, 'The very object itself, together with its essence, purpose, sense of fullness of its presentation, the Cubists thought were also unnecessary'.

5 Shchukin owned Picasso's *Table, Violin and Glasses* of 1913, now in The Hermitage Museum.

6 The Bauhaus version of Malevich's text was in certain respects unfaithful to its original, probably because of difficulties in translating Malevich's idiosyncratic prose into German.

7 Kandinsky, *Complete Writings on Art*, ed. Kenneth C. Lindsay and Peter Vergo, New York, 1994, p. 94.

8 Photographs of exhibitions held during Malevich's lifetime sometimes show the same paintings hung differently in terms of their orientation.

9 Preface to *Suprematism. 34 Drawings*, probably prepared at the time of the big Moscow retrospective. See *Essays on Art*, 15–32 (2 vols.), ed. Troels Andersen, with translations by Zenia Glowacki-Prus and Arnold McMillin, London 1968. All passages quoted in this essay are taken from this edition unless otherwise stated.

10 *Philosophie als Denken der Welt gemässe dem Princip des kleinsten Kraftmasses*, Leipzig, 1876, p. 6.

11 See Susan Compton, 'Malevich and the fourth dimension', *Studio*, April 1974, and Milner, op. cit., p. 131.

12 *Non-Objective Creation and Suprematism*, 1919.

13 *Suprematism, 34 Drawings*, 1920.

14 *The Philosophy of History*, p. 56.

15 *Suprematism, 34 Drawings.*

16 'God is Not Cast Down', *Collected Writings*, p. 196.

17 Reprinted in Sophie Lissitzky-Küppers, *El Lissitzky*, London, 1968, pp. 334–44; see esp. p. 339.

18 *The Suprematist Mirror*, 1923, cited in A.B. Nakov, *Malévitch; Ecrits*, Paris, 1975, pp. 227–8.

19 'On the New Systems in Art', 1919. *Essays on Art*, vol. 1, p. 92.

20 Quoted in Ronald Hunt, 'The Constructivist ethos: Russia 1913–32', *Art Forum*, New York. Sept./Oct. 1967.

21 The drawing, probably of 1923–4, is in the State Russian Museum.

3 Kandinsky and the sound of colour

1 'On Stage Composition', 1912, *Kandinsky, Complete Writings On Art*, ed. Kenneth C. Lindsay and Peter Vergo, New York, 1994, p. 259 (henceforth *C.W.*).

2 'Reminiscences', 1913, *C.W.*, p. 364.

3 *Catalogue of the Second Exhibition of the Neue Künstler-Vereinigung, Munich*, 1910–11, *C.W.*, p. 82.

4 *C.W.*, pp. 357–83.

5 Ibid., pp. 368–9.

6 Peg Weiss, *Kandinsky and Old Russia; The Artist as Ethnographer and Shaman*, New Haven and London, 1995, p. 46.

7 'Letters from Munich', 1909–10, *C.W.*, pp. 55–8.

8 See Jonathan Fineberg, *Kandinsky in Paris, 1906–07*, Ann Arbor, Mich., 1984 (Studies in the Fine Arts: The Avant-Garde 44).

9 'Letters from Munich', 1909–10, *C.W.*, p. 80.

10 Letter of 7 July 1907, quoted in Jelena Hahl-Koch, *Kandinsky*, New York and London,1993, p. 110.

11 'Whither the New Art?', 1911, *C.W.*, p. 101.

12 'The Battle for Art', 1911, *C.W.*, p. 107.

13 Arthur Schopenhauer, *Schriften über Musik*, ed. Karl v. Stabenow, Regensburg, 1922, p. 159.

14 'On the Spiritual in Art', 1912, *C.W.*, p. 206.

15 Letter of 23 October 1910, quoted in Hahl-Koch, op. cit., p. 155.

16 *C.W.*, p. 218.

17 I am particularly indebted to Magdalena Dabrowski's *Kandinsky's Compositions*, The Museum of Modern Art, New York, 1995.

18 *C.W.*, p. 218.

19 *Content and Form*, 1910–11, p. 87.

20 In a letter of 21 April 1940, quoted in Hahl-Koch, op. cit., p. 331.

21 *C.W.*, p. 160.

22 'Cologne Lecture', 1914, *C.W.*, p. 395.

23 Ibid., p. 397.

24 *Reminiscences/Three Pictures*, 1913, *C.W.*, p. 384.

25 Weiss, op. cit. (note 6), p. 87.

26 Peter Vergo, *Kandinsky: Cossacks*, London: Tate Gallery, 1986.

27 See Jelena Hahl-Koch (ed.), *Arnold Schoenberg-Wassily Kandinsky, Letters, Pictures and Documents*, trans. John C. Crawford, London and Boston, Mass., 1984.

28 *C.W.*, pp. 206–7.

29 Ibid., p. 746.

30 Quoted in Weiss, op. cit., p. 94. Weiss's discussion of Kandinsky's views on the healing powers of art is the fullest.

31 'Cologne Lecture', 1914, *C.W.*, p. 399.

32 Ibid., p. 393.

33 'Interview with Karl Nierendorf', 1937, *C.W.*, p. 806.

34 For a detailed analysis of the picture see Hahl-Koch, op. cit., pp. 181, 184.

35 'Reminiscences/Three Pictures', 1913, *C.W.*, pp. 385–8.

36 'On the Spiritual in Art', 1912, *C.W.*, p. 185.

37 'Reminiscences/Three Pictures', 1913, *C.W.*, pp. 389–91.

38 'Assimilation of Art', 1937, *C.W.*, p. 802.

39 'On the Spiritual in Art', 1912, *C.W.*, p. 170.

40 Ibid., p. 166.

41 Ibid., p. 116.

42 *C.W.*, p. 396.

43 Will Grohmann, *Kandinsky*, Paris, 1930, p. 42.

44 'Foreword to the Catalogue of the First International Art Exhibition, Düsseldorf', 1922, *C.W.*, p. 478.
45 'The Psychology of the Productive Personality', 1929, *C.W.*, p. 740.
46 Hahl-Koch, op. cit., p. 284.
47 Ibid., pp. 284, 289 (reply to a questionnaire by Paul Plaut in 1929).
48 'Reflections on Abstract Art', 1931, *C.W.*, p. 769.
49 Quoted in Hahl-Koch, op. cit., p. 323.
50 Ibid., p. 331.
51 'Interview with Karl Nierendorf', 1937, *C.W.*, p. 807.
52 Quoted in Hahl-Koch, op. cit., p. 355.

4 Pollock and the search for a symbol

1 This picture has frequently been ascribed to 1937 because it was listed under that date at the Metropolitan Museum's exhibition 'Artists for Victory', December 1942–February 1943. *Jackson Pollock, A Catalogue Raisonné* (4 vols.), ed. Francis Valentine O'Connor and Eugene Victor Thaw, New Haven and London, suggests a date *c.* 1934–8. On purely visual grounds it is unlikely that the work could have been executed before reproductions of Orozco's Hospicio Cabañas cycle first went on view at the Hudon D. Walker Gallery in New York in the autumn of 1939.
2 Quoted in Stephen Polcari, *Abstract Expressionism and the Modern Experience*, Cambridge, 1991, p. 5.
3 Michael Leja, *Reframing Abstract Expressionism*, New Haven and London, 1933. The theme is central to Leja's arguments throughout the book.
4 John D. Graham, 'Primitive Art and Picasso', *Magazine of Art*, April 1937, pp. 236–9, 260.
5 Quoted in Jeffrey Potter, *To a Violent Grave*, New York, 1985, p. 197.
6 John D. Graham, *Systems and Dialectics of Art*, New York, 1937 (reissued in a revised and annotated form by the Johns Hopkins Press, Baltimore and London, 1971).
7 Ibid., p. 110.
8 Ibid., p. 194.
9 This was published first in America in 1916 by Moffatt Yard, New York.
10 Leland Wyman, *Treaty on Navajo Sand Painting*, Boston University, 1916.
11 Jung's *Wandlungen und Symbole der Libido*, first published in 1912 and reprinted in second and third editions, had been only sparsely illustrated. After extensive revisions by the author, the fourth edition appeared in 1952 under the title *Symbole der Wandlung* and included many more illustrations from a wide variety of cultures. This version was published in an English translation by R.F.C. Hull as *Symbols of Transformation*, New York and London, 1956. For the legend cited here see pp. 317–18.
12 Dr Joseph Henderson: 'He [Pollock] did not have free associations.' Quoted in B.H. Friedman, *Jackson Pollock, Energy Made Visible*, London, 1972, p. 41.
13 *Symbols of Transformation*, op. cit., p. 372
14 *Possibilities 1*, ed. Robert Motherwell and Harold Rosenberg, 1947–8 (only one issue appeared).
15 In 'The Sublime is Now', *Tiger's Eye*, December 1948, pp. 51–3.
16 From Pollock's journals and notes, quoted in Friedman, op. cit. (note 12), p. 228.
17 Ibid., pp. 64–5.
18 See Leja, op. cit. (note 3), pp. 187–201, and T.J. Clark, 'Jackson Pollock's Modernism', in *Reconstructing Modernism: Art in New York, Paris and Montreal 1945–64*, Cambridge, Mass., 1990.
19 'Talk of the Town, *New Yorker*, 5 August 1950, p. 16.
20 Selden Rodman, *Conversations with Artists*, New York, 1957, p. 82.
21 Tony Smith, quoted in Steven Naifeh and Gregory White Smith, *Jackson Pollock, An American Saga*, London, 1992, pp. 1–5.
22 *Catalogue Raisonné*, vol. 4, p. 275.

5 Newman, Rothko, Still and the reductive image

1 Clement Greenberg, *The Late Thirties in New York Art and Culture*, London, 1973, p. 230.
2 Fewer than 180 of Still's works have left his studio to date, although 750 oil paintings and 1,459 works on paper are in his estate. See *Clyfford Still, 1904–1980, The Buffalo and San Francisco Collections*, ed. Thomas Kellein, Munich, 1992, p. 11.
3 See James E.B. Breslin, *Mark Rothko, A Biography*, Chicago and London, 1993, p. 127.
4 Louis Aragon, Fragments of a Lecture given in Madrid at the Residencia de Estudiantes, 18 April 1925. Quoted in Maurice Nadeau, *The History of Surrealism*, New York, p. 111.
5 Edward Alden Jewell.
6 Clement Greenberg, 'Art', in *The Nation* CLXV, no. 23 (6 December 1947), p. 360.
7 Quoted in Sidney Janis, *Abstract and Surrealist Art in America*, New York, 1944, p. 118.
8 The term was not used by Rothko himself and only came to refer to this group of paintings after the artist's death.
9 'A Statement by the Artist', in *Clyfford Still, Thirty-three Paintings in the Albright-Knox Art Gallery* (exhibition catalogue), Buffalo, Albright-Knox Art Gallery, 1966, pp. 16–18.
10 *A Companion to Aesthetics*, ed. David Cooper, Oxford, 1996, p. 306.
11 Ibid.
12 *Thus Spake Zarathustra: Fourth Part; On the Higher Man*, 1892, Section 17.
13 Albright-Knox Art Gallery catalogue, Buffalo, 1966.
14 Stephen Polcari, *Abstract Expressionism and the Modern Experience*, Cambridge, 1991, p. 95.
15 J. Benjamin Townsend, *Interview with Clyfford Still*, Albright-Knox Art Gallery, Buffalo, Summer 1961.
16 Polcari, op. cit., p. 109.
17 'Las formas artisticas del Pacifico', *Ambos Mundos* 1, reprinted in English in *Studio International* 179, February 1970, pp. 70–1.
18 Thomas B. Hess, *Barnett Newman*, New York, 1969, p. 31.
19 'The Ideographic Picture' (Foreword to catalogue), Betty Parsons Gallery, New York, 20 January–8 February 1947.

6 Newman, Rothko, Still and the abstract sublime

1 Harold Rosenberg, *Barnett Newman*, New York, 1978, p. 7.
2 Thomas Hess, *Barnett Newman*, Tate Gallery catalogue, London, 1972, p. 32. Hess's essay differs very slightly from that published in 1971 to accompany the same exhibition when it was shown in New York at The Museum of Modern Art. It was in 1972 that I met Hess and talked to him about Newman. I am much indebted to him.
3 Ibid., p. 32.
4 Ibid., p. 34.
5 Ibid., p. 52. Hess is quoting Scholem.
6 See, for example, Clement Greenberg, *American Type Painting*, 1955; reprinted in *Art and Culture*, London, 1973, pp. 208–30.
7 'After Abstract Expressionism', *Art International*, October 1962.
8 Statement of 1947. *Pollock, Catalogue Raisonné* (ed. Frances Valentine O'Connor and Eugene Victor Thaw), New Haven and London, 1978, vol. IV, p. 238.
9 The title of this essay harks back to an article by Robert Rosenblum, 'The Abstract Sublime', *Art News* LIX, no. 10, February 1961.
10 *Tiger's Eye* vol. 1, no. 1, 15 December 1948, pp. 51–3.
11 Quoted in Thomas Hess, *Barnett Newman*, New York, 1969, p. 38
12 Hess, Tate Gallery catalogue, 1972, p. 47.
13 Ibid., p. 50.
14 Doris Green Sackler, 'Frontiers of Space', *Art in America*, 2 (Summer 1962), pp. 86–7.
15 Hess in conversation with the author, September 1972.
16 In Tate Gallery catalogue, 1972, p. 44.
17 Ibid., p. 50.
18 On several occasions Still stressed that his interest in the concept of the sublime went back to his student days; he also mentioned this in conversation with the author in 1979.
19 Statement in the catalogue to the exhibition held at the Albright-Knox Art Gallery, Buffalo, N.Y., 1966, pp. 16–18 (see ch. 5, note 9).
20 In an interview with J. Benjamin Townsend, Albright-Knox Art Gallery, Buffalo, Summer 1961.
21 Still exhibited at the Albright-Knox Art Gallery in Buffalo in 1959. The following year he taught at a summer session at the University of Colorado, Boulder.
22 Townsend interview.
23 *Clyfford Still*, The Metropolitan Museum of Art, New York, 1979, p. 27.
24 Ibid., p. 29.
25 James E. B. Breslin, *Mark Rothko, A Biography*, Chicago and London, 1993, p. 332.
26 Ibid., p. 475.
27 *Tiger's Eye*, vol. 1, no. 9 (October 1949), p. 114.
28 *Mark Rothko – A Retrospective Exhibition. Paintings 1945–1960*, with texts by Robert Goldwater, Bryan Robertson and Peter Selz, London, 1961, p. 21.
29 Ibid.
30 Quoted in Andrew Causey, 'Rothko Through His Paintings', *Studio International*, April 1972, p. 149.
31 After all, it was only with the superb Mondrian exhibition mounted in Holland and America in 1995–6 that the artist's work of the 1930s was rescued from the neglect to which it had been consigned.
32 Statement written by Newman for *Art Now: New York*, vol. 1, no. 3, March 1969, n.p.
33 Ibid.

List of illustrations and sources

The publishers would like to thank the following for their help and advice in the preparation of the book's illustrations: David Anfam, The Max, Binia and Jakob Bill Foundation, The St Petersburg Museum of Theatre and Music, The Pollock-Krasner House, Barbara and Justin Kerr, Kate Rothko Prizel, Christopher Rothko, Marion Kahan, Mrs Clyfford Still, Collection Onnasch, The Barnett Newman Foundation, Denise and Andrew Saul, The Mitchell-Innes & Nash Gallery.

Dimensions are given in centimetres, followed by inches (for larger works feet and inches), height before width and (where applicable) depth.

1 Mondrian and the architecture of the future

1 Mondrian, *The Jacobskerk, Winterswijk*, pencil, charcoal, pastel, watercolour and gouache on paper, 1898, 75 x 50 (29½ x 19⅝). Private Collection. Photograph: Christie's Images Ltd, 1999. © Piet Mondrian 2000, Mondrian/Holtzman Trust c/o Beeldrecht, Amstelveen/DACS, London.
2 Mondrian, *Composition II with Blue*, oil on canvas, *c.* 1936–42, 62 x 60.3 (24⅜ x 23¾). National Gallery of Canada, Ottawa. Purchased 1970. © Piet Mondrian 2000, Mondrian/Holtzman Trust c/o Beeldrecht, Amstelveen/DACS, London.
3 Mondrian, *Evening on the Gein with Isolated Tree*, oil on canvas, *c.* 1907–8, 65 x 86 (25⅝ x 33⅞). Collection Haags Gemeentemuseum, Den Haag. © Piet Mondrian 2000, Mondrian/Holtzman Trust c/o Beeldrecht, Amstelveen/DACS, London.
4 Mondrian, *Evening; Red Tree*, oil on canvas, 1908, 70 x 99 (27½ x 39). Collection Haags Gemeentemuseum, Den Haag. © Piet Mondrian 2000, Mondrian/Holtzman Trust c/o Beeldrecht, Amstelveen/DACS, London.
5 Mondrian, *Mill in Sunlight*, oil on canvas, 1908, 114 x 87 (44⅞ x 34¼). Collection Haags Gemeentemuseum, Den Haag. © Piet Mondrian 2000, Mondrian/Holtzman Trust c/o Beeldrecht, Amstelveen/DACS, London.
6 Mondrian, *Red Mill at Domburg*, oil on canvas, 1911, 150 x 86 (59 x 33⅞). Collection Haags Gemeentemuseum, Den Haag. © Piet Mondrian 2000, Mondrian/Holtzman Trust c/o Beeldrecht, Amstelveen/DACS, London.
7 Mondrian, *Still Life with Ginger Pot II*, oil on canvas, 1911–12, 95.2 x 120 (37½ x 47¼). Solomon R. Guggenheim Museum, New York. Photograph David Heald. © The Solomon R. Guggenheim Foundation, New York (FN 294.76). © Piet Mondrian 2000, Mondrian/Holtzman Trust c/o Beeldrecht, Amstelveen/DACS, London.
8 Paul Cézanne, *Still Life with Ginger Jar*, oil on canvas, *c.* 1895, 72.3 x 59 (28½ x 23¼). © Reproduced with the Permission of The Barnes Foundation™, Merion, PA. All Rights Reserved.
9 Mondrian, *Tableau No. 2, Composition No. VII*, oil on canvas, 1913, 104.4 x 113.6 (41⅛ x 44¾). Solomon R. Guggenheim Museum, New York. Photograph David Heald. © The Solomon R. Guggenheim Foundation, New York (FN 49.1228). © Piet Mondrian 2000, Mondrian/Holtzman Trust c/o Beeldrecht, Amstelveen/DACS, London.
10 Picasso, *Soldier and Girl*, oil on canvas, 1911. Private Collection, Paris © Succession Picasso /DACS 2000.
11 Picasso, *Ma Jolie* (*Woman with a Zither or Guitar*), oil on canvas, 1911–12, 100 x 65.4 (39⅜ x 25¾). The Museum of Modern Art, New York. Acquired through the Lillie P. Bliss Bequest. Photograph © 2000 The Museum of Modern Art, New York © Succession Picasso/DACS 2000.
12 Mondrian, *Composition in Oval with Colour Planes 2*, oil on canvas, 1914, 113 x 84.5 (44½ x 33¼). Collection Haags Gemeentemuseum, Den Haag. © Piet Mondrian 2000, Mondrian/Holtzman Trust c/o Beeldrecht, Amstelveen/DACS, London.
13 Mondrian, *Composition 1916*, oil on canvas (with wooden strip at bottom edge), 119 x 75.1 (46⅞ x 29⅝). Solomon R. Guggenheim Museum, New York. Photograph David Heald. © The Solomon R. Guggenheim Foundation, New York (FN 49.1229). © Piet Mondrian 2000, Mondrian/Holtzman Trust c/o Beeldrecht, Amstelveen/DACS, London.
14 Mondrian, *Composition No. 10 in Black and White; Pier and Ocean*, oil on canvas, 1915, 85 x 108 (33½ x 42½). © Rijksmuseum Kröller-Müller, Otterlo, The Netherlands. © Piet Mondrian 2000, Mondrian/Holtzman Trust c/o Beeldrecht, Amstelveen/DACS, London.
15 Mondrian, *Composition in Colour B*, oil on canvas, 1917, 50 x 44 (19⅝ x 17⅜). © Rijksmuseum Kröller-Müller, Otterlo, The Netherlands. © Piet Mondrian 2000, Mondrian/Holtzman Trust c/o Beeldrecht, Amstelveen/DACS, London.
16 Bart van der Leck, *Geometrical Composition I*, oil on canvas, 1917, 95 x 102 (37⅜ x 40⅛) © Rijksmuseum Kröller-Müller, Otterlo, The Netherlands. © DACS 2000.
17 Mondrian, *Composition with Grid 1* (*Lozenge*), oil on canvas, 1918, vertical axis 121 (47⅝). Collection Haags Gemeentemuseum, Den Haag. © Piet Mondrian 2000, Mondrian/Holtzman Trust c/o Beeldrecht, Amstelveen/DACS, London.
18 Mondrian, *Composition with Grid 8; Checkerboard with Dark Colours*, oil on canvas, 1919, 84 x 102 (33⅛ x 40⅛). Collection Haags Gemeentemuseum, Den Haag. © Piet Mondrian 2000, Mondrian/Holtzman Trust c/o Beeldrecht, Amstelveen/DACS, London.
19 Mondrian, *Composition with Colour Planes and Grey Lines 1*, oil on canvas, 1918, 49 x 60.5 (19¼ x 23⅞). Private Collection. Photograph: Archive Max Bill c/o Max, Binia and Jakob Bill Foundation, Adligenswil, Switzerland. © Piet Mondrian 2000, Mondrian/Holtzman Trust c/o Beeldrecht, Amstelveen/DACS, London.
20 Mondrian, *Composition A; Composition with Black, Red, Grey, Yellow and Blue*, oil on canvas, 1920, 91.5 x 92 (36 x 36½). Galleria Nazionale d'Arte Moderna, Rome. Su concessione del Ministero per I beni e le Attività Culturali. © Piet Mondrian 2000, Mondrian/Holtzman Trust c/o Beeldrecht, Amstelveen/DACS, London.
21 Mondrian, *Composition with Yellow, Red, Black, Blue and Grey*, oil on canvas, 1920, 51.5 x 61 (20¼ x 24). Stedelijk Museum, Amsterdam. © Piet Mondrian 2000, Mondrian/Holtzman Trust c/o Beeldrecht, Amstelveen/DACS, London.
22 Mondrian, *Composition with Red, Blue, Yellow and Black*, oil on canvas, 1929, 45.1 x 45.3 (17¾ x 17⅞). Solomon R. Guggenheim Museum, New York. Gift, Estate of Katherine S. Dreier, 1953. Photograph David Heald. © The Solomon R. Guggenheim Foundation, New York (FN 53.1347). © Piet Mondrian 2000, Mondrian/Holtzman Trust c/o Beeldrecht, Amstelveen/DACS, London.
23 Mondrian, *Composition with Yellow and Double Line*, oil on canvas, 1932, 45.3 x 45.3 (17⅞ x 17⅞). Scottish National Gallery of Modern Art. © Piet Mondrian 2000, Mondrian/Holtzman Trust c/o Beeldrecht, Amstelveen/DACS, London.
24 Mondrian, *Trafalgar Square*, oil on canvas, 1939–43, 145.2 x 120 (57⅛ x 47¼). The Museum of Modern Art, New York. Gift of Mr and Mrs William A.M. Burden. Photograph © 2000 The Museum of Modern Art, New York. © Piet Mondrian 2000, Mondrian/Holtzman Trust c/o Beeldrecht, Amstelveen/DACS, London.
25 Mondrian, *Broadway Boogie Woogie*, oil on canvas, 1942–3, 127 x 127 (50 x 50). The Museum of Modern Art, New York. Given anonymously. Photograph © 2000 The Museum of Modern Art, New York. © Piet Mondrian 2000, Mondrian/Holtzman Trust c/o Beeldrecht, Amstelveen/DACS, London.
26 Mondrian, *Victory Boogie Woogie* (unfinished), oil on canvas, 1942–4, diagonal 178.4 (70¼). Private Collection. Photograph: Instituut Collectie Nederland. © Piet Mondrian 2000, Mondrian/Holtzman Trust c/o Beeldrecht, Amstelveen/DACS, London.

2 Malevich and the ascent into ether

27 Malevich, *The Triumph of Heaven* (study for a fresco), tempera on cardboard, 1907, 72.5 x 70 (28½ x 27⅝). The State Russian Museum, St Petersburg, Russia.
28 Malevich, *Self-Portrait*, gouache on paper, *c.* 1908–9, 27 x 26.8 (10⅝ x 10½). State Tretyakov Gallery, St Petersburg, Russia.
29 Malevich, *Finished Portrait of Ivan Kliun*, oil on canvas, 1913, 112 x 70 (44⅛ x 27⅝). The State Russian Museum, St Petersburg, Russia. Photograph: AKG London.
30 Malevich, *Bather*, gouache on paper, 1911, 105 x 69 (41⅜ x 27⅛). Stedelijk Museum, Amsterdam.
31 Matisse, *La Danse*, oil on canvas, 1910, 258.1 x 389.8 (101⅝ x 153½). The State Hermitage Museum, St Petersburg, Russia. © DACS 2000.
32 Malevich, *The Chiropodist at the Bath House*, gouache on paper, *c.* 1911–12, 77.7 x 103 (30⅝ x 40½). Stedelijk Museum, Amsterdam.
33 Malevich, *The Knife Grinder: Principle of Flickering*, oil on canvas, 1913, 79.5 x 79.5 (31⅜ x 31⅜). Yale University Art Gallery, New

Haven, Connecticut. Gift of Collection Société Anonyme.
34 Fernand Léger, *Woman in Blue*, oil on canvas, 1912, 194 x 130 (76 3/8 x 51 1/8). Öffentliche Kunstsammlung Basel, Kunstmuseum, Donation Raoul La Roche 1952. Photograph: Martin Bühler. © ADAGP, Paris, and DACS, London 2000.
35 Marcel Duchamp, *Nude Descending a Staircase, No. 2*, oil on canvas, 1912, 147 x 89.2 (57 7/8 x 35 1/8). Philadelphia Museum of Art: The Louise and Walter Arensberg Collection. Photograph: Graydon Wood, 1994. © ADAGP, Paris, and DACS, London 2000.
36 Gino Severini, *Blue Dancer*, oil on canvas, 1912, 60.5 x 49.5 (23 7/8 x 19 1/2). Collection Mattioli, Milan. Photograph: Scala, Florence. © ADAGP, Paris, and DACS, London 2000.
37 Picasso, *Female Nude in an Armchair*, oil on canvas, 1909–10, 92.3 x 73.3 (36 3/8 x 28 7/8). The State Hermitage Museum, St Petersburg, Russia. © Succession Picasso/DACS 2000.
38 Malevich, *Head of a Peasant Girl*, oil on canvas, 1913, 80 x 95 (31 1/2 x 37 3/8). Stedelijk Museum, Amsterdam.
39 Malevich, *Woman at the Advertising Column*, oil and collage on canvas, 1914, 71 x 64 (28 x 25 3/8). Stedelijk Museum, Amsterdam.
40 Abstract paintings by Malevich at the exhibition 0.10, Petrograd, 1915. Photograph: Klaus Hurrgimalla, Frankfurt.
41 Picasso, *Table with Violin and Glasses*, oil on canvas, 1913, 65 x 54 (25 5/8 x 21 1/4). The State Hermitage Museum, St Petersburg, Russia. © Succession Picasso/DACS 2000.
42 Malevich, *Black Square*, oil on canvas, 1915, 106.2 x 106.5 (41 3/4 x 41 7/8). State Tretyakov Gallery, Moscow.
43 Vladimir Tatlin, *Corner Counter-Relief*, iron, aluminium and primer, displayed at the exhibition 0.10, Petrograd, 1915. Photograph: VAAP, Moscow. © DACS 2000.
44 Malevich, set design for Act I, Scene Three of *Victory over the Sun*, pencil on paper, 1913, 17.7 x 22.2 (7 x 8 3/4). St Petersburg Museum of Theatre and Music, St Petersburg, Russia.
45 Malevich, *The Aviator*, oil on canvas, 1914, 125 x 65 (49 1/4 x 25 5/8). The State Russian Museum, St Petersburg, Russia. Photograph: AKG London.
46 Malevich, *Painterly Realism of a Football Player: Colour Masses in the Fourth Dimension*, oil on canvas, 1915, 70 x 44 (27 5/8 x 17 3/8). Stedelijk Museum, Amsterdam.
47 Malevich, *Suprematist Painting: Aeroplane in Flight (Airplane Flying)*, oil on canvas, 1915, 58.1 x 48.3 (22 7/8 x 19). The Museum of Modern Art, New York. Purchase. Photograph © 2000 The Museum of Modern Art, New York.
48 Malevich, *Suprematist Painting*, oil on canvas, 1916–17, 97.8 x 66.4 (38 1/2 x 26 1/8). The Museum of Modern Art, New York. Photograph © 2000 The Museum of Modern Art, New York.
49 Malevich, *Suprematist Painting*, oil on canvas, 1917–18, 97 x 70 (38 1/8 x 27 1/2). Stedelijk Museum, Amsterdam.
50 Malevich, Suprematist Painting, oil on canvas, 1917–18, 97 x 70 (38 1/8 x 27 1/2). Stedelijk Museum, Amsterdam.
51 Malevich, *White Square on White*, oil on canvas, 1918, 79.4 x 79.4 (31 1/4 x 31 1/4). The Museum of Modern Art, New York. Photograph © 2000 The Museum of Modern Art, New York.
52 Malevich, *The Sportsmen*, oil on canvas, *c.* 1928–32, 142 x 164 (55 7/8 x 64 5/8). The State Russian Museum, St Petersburg, Russia. Photograph: AKG London.
53 Malevich, *Alpha*, model in plaster of Paris, 1920, 33 x 37 x 84.5 (13 x 14 5/8 x 33 1/4). The State Russian Museum, St Petersburg, Russia.

3 Kandinsky and the sound of colour

54 Kandinsky, *Motley Life*, tempera on canvas, 1907, 129.9 x 162.6 (51 1/8 x 64). Städtische Galerie im Lenbachhaus, München. © ADAGP, Paris, and DACS, London 2000.
55 Kandinsky, *Composition X*, oil on canvas, 1939, 130 x 195 (51 1/8 x 76 3/4). Kunstsammlung Nordrhein-Westfalen, Düsseldorf/photograph: Walter Klein, Düsseldorf. © ADAGP, Paris, and DACS, London 2000.
56 André Derain, *Trois Arbres, L'Estaque*, oil on canvas, 1906, 100.3 x 79.9 (39 1/2 x 31 1/2). Art Gallery of Ontario, Toronto. Gift of Sam and Ayala Zacks, 1970. © ADAGP, Paris, and DACS, London 2000.
57 Kandinsky, *Murnau: Kohlbruberstrasse*, oil on cardboard, 1908, 71.4 x 97.5 (28 1/8 x 38 3/8). Orix Collection, Tokyo. © ADAGP, Paris, and DACS, London 2000.
58 Kandinsky, *Improvisation 9*, oil on canvas, 1910, 110 x 110 (43 1/4 x 43 1/4). Staatsgalerie, Stuttgart. © ADAGP, Paris, and DACS, London 2000.
59 Henri Matisse, *Le Bonheur de vivre*, oil on canvas, 1905–6, 175 x 241 (69 1/8 x 94 7/8). © Reproduced with the Permission of The Barnes Foundation™, Merion, PA. All Rights Reserved © Succession H. Matisse/ DACS 2000.
60 Kandinsky, Sketch for *Composition II*, oil on canvas, 1909–10, 97.5 x 131.2 (38 3/8 x 51 5/8). Solomon R. Guggenheim Museum, New York. Photograph David Heald. © The Solomon R. Guggenheim Foundation, New York (FN 45. 961). © ADAGP, Paris, and DACS, London 2000.
61 Kandinsky, *All Saints I*, painting on glass, 1911, 34.6 x 40.6 (13 5/8 x 16). Städtische Galerie im Lenbachhaus, München. © ADAGP, Paris, and DACS, London 2000.
62 Kandinsky, *All Saints I*, oil on cardboard, 1911, 34.6 x 40.6 (13 5/8 x 16). Städtische Galerie im Lenbachhaus, München. © ADAGP, Paris, and DACS, London 2000.
63 Kandinsky, *Composition IV*, oil on canvas, 1911, 159.5 x 250.5 (62 3/4 x 98 5/8). Kunstsammlung Nordrhein-Westfalen, Düsseldorf/photograph: Walter Klein, Düsseldorf. © ADAGP, Paris, and DACS, London 2000.
64 Kandinsky, *Impression III (Concert)*, oil on canvas, 1911, 76.8 x 100 (30 1/4 x 39 3/8). Städtische Galerie im Lenbachhaus, München. © ADAGP, Paris, and DACS, London 2000.
65 Kandinsky, *Sketch for Composition V*, oil on canvas, 1911, 94.6 x 139.1 (37 1/4 x 54 3/4). The State Hermitage Museum, St Petersburg. © ADAGP, Paris, and DACS, London 2000.
66 Kandinsky, *Composition V*, oil on canvas, 1911, 192.7 x 275 (75 7/8 x 108 1/4) Private Collection © ADAGP, Paris, and DACS, London 2000.
67 Kandinsky, *Picture with a Circle*, oil on canvas, 1911, 139.1 x 111.1 (54 3/4 x 43 3/4). State Museum of Art, Tbilisi, Republic of Georgia. © ADAGP, Paris, and DACS, London 2000.
68 Kandinsky, *Small Pleasures*, oil on canvas, 1913, 109.8 x 119.7 (43 1/4 x 47 1/8). Solomon R. Guggenheim Museum, New York. Photograph David Heald. © The Solomon R. Guggenheim Foundation, New York (FN 43.921). © ADAGP, Paris, and DACS, London 2000.
69 Kandinsky, *Composition VI*, oil on canvas, 1913, 194 x 294 (76 3/8 x 115 3/4). The State Hermitage Museum, St Petersburg, Russia. © ADAGP, Paris, and DACS, London 2000.
70 Kandinsky, *Improvisation Deluge*, oil on canvas, 1913, 87.3 x 151.1 (34 3/8 x 59 1/2). Städtische Galerie im Lenbachhaus, München. © ADAGP, Paris, and DACS, London 2000.
71 Kandinsky, *Painting with a White Border*, oil on canvas, 1913, 140.3 x 200.3 (55 1/4 x 78 7/8). Solomon R. Guggenheim Museum, New York. Gift of Solomon R. Guggenheim, 1937. Photograph Robert E. Mates. © The Solomon R. Guggenheim Foundation, New York (FN 37. 245). © ADAGP, Paris, and DACS, London 2000.
72 Kandinsky, *Composition VII*, oil on canvas, 1913, 200 x 300 (78 3/4 x 118 1/8). State Tretyakov Gallery, Moscow. © ADAGP, Paris, and DACS, London 2000.
73 Kandinsky, *Composition VIII*, oil on canvas, 1923, 140 x 200 (55 1/8 x 78 3/4). Solomon R. Guggenheim Museum, New York. Gift of Solomon R. Guggenheim, 1937. Photograph David Heald. © The Solomon R. Guggenheim Foundation, New York (FN 37. 262). © ADAGP, Paris, and DACS, London 2000.
74 Kandinsky, *Composition IX*, oil on canvas, 1936, 114 x 194.9 (44 7/8 x 76 3/4). Cliché Musée National d'Art Moderne, Paris. © ADAGP, Paris, and DACS, London 2000.

4 Pollock and the search for a symbol

75 José Clemente Orozco, *Prometheus*, fresco, 1936, 609.6 x 854.7 (20 ft x 28 ft 6 in.). Montgomery Gallery, Pomona College, Frary Hall, Claremont, California. Reproduction Rights Reserved. © DACS 2000.
76 José Clemente Orozco, *Man in Flames*, cupola decoration, 1938–9. Hospicio Cabañas, Guadalajara, Mexico. © DACS 2000.
77 Pollock, *The Flame*, oil on canvas, *c.* 1940, 51.1 x 76.2 (20 1/8 x 30). The Museum of Modern Art, New York. Enid A. Haupt Fund. Photograph © 2000 The Museum of Modern Art, New York. © ARS, NY, and DACS, London 2000.
78 José Clemente Orozco, *The Epic of American Civilisation: Ancient Human Sacrifice (Panel 3)*, fresco 1932–4. Commissioned by the Trustees of Dartmouth College, Hanover, New Hampshire. © DACS 2000.
79 Pollock, *Untitled (Naked Man with Knife)*, oil on canvas, *c.* 1938–41, 127 x 91.4 (50 x 36). © Tate Gallery, London 2000. © ARS, NY, and DACS, London 2000.
80 Pollock, *Birth*, oil on canvas, *c.* 1938–41, 46 x 21.7 (18 1/8 x 8 5/8). © Tate Gallery, London 2000. © ARS, NY, and DACS, London 2000.
81 Pollock, *Moon Woman Cuts the Circle*, oil on canvas, *c.* 1943, 106.7 x 101.6 (42 x 40). Cliché Musée National d'Art Moderne, Paris. © ARS, NY, and DACS, London 2000.
82 Kwakiutl mask. Whereabouts unknown.
83 Inuit mask from the Lower Yukon area. Museum of Anthropology, University of California.
84 Yu'pil grinning mask with divided countenance. Collected in Good News Bay, Alaska, *c.* 1920, 30 long (11 7/8). Photograph: National Museum of the American Indian, Smithsonian Institution (N22588).
85 Pollock, *Male and Female in Search of a Symbol*, oil on canvas, 1943, 109.2 x 170 (43 x 67). Private Collection. Photograph: Pollock-Krasner House, East Hampton, NY. © ARS, NY, and DACS, London 2000.
86 Maya relief (wall panel 3) from Piedras Negras, Guatemala, late eighth century. Museo Nacional, Guatemala City. Photo: © Justin Kerr # 4892.
87 '*Osiris in the Cedar Coffin*', drawing after an

ancient Egyptian relief at Dendera. After the *Collected Works of C.G. Jung*, vol. 5 *Symbols of Transformation*, London and New York 1956.

88 Pollock, *Guardians of the Secret*, oil on canvas, 1943, 122.9 x 191.5 (48 3/8 x 75 3/8). San Francisco Museum of Modern Art. Albert M.Bender Collection, Albert M. Bender Bequest Fund Purchase. © ARS, NY, and DACS, London 2000.

89 Pollock, *Pasiphaë*, oil on canvas, 1943, 142.6 x 243.8 (56 1/8 x 96). The Metropolitan Museum of Art, New York. Rogers, Fletcher and Harris Brisbane Dick Funds and Joseph Pulitzer Bequest, 1982. © ARS, NY, and DACS, London 2000.

90 Joan Miró, *Nude*, oil on canvas, 1926, 92.4 x 73.7 (36 3/8 x 29). Philadelphia Museum of Art: Louise and Walter Arensberg Collection.© ADAGP, Paris, and DACS, London 2000.

91 Pollock, *Mural*, oil on canvas, 1943, 247 x 605 (8 ft 1 1/4 in. x 19 ft 10 in.).The University of Iowa Museum of Art, Gift of Peggy Guggenheim, 1959.6. © The University of Iowa Museum of Art, All Rights Reserved. © ARS, NY, and DACS, London 2000.

92 André Masson, *Furious Suns*, pen and ink, 1925, 42.2 x 31.7 (16 5/8 x 12 1/2). The Museum of Modern Art, New York. Purchase. Photograph © 2000 The Museum of Modern Art, New York. © ADAGP, Paris, and DACS, London 2000.

93 Vasily Kandinsky, *Study for Composition VII*, watercolour and India ink on paper, dated 1910 on the print 1913, 49.8 x 65.1 (19 5/8 x 25 5/8). Cliché Musée National d'Art Moderne, Paris, © ADAGP, Paris, and DACS, London 2000.

94 Pollock, *Drawing*, brush, pen and black and coloured inks, pastel, gouache and wash on paper, *c.* 1946, 57.2 x 78.4 (22 1/2 x 30 7/8). Private Collection. Photograph: Pollock-Krasner House, East Hampton, NY © ARS, NY, and DACS, London 2000.

95 Pollock, *Gothic*, oil on canvas, 1944, 215.5 x 142.1 (7 ft 0 7/8 in. x 4 ft 8 in.). The Museum of Modern Art, New York. Bequest of Lee Krasner. Photograph © 2000 The Museum of Modern Art, New York. © ARS, NY, and DACS, London 2000.

96 Pollock, *Eyes in the Heat*, oil (and enamel?) on canvas, 1946, 137.2 x 109.2 (54 x 43). Peggy Guggenheim Collection,Venice, The Solomon R. Guggenheim Foundation.© ARS, NY, and DACS, London 2000.

97 Pollock, *Full Fathom Five*, oil on canvas, 1947, 129.2 x 76.5 (50 7/8 x 30 1/8). The Museum of Modern Art, New York. Gift of Peggy Guggenheim. Photograph © 2000 The Museum of Modern Art, New York. © ARS, NY, and DACS, London 2000

98 Pollock, *Cathedral*, oil and mixed media on canvas, 1947, 180.3 x 88.9 (71 x 35). Dallas Museum of Fine Arts, Gift of Mr and Mrs Bernard Reis, 1950. © ARS, NY, and DACS, London 2000.

99 Pollock, *No. 1A*, oil and enamel on unprimed canvas, 1948, 172.7 x 264.2 (5 ft 8 in. x 8 ft 8 in.). The Museum of Modern Art, New York. Purchase. Photograph © 2000 The Museum of Modern Art, New York. © ARS, NY, and DACS, London 2000.

100 Pollock, *Lavender Mist*, oil and enamel and aluminium paint on canvas, 1950, 221 x 299.7 (7 ft 3 in. x 9 ft 10 in.). Ailsa Mellon Bruce Fund, © 1999 Board of Trustees, National Gallery of Art, Washington. Photograph: Richard Carafelli. © ARS, NY, and DACS, London 2000.

101 Pollock, *Cut Out*, oil on paper cut out over canvas, 1948, 77.5 x 59.7 (30 1/2 x 23 1/2). Ohara Museum of Art, Kurashiki, Japan. © ARS, NY, and DACS, London 2000.

102 Pollock, *Out of the Web*, oil and enamel on masonite, cut-out, 1949, 121.9 x 243.8 (48 x 96). Staatsgalerie Stuttgart. © ARS, NY, and DACS, London 2000.

103 Pollock, *Autumn Rhythm*, oil on canvas, 1950, 266.7 x 525.8 (8 ft 9 in. x 17 ft 3 in.). The Metropolitan Museum of Art, George A. Hearn Fund, 1957 (57.92). Photograph © 1998 The Metropolitan Museum of Art. © ARS, NY, and DACS, London 2000.

104 Pollock, *Echo*, enamel on unprimed canvas, 1951, 233.4 x 218.4 (7 ft 7 7/8 in. x 7 ft 2 in.). The Museum of Modern Art, New York. Acquired through the Lillie P. Bliss Bequest and the Mr and Mrs David Rockefeller Fund. Photograph © 2000The Museum of Modern Art, NewYork. © ARS, NY, and DACS, London 2000.

105 Pollock, *Ocean Greyness*, oil and duco on canvas, 1953, 146.7 x 229 (57 3/4 x 90 1/8). Solomon R. Guggenheim Museum, New York. Photograph: Robert E. Mates. © The Solomon R. Guggenheim Foundation, New York (FN 54. 1408). © ARS, NY, and DACS, London 2000.

106 Pollock, *Composition with Masked Forms*, oil on canvas, 1941, 70.5 x 127 (27 3/4 x 50). Private Collection. Photograph: Pollock-Krasner House, East Hampton, NY/Lances. © ARS, NY, and DACS, London 2000.

107 Pollock, *Blue Poles*, oil, enamel and aluminium paint with glass on canvas, 1952, 212.9 x 489 (6 ft 11 7/8 in. x 16 ft 0 1/2 in.). Collection: National Gallery of Australia, Canberra © ARS, NY, and DACS, London 2000.

108 Pollock, *The Deep*, oil and enamel on canvas, 1953, 220.3 x 150.2 (86 3/4 x 59 1/8). Cliché Musée National d'Art Moderne, Paris. © ARS, NY, and DACS, London 2000.

109 Pollock, *Easter and the Totem*, oil on canvas, 1953, 208.6 x 147.3 (6 ft 10 1/8 in. x 4 ft 10 in.). The Museum of Modern Art, New York. Gift of Lee Krasner in memory of Jackson Pollock. Photograph © The Museum of Modern Art, New York. © ARS, NY, and DACS, London 2000.

110 Pollock, *Male and Female*, oil on canvas, 1942, 185.4 x 124.5 (73 x 49). Philadelphia Museum of Art: Gift of Mr and Mrs H.Gates Lloyd. Photograph: Graydon Wood. © ARS, NY, and DACS, London 2000.

111 Pollock, *Scent*, oil on canvas, 1953–5, 198.1 x 146.1 (78 x 57 1/2). Collection of David Geffen, Los Angeles, courtesy of Mitchell-Innes & Nash. © ARS, NY, and DACS, London 2000.

112 Pollock, *Search*, oil and enamel paint on canvas, 1955, 146 x 228.6 (57 1/2 x 90). Private Collection. Photograph: Pollock-Krasner House, East Hampton, NY. © ARS, NY, and DACS, London 2000.

5 Newman, Rothko, Still and the reductive image

113 Mark Rothko, *Subway Scene*, oil on canvas (hardboard), 1938, 86.4 x 117.5 (34 x 46 1/4). Collection Kate Rothko Prizel. © Kate Rothko Prizel & Christopher Rothko/ARS, NY, and DACS, London 2000.

114 Mark Rothko, *Black on Maroon*, oil on canvas, 1958, 182.9 x 114.3 (72 x 45). © Tate Gallery, London 2000. © Kate Rothko Prizel & Christopher Rothko/ARS, NY, and DACS, London 2000.

115 Adolph Gottlieb, *The Voyager's Return*, oil on canvas, 1946, 96.2 x 75.9 (37 7/8 x 29 7/8). The Museum of Modern Art, New York. Gift of Mr and Mrs Roy R. Neuberger. Photograph © 2000 The Museum of Modern Art, New York. © Adolph Gottlieb Foundation/DACS, London/VAGA, New York 2000.

116 Mark Rothko, *Omen of the Eagle*, oil and graphite on canvas, 1942, 65.4 x 45.1 (25 1/2 x 17 3/4). Gift of the Mark Rothko Foundation. © 2000 Board of Trustees, National Gallery of Art, Washington. © Kate Rothko Prizel & Christopher Rothko/ARS, NY, and DACS, London 2000.

117 Joan Miró, *The Family*, vine charcoal, white pastel and red conté on oatmeal paper, 1924, 74.9 x 104.1 (29 1/2 x 41). The Museum of Modern Art, New York. Gift of Mr and Mrs Jan Mitchell. Photograph © 2000 The Museum of Modern Art, New York. © ADAGP, Paris, and DACS, London 2000.

118 Mark Rothko, *Slow Swirl at the Edge of the Sea*, oil on canvas, 1944, 191.4 x 215.2 (6 ft 3 3/4 in. x 7 ft 0 3/4 in.). The Museum of Modern Art, New York. Bequest of Mrs Mark Rothko through the Mark Rothko Foundation, Inc. Photograph © 2000 The Museum of Modern Art, New York. © Kate Rothko Prizel & Christopher Rothko/ARS, NY, and DACS, London 2000.

119 Mark Rothko, *Entombment 1*, gouache on paper, 1946, 51.8 x 65.4 (20 3/8 x 25 3/4). Collection of Whitney Museum of American Art. Photograph © 2000 Whitney Museum of American Art. © Kate Rothko Prizel & Christopher Rothko/ARS, NY and DACS, London 2000.

120 Mark Rothko, *Untitled (Multiform)*, oil on canvas, 1948, 225.7 x 165.1 (7 ft 4 7/8 in. x 5 ft 5 in.). Collection Kate Rothko Prizel. © Kate Rothko Prizel & Christopher Rothko/ARS, NY, and DACS, London 2000.

121 Mark Rothko, *Number 15*, oil on canvas, 1948, 131.8 x 74 (51 7/8 x 29 1/8). Gift of the Mark Rothko Foundation. © 2000 Board of Trustees, National Gallery of Art, Washington. © Kate Rothko Prizel & Christopher Rothko/ARS, NY, and DACS, London 2000.

122 Clyfford Still, *1944-G*, oil on canvas, 1944, 173.3 x 80.3 (68 1/4 x 31 5/8). San Francisco Museum of Modern Art. Gift of the Artist. Reproduced with permission of Mrs Clyfford Still.

123 Clyfford Still, *Untitled* (formerly *Striding Man*), oil on canvas, 1934, 146.4 x 80.3 (57 5/8 x 31 5/8). San Francisco Museum of Modern Art. Gift of the Artist. Reproduced with permission of Mrs Clyfford Still.

124 Clyfford Still, *1937–38-A*, oil on canvas, 1938, 119.4 x 85.1 (47 x 33 1/2). Albright-Knox Art Gallery, Buffalo, NY. Gift of Clyfford Still, 1964. Reproduced with permission of Mrs Clyfford Still.

125 Picasso, *Woman Seated in a Red Armchair*, oil on canvas, 1932, 130 x 97.5 (51 1/8 x 38 3/8). Musée Picasso, Paris. © Photo RMN/R.G. Ojeda. © Succession Picasso/DACS 2000.

126 Shaman Mnemonic System of the Grand Medicine Society, in H.R. Schoolcraft, *Information respecting the History, Condition and Prospect of the Indian tribes of the United States*, 1853.

127 Clyfford Still, *1936–7 No. 2*, oil on canvas, 1936–7, 161.6 x 84.1 (63 5/8 x 33 1/8). San Francisco Museum of Modern Art. Gift of the Artist. Reproduced with permission of Mrs Clyfford Still.

128 Clyfford Still, *1938-N No. 1*, oil on canvas, 1938, 78.6 x 64 (30 7/8 x 25 1/4). San Francisco Museum of Modern Art. Photograph: Ben Blackwell. Gift of the Artist. Reproduced with permission of Mrs Clyfford Still.

129 Clyfford Still, *1943-J*, oil on canvas, 1943, 177.2 x 79. 4 (69 3/4 x 31 1/4). San Francisco Museum of Modern Art. Gift of the Artist. Reproduced with permission of Mrs Clyfford Still.

130 Clyfford Still, *Untitled 1937*, oil on canvas, 1937, 108.9 x 78.1 (42 7/8 x 30 3/4). San Francisco Museum

of Modern Art. Gift of the Artist. Reproduced with permission of Mrs Clyfford Still.
131 Clyfford Still, *1945-H*, oil on canvas, 1945, 230 x 175 (7 ft 63/8 x 5 ft 87/8). San Francisco Museum of Modern Art. Gift of the Artist. Reproduced with permission of Mrs Clyfford Still.
132 Clyfford Still, *Untitled, 1936*, oil on burlap, 1936, 63.2 x 42.9 (247/8 x 167/8). San Francisco Museum of Modern Art. Gift of the Artist. Reproduced with permission of Mrs Clyfford Still.
133 Clyfford Still, *1941–2-C*, oil on canvas, 1942, 108 x 81.3 (42½ x 32) Albright-Knox Art Gallery, Buffalo, NY. Gift of the Artist. Reproduced with permission of Mrs Clyfford Still.
134 Arnold Böcklin, *Island of the Dead*, oil on wood, 1880, 73.7 x 121.9 (29 x 48). The Metropolitan Museum of Art, New York, Resinger Fund, 1926.
135 Max Ernst, *Le Baiser*, oil on canvas, 1927, 128.9 x 161.3 (50¾ x 63½). Peggy Guggenheim Collection,Venice, Solomon R. Guggenheim Foundation. Photo: Robert E. Mates. © ADAGP, Paris, and DACS, London 2000.
136 Clyfford Still, *Untitled (Self-Portrait)*, oil on canvas, 1946, 180 x 106.5 (707/8 x 417/8). San Francisco Museum of Modern Art. Gift of Peggy Guggenheim. Reproduced with permission of Mrs Clyfford Still.
137 Max Ernst, *The Horde*, oil on canvas, 1927, 115 x 146 (45¼ x 57½). Stedelijk Museum, Amsterdam © ADAGP, Paris, and DACS, London 2000.
138 Clyfford Still, *Untitled 1945*, oil on canvas, 1945, 227 x 170 (91 x 68). Private Collection. Reproduced with permission of Mrs Clyfford Still.
139 Joan Miró, *Dog Barking at the Moon*, oil on canvas, 1926, 73 x 92 (28¾ x 36¼). Philadelphia Museum of Art: A.E. Gallatin Collection. © ADAGP, Paris, and DACS, London 2000.
140 Clyfford Still, *1945-K*, oil on canvas, 1945, 127 x 79 (50 x 31). Albright-Knox Art Gallery, Buffalo, NY. Gift of Clyfford Still, 1964. Reproduced with permission of Mrs Clyfford Still.
141 Clyfford Still, *September 1946*, oil on canvas, 1946, 152.4 x 69.9 (60 x 27½). Albright-Knox Art Gallery, Buffalo, NY. Gift of Clyfford Still, 1964. Reproduced with permission of Mrs Clyfford Still.
142 Barnett Newman, *Pagan Void*, oil on canvas, 1946, 83.8 x 96.5 (33 x 38). Gift of Annalee Newman, in honour of the 50th Anniversary of the National Gallery of Art, Washington. © 2000 Board of Trustees, National Gallery of Art, Washington. © ARS, NY, and DACS, London 2000.
143 Barnett Newman, *Genetic Moment*, oil on canvas, 1947, 96.5 x 71(38 x 28). © Fondation Beyeler, Riehen/Basel. © ARS, NY, and DACS, London 2000.
144 Clyfford Still, *January 1947*, oil on canvas, 1947. 157.5 x 114.3 (62 x 45). Albright-Knox Art Gallery, Buffalo, NY. Gift of Clyfford Still, 1964. Reproduced with permission of Mrs Clyfford Still.
145 Barnett Newman, *The Command*, oil on canvas, 1946, 122 x 91.5 (48 x 36). Öffentliche Kunstsammlung Basel, Kunstmuseum. Gift of Mrs Annalee Newman 1988. © ARS, NY, and DACS, London 2000.
146 Barnett Newman, *The Beginning*, oil on canvas, 1946, 101.6 x 75.6 (40 x 29¾). Through prior gift of Mr and Mrs Carter H. Harrison, 1989.2, photograph courtesy of The Art Institute of Chicago. © ARS, NY, and DACS, London 2000.

6 Newman, Rothko, Still and the abstract sublime

147 Barnett Newman, *Onement 1*, oil on canvas, 1948, 69.2 x 41.2 (27¼ x 16¼). The Museum of Modern Art, New York. Gift of Annalee Newman. Photograph © 2000 The Museum of Modern Art, New York. © ARS, NY, and DACS, London 2000.
148 Alberto Giacometti, *Man Pointing*, bronze, 1947, 178 x 95 x 52 (70⅛ x 373/8 x 20½). © Tate Gallery, London 2000. Photograph: F.L. Kenett. © ADAGP, Paris, and DACS, London 2000.
149 Clyfford Still, *July 1945-R*, oil on canvas, 1945, 175.3 x 81.3 (69 x 32). Albright-Knox Art Gallery, Buffalo, NY. Gift of Clyfford Still, 1964. Reproduced with permission of Mrs Clyfford Still.
150 Barnett Newman, *Adam*, oil on canvas, 1951–52, 238.8 x 172.1 (94 x 67¾). © Tate Gallery, London 2000. © ARS, NY, and DACS, London 2000.
151 Barnett Newman, *Eve*, oil on canvas, 1950, 242.9 x 202.9(955/8 x 797/8). © Tate Gallery, London 2000. © ARS, NY, and DACS, London 2000.
152 Barnett Newman, *Anna's Light*, acrylic on canvas, 1968, 276 x 611 (7 ft 05/8 in. x 20 ft 0½ in.). Collection of Kawamura Memorial Museum of Art, Sakura-shi, Japan. © ARS, NY, and DACS, London 2000.
153 Barnett Newman, *Achilles*, oil on canvas, 1952, 200.4 x 200 (95⅛ x 79⅛). Gift of Annalee Newman, in honour of the 50th Anniversary of the National Gallery of Art, Washington. © 2000 Board of Trustees, National Gallery of Art, Washington. © ARS, NY, and DACS, London 2000.
154 Barnett Newman, *Vir Heroicus Sublimis*, oil on canvas, 1950–1, 242.2 x 541 (7 ft 113/8 in. x 17 ft 9 in.). The Museum of Modern Art, New York. Gift of Mr and Mrs Ben Heller. Photograph © 2000 The Museum of Modern Art, New York. © ARS, NY, and DACS, London 2000.
155 Barnett Newman, *Cathedra*, oil on canvas, 1951, 240 x 543.5 (7 ft 10½ in. x 17 ft 9 in.). Stedelijk Museum, Amsterdam. © ARS, NY, and DACS, London 2000.
156 Barnett Newman, *Uriel*, oil on canvas, 1955, 243.6 x 548.6 (8 ft x 18 ft). Collection Onnasch, Berlin. On loan to the Hamburger Kunsthalle. © ARS, NY, and DACS, London 2000.
157 Clyfford Still, *1947–48-W No. 2*, oil on canvas, 1948, 275.6 x 223.5 (9 ft x 7 ft 4 in.). Albright-Knox Art Gallery, Buffalo, NY. Gift of Clyfford Still, 1964. Reproduced with permission of Mrs Clyfford Still.
158 Clyfford Still, *1949-H*, oil on canvas, 1949, 203.2 x 175.3 (80 x 69). Albright-Knox Art Gallery, Buffalo, NY. Gift of Clyfford Still, 1964. Reproduced with permission of Mrs Clyfford Still.
159 Clyfford Still, *November 1950*, oil on canvas, 1950, 203.2 x 172.7 (80 x 68). Albright-Knox Art Gallery, Buffalo, NY. Gift of Clyfford Still, 1964. Reproduced with permission of Mrs Clyfford Still.
160 Clyfford Still, *1951-L No. 2*, oil on canvas, 1951, 289.6 x 243.8 (9 ft 2 in. x 8 ft). Albright-Knox Art Gallery, Buffalo, NY. Gift of Clyfford Still, 1964. Reproduced with permission of Mrs Clyfford Still.
161 Clyfford Still, *1957-D No. 1*, oil on canvas, 1957, 287 x 403.9 (9 ft 5 in. x 13 ft 3 in.). Albright-Knox Art Gallery, Buffalo, NY. Gift of Seymour H. Knox, 1959. Reproduced with permission of Mrs Clyfford Still.
162 Mark Rothko, *Untitled 1948*, oil on canvas, 1948, 126.4 x 111.7 (49¾ x 44). Gift of the Mark Rothko Foundation. © 2000 Board of Trustees, National Gallery of Art, Washington. © Kate Rothko Prizel & Christopher Rothko/ARS, NY, and DACS, London 2000.
163 Mark Rothko, *Untitled 1949*, oil on canvas, 1949, 142.2 x 83.8 (56 x 33). The Metropolitan Museum of Art, Gift of the Mark Rothko Foundation, 1985 (1985.63.3). Photograph by Lynton Gardiner. Photograph © 1986 The Metropolitan Museum of Art. © Kate Rothko Prizel & Christopher Rothko/ARS, NY, and DACS, London 2000.
164 Arshile Gorky, *The Sun, the Dervish in the Tree*, oil on canvas, 1944, 90.8 x 119.4 (35¾ x 47). Collection Denise and Andrew Saul, New York. Photograph: Zindman/Fremont. © ADAGP, Paris, and DACS, London 2000.
165 Mark Rothko, *No. 10*, 1950, oil on canvas, 1950, 229.6 x 145.1 (7 ft 63/8 in. x 4 ft 9⅛ in.). The Museum of Modern Art, New York. Gift of Philip Johnson. Photograph © 2000 The Museum of Modern Art, New York. © Kate Rothko Prizel & Christopher Rothko/ARS, NY, and DACS, London 2000.
166 Mark Rothko, *Green, Red on Orange*, oil on canvas, 1951, 236.2 x 149.9 (93 x 59). Collection Denise and Andrew Saul, New York. © Kate Rothko Prizel & Christopher Rothko/ARS, NY, and DACS, London 2000
167 Mark Rothko, *Red, Dark Green, Green*, mixed media on canvas, 1952, 243.2 x 207.7 (95¾ x 81¾) Private collection. Photograph: Rick Meoli. © Kate Rothko Prizel & Christopher Rothko/ARS, NY, and DACS, London 2000.
168 Mark Rothko, *Number 8*, oil on canvas, 1952, 205.1 x 173 (80¾ x 68⅛). © Christie's Images Ltd, 1999. © Kate Rothko Prizel & Christopher Rothko/ARS, NY, and DACS, London 2000.
169 Mark Rothko, *Light Red over Black*, oil on canvas, 1957, 232.7 x 152.7 (915/8 x 60⅛). © Tate Gallery, London 1999. © Kate Rothko Prizel & Christopher Rothko/ARS, NY, and DACS, London 2000.
170 Barnett Newman, *Who's Afraid of Red, Yellow and Blue I*, oil on canvas, 1966, 190.5 x 122 (75 x 48). Collection of David Geffen, Los Angeles. Photo courtesy of Mitchell-Innes & Nash. © ARS, NY, and DACS, London 2000.
171 Barnett Newman, *Who's Afraid of Red, Yellow and Blue IV*, oil on canvas, 1969–70. 274 x 603 (9 ft x 19 ft 9 in.). © bpk, Staatliche Kunsthalle, Berlin. © ARS, NY, and DACS, London 2000.
172 Barnett Newman, *Shining Forth (to George)*, oil on canvas, 1961, 290 x 442 (9 ft 6 in. x 14 ft 6 in.). Cliché Musée National d'Art Moderne, Paris. © ARS, NY, and DACS, London 2000.

Index

Text page references are followed, where appropriate, by caption numbers shown in italics. See also List of illustrations and sources, pp. 235ff.